Human Rights Protection System in China

Pinghua Sun

Human Rights Protection System in China

Sponsored by Chinese Fund for the Humanities
and Social Sciences (本书获中华社会科学基金资助)

Springer

Pinghua Sun
School of Foreign Languages
China University of Political Science
and Law
Beijing
People's Republic of China

ISBN 978-3-642-39662-5 ISBN 978-3-642-39663-2 (eBook)
DOI 10.1007/978-3-642-39663-2
Springer Heidelberg New York Dordrecht London

Library of Congress Control Number: 2013945142
Sponsored by Chinese Fund for the Humanities and Social Sciences (本书获中华社会科学基金资助)

Printed on acid-free paper

Springer is part of Springer Science+Business Media (www.springer.com)

Preface

I started to think about human rights protection system in China when I was working on my Ph.D. dissertation entitled *The Study of the Universal Declaration of Human Rights* (UDHR) in 2008. In fact, at that time, I viewed issues from the perspective of the influences made by the UDHR. I read extensively including both Chinese and English literature, and many documents issued by the government, such as the white papers: *Human Rights in China* (1991), *China's Efforts and Achievements in Promoting the Rule of Law* (2008), and so on. Based on this extensive reading, I found that human rights protection system in China was a very important topic to be further explored.

In 2009, I applied for the research subprogram of the third stage of "211 Program" of China University of Political Science and Law. The subprogram is: *Equity and Justice, Efficiency, and Human Rights Protection of Chinese Judicial Practice Viewed from the Perspective of Judicial Language* (The Subprogram No. 10108329). The program provided financial support for the initial research of this book. In 2010, I successfully applied for the program for young teachers to be further promoted abroad with an invitation from the University of Exeter. In the same year, I applied for the inclusion of the first "National Philosophy and Social Science Research Excellence Library" with my doctoral thesis (Sun, 2009)—*The Study of the Universal Declaration of Human Rights*, which was successfully incorporated into the "National Social Science Foundation Post-funded Projects" (its number of approval: 10FFX010). These research projects further facilitated my research in human rights protection system in the Chinese context.

In February 2011, I went to the UK to continue with my research. During my time at the UK, I proposed and taught a postgraduate level module on *Human Rights in China* as a course for MA students in the School of Law (LAWM706), the University of Exeter. Before starting the course, I recognized that the Western world should know more about the progress and achievements of human rights protection in China. Therefore, I designed the teaching module including five topics: 1. Nature and Development of Human Rights in China; 2. Socialist Legal System with Chinese Characteristics; 3. Judicial Protection System with Chinese Characteristics; 4. Human Rights Education and Research in the Chinese Context; 5. New Development of Human Rights Protection in China. In order to meet the requirements of teaching, I started to write English articles about human rights protection system in China, which further facilitated and encouraged my research.

Based on the previous research projects and the teaching module, this book focuses on human rights protection system in China. The first chapter is based on the delivery of the first lecture for MA students at the School of Law at Exeter. The following six chapters systematically introduce the dynamic development and progress of human rights protection in China, attaching great importance to the first white paper on *Human Rights in China*, "The state respects and guarantees human rights" included in the Constitution, the *National Human Rights Action Plan* as a milestone, and then putting forth fundamental principles for achieving international human rights standards and specific measures to improve human rights protection standards in China. Then the book further discusses "Foundations of human rights guarantee in contemporary China" and "Human rights, culture and their reconstruction in the Chinese context". The last two chapters include "Several issues on the formation of a socialist legal system with Chinese characteristics" and "Judicial protection of human rights in China". With 11 chapters as its main content, the present book will generally introduce human rights protection system in China.

In appendices, the book covers the introduction of the teaching module: *Human Rights in China* (LAWM706), four important documents on human rights in China, as well as a list of the author's major articles and works in the past 10 years.

This book is a starting point rather than a conclusion in exploring human rights protection system in China, and there are a lot of issues worthy of further studies. However, it will serve as a window, through which the western world will have a better understanding of theory and practice of human rights protection in the Chinese context.

Hopefully, as a final academic achievement for China Academic Translation Project of the National Social Science Fund—*Socialist Protection System of Human Rights with Chinese Characteristics* (its number of approval: 12WFX001), this book will lay a foundation for further exploration of this area and play a part in the communication with the western academia.

May 2013 Pinghua Sun

Acknowledgments

I would like to take this opportunity of publication to express my wholehearted appreciations to those who have helped me in the process of my human rights research and writing. First of all, I am extremely grateful to Prof. Yang Yuguan, my Ph.D. supervisor, for his intellectual inspiration, constructive advice, and meticulous guidance through the process of my research. His unfailing encouragement and support has carried me through many a sleepless night as I strove to complete this book, especially during the critical phase of finalizing the drafts.

I am deeply indebted to Dr. Michael K. Addo, Senior Lecturer of the Law School of the University of Exeter, and a Member of the United Nations Working Group on the Issue of Human Rights and Transnational Corporations and Other Business Enterprises, who was always ready to provide me with stimulating ideas and insightful opinions regarding any issue relevant to human rights research. I greatly benefited from the communication with Dr. Michael Addo, who gave me unselfish support and invaluable suggestions, aiding me more than I could say in the whole process of my stay at the University of Exeter from February 2011 to February 2012.

I am immensely grateful to the Chinese Government, China Scholarship Council, China University of Political Science and Law (CUPL). The Chinese Government provided financial support for my further study of the *Universal Declaration of Human Rights* (Research Project No. 10FFX010, sponsored by National Planning Office of Philosophy and Social Science); China Scholarship Council awarded me a scholarship covering the returning international airfare and the living stipend during my 1-year visit in the United Kingdom (UK); CUPL agreed to let me take a year's sabbatical. All these support and encouragement enabled me to finish the first draft of this book during my stay in the UK.

I would like to express my gratitude to the University of Exeter and its Law School. The University of Exeter attached great importance to my research, timely awarding me a scholarship during my stay in the UK. The Law School invited me to run a course named "Human Rights in China" for its postgraduates. This course not only provided me with the opportunity to communicate with MA students in class, but also encouraged and promoted my research in this human rights area systematically. In the process of my teaching, the Law School provided me with ongoing support and encouragement. Meanwhile, I was invited to attend the 47th

Session of the United Nations Committee on Economic, Social and Cultural Rights in Geneva, from which I benefited a lot. In addition, Senior Administrator Tom Begbie, provided me with much help in many aspects. Mr. Michael Sanderson read the English abstract carefully and made some modifications and corrections, which provided a better version of abstract.

I would like to acknowledge my debt to my CUPL colleagues from the School of Foreign Languages. Prof. Li Li, Dean of the School, has given me much selfless help, active support, and insightful guidance in the whole process of my research. Prof. Zhang Qing, Vice Dean of the School, has frequently encouraged me whenever I have difficulties. Some of my other colleagues, including Gao Jing, Liu Yan, Zhang Zhuojuan, Wang Dongmei and Li Dan, have provided me with great help in the writing process of the first draft. In addition, I would like to thank my MA students, including Thomas Bacon, Wang Xiangfeng and Qu Xin, who have helped me in different writing stages. Dr. Horace W. H. Yeung, from the School of Law, the University of Leicester, has supported me in the proofreading of Chapter 11. Without their support, encouragement and help, it would be impossible for me to get this book ready in an English version in such a short period of time. Of course if any errors remain, they are my sole responsibility.

I feel grateful to Prof. Chen Youwu from Guangzhou University, Prof. Xiao Junyong from the University of International Relations and Prof. Tang Jianfei from Jiangxi University of Finance and Economics. I have been approved to include my translation of their articles in this book. Their articles were originally published in *China Legal Science*. I would like to give my thanks to Li Zhongcheng, Deputy Director of Malfeasance Prosecutor's Office of the Supreme People's Procuratorat, who agreed to include my English translation of his article in the present book, which has deepened our understanding of the whole system of judicial human rights protection in the Chinese context. In particular, I would like to express my heartfelt gratitude to Wang Zhaoguo, Vice-chairman of the Standing Committee of the National People's Congress (NPC), who authorized me to translate his article into English for its inclusion in the present book as a core chapter, which has not only deepened our understanding of the Chinese socialist legal system, but also greatly increased the authority of the book.

I am especially grateful to the Chinese Government for its financial support. As a final achievement for China Academic Translation Project of the National Social Science Fund—*Socialist Protection System of Human Rights with Chinese Characteristics*, its number of approval: 12WFX001, this book has been sponsored by Chinese Fund for the Humanities and Social Sciences. This financial support has played an important role in writing, translating, revising, modifying and finalizing the draft, which has led to its publication of the first book with such a theme published in English outside China.

I must give my thanks to Prof. Lucia Serena Rossi from the University of Bologna, Italy. In May 2012, it was Prof. Rossi who invited me to attend the International Conference of the China-EU Fundamental Rights at the University of Bologna, Italy. At the conference, I was invited to deliver a speech entitled "*Fundamental Principles for Achieving International Human Rights Standards in*

China", which is included in *Fundamental Rights in Europe and China: Regional Identities and Universalism* published in Italy (2013), promoting exchanges and cooperation in the field of human rights between the East and the West. Meanwhile, this experience has promoted my current research in the field of the development of human rights in China.

I must give my thanks to Prof. Paul Finkelman from Albany Law School of the Union University, the United States. In February 2013, Prof. Paul Finkelman invited me to be a panelist of the International Human Rights Symposium—"Human Trafficking and Sex Slavery in the Modern Era" held in Albany, New York, the United States. I attended two panels including both "International Perspectives on Human Trafficking" and "Issues in Domestic Law Enforcement of Human Trafficking" as a panelist, making two speeches. Based on the panel speeches, I wrote an article entitled "*Human Trafficking and Sex Slavery in the Modern World*", which will be published in the journal *Albany Government Law Review* in 2013. In particular, during my stay at Albany Law School, I was invited to give a speech entitled "The Development of Human Rights in China" to the law students and professors there, which not only played a role in communicating with the American scholars, but also facilitated my research in the protection system of human rights in China.

I must express my heartfelt gratitude to the leading scholars for their encouragement and support in my human rights studies. These scholars include Michael K. Addo (Member of the United Nations Working Group on the Issue of Human Rights and Transnational Corporation and Other Business Enterprises), Xu Xianming (Professor of Law and President at Shandong University), Huang Jin (Professor of Law and President of China University of Political Science and Law), Benjamin Liebman (Professor of Law and Director of the Center for Chinese Legal Studies at Columbia Law School). Knowing the book to be published, they are delighted to give their insightful comments on the book and make their warmhearted recommendations to the readers, which not only encourage me greatly in my human rights studies, but also heighten and broaden the social influence of this book globally.

I owe a debt of gratitude to the world-known publisher, Springer, which agreed to publish the book in an English edition. Editor Leana (Li Yan from Springer Asia) and Dr. David (Dr. S. A. Shine David from Scientific Publishing Services Ltd) have helped a lot at the editorial and typesetting stages. All their successful support has contributed to its timely publication of the book.

Thanks as ever, to my wife Wang Huaying for her unfailing support and encouragement. She accompanied me to participate in my academic activities in the United Kingdom, in Italy, and in the United States.

May 2013 Pinghua Sun

Contents

Abbreviations

BBS	Bulletin Board Services
BC	Before Christ
CASS	Chinese Academy of Social Sciences
CPC	Communist Party of China
CPPCC	Chinese People's Political Consultative Conference
CUPL	China University of Political Science and Law
FAO	Food and Agriculture Organization
GDP	Gross Domestic Product
HRC	Human Rights Council
ICCPR	International Covenant on Civil and Political Rights
ICESCR	International Covenant on Economic, Social and Cultural Rights
ILO	International Labor Organization
KMT	Kuomintang
LAWM	Law Course for Master Program
MA	Master
NPC	National People's Congress
OHCHR	UN's Office of the High Commissioner for Human Rights
P. C. Chang	Pengchun Chang or Peng Chun Chang (Zhang Pengchun)
PRC	People's Republic of China
ROC	Republic of China
SAR	Special Administrative Regions
SIPO	State Intellectual Property Office
UDHR	Universal Declaration of Human Rights
UNESCO	UN Educational, Scientific and Cultural Organization
UN	United Nations
UPR	Universal Periodic Review
US	United States
WHO	World Health Organization
WTO	World Trade Organization

Abstract

China has made considerable progress in the protection of human rights since the beginning of political reform and the process of opening-up to the outside world. It was in 2004 that the *Constitution of the People's Republic of China* was amended to stipulate that "the state respects and guarantees human rights", thus signaling that human rights protection in China has entered into a new stage of development. However, despite these developments, Western society does not yet know much about progress made by China in this area. The present book will introduce a general survey of the current situation and progress in China's human rights protection to the international community based on the author's preliminary study of the human rights protection system in China.

This book is divided into 11 chapters and seeks to discuss China's human rights protection system systematically with respect to the latest developments in human rights protection. Chapter 1 starts with the concept of human rights, discussing the role of human rights in China's traditional culture and the concept of human rights as understood in Confucian philosophy. This chapter takes the work of Peng-Chun Chang (P. C. Chang) as a key example, discussing the important contributions made by the Chinese representative to the drafting of the *Universal Declaration of Human Rights*. According to statements by western scholars P. C. Chang succeeded in persuading the international community to include Confucian doctrines in the Declaration. This is a significant and frequently overlooked contribution by China to the development of the international human rights regime. This chapter ends with a brief summary of the three prominent features of the Chinese human rights protection. Chapter 2 briefly introduces China's main human rights movements in modern history from a historical perspective, including the discussion of the Chinese Communist Party's struggle for human rights and the revival and new developments of human rights in China. Chapter 3 has a systematic analysis of the first white paper on *Human Rights in China*, including the drafting background, the basic content and its significance. Chapter 4 has an in-depth discussion of the incorporation of the principle "the state respects and guarantees human rights" into the Constitution, including a summary of several amendments relevant to the inclusion of "human rights into the Constitution" and their substantive content and significance. Chapter 5 studies the *National Human Rights Action Plan* as a milestone from the following perspectives: the background of the action plan, the specific content, implementation measures, and their significance. Chapter 6 puts forward 10 fundamental principles for achieving international human rights standards in China and suggests how these principles might form the basis of systematic theory for human rights protection in the Chinese context. Chapter 7 puts forth important measures to improve human rights protection in China, strengthen and improve human rights protection system by human rights legislation, and enhance the ability of the government officials to manage state's affairs according to law. Specifically, this includes the establishment of national human rights institutions and the development of a mid-to-long-term action plan to implement the constitutional principle of human rights protection. Chapter 8 analyzes four aspects of human rights protection in contemporary China including national foundation, economic foundation, political foundation, and the foundation of the rule by law. Chapter 9 discusses human rights, culture and its reconstruction in the Chinese context, covering the close relationship between human rights and culture and the reconstruction of human rights culture in China. Chapter 10 studies the issues on the formation of a socialist legal system with Chinese characteristics, starting with the formation of a socialist legal system with Chinese characteristics, exploring the basic features and significance of the socialist legal system with Chinese characteristics, and ending with playing a further important role of local legislation. Chapter 11 discusses judicial protection of human rights in China, starting with the analysis of the characteristics of human rights protection in China's criminal justice and focusing on human rights protection of the victims, the suspects, the defendants, and the criminals in order to discuss in detail the judicial protection of human rights in criminal justice.

The appendices describe "Human Rights in China", a course run by the author at the School of Law in the University of Exeter and journal articles and works published by the author in the past 10 years. In addition, this book contains four important human rights instruments issued by the Chinese Government in recent years, including "China's Efforts and Achievements in Promoting the Rule of Law" released in 2008, "The Socialist System of Laws with Chinese Characteristics" released in 2011, "National Human Rights Action Plan (2012–2015)" released in 2012, and "Judicial Reform in China" released in 2012. These important human rights instruments further highlight the fact that the Chinese Government has attached great importance to the protection of human rights and at the same time measures taken to promote the development of a system for the protection of human rights in China have played a key role in this area.

Chapter 1
Confucian Philosophy and Its Historical Contributions to Human Rights

Abstract Though the academics have not reached a consensus about the definition of the term, human rights, based on human's natural and social attributes, are regarded as a measure of value of social progress and civilization. Confucian philosophy as a typical representative of the eastern wisdom contains sufficient ideas of human rights, which have made outstanding contributions to the Universal Declaration of Human Rights (UDHR), which serves as a foundation for international human rights regime. These historical contributions were made by the efforts of the Chinese representative, P. C. Chang, who successfully got *Rén* (conscience or benevolence) included in the first article of the UDHR. The nature of human rights in China can be described to be developmental, systematic, and protective. These features show us that the research in this area is a significant and promising one.

As a measure of value of human progress and civilization, human rights are important parameters in judging social development. The growth, development, and full realization of human rights are not only identical with the development of society, but also go hand in hand with the development of history, culture, economy, and science and technology. Different scholars have given different definitions to human rights. Up to now, we have not reached a consensus in academia. Therefore, it is very hard to give a definition to human rights, which can be approved and recognized by all scholars. However, we have to give our definition to human rights before we can further discuss other issues relevant. On the basis of the discussion of the concept of human rights, this chapter will focus on Confucian philosophy and its contributions to human rights.

P. Sun, *Human Rights Protection System in China*,
DOI: 10.1007/978-3-642-39663-2_1,

1.1 The Concept of Human Rights

As we have known, the famous Italian poet—Dante (1265–1321), firstly put forth human rights in his book entitled in Latin—*De Monarchia* (*Monarchy*), in which Dante said: "But the foundation of the empire is human right" [1]. He also said: "The empire is not allowed to do anything which is in conflict with human right" [1]. Without respecting and protecting human rights, the state will lose the foundation for its existence. Therefore, human rights are endowed with lofty missions. They are moral and basic rules that the state should obey.

Nowadays, human rights have not only become an important topic for politicians, but also become a common standard of achievement for all peoples and all nations. However, we find it difficult to define human rights. Different scholars have given different definitions. No definition has been authoritatively recognized in the whole world. In this case, I have to list a few definitions as follows:

> Human rights are the rights approved, supported and guaranteed by certain ethics and moralities, which people should enjoy [2].

> Human rights are the rights of human as a human to be enjoyed, which are essentially moral rights rather than legal rights [3].

> Human rights are rights of human beings in brief, which are based on human natural and social properties [4].

> Human rights are the rights that people should enjoy, which are based on human natural characteristics, with social nature as their essence and which belong to human beings as humans are treated as human persons [5].

> Human rights are the rights of human as a human, … the rights of enabling human to be human, … the rights of enabling human to be dignified, … and the rights of enabling human to be dignified and fully developed [6].

A definition given by an American scholar—Donnelly:

> What are human rights? Literally, they are the rights of humans. More precisely, human rights are the rights one has simply because one is a human being"[7]. "The very term human rights indicates both their nature and their source: they are the rights that one has simply because one is human" [8]. "Human rights are a special type of right. Most fundamentally, they are paramount moral rights" [9].

Vincent discussed the grounding of human rights, and he believes: "Human rights are the rights that everyone has, and everyone equally, by virtue of their very humanity. They are grounded in an appeal to our human nature" [10]. Then he analyzed human nature from three angles: physical nature, moral nature, and the nature of rudimentarily necessary for the enjoyment of a dignified life. Regarding physical nature, Vincent believes,

> Being human involves, generally, having certain physical characteristics—from the standard number of arms and legs, to the need, say, for food, to vulnerability to violence, to a variety of capacities to reason, learn, make and use tools and so on. From a comprehensive physical profile along these lines, a pattern might emerge showing a set of needs requiring to be met if human survival and well-being are to be assured" [11].

As for the moral nature, Vincent claims that "(t)his is a second, and deeper, appeal not to this or that capacity or need, but to notion of human potentials in the achievement of which we recognized the concept of human dignity" [10]. The nature of rudimentarily necessary for the enjoyment of a dignified life is relevant to basic rights including the rights to subsistence and security.

On the basis of analysis of the definitions given by both Chinese and Western scholars, I have also tried to give a definition in detail. My definition to human rights is shown as follows:

> Human rights are the rights that everyone enjoys in reality and the rights everyone should enjoy according to their natural and social attributes. Human rights derive from human dignity and worth inherent, and freedom and equality are fundamental principles of human rights. Human rights are moral rights, but they must be guaranteed by law. The realization of human rights is a dynamic process from the deserved rights to the legitimate rights, and from the legitimate rights to the practical rights. Therefore, human rights are influenced by all the political, economic, social, cultural, historical, legal system and other factors. Guarantee of everyone's equal enjoyment of rights is the ultimate goal being pursued by human rights [12].

Here I would like to give a further explanation to my definition above to human rights: The subjects of human rights are human beings, while the objects of human rights are rights. In the sense of law, human rights are human beings' fundamental rights, but as far as the attributes are concerned, human rights have their own complicated features:

According to natural attributes, everyone has his rights that should be enjoyed as a human being. The concept of human rights emerged when society developed to a certain stage. In a slavery society, slavers enjoyed neither freedom nor the right to life. In that case, a slaver could never meet the conditions to be a human being. In fact, slavers could not enjoy human rights. With the development of productive force, excessive products were produced, while settling down the belongings of the excessive products made some interests, which led to the emergence of human rights.

In fact, the implications of human rights develop constantly with the development of society. "Human beings always exist within a certain society. Rights also originate and develop within a certain society. A human being separated from society does not have any right, just as Robinson Crusoe living on a deserted island, although accompanied by Friday, did not enjoy any rights" [13]. In the light of social attributes, human rights show certain social relations between individuals, between individual and groups, between individual and the state. Among these relations, when people's rights are violated in reality, the state should take the responsibility to protect those human rights. However, "(o)ur society today is still far from being the Great Harmony, therefore, legal rights will inevitably be the rights stipulated or recognized by the State power" [13]. The state should take measures of intervention according to law to deal with illegal violation of human rights. In society, the practical human rights of human beings need to be protected by the state.

However, the implications of human rights vary from one period to another, from one country to another because of the traditional and cultural diversities. Since people began to realize the importance of human rights, the process of pursuing human rights has been a process of enriching the concrete content of human rights continuously, and a process of everyone gradually and progressively gaining equal rights. The ultimate goal is that all the people in the world can have equal rights before law.

1.2 Confucian Philosophy as a Typical Representative of a Chinese Culture

Though the term of human rights was not clearly put forth in the Chinese traditional culture, Confucian philosophy, as a typical representative of a Chinese traditional culture, contains sufficient ideas of human rights. Confucian philosophy not only laid an emphasis on understanding others, tolerance and compromise between each other, and on showing sympathy to others, but also claimed the conscience of human beings, social harmony, moral educational functions, social order, and creativities. Human rights originate from human dignity, while human dignity comes from human beings' reason and conscience, which distinguishes human beings from animals.

1.2.1 The Core Concept of Confucian Philosophy

Rén (仁, rén) is the core concept of Confucian philosophy, which was coined by Kong Zi (孔子, Kǒngzǐ, K'ung Tse, 551–479 B.C.), an ancient Chinese philosopher whose ideas encouraged justice and peace by teaching social and moral principles which had a great influence on Chinese society, and whose *Analects* contains a collection of his sayings and dialogs compiled by disciples after his death. *Rén* was translated by P. C. Chang [14] into "two-man-mindedness," which was well known in the Western world as "conscience" (良心, lángxīn). In fact, the term of conscience was first coined by Meng Zi (孟子, Mèngzǐ, Meng Tse, 372–289 B.C.), a Chinese Confucian philosopher who taught that people are innately good and that one's nature can be enhanced or perverted by one's environment, and whose *Works of Mencius* is also very influential in the world.

Here I would like to introduce more about Meng Zi's thoughts. Meng Zi, known to the Western world as Mencius, was the first great thinker to extend the teachings of Confucius. His teachings tended to increase the self-respect and self-confidence of man. He taught that the nature of man was good, and that the difference between man and animals, though very small, should be stressed and could be cultivated. One of the implications of this teaching of the essential goodness of the nature of man is the fundamental respect for what is "human" in all men. He emphasized the rights of the people as well as the obligation of the ruler to provide for the good of the people.

1.2.2 Emphasis on People's Dignity

Confucian philosophy lays an emphasis on people's dignity, from which human rights originate. The Master said, "The commander of the army may be carried off, but the will of the common man can not be made to change" (Sān-jǔn kěyǐ duóshuàiyě, pǐfū bùkě duózhìyě. 三军可以夺帅也，匹夫不可夺志也。[15]). This shows that Confucius valued individual's willingness regardless of his status. The Master said, "Do not do to others what you wouldn't like yourself" (Jǐ suǒ bù yù, wù shī yǔ rén. 己所不欲，勿施于人。). This has become a golden rule for human beings of the modern and civilized world. With regard to government, Meng Zi thought that the people were the most important element; the institutions were the next; the sovereign the least important (Mín wèi guì, shèjì cìzhī, jūn wèi qīng. 民为贵，社稷次之，君为轻。).

1.2.3 The Age of Grand Harmony

As a statement of the ideal of economic and social adjustment in the world, Confucius formulated the following thoughts some 2,500 years ago, which expresses even today the dream of all mankind. The passage is as follows:

> When the Dadao or Grand Way prevails, the world is for the welfare of all. Officers are selected because of their virtue and competence. Mutual confidence is promoted and peaceful relations are maintained. People regard not only their own parents as parents, nor only their own children as children. Previsions are made for the aged, employment is provided for the able-bodied, and education is afforded to the young. Widows and widowers, orphans and the childless, the deformed and diseased, are all cared for. Men have their occupations and women have their homes. Surplus goods are not to be wasted; they need not be kept as one's own. Labor is not to be idle; work is not necessarily for self only. Scheming and intrigues are repressed and banditry and rebellion do not arise. As a result, there is no need of shutting the house-gate at night. Such is the Age of Grand Harmony [16].

The quotation is a vivid picture, showing us an ideal society, in which people will achieve the highest and ultimate goal in realizing economic and social rights. Some people believed that this was the first chapter of human rights in the history of human beings. It was about 17 centuries earlier than the *Magna Carta* of 1215. As P. C. Chang once pointed out in his lecture to the Economic and Social Council of the United Nations, "people all over the world are longing for a rising standard of living and, for some of them, a rising standard of living means at present a stay from starvation. The conscience of the world cannot be set at ease unless action is taken towards that goal" [17].

1.2.4 Morality Rather than Interests

Confucian philosophy cherishes morality rather than interests. The Master said, "A man of morality will never live in solitude; he will always bring companions" (Dé bù gū, bì yǒu lín. 德不孤，必有邻。). The Master also said, "A gentleman is conscious only of justice, a petty man, only of self-interest" (Jūnzǐ yùyúyì, xiǎorén yùyúlì. 君子喻于义，小人喻于利。). According to Confucius, "He who engages solely in self-interested actions will arouse continual discontent" (Fàng yú lì ér xíng, duōyuàn. 放于利而行，多怨。). The Master also said, "Wealth and rank unrighteously obtained seem to me as insubstantial as floating clouds" (Bùyì érfù qiěguì, yú wǒ rú fúyún. 不义而富且贵，于我如浮云。). From the quotations above, we can safely draw a sound conclusion: In the Chinese tradition, people would rather give up wealth and interests than put themselves into an unrighteous position, which serves as a fundamental moral rule. Therefore, the Chinese cultural tradition leads to this kind of phenomenon: People put great stress upon duties and obligations and look down upon interests and rights.

At the same time, the Chinese traditional culture would lay emphasis on people's responsibilities and duties to others, to society and to the country rather than claim rights in their social life. Much more attention has been given to moral standards concerning the relationship between rights and duties. People would not only pursue private rights, but also take their obligations. While one respects and protects self rights, one must set a position for his or her duties and obligations to others. That is to say, people can enjoy their natural rights, but at the same time they have to carry out their duties and responsibilities as in the social relations. Only in this way can people avoid being too selfish, which will make the whole society a civilized one.

Human rights is a great term, however, only seeking to enjoy rights without taking responsibilities seems too selfish. If everyone is just to seek one's own interest and rights without taking care of others' equal interest and rights, the whole world will bring to its end. Human rights career is an endless business, but over pursuing self rights will lead to the opposite side, on which one's greedy feeling would be further expanded. By contrast, the resources are limited, while pursuing personal human rights, people will take advantage of the limited resources, which may belong to the following generations. Once the resources were used up, human beings would find it difficult to survive. In this case, in order to save the whole world and to save human beings, we have to learn from Confucian philosophy.

1.2.5 Social Harmony

According to Confucius, it is the highest goal to pursue social harmony. The Master said, "In carrying out the rites it is harmony that is prized". (Lǐ zhī yòng, hé wèi guì. 礼之用，和为贵。) Here harmony refers to a relationship between the body and heart of human beings, between human and human, between human and society, between human and nature (natural world). This brilliant idea should become a common moral standard of the whole world, which will bring people peace, happiness, and harmony. World lasting peace cannot be divorced from this moral standard. China is a peace-loving country where morality is prized and social harmony is advocated. In some sense, the concept of harmony is a wonderful contribution to the theory of the international human rights protection. The contemporary world should regard this principle as a common moral standard.

1.3 Historical Contributions to the Drafting of the UDHR

I would like to take an example of the drafting practice of the *Universal Declaration of Human Rights* (UDHR) in order to show how Confucian philosophy and human rights conceptions became the origin of the UDHR, which serves as an important milestone in the history of international human rights protection system. Associating the establishment of international human rights protection system, I will give detailed explanations about the contributions that Chinese culture and eastern wisdom have ever made to international human rights regime. My focus is on P. C. Chang's contributions to the drafting of the UDHR.

1.3.1 The Chinese Representative, P. C. Chang

In the process of establishing the international human rights regime, a Chinese representative, P. C. Chang [18] (Pengchun Chang, now spelling Zhang Pengchun), by using eastern wisdom, successfully persuaded the world to adopt the core concepts of Confucian philosophy in the process of the drafting of the UDHR.

In January of 1946, the Organization Meeting of the United Nations convened in London, England, and the United Nations was officially founded. P. C. Chang attended the first conference of the United Nations. He was assumed the position of Resident Chief Delegate (Ambassador rank) to the Economic and Social Council of United Nations and Vice Chairman of the Commission on Human Rights. As a Chinese representative to the Economic and Social Council of the United Nations, P. C. Chang made three speeches. The first speech was delivered at Opening Meeting of the First Session of the Economic and Social Council—London, January 23, 1946. The title of this speech is *A New Loyalty*. Another speech "*War Against Microbes*" was made by P. C. Chang proposing the Resolution on the Calling of an International Health Conference at a meeting of the First Session of the Economic and Social Council—London, February 7, 1946. The third speech "*World Significance of Economically 'Low-Pressure' Areas*" was delivered at a meeting of the Second Session of the Economic and Social Council —New York, June 4, 1946.

After returning to New York, he suggested organizing the World Health Organization (WHO) and drafted the *Universal Declaration of Human Rights*. According to the French representative, P. C. Chang was instrumental in selecting the proper wording for that declaration. His second son Chang Yuanfeng also wrote an article recalling his impression on P. C. Chang's participation in the discussion about the UDHR as follows:

> It was the summer of 1947, the family was living in Garden City, L. I., N. Y, I finished my college freshman year and didn't have a summer job. Since I was home, my father made me attend his meetings. He was vice chairman (chair-woman was Mrs. Eleanor Roosevelt) on the United Nations Commission on Human Rights. The purpose of those meetings was to draft a Declaration of Human Rights. The meetings were held in the company auditorium of the Sperry Gyroscope plant. I always sat in the fourth row, watched and listened to the Commission members debating around a table set up on the stage. … Day after day, they debated what would constitute basic human rights, and how it should be clearly stated in the document so that there would not be any misunderstanding or misinterpretation. My father repeated many times the phrase "Man's inhumanity to man". You know, Mrs. Roosevelt was the chairwoman, but every time there was a question about phrasing or logic, everyone would defer to my father. He was the one who wrote that Universal Declaration of Human Rights" [19].

In P. C. Chang's life, he shifted his interest and foci from time to time, but he had a clear focus on modernization according to his own explanation. First, he is an educator and playwright, then as a philosopher and diplomat, last as an expert in human rights by taking advantage of his profound knowledge in different disciplines. It was just thanks to his extensive knowledge that he could play an important role in the drafting of the UDHR. Intellectually, P. C. Chang and Malik [20] were dominant in the work of Commission on Human Rights according to the memoirs by John Humphrey [21] and Mary Glendon [22]. Sumner Twiss [23] also believed that P. C. Chang made noncomparative contributions to the drafting of the UDHR.

As far as P. C. Chang's contributions to the drafting of the UDHR were concerned, we can see that the contributions were made in different stages: in the drafting committee (at First Session), in the Commission on Human Rights (at First and Third Session) and in the Third Committee, General Assembly. As a master of language art, P. C. Chang made outstanding contributions to the drafting of the UDHR. However, hardly a word was uttered about the very substantive input he himself brought to the process that spawned the great document. This reminds me of his style name Zhongshu (仲述, zhòngshù), among which Zhong (仲, zhòng) refers to Confucius, and shu (述, shù) was quoted from Confucian doctrine: "The Master said, 'I have transmitted what was taught to me without making up anything of my own. I have been faithful to and loved ancient culture. I would compare myself to Old Peng who was fond of talking about the good old days'" (zǐyuē: shù ér bùzuò, xìn ér hàogǔ, què bǐyú wǒ lǎopéng. "子曰：'述而不作，信而好古，窃比于我老彭。'" [15]).

It is just because P. C. Chang hardly uttered a word about his great contributions to the UDHR but the UDHR was an important milestone in establishing the international human rights regime that we should conduct a research relevant to his contributions. In my research, the major research methods adopted can be called triangulations. In another word, P. C. Chang's contributions will be triangulated from at least three different angles. One angle is from the viewpoint on him of the Western scholars. Another angle is from P. C. Chang's own relevant lectures, speeches, and works. The third angle is from P. C. Chang's colleagues while he participated in the drafting process, such as Eleanor Roosevelt [24], Charles Malik, René Cassin [25] and John Humphrey [26]. Other angles can be also possible from both Chinese and Western scholars' comments, and statements of P. C. Chang's family members, friends, and students or others.

1.3.2 John Humphrey's Memoirs

When John Humphrey recalled the first session of the Commission (1947), in his fifth chapter of his memoirs, he firstly made a brief introduction to Mrs. Roosevelt. Then he introduced the Chinese representative P. C. Chang, giving a positive assessment. He wrote:

> The vice-chairman was P. C. Chang, who also represented China in the Economic and Social Council. I was at first put off by his somewhat gruff manner and his uninhibited criticisms of the Secretariat, but I soon learned to appreciate his great human qualities and we became friends. He was a master of the art of compromise and, under cover of a quotation from Confucius, would often provide the formula which made it possible for the Commission to escape from some impasse [27].

He continued to make a comparison between P. C. Chang and Charles Malik of Lebanon. Humphrey believed that both P. C. Chang and Charles Malik were scholars, and they dominated the Commission intellectually. However, they had different philosophies. Chang was a pragmatist (he called himself a pluralist), while Malik was a Thomist. Therefore, they were usually in disagreement. According to the comments on P. C. Chang from Humphrey's Diary on December 4, 1948, "In intellectual stature he towers above any other member of the committee. I also like his philosophy" [28].

In Humphrey's memoirs, he made a clear statement about the dominant role played by P. C. Chang, who made an important contribution to the procedures of drafting a declaration. Mrs. Roosevelt hoped the Commission would discuss the Secretariat's suggestions: a declaration or a convention. Some other suggestion is the possibility of amending the Charter. Because Mrs. Roosevelt wanted the Commission to start drafting the declaration at once, while her colleagues thought that they should have a general discussion at least. When they had no idea about the working procedures, P. C. Chang gave a practical solution, which settled down the problem at last. According to Humphrey's memoirs, "P. C. Chang, who was nearly always ready with a practical solution, then suggested that the Commission should not vote on the matter but should proceed on the assumption that the Bill would be drafted as a resolution for adoption by the General Assembly, i.e. as a declaration. It was on this assumption that I later prepared my draft" [29].

In his memoirs, Humphrey recalled who would take the responsibility of drafting the declaration. It described as follows: Mrs. Roosevelt wanted the drafting committee to start the work at once. She invited P. C. Chang, Malik, and Humphrey to have tea in her Washington Square apartment on that Sunday following the adjournment. However, "Chang and Malik were too far apart in their philosophical approaches to be able to work together on a text" [30]. They talked a lot with getting nowhere. At last, P. C. Chang suggested that Humphrey should put his other duties aside for 6 months and study Chinese philosophy, after which he might be able to prepare a text for the committee [30]. Chang adopted an implicit strategy to mean that the Western influences might be too great. This story had laid a foundation for Chang's incorporating Confucian ideas in the declaration.

It was because of P. C. Chang's proposal that the components of the *International Bill of Human Rights* was further confirmed, consisting of a declaration, covenants, and measures of its implementation. This had clarified the ideas and framework of the international human rights protection system. In his memoirs, Humphrey wrote:

> Much of the discussion still turned on the form of the Bill. Mrs. Roosevelt said that, since it was to be adopted by the General Assembly, it should be a declaration. This could be followed by treaties on particular subjects which would be binding on the states which ratified them, or there might be a convention containing the substance of the Declaration. In that case both instruments might be presented to the General Assembly at the same time. P. C. Chang envisaged three instruments: a declaration 'drafted in simple phrases', a commentary on each of its articles, and proposals for its implementation. Later he suggested the formula for a tripartite bill—declaration, a convention, and measures of implementation—which was finally adopted [31].

With regard to the origin of human rights, P. C. Chang suggested a persuasive solution. As a result, an endless debate was successfully avoided about the origin of human rights from between God and the nature or between deity and Creator. Details relevant to these debates were described clearly in Humphrey's memoirs as follows:

> But the most controversial issue to which the article gave rise was whether it should contain some reference to the Deity. At the second session of the Human Rights Commission, and again at the second session of the Drafting Committee, Malik had unsuccessfully tried to bring a reference to the Creator into the article on the family. Now it was the Brazilian delegation which wanted Article 1 to say that human beings are created in the image of God. The article as it then stood said that human beings are endowed 'by nature' with reason and conscience, and the Brazilians wanted this statement to be preceded by a reference to the Deity. But Count Carton de Wiart of Belgium, fearing an endless philosophical debate, moved that the words 'by nature' be deleted. P. C. Chang supported him in a speech in which he pleaded for 'two-man-mindedness' and asked the delegates not to impose philosophical concepts such as natural law on countries where they are alien to the thinking of many millions of people. The words 'by nature', he added,

'had a ring of Rousseau and evoked memories of the theory that man was naturally good.' In the result, the Belgian amendment to delete the words was adopted and the Brazilians withdrew their amendment. ... The result was that the Universal Declaration of Human Rights mentions neither God nor nature [32].

1.3.3 Sumner Twiss's Comments

Professor Sumner Twiss's research is a typical one relevant to Confucian contributions to the drafting of the UDHR. His ideas and thoughts are reflected in his two articles: *Confucian ethics, concept-clusters, and human rights* [23], and *Confucian contributions to the Universal Declaration of Human Rights: A historical and philosophical perspective* [33].

In his first article, Twiss believes:

> Although his higher education was pursued in U. S. universities (Clark and Columbia), Chang was significantly shaped by classical Confucian thought. He wrote and lectured extensively about its relevance to the modern world. Chang was consistently characterized by his peers as the towering intellect of the Commission on Human Rights and of the Third Committee who more than anyone else was responsible for imparting a universal rather than purely Western character to the UDHR. Given his role and influence in crafting the declaration, he is a particularly authoritative source for its proper interpretation [34].

Twiss views P. C. Chang's interventions from the perspectives of comparing different ethics and religions. "There is a deeper lesson to draw from Chang's interventions. He appears to be engaged in a project of constructive comparative ethics, one that is self-consciously trying to find conceptual and normative bridges between Confucian moral thought and Western ethics in a manner that forges new angles on both traditions and how they might learn from one another" [23].

Twiss also shows us how P. C. Chang had managed to persuaded the Western world to learn from Confucian philosophy.

> By emphasizing the interdependence of human rights and duties, Chang seems to be trying to open the Confucian tradition to a new moral conceptual category (rights). At the same time, however, in emphasizing the importance of the li (decorum, civility, manners) and linking these to the struggle to uphold noble principles (human dignity and rights), he also looks like he is suggesting that the Western tradition for its part could benefit from incorporating that distinctively Confucian moral-conceptual category [23].

Twiss explains the process of P. C. Chang's intervention clearly by adding:

> Furthermore, in using Mencian language to (re)describe aspects of eighteenth century European philosophy, Chang appears to be demonstrating that there are important similarities or parallels between the two traditions that ought to be embraced as the basis for the common project of the genuine humanization of the world. He is, in effect, showing us how to construct an intercultural concept-cluster of person, community, relational autonomy, human rights, civility, and responsibility for others that could be used by all the peoples of the world [35].

In his second article, on the basis of researching the official United Nations records of 1947–1948, and by referring to John Humphrey's diaries, Twiss has determined:

> The Chinese delegate P. C. Chang introduced a number of Confucian ideas, strategies, and arguments into the deliberative process leading up to the final formulation of the UDHR, adopted on December 10, 1948, by the UN General Assembly. This Confucian contribution is considerably more extensive and influential than has ever been reported previously. Chang was described by Humphrey as the towering intellect of the Third Committee (which debated and approved the final UDHR draft sent to the General Assembly) who more than anyone else was responsible for imparting a universal rather than a purely Western character to the UDHR [36].

Twiss is a distinguished professor of human rights, ethics, and religion from Florida State University, his high appraisal of P. C. Chang's contributions to the UDHR clearly shows us that P. C. Chang's contributions were thought highly of by the Western world.

In this article, Twiss analyzes Confucian contributions to the UDHR from a historical and philosophical perspective. This article consists of three parts. The first part is about P. C. Chang's biographical background, except for some inexact information, it is well organized. The second part is about intellectual influences on P. C. Chang by Dewey and Chinese culture, especially Confucianism. It is because these influences that P. C. Chang formed a propensity to use Confucian thought. Twiss further discusses P. C. Chang's lectures and addresses in the years immediately preceding his work with the Commission on Human Rights. "Two sets of talks are particularly revealing of the way that he interlaces Chinese thoughts and Western sources" [36]. Then, Twiss continues to discuss P. C. Chang's three 1946 addresses to the UN Economic and Social Council, "Chang is equally bold (and arguably Confucian) in his conception of the council's role and practical work" [36].

After detailed discussion about P. C. Chang's propensity to use Confucian thought, Twiss believes that P. C. Chang had the following traits, and the last three of them were carried into his work on the UDHR.

1. *An abiding commitment to modernization in Chinese education, society, and culture, construed along the lines of Dewey's thought, self-critically combining aspects of old and new.*
2. *A passionate commitment to the humanistic elements and vision of Confucian thought.*
3. *A deep interest in constructive comparative thought that attempts to reconcile the humanistic values of the Confucian tradition with those of Western traditions.*
4. *A propensity to use Confucian ideas to advance his case for self-critical and humanized modernization in the world* [36].

The third part of this article focuses on P. C. Chang's strategic contributions, specific articles, and comparative philosophy. With regard to strategic contributions, Twiss points out:

> The historical record shows that Chang argued vigorously and successfully for the position that the UDHR should (1) be conceived as the basis and program for the humanization of mankind (here Chang appealed to the Confucian idea of man's moral nature or capacity to become truly human in the sense of moral growth and achievement); (2) incorporate a large measure of pragmatic agreement on norms of conduct despite persisting differences of philosophy and ideology among peoples of the world (here Chang appealed to the Confucian emphasis on the art of living—as contrasted with metaphysics—together with making the argument that no representatives should insist on including controverted metaphysical or theological concepts in the declaration); (3) be written in a manner readily comprehensible to all people (here Chang implicitly used the Confucian emphasis on the priority of the people to support his view that UDHR was to be a people's document, not a scholar's or a lawyer's) [36].

On the matter of specific articles, Twiss quotes a lot from the UN records, which clearly shows that Chang's Confucian background played a large role in the whole process. Chang successfully introduced *ren* (仁, rén) and *li* (礼, lǐ) into the drafting process of the UDHR and made the crucial mediating intervention in the Third Committee's debate about the origin of human rights.

Regarding comparative philosophy, Twiss gives a brief summary as follows: "he (Chang) self-consciously tried to find normative and conceptual bridges between Confucian moral thought and Western European philosophy in a way that forged new angles of vision on both traditions and how they might learn from each other" [36]. Twiss believes that Chang tried to build a bridge between Eastern and Western traditions by (1) linking human rights to humanization, (2) emphasizing the interdependence of rights and duties, (3) highlighting the significance of "the spirit of brotherhoods" as a moral concept shared by both East and West, (4) identifying mankind's moral capacity as another philosophical bridge or similarity between East and West, (5) demonstrating how freedom of religion could be soundly protected by both Eastern and Western traditions, and (6) demonstrating how Eastern and Western traditions could agree on certain fundamentals of human governance.

After reading Twiss's articles, we can have a better understanding of Chinese traditional culture, particularly the outstanding contributions made by Confucian philosophy to the drafting of the UDHR, which serves a milestone for the international human rights regime.

1.3.4 My Research Findings

Zhang Pengchun (P. C. Chang) made outstanding contributions to the drafting process of the UDHR with the help of his profound knowledge and distinguished intelligence. I have summarized his contributions from the following aspects [37]: (1) Putting forth the drafting plan and identifying the nature of the UDHR; (2) Insisting on Chinese traditional culture and successfully integrating Confucian thoughts into the UDHR; (3) Insisting on the universality of human rights and solving the problems of the origin of human rights; (4) Sticking to the principle of simplicity and easiness and making a strict structure; (5) Taking advantage of Chinese wisdom and creatively breaking impasses to mediate disputes; (6) Dominating the language discourse in the drafting process with his profound knowledge; (7) Placing stress on economic, social, and cultural rights and putting forth tolerance and the concept of harmonious society; (8) Viewing issues from philosophical perspective and interpreting Chinese views on human rights to the world. In a word, P. C. Chang played an important part in the whole process of the drafting of the UDHR, and made outstanding contributions to the UDHR, which was admired particularly by American scholars.

Only before the release of the *Universal Declaration of Human Rights*, Malik spoke highly of P. C. Chang's contributions to the initial stage of the drafting on December 9, 1948. He said:

> It is impossible even to begin to name the hundreds of individuals and institutions that had something to do, directly or indirectly, with our work in its initial stages. However, I must refer to Dr P. C. Chang, the distinguished vice-chairman of the Commission and drafting committee. He never failed to broaden our perspective by his frequent references to the wisdom and philosophy of the Orient and, by a special drafting gift, was able happily to rectify many of our terms [38].

Chang resigned from the UN in 1952 because of his worsening heart condition, and he died in 1957. John Humphrey, on hearing the news, wrote in his diary: "P. C. Chang is dead. Of all the delegates who came into the Council, he was the one with whom I felt most in spiritual and intellectual communion. And the one I like the best. … He was a scholar and, in a way, an artist although he performed his diplomatic functions well in spite of these superior gifts. What a giant he seems in contrast with the time-servers" [39]. In some sense, his contributions were the ones that Chinese civilization, wisdom of the people, splendid traditional culture made. This reflects in the first article of the *Universal Declaration of Human Rights*: "All human beings are born free and equal in dignity and rights. They are endowed with reason and conscience and should act towards one another in a spirit of brotherhood."

1.4 The Nature of Human Rights in China

The nature of human rights protection in China can be analyzed in the following three characteristics of being developmental, systematic, and protective.

1.4.1 Developmental Characteristic

Everything in the world is in motion, but changes need to satisfy the requirements, which may include time, economic, political, and cultural factors. China belongs to the developing socialist countries, in which the economic foundation is quite weak. In this case, if we would fully reach the international standards, it seems impractical. It is a progressive process of human rights protection in China. However, as Professor Xia Yong says:

> History is over, and the present is becoming history. Chinese culture has existed and developed and is being continuously created. Over the past one hundred years, great changes have taken place in the various factors which determined the lack of regard for human rights in Chinese traditional society. Social harmony cannot be achieved and promoted by relying on rites, religion and power alone. The Chinese people are advocating and promoting human rights together with people all over the world [40].

The International Covenant on Economic, Social and Cultural Rights (ICESCR) sets a series of standards for member states. China has joined ICESCR and submitted its national report in 2008 about the implementation of this Covenant in China. In the review of China's report, Chinese representative took an active part in the dialog, which had achieved a very good reputation in the whole world. Great achievements and new development of human rights protection system in China were highly appraised by the UN Committee on Economic, Social and Cultural Rights.

1.4.2 Systematic Characteristic

In the Western countries, people used to attach an importance to the so-called "first generation rights," which covers civil rights and political rights. By contrast, in the socialist countries, people gave more attention to the so-called "second generation rights," which covers economic, social and cultural rights; while in the developing countries, people show great concern with the so-called "third generation rights," which covers the right to subsistence and the right to development. A famous Chinese scholar of human rights, Xu Xianming, once put forth the fourth generation rights [41], namely, the right to harmony, which covers a series of new rights, such as the environmental right, the rights of coming generations. Though it is still a controversial concept, but in fact, taking the future of human beings into considerations, harmony is the highest wisdom for the existence of the world.

The concept of the right to harmony will undoubtedly contribute to the discourse of international human rights protection in the future. Professor Xia Yong once pointed out as follows:

> When giving consideration to human rights from the concept of harmony, we should no longer proceed from absolute rights of abstract individuals to establish the relations of rights and obligations. Rather, we should study and practice human rights in the context of particular social relations. Here, special attention should be paid to efforts to seek coordination among various individuals and between various nations and cultures. Only in this way will it be possible to master completely all relevant factors, ancient and modern, Chinese and Western, and create new ones [40].

China is a developing socialist country, systematic protection of human rights is highly advocated, covering protection of all kinds of human rights, regardless of the first-generation rights, the second-generation rights, the third-generation rights, and the fourth-generation rights.

1.4.3 Protective Characteristics

In China, a clear tendency is to shift the characteristic of management to the protective characteristic. This tendency can be further explored from the following aspects: safeguarding rights by laws is a transparent trait. In China, a socialist system of laws with Chinese characteristics has been formed. This is a great achievement for a great country. Wang Zhaoguo once said:

> Over 30 years of reform and opening up, under the leadership of the Communist Party of China, after unremitting efforts in all areas, so far, China has developed 237 pieces of the Constitution and existing laws, more than 690 pieces of administrative regulations, and more than 8,600 pieces of local laws and regulations. China has laws to obey generally in all aspects of economic, political, cultural, social, and ecological civilization constructions [42].

Showing concern with the rising of people's living standards is also reflected in the Chinese context. This is because in China people extremely lay stress upon economic, social and cultural rights, which is in line with the Chinese traditional culture. On the other hand, ideals of enjoying human rights should firstly be confirmed by the law, which enables the deserved rights (human rights ideals) to become legitimate rights. Meanwhile, the legitimate rights should be practically guaranteed in reality not only by the State's respecting human rights but also by its promoting and safeguarding human rights. In this case, the State will have a lot of obligations to take. In order to protect people's rights, the Chinese government has made great efforts in promoting and safeguarding people's fundamental freedoms and rights and made great contributions to the construction of harmonious society, where everyone can enjoy their fundamental freedoms and rights. However, China, as I have mentioned above, is a developing country, having a lot of work to do in the field of human rights protection.

1.5 Conclusion

From the discussion above, we can safely draw a sound conclusion. In the Chinese traditional culture, no concept of human rights was clearly put forth, but the underlying ideals of human rights in the Chinese tradition are splendid and brilliant, they are even the great goals for the whole world to struggle to reach. Harmony, tolerance, benevolence, rites, virtue, morality, concern with others, and so on will play an important role in correcting ultra-individualism, egomania and antagonism contained in Western traditional human rights and in reconstructing the theory of international human rights discourse. In addition, from the perspective of Chinese modern history, China has put painstaking efforts to winning national independence, people's prosperity, economic development, social harmony, and promoting, improving the conditions of human rights protection, meanwhile, China has taken an active part in the international human rights cooperation and communication, and has made great contributions to the establishment of the international human rights protection system.

References

1. Dante. (1999). *Monarchy*. (P. Shaw, Trans) (p. 82). Cambridge: Cambridge University Press.
2. Li, B. (2005). *Human rights law* (p. 17). Beijing: Higher Education Press.
3. Xia, Y. (1992). *The origin of the concept of human rights—A historical philosophy of rights*. (p. 213). Beijing: China University of Political Science and Law Press.
4. Yang, Y. (2008). *Influence of international human rights law on China's criminal and judicial reform*. (p. 1). Beijing: China Legal Publishing House.
5. Zhuo, Z. (2003). *The rule of law and the state* (p. 43). Beijing: Law Press.
6. Xu, X. (2004). An endless study of human rights—speech at the closure of seminar between Chinese and American academics. *Tribune of Political Science and Law, 2*, 36–38.
7. Donnelly, J. (1985). *The concept of human rights* (p. 1). London/New York: Croom Helm Ltd.
8. Donnelly, J. (1998). *International human rights*. (p. 18.) (2 ed.). Boulder: Westview Press.
9. Donnelly, J. (1998). *International human rights*. (p. 19.) (2 ed.). Boulder: Westview Press.
10. Vincent, R. J. (1986). *Human rights and international relations* (p. 13). Cambridge: Cambridge University Press.
11. Vincent, R. J. (1986). Human rights and international relations (p. 14). Cambridge: Cambridge University Press.
12. Sun, P. (2012). *The study of the Universal Declaration of Human Rights* (pp. 4–5). Beijing: Peking University Press.
13. Han, Y. (1996). Legal protection of human rights in China. In P. R. Baehr et el. (Eds.), *Human rights: Chinese and Dutch perspectives*. (pp. 91–101). The Hague/London/Boston: Martinus Nijhoff Publishers.
14. P. C. Chang was a Chinese representative to the United Nations Economic and Social Council. (1946–1948). He participated in the drafting process of the *Universal Declaration of Human Rights* as a vice-chairman of the Commission on Human Rights, taking advantage of Confucian philosophy in the drafting process and making great contributions in mediation and solving disputes.
15. Li, T. (1991). *The analects of Confucius*. Jinan: Shandong University Press.
16. Cited from Peng-chun Chang, "World significance of economically 'low pressure' areas," Speech at the Second Session of the Economic and Social Council, June 4, 1946, reprinted in Ruth H. C. & S.-C. Cheng. (Eds.), *Peng Chun Chang 1892–1957: Biography & collected works*. Privately printed, 1995. pp. 151–153./Also refer to Glendon, M. A. (2001). *A world made new: Eleanor Roosevelt and the Universal Declaration of Human Rights* (p. 185). New York: Random House.
18. Pengchun Chang, or P. C. Chang (1892–1957), whose style name was Zhongshu, was born in Tianjin on April 22nd, 1892. He was an international renowned educator, philosopher, playwright, diplomat, human rights activist and the main drafter of the *Universal Declaration*

of Human Rights. P. C. Chang had a western education background, who was one of Professor Dewey's favorite students at Columbia University and the first doctor in education in China's history (1924). He was also a planner of Nankai University as an Acting Principal (1917–1919) and a contributor as a Dean to Tsinghua University (1923–1926). He taught at Tsinghua University (1923–1926), Nankai University (1926–1937), University of Chicago (1931), School of the Art Institute of Chicago, University of Hawaii (1933–1934) and Columbia University (1945). He was also a famous educator of drama and director, and the mentor of the renowned playwright Cao Yu. He edited the play "New Village" which was considered as "iconic works of modern Chinese dramas" by historians. P. C. Chang was also an excellent diplomat, and he was the former Minister Plenipotentiary and Envoy Extraordinary to Turkey (1940–1942) and ambassador to Chile (1942–1945). From January 10th, 1946 to February 14th, the first conference of the UN General Assembly was held in London. P. C. Chang, as one of China's four official representatives, attended the conference. During the conference of the General Assembly he was appointed Resident Chief Delegate (with an ambassador rank) to the UN Economic and Social Council (1946–1952). From 1947 to 1948, P. C. Chang served as vice chairman of the UN Commission on Human Rights and vice chairman of the Drafting Committee, making outstanding contributions to the drafting the *Universal Declaration of Human Rights*. On July 19th, 1957, Chang died from a heart attack at the age of 65 in New Jersey, the US. Regarding a further life story of P. C. Chang, see Sun, Pinghua. 2011. "P. C. Chang: A world-renowned human rights activist." in *Human Rights* 6. 40–45.

19. Chang, Y. (1995). Thoughts on my beloved father. In Ruth H. C. & S.-C. Cheng (Eds.), *Peng Chun Chang 1892–1957: Biography & collected works* (p. 179). Privately printed.
20. Charles Malik (1906–1987) was the representative of Lebanon. He was a Doctor of Philosophy at Harvard University. He attended San Francisco Conference in 1945, and served as Lebanon ambassador to the United States (1945–1955). He served almost all the important positions in the UN: Rapporteur of the Commission of Human Rights (1947–1948), Chairman of the UN Economic and Social Council (1948), Chairperson of the Commission on Human Rights (1951), and President of the thirteenth session of the UN General Assembly (1958–1959). In the process of drafting the *Universal Declaration of Human Rights*, he served as Rapporteur and the chairman of the Third Committee in the autumn of 1948, and chaired the debate of the Third Committee. He and Chinese representative P. C. Chang are considered to intellectually dominate the work of the Commission on Human Rights.
21. Humphrey, J. P. (1983). The memoirs of John P. Humphrey, the first Director of the United Nations Division of Human Rights. *Human Rights Quarterly* 5(4), 387–439.
22. Glendon, M. A. (2001). *A world made new: Eleanor Roosevelt and the Universal Declaration of Human Rights*. New York: Random House.
23. Twiss, S. B. (2007). Confucian ethics, concept-clusters, and human rights. In M. Chandler & R. Littlejohn (Eds.), *Polishing the Chinese mirror: Essays in honor of Henry Rosemont, Jr* (pp. 50–67). New York: Global Scholarly Publications.
24. Eleanor Roosevelt (1884–1962) was the US representative of the UN General Assembly and of the Commission on Human Rights (1946–1952). She was also the first Chair of the Commission on Human Rights (1947–1948), who led the drafting process of the *Universal Declaration of Human Rights*. Although she was not an expert in this field, her commitment and efforts for the Declaration won her great reverence.
25. René Cassin (1887–1976) was the representative of France of the Commission on Human Rights and of the Drafting Committee (1947–1948). He then served as vice chair of the Commission on Human Rights (1949) and Chair of the Commission (1955). He served as Law Professor at Paris University, who was an enthusiastic human rights expert in international law. As the representative of international organizations in the drafting of the UN Charter, René Cassin insisted explicitly incorporating respect for human rights and the dignity into the Charter. He was not only responsible for the drafting of the first draft of the *Universal Declaration of Human Rights*, but an effective mediator between the Committee and those who held different concepts of human rights. He devoted all his life to the cause of

human rights. Regarding his contributions to the cause of human rights and the drafting of the *Universal Declaration of Human Rights*, he was awarded the Nobel Peace Prize in 1968. According to the forty-seventh footnote in *Humphrey's Diary* Vol.1 P. 21-22, although he was drafted the first draft of the *Universal Declaration of Human Rights* and was known as the father of the Declaration, his contribution was somewhat exaggerated.

26. John Humphrey (1905–1995) was a Canadian. He served as a Dean of the Department of McGill University in Canada. He was the director of the Human Rights Division at the Secretariat of the United Nations in 1946. He combined his knowledge in international law and his support for the international human rights protection. He contributed a great deal in coordinating the disputes in various human rights philosophies. The most phenomenal contribution was his 408-paged draft outline of an International Bill of Human Rights for the Commission, which is also called the Secretariat's Outline or Humphrey's Draft. This outline included 30 definitions, list of rights and proposals from governments and nongovernmental organizations, which laid the foundation for the drafting of the declaration.
27. Humphrey, J. P. (1983). The memoirs of John P. Humphrey, the first Director of the United Nations Division of Human Rights. *Human rights Quarterly* (5/4), 387–439. (pp. 396–397.)/ Also see: Humphrey, J. P. (1984). *Human rights and the United Nations: A great adventure* (p. 23). New York: Transnational Publishers.
28. Hobbins, A. J. (Ed.). (1994). *On the edge of greatness: The diaries of John Humphrey, first Director of the United Nations Division of Human Rights* (Vol. 1.). (p. 88.) 1948–1949. Montreal: McGill University Libraries.
29. Humphrey, J. P. (1983). The memoirs of John P. Humphrey, the first Director of the United Nations Division of Human Rights. *Human rights Quarterly* (5/4), 387–439. (p. 400.)/Also see: Humphrey, J. P. (1984). *Human rights and the United Nations: A great adventure* (p. 26). New York: Transnational Publishers. UN Document: E. EN.4/SR.7. (p. 3.).
30. Humphrey, J. P. (1983). The memoirs of John P. Humphrey, the first Director of the United Nations Division of Human Rights. *Human Rights Quarterly* (5/4), 387–439. (p. 403).
31. Humphrey, J. P. (1983). The memoirs of John P. Humphrey, the first Director of the United Nations Division of Human Rights. *Human Rights Quarterly* (5/4), 387–439. (p. 416).
32. Humphrey, J. P. (1983). The memoirs of John P. Humphrey, the first Director of the United Nations Division of Human Rights. *Human Rights Quarterly* (5/4), 387–439. (pp. 427–428).
33. Twiss, S. B. (2009). Confucian contributions to the Universal Declaration of Human Rights: A historical and philosophical perspective. In A. Sharma (Ed.), *The world's religions after September 11*: (Vol. 2, Chap. 14, pp. 153–173). Religion and human rights. Westport, Connecticut and London: Praeger.
34. Twiss, S. B. (2007). Confucian ethics, concept-clusters, and human rights. In M. Chandler & R. Littlejohn (Eds.), *Polishing the Chinese mirror: Essays in honor of Henry Rosemont, Jr.* (pp. 50–67, p. 60). New York: Global Scholarly Publications.
35. Twiss, S. B. (2007). Confucian ethics, concept-clusters, and human rights. In M. Chandler & R. Littlejohn (Eds.), *Polishing the Chinese mirror: Essays in honor of Henry Rosemont, Jr.* (pp. 50–67). New York: Global Scholarly Publications.
36. Twiss, S. B. (2009). Confucian contributions to the Universal Declaration of Human Rights: A historical and philosophical perspective. In A. Sharma (Ed.), *The world's religions after September 11*: (Vol. 2, Chap. 14, pp. 153–173) Religion and human rights. Westport, Connecticut and London: Praeger.
37. Sun, P. (2012). *The study of the Universal Declaration of Human Rights* (pp. 93–112). Beijing: Peking University Press.
38. Malik, C. (2000). December 9, 1948, Speech to the General Assembly. In H. C. Malik (Ed.), *The challenge of human rights: Charles Malik and the Universal Declaration* (p. 121). Oxford: Centre for Lebanese Studies.
39. Humphrey, On the Edge of Greatness, 232–233. Cited in M. A. Glendon. 2001. *A world made new: Eleanor Roosevelt and the Universal Declaration of Human Rights* (pp. 211–212.). New York: Random House.

40. Xia, Y. (1996). Human rights and Chinese tradition. In P. R. Baehr et al. (Eds.), *Human rights: Chinese and Dutch perspectives* (pp. 89–90). The Hague/London/Boston: Martinus Nijhoff Publishers.
41. Xu, X. (2006). The right to harmony: The fourth generation human rights. *Human Rights, 2*, 30–32.
42. Wang, Z. (2010). Several issues on the formation of a socialist legal system with Chinese characteristics. *People's Daily.* November 15th. p. 6.

Chapter 2
The Dynamics of Human Rights Protection in China

Abstract In modern history, Human Rights Movement and Civil Rights Protection Movement had profound influence. The founding of the People's Republic of China on October 1, 1949 set a significant milestone. Though China has learned a bitter lesson from the "cultural revolution," it has also witnessed new developments in human rights protection. The release of white paper on Human Rights in China in 1991, the inclusion of "the state respects and guarantees human rights" in the Constitution in 2004, and the release of National Human Rights Action Plan of China in 2009, have marked the progressive development of human rights protection in China, and have made important contributions to the international human rights career.

In modern history, several events (e.g., The New Culture Movement, The Provincial Constitutionalism Movements, the Movements for Compensation of Unjust Verdict in the 1930s, the Human Rights Movements between 1929 and 1931 and the Civil Rights Protection Movement) showed the awareness and pursuit of human rights in China [1]. Among the events, the impact of the last two was most profound. New possibilities in progress of human rights were opened up by overthrowing the three mountains (of imperialism, feudalism, and bureaucrat-capitalism) that had suppressed Chinese people and by the founding of the People's Republic of China (PRC) in 1949. It is the founding of new China that has created the favorable national and international environments for Chinese people to enjoy human rights.

The founding of the PRC on October 1, 1949, is a milestone in human rights development for the whole world community. Chinese people, led by the Communist Party, fought bloody battles for more than two decades and finally overthrew the rule of imperialism, feudalism and bureaucrat-capitalism, and terminated almost the century-long humiliating history for Chinese nation. As the country won independence, its people were thus emancipated from oppression. Since the founding of new China, great achievements have been made in human rights protection, despite the bitter experience of "cultural revolution". Especially after the reform and opening-up, China's economy develops fast and its people's living

P. Sun, *Human Rights Protection System in China*,
DOI: 10.1007/978-3-642-39663-2_2, © Springer-Verlag Berlin Heidelberg 2014

standard has been improved. The rights enjoyed by its people are being increasingly enriched. The general level of human rights protection is being improved. Objectively speaking, thousands of years' cultural tradition, Marxism and communist party's experience accumulated from practice are determining the progress and direction in the cause of human rights in China.

Just before the founding of new China, civil rights protection was put forward in the Common Program of Chinese People's Political Consultative Conference (CPPCC), the first complete constitutional program of new democracy, adopted on September 29, 1949. After the founding of new China, the content and scope of human rights protection have tremendously been enriched and expanded through the promulgation of four successive versions of Constitutions of 1954, 1975, 1978, and 1982, and through four amendments of the fourth version respectively made in 1988, 1993, 1999, and 2004. In a word, over the past six decades after the founding of new China, the cause of human rights has gone through the catastrophe of "cultural revolution" and learned the painful lesson from it on the one hand, and on the other hand has made new great progress too.

2.1 Main Human Rights Movements in Modern History of China

Two movements have exerted profound impacts in modern history of China, namely, the Human Rights Movement and Civil Rights Protection Movement that took place in late 1920s and early 1930s.

2.1.1 Human Rights Movement

In late 1920s and early 1930s, college professors that had education background from Europe and America started the Human Rights Movement, demanding constitutional protection of human rights. This movement is "the political movement that was themed only human rights" [2]. It was led by Hu Shi, Luo Longji, and Liang Shiqiu, etc., who formed the "Human Rights School" with the journal of *New Moon* (*XinYue*) as a front to express their opinions. The article entitled "*Human Rights and Provisional Constitution*" by Hu Shi was so powerful that it seemed to "have shot the first cannon in human rights movement" [3]. Later, Hu Shi published several similar articles successively in this journal like "*When Can We Have Constitution.*" Meanwhile, Luo Longji also published articles like "*On Human Rights*" and "*Warning for Those Who Oppress Freedom of Speech.*" Liang Shiqiu published articles like "*On Unity of Thoughts.*" Some of these articles were later compiled in *Collection of Human Rights,* which played an important role in exposing and criticizing the abuse of human rights and the absence of human rights protection under the rule of the Kuomintang (KMT).

First, in Human Rights Movement, the "Human Rights School" disclosed and criticized the fact that human rights could not be protected under the rule of KMT. In "*Human Rights and Provisional Constitution,*" Hu Shi first questioned and criticized the so called human rights protection by analyzing the "*Human Rights Protection Decree*" issued by the KMT on April 20, 1930. After demonstrating the opposite to the KMT's proclamation with hard facts, Hu proposed "to truly protect human rights, the rule of law must be established. The first thing is to draw up a constitution of the Republic of China (ROC). Or at least draft a transitional constitution" [4].

Second, the "Human Rights School" put forward the idea of protecting human rights through constitution. In "*When Can We Have Constitution,*" Hu Shi explicitly asserted that "a constitution should be adopted, and any office of the municipal government shall not exceed the limit of their rights stipulated by constitution, and shall not infringe on people's rights—this is the practice of democracy. For the nation at the infant stage of democracy, not only its people need such practice, but also its government needs too" [5]. In fact, these words explicitly raised the question of protecting human rights through constitution.

Third, this school defined human rights. Luo Longji noted in "*On Human Rights,*" "Human rights, to put it simply, are the rights to be human. These rights are the necessary conditions for being human" [6]. In this school, Luo Longji is the one that went furthest in the research into human rights. He not only initiated the theory of the necessary conditions, but also substantiated the content of human rights that should cover not only the rights to food, clothes, accommodation so as to sustain life, but also the rights to happiness, individuality, and development [7]. What is more, he also illustrated the relation between human rights and nation, law, practice, location, etc. He thus was the one among the scholars of this school that gave the most systematic explanation of human rights. Profoundly influenced by Western theory and thoughts on human rights, Luo Longji could still take account of the social reality of China to expound human rights. Even today, some of his original ideas are still enlightening.

Finally, this school advocated that freedom of thought and speech is the most significant content of human rights. Liang Shiqiu argued that "we need freedom of thought, freedom to express our thoughts. We need law to ensure such freedom" [4]. He further proposed that "we wish freedom of thought for everyone, and must support liberal education" [4]. Luo Longji pointed out in "*Warning for Those Who Oppress Freedom of Speech,*" "Freedom of speech means the freedom from the interference of law. It means the congress cannot make law to prohibit people's speech" [8].

In the Human Rights Movement, the criticism of the KMT government for not protecting human rights exerted undoubtedly some actual influence on the KMT so that they would restrain their Fascist arrogance. This movement is considered to be "the only real human rights movement, and the most significant enlightenment movement on thoughts of human rights" [9]. The "Human Rights School," after studying, assimilating and digesting Western philosophy of human rights, systematically raised their theories of human rights with reference to China's social reality. "Their theories are not only significant at that time, but also lend themselves to today' thoughts" [10].

2.1.2 Civil Rights Protection Movement

Later on December 18, 1932, Song Qingling, Cai Yuanpei, and Yang Xingfu proclaimed their manifesto, and started to organize and lead China League for Civil Rights. The League was officially founded on December 29, and presided by Song Qingling. The League specified its tenet as "to arouse the pubic awareness to protect civil rights" [11]. Its members could generally communicate in English and thus could win international support. With its rigorous tenet for organizing the league and its activities, it successfully rescued Communist Party members like Chen Duxiu, Chen Geng, Mu Chengzhi and the writer Ding Ling. The League's activities were terminated by the assassination of one of its leader, Yang Xingfu by the reactionary authorities. However, this movement played an important role in the history of China's human rights.

2.2 The History of Fighting for Human Rights by the Communist Party of China

At its early time, the Communist Party took a succession of measures to protect human rights. In 1922, it raised the question of protecting freedom of various kinds, like the one of association, assembly, speech, and press in its "*First Proposal to the Current Political Situation.*" In 1923, the famed Great Demonstration on February 7th shouted the slogan: "Fighting for freedom, fighting for human rights." In 1934, the "*Constitution Outline of the Chinese Soviet Republic*" stipulated the rights to participation in political affairs, to freedom and to education. In 1941, the "*Administration Outline for the Border Areas of Shaanxi, Gansu and Ningxia*" provided general human rights for the people fighting the Anti-Japanese War, including the freedom to speech, assembly, association, religious belief, residence, migration etc. In 1942, the "*Shandong Provincial Regulations for Human Rights Protection*" stipulated the legal measures for protecting personal rights.

After the victory of Anti-Japanese War, the KMT government ignored the outcries of the Communist Party and the people, waged the Civil War and carried out the Nazi-like dictatorial rule, under which the patriotic democratic personages were arrested, imprisoned, and massacred, and the people were completely deprived of their democratic and personal rights. To counter the KMT's dictatorial rule, the Communist Party led the people in launching the democratic movement to "fight against hunger, persecution, Civil War" and to "fight for freedom, democracy, human rights," which contributed to the final victory of China's New Democratic Revolution. In 1946, "*The Constitutional Principle for Border Areas of Shaanxi, Gansu and Ningxia*" stipulated "the people shall enjoy six basic rights," and provided the measures to ensure such rights, e.g. "The government shall provide material help, shall reduce rents and interests to improve workers' living standard, and shall develop education, medical care and medical equipments" [12]. The above-mentioned laws and regulations all provide precious experience for developing and improving the human rights protection system of China.

On September 20, 1954, in its first conference, the first National People's Congress adopted the first *Constitution of the People's Republic of China (PRC)*, which is the first constitution of socialist nature in China's history. It was based on the *Common Program of CPPCC*. Chairman Mao participated in and led the whole process of drafting the constitution. This constitution established China's political system and the basic system of constitutional government, reflected the will and interests of the people and thus was a good fundamental charter.

The basic contents and principles of the 1954 constitution laid a solid foundation for the later development of constitution and constitutionalism. Unfortunately, with the advent of "cultural revolution", this constitution, drafted with the participation of Chairman Mao, was reduced to shadow, and a catastrophe in human rights protection started. In 1957, with the acting of numerous historical factors, the ultra-left trend of thought prevailed. Large numbers of cadres and intellectuals were oppressed and labeled as the Rightists. The total number of the alleged innocent Rightists amounted to 3.17 million [13]. In 1959, the Lushan Conference mistakenly made the resolution, namely the "Decision on the Mistakes Made by the Anti-Party Clique Headed by Peng Dehuai." The nihilism of law began to prevail over the dignity and authority of the constitution.

Three decades has passed since the "cultural revolution", during the period of which democracy and law were ruthlessly overridden, basic freedom and human rights deprived, and the whole country thrown into chaos. This bitter experience is still remembered by the Party, the country and the people. The people have learned the lesson that there will be no basic freedom and human rights without democracy and rule of law.

On the one hand, China should practice the rule of law, should develop its socialist democracy and legal system, which had been disastrously damaged by the "cultural revolution". At that time, man's dignity and value were completely deprived, personal safety and freedom not protected, and the whole country and society in a chaotic state, with the absence of democracy and of the rule of law. This agonizing experience has taught us that China should be ruled by law, and should develop socialist democracy and the rule of law so as to guarantee its long-term peace and order, enhance its people's well-being and push forward its socialist cause. To govern China by law, the authority of the rule of law should be established, and any organization and individual shall comply with the state law, shall not enjoy the privilege to override the law.

On the other hand, China should protect human rights, and should build and develop a harmonious society. Human rights protection plays a decisive role in China's socialist cause. In 2004, "the state respects and guarantees human rights" was included in China's *Constitution*. Thus, to respect and guarantee human rights has become a constitutional principle and has become the essential content in developing China's legal system. Therefore, to develop socialist human rights has become one important task for the Party and the country, and one major task of China's socialist construction in new period. A harmonious society cannot do without respecting and protecting human rights. The ambitious goal of a harmonious society can only be realized after the human rights are adequately respected and protected. To protect human rights is the core nature of a harmonious society, and a harmonious society must be one in which human rights are entirely protected.

2.3 The Rejuvenation of Human Rights Cause in China

After the founding of new China, some progress was made in the building of constitutionalism. But this progress was suspended by the "cultural revolution," the end of which was brought about by the crushing of the *Gang of Four* in October 1976, and was declared by the 11th CPC Conference in August 1977. The constitution adopted in 1975 was found to have severe problems, and thus it was put on the agenda to revise the Constitution. The third Constitution of PRC was adopted by the first conference of the fifth NPC on March 5, 1978. It made amendments to the 1975 constitution and put wrongs to rights. It basically resumed the provisions of the 1954 constitution about civil rights and structuring of government offices and their functions and powers. However, this constitution was "transitional" due to its historical context. It still showed inadequacy despite containing some right contents [14]. It failed to eradicate the ultra-left thoughts, the residue of the "cultural revolution." It still contained some incorrect political views and some impractical provisions.

The incorrect political views and thoughts were only corrected after the mass debate, which was brought about by a special commentator article titled "*Practice Is the Only Criterion to Test Truth*" published on *Guangming Daily*. The debate "stirred up the tide of liberating minds in Chinese academia" [15]. The mistakes of the "cultural revolution" were thoroughly sorted out by the Third Plenary Session of the 11th CPC Central Committee. It was in this session that lessons were summed up and learned from the practice after the founding of new China, correct principles and policies made, civil rights protection specified, the idea that all men are equal before law raised, and democracy and rule of law emphasized. This session marked the new beginning of the cause of human rights, and signified the historical turn in the history of new China. Furthermore, the political line "to free our mind, to seek truth from facts" and the principle "*Practice Is the Only*

Criterion to Test Truth" were established in the Sixth Plenary Session of the 11th CPC Central Committee in June, 1981. In 1979, seven laws were promulgated successively, namely, the Criminal Law, the Criminal Procedural Law, Organic Law of the PRC on the Local People's Congresses and Local People's Governments, Electoral Law of the PRC on the National People's Congress and the Local People's Congresses, Organic Law of the People's Court of the PRC, Organic Law of the People's Procuratorate of the PRC and Sino-foreign Joint Venture Law. The guiding principle for making such laws was to ensure citizen's lawful rights.

The fourth Constitution of PRC was adopted by the fifth session of fifth NPC on December 4, 1982, in order to adapt to the new situation of the reform and opening up. This constitution is sill in effect. It carried forward and developed the basic principles of the 1954 Constitution, summed up scientifically and profoundly the experience of Chinese socialism development, and assimilated precious experience from international constitution drafting. It entered the "Four Cardinal Principles" and carried out them from its beginning to end. It specified that China hereafter shall concentrate all its efforts on socialist construction and modernization. It provided that all citizens are equal before law. In a word, this 1982 Constitution is a fundamental charter of Chinese characteristics that accommodates to the need of China's socialist construction and modernization. It has undergone four amendments, each of which has greatly pushed forward China's socialist construction and modernization.

On November 1, 1991, Chinese government issued its first white paper on human rights—*Human Rights in China*,which marked the entry of "human rights" as a political notion into China's political life. It illustrated objectively the human rights practice in China, and put forward China's propositions on human rights. The Chinese government for the first time raised the banner of human rights with assured justice, thus preserved China's international reputation and brought about favorable influence at home and abroad.

"The state respects and guarantees human rights" became a constitutional principle and was for the first time written into the fourth Constitution Amendment [16], which was reviewed and adopted by the second session of the tenth NPC. This marked the new age China has stepped into in terms of human rights protection. This entry of human rights into the Constitution is a new milestone for China. If human rights were considered man's ideals or imperatives before, then after this amendment, human rights have become a constitutional principle and become lawful. Undoubtedly, this is a big leap forward in the cause of human rights and provides legal basis for the exercise of human rights.

National Human Rights Action Plan of China (2009–2010) was issued by the Information Office of the State Council. This plan is "the first human-rights-themed national plan, and is a policy paper of the action program to put into practice the constitutional principle 'the state respccts and guarantees human rights' and advance China's human rights cause" [17]. It provides not only the guarantee of economic, social and cultural rights, the civil rights and political rights, but also the measures to ensure the rights for ethnic minorities, women, children, old people, and the disabled. Besides, it also maps out human rights education, performing international human rights duties, and the communication and cooperation in human rights in the international arena. It has established a joint-conference review system. Its measures are specific, proper, feasible, and workable and above all fit for the specific national situations. It will greatly contribute to the development of China's human rights cause.

Over the past few years, China has been actively seeking cooperation and dialogue with the international community, has contributed tremendously for the international human rights cause, and has made great achievements that have attracted world-wide attention. On December 9, 2008, Wang Chen, Director of the Information Office of the State Council, pointed out in an exclusive review by the journal *Human Rights*, "China human rights cause has made progress of historic significance. China's human rights practice is at the best time" [18]. The major achievements he believed are seen in the following five aspects: "First, unprecedented attention has been given to respecting and safeguarding human rights, which has become an important principle for the CPC and Chinese government in managing state affairs. Second, the people's rights to subsistence and development have been ensured in an unprecedented way. Third, the people's civil rights and political rights have been practically guaranteed. Fourth, the people's economic, social and cultural rights have been continuously improved. Fifth, the international communication and cooperation have been constantly expanded" [18].

2.4 Progress of China's Human Rights Viewed by Human Rights Experts

Since the founding of the PRC in 1949, both practice and theory of human rights in China have made great progress. Particularly in the past 30 years, the cause of China's human rights has made great achievements, which are obvious to the whole world. Professor Qi Yanping and Zang Zhen once systematically reflected on the progress and development of Chinese human rights since the reform and opening up 30 years ago, believing that the human rights protection thought has been established, the human rights theoretical system has been formed, the human rights safeguarding system has been improved, and the human rights safeguarding practice has made a progress [19].

2.4.1 The Establishment of Human Rights Protection Thought

Regarding the establishment of human rights protection thought, Professor Qi and Zang believed that it has included two aspects: one is the establishment of rights first concept, changing from duty first to right first and changing from power first to rights first; another is the establishment of human rights protection concept. They point out:

> China's human rights legal circle has reached a consensus in the classification of human rights, namely, the deserved, legitimate and practical rights. The real condition of human rights of a country is just the proportion among the three types. If the deserved becomes the legitimate and the latter becomes the practical, the proportion of the three is one, meaning the ideal reality of human rights. In contrast, if there is a big gap in the proportion, the country's human rights situations are not good. The human rights situation of a country should not be judged by only one type. If we regard the legitimate human rights as the practical ones, the protection of human rights will only stay at the legal level. Such judgment is not conducive to human rights practice [19].

After further analysis from the political circles, Professor Qi and Zang summarized as follows: "The concept of human rights protection has been gradually established, with deepened research and knowledge about human rights among academic and political circles, and social, economic and cultural development and people's knowledge of the importance of human rights issue. The protection of human rights has become a basic principle and core value for the construction of a complete, systematic legal system and of a socialist country under the rule of law" [19].

2.4.2 *The Form of Human Rights Theoretical System*

With reference to the formation of human rights theoretical system, Professor Qi and Zang discuss the extension of human rights subjects and the improvement of human rights content. When discussing the extension of human rights subjects, they insist that "the 30 years of the development of China's human rights subjects theory is represented by two marked changes, namely, 'from limited subjects to general subjects' and 'from general subjects to special subjects'" [19].

Then they move on to discuss the improvement of human rights content, stating that China not only views all the social members as subjects of human rights protection, but also attach great importance to all kinds of human rights, setting the highest priority for the right to subsistence and the right to development. They strongly insist that "to a country and a person, man's subsistence right comes first. Without subsistence rights, there will be no other human rights at all" [19]. They continue with the following statement: "The right to development mainly means the right of all members of society to share all kinds of fruits brought by the overall social progress and development" [19]. Then they summarize that "over the past 30 years, China has basically set up the human rights theoretical system with Chinese characteristics, which regards everyone (all members of society) as its subjects and the rights to subsistence and development as core contents" [19].

2.4.3 The Improvement of Human Rights Safeguarding System

The improvement of human rights safeguarding system can be analyzed from the following perspectives: first, China has made remarkable achievements in the legislation area.

> The socialist legal system with Chinese characteristics has basically been established. The system, consisting of seven law divisions and three tiers of laws and regulations, has the constitution as its core, the laws its main body and includes regulatory documents such as administrative and local regulations. The laws have covered the country's economic, political, cultural and social life, providing a strong legal backing for rule by law and the building of a socialist country under the rule of law and safeguard of all human rights [19].

Similarly, another Chinese expert, Han Yanlong, believes that "China has developed a relatively complete human rights law system compatible with its current level of political, social, and economic development. This system consists of the following four parts: the Constitution, the laws, the administrative regulations, and local regulations" [20]. Han further summarizes the following characteristics of China's human rights law system:

> (1) It consists of both provisions stipulated in the Constitution and provisions stipulated in general law. It should be mentioned that China belongs to the continental law system, and legal precedents could not be taken as the basis for the administration of law, but only as references. The judicial interpretations of the Supreme People's Court and the Supreme People's Procuratorate should be regarded as a part of China's human rights law system, playing an important role in the judicial practice. … (2) It consists of both comprehensive or principled legislations and specific human rights protection laws. … (3) It consists of both the legislations of the Central Government and those of local governments. A wide range of issues is dealt with by local regulations, which are formulated under the premise that they shall not contravene the Constitution and the laws [21].

In China, the Constitution, drafted and ratified by highest organ of the state power, is the fundamental law of the country. Therefore, the Constitution has supreme legal effect in the Chinese system of law. The citizen's fundamental rights and freedom stipulated in the Constitution are sacred and inalienable, and no laws and regulations may contravene the Constitution. Laws specify and supplement some of the citizen's rights provided in the Constitution and they are drafted and ratified by the National People's Congress or its Standing Committee. Administrative regulations are promulgated by the highest organ of administration and the ministries and commissions under it while local regulations are formulated and promulgated by the local people's congresses of provinces, autonomous regions and municipalities directly under the Central Government, according to the actual situation in their respective areas.

2.4.4 Progress in Human Rights Safeguarding Practice

In 2004, "the State respects and guarantees human rights" was written into the Constitution, which turned a new leaf for human rights protection in China. When talking about its significance of the inclusion of human rights concept into the Constitution, Professor Qi and Zang made the following statement from five different aspects:

> The first is the modification on the outlook on subject of human rights, which changes the formerly used citizen subject into the adjusted subject of 'everyone' or 'all people'. The change challenges the differentiation outlook of subject and legislation and the dual structure of rights. The second is the change from closedness to openness of the established human rights system. The third is about the human rights standard and value. … The international human rights standards, are also the country's domestic ones except for declared reservations. The human rights modifications unite domestic and international standards. The fourth is the adjustment of governance idea. 'Governance for the people' should be transformed into legal judgment to safeguard human rights. The 'for the people' in governance should become 'for the people's rights' in law. The fifth is the modification on law enforcement idea. The state respects and safeguards human rights, indicating law enforcement departments should regard this as their own duties [19].

Progress in human rights safeguarding practice is also a focus in Professor Qi and Zang's article, subdividing this section into four components: (1) rights to subsistence and development; (2) citizen's rights and political rights; (3) economic, social and cultural rights; and (4) judicial safeguard of human rights. At last, the article gives a very good summary:

> The 30 years of reform and opening up is also a period of China's all round economic, social and cultural development and of the flourish of its human rights undertakings, which have experienced a fundamental change from being a cold field to being a hot issue. In the 30 years, China's human rights thought was established, its human rights theoretical system formed, human rights safeguarding system improved and human rights safeguarding practice promoted. The report of the 17th CPC National Congress said 'we must respect and safeguard human rights' in the part of speeding up the building of a socialist country governed by law. It puts more emphasis on the relationship between human rights and rule of law. Human rights are changed from a political concept to a legal one. Human rights become legal rights which make it a legal duty for the state to respect and safeguard human right. This not only points out the direction for the development of China's human rights undertakings, is also the action principle and guidance for us to push forward human rights work and strengthen the construction of human rights thought and theory. It is believed China's human rights undertakings will achieve greater progress with the deepening of political system reform and sustained economic and social development [19].

However, when we talked about socialist legal system with Chinese characteristics, we had better answer the following questions: (1) Why can we say that socialist legal system with Chinese characteristics has basically been established and confirmed in 2010? (2) What are the fundamental characteristics of this socialist legal system? (3) What is the significance of the formation of Chinese socialist legal system? Circling around the three questions listed above, I would mainly refer to Wang Zhaoguo's speech [22] at the Sixteenth National Symposium on the local legislation (See Chap.10). To introduce his ideas to the Western scholars, I would like to translate Wang's speech from Chinese into English as Chap.10. The original Chinese version of this article can be found in *People's Daily*, November 15th, 2010.

References

1. Xu, X. (Ed.). (2008). *Human rights principles* (p. 40). Beijing: China University of Political Science and Law Press.
2. Xu, X. (Ed.). (2008). *Human rights principles* (p. 43). Beijing: China University of Political Science and Law Press.
3. Xu, X. (Ed.). (2008). *Human rights principles* (p. 44). Beijing: China University of Political Science and Law Press.
4. Ouyang, Z. (Ed.). (1998). *Collected works of Hushi 5* (p. 527). Beijing: Peking University Press.
5. Ouyang, Z. (Ed.). (1998). *Collected works of Hushi 5* (p. 538). Beijing: Peking University Press.
6. Ouyang, Z. (Ed.). (1998). *Collected works of Hushi 5* (p. 541). Beijing: Peking University Press.
7. Ouyang, Z. (Ed.). (1998). *Collected works of Hushi 5* (p. 543). Beijing: Peking University Press.
8. Ouyang, Z. (Ed.). (1998). *Collected works of Hushi 5* (p. 562). Beijing: Peking University Press.
9. Xu, X. (Ed.). (2008.). *Human rights principles* (p. 53). Beijing: China University of Political Science and Law Press.
10. Xu, X. (Ed.). (2008). *Human rights principles* (p. 53). Beijing: China University of Political Science and Law Press.
11. See article 2 of "*Charter for China League for Civil Rights*" (1979), published in *China League for Civil Rights* (p. 3). China Social Academy Press.
12. Hu, J., & Han, D. (1993). *Contemporary human rights protection system* (p. 296). Beijing: China University of Political Science and Law Press.
13. Guo, D. (2009). The original intention of Mao for launching the movement of rectifying the incorrect style of work. *Yanhuang Chunqiu, 2*, 10–16.
14. Yu, Z. (2004). *Constitutional jurisprudence* (p. 62). Beijing: China University of Political Science and Law Press.
15. Qu, X. (2009). Main doctrines for human rights over the past three decades after the opening up and reforming. In X. Xu (Ed.), *Human Rights Research* (Vol. 8, p. 1). Jinan: Shandong People's Press.
16. The four partial amendments of *Constitution* of PRC will be discussed in part 3 of this chapter.
17. Wang, C. (2009). Major measures to advance the all-round development of human rights in China. *China Daily*. April 15th, p. 8.
18. Wang, C. (2008). China's human rights have made a historic progress. *Human Rights, 6*, 2–7.
19. Qi, Y., & Zang, Z. (2008). Progress and reflection: China's human rights in the past 30 years. *Human Rights, 3*, 19–26.
20. Han, Y., et al. (1996). Legal protection of human rights in China. In P. R. Bachr (Ed.), *Human rights: Chinese and Dutch perspective* (pp. 91–101). The Hague: Martinus Nijhoff Publisher.

21. Han, Y. (1996). Legal protection of human rights in China. In P. R. Bachr, et el. (Eds.), *Human rights: Chinese and Dutch perspective* (pp. 91–101). The Hague: Martinus Nijhoff Publisher.
22. Wang, Z. (2010). Several issues on the formation of a socialist legal system with Chinese characteristics. *People's Daily*. November 15th, p. 6.

Chapter 3
The First White Paper: Human Rights in China

Abstract The first white paper—Human Rights in China was released by the Chinese government in 1991. This white paper regarded full implementation of human rights as a great ideal and loft goal that human beings have been pursuing. The release of this white paper broke the forbidden area of human rights research, and it exhibited great achievements of human rights protection in China by clarifying the attitudes and principles of the Chinese government to human rights. It maintained the international image of China and laid a foundation for human rights protection career in China. The white paper has become a milestone in the history of Chinese human rights development.

On November 1, 1991, the Information Office of the State Council of the People's Republic of China published *Human Rights in China*, which is the first white paper on human rights issued by our government. The white paper distinguishes "human rights" as the "great term", making it a glorious ideal and lofty goal to enjoy human rights to their full extent. For the first time since the founding of the People's Republic of China, the Chinese government holds high the banner of human rights to show the world the human rights achievements and its corresponding attitudes. As an important milestone, such a positive attitude towards the new phase of international human rights cause writes a brilliant page in the history of China's human rights. Professor Qu Xiangfei thought, "The door finally opens to human rights study after the release of the white paper on human rights. With the blind rejection changed into a stirring of interest in human rights, the research and the protection system on human rights begin to get on the right track in China" [1]. Professor Dong Yunhu thought, "This is the first official document on human rights announced by the Chinese government. It greatly pushes forward the development of theory and practice, worthy of a major landmark in the history of China's human rights" [2].

P. Sun, *Human Rights Protection System in China*,
DOI: 10.1007/978-3-642-39663-2_3, © Springer-Verlag Berlin Heidelberg 2014

3.1 Background and Process in Drafting the White paper

During the "cultural revolution" decade from 1957 to 1976, human rights protection was severely damaged due to the political unrest. The principles set by the Constitution in 1954, on which a sequence of systems had been based, did not function normally. "The Constitution and human rights protection system suffered seriously, i.e., 'no constitution' and 'disordering' reigned" [3]. The "cultural revolution" is considered to be "a vacancy in the history of human rights protection system since the founding of China" [4]. After the downfall of the "Gang of Four" in 1976, the government decided timely policies to restore order and establish new Constitution in 1978. Although many problems remained, the Constitution truly restored a number of important rights and freedoms provided by the 1954 Constitution and made provisions in the aspect of protection system, which is undoubtedly a big step forward compared with the 1975 Constitution . Since the Third Plenary Session of the 11th Central Committee of the Chinese Communist Party, China has adhered to the principle in legal system that "there shall be laws to abide by, everyone should abide by the law, the law must be enforced strictly, and those who violate the law must be dealt with", with the grievances redressed, government legal organization reestablished and strengthened, and human protection guaranteed institutionally. In 1982, the Constitution of the People's Republic of China was established and issued, which makes human rights protection system proceed along a normal track in China.

In the international community , the US-led Western countries, however, have been using "human rights" as a means to attack China, attempting to occidentalize and disunite China and launching anti-China campaign frantically in the name of human rights. Especially from the late 1980s to the early 1990s, due to the radical changes in Eastern Europe and the disintegration of the Soviet Union, the US leveled a blast at China, advertising its own social system and values as the only standard by pushing hegemonism and power politics in the name of "human rights". Professor Dong Yunhu points out:

> Linking the so-called 'human rights issue' with the relation with China, they, in the name of quelling the political turmoil in Beijing, passed resolutions, published reports and slandered the socialist China without any constraint. Moreover, such international organizations as the United Nations were manipulated to pass the anti-China resolution with the purpose of pressing and besiege China in an all-round way, which caused waves of anti-China storm and smeared the international image of China. That not only undermined China's national sovereignty and external relations, but interfered with China's reform, development and stability [2].

Facing the "anti-China campaign " represented by the US, the third generation of collective central leadership with Jiang Zemin at the core attached great importance to human rights issue. They reviewed regularly the theory and practice of socialist construction and analyzed profoundly the changing international situations. With Marxist theory as a guide, the nature of human rights was understood further and the dialectical relation between socialist system and human rights analyzed thoroughly. In response to the major decisions of international human rights, they strategically took advantage of the Marxist concept to look at "democracy, freedom and human rights" [5], and "held high the banner of human rights timely to cope with the international human rights struggle" [2]. On March 2, 1991, the Propaganda Department of the CPC Central Committee held mini-symposium on human rights issue, conveying the comments on human rights by Jiang Zemin who requested to carry out human rights research [6].

It was against this background that the Chinese government drafted and issued the first white paper on human rights—*Human Rights in China*. In accordance with the instructions on human rights research from the central authority leader, the State Council Information Office decided to draft and issue the first white paper on human rights in order to help the domestic and international community to know comprehensively, systematically and accurately the fact that Chinese people enjoyed human rights. Zhu Muzhi , with Zeng Jianhui and Zhou Jue as assistants, chaired and participated in the drafting. Headed by Li Yuanchao the Secretary of the First Office of the State Council Information Office, a writing group was organized, which included Li Yuanchao, Qian Xiaoqian , Tian Dan , Dong Yunhu , Liu Fenzhi , Xu Jianyi and Zou Encheng [7].

During the process of drafting, the State Council Information Office asked ministries and commissions of the CPC Central Committee and the Institute of Law of Chinese Academy of Social Sciences (CASS) to provide elaborate data on human rights construction and held frequent symposiums. After the Central Government and the departments closely relevant with human rights looked into the content and structure repeatedly, the State Council Information Office published the white paper *Human Rights in China* on November 1, 1991. The first white paper on human rights is couched by the collective wisdom of generations, which uses detailed data to fully demonstrate the great achievements the Chinese government has made on human rights and expresses concisely the stance and principles on human rights in China.

3.2 Basic Content in the White Paper

The white paper *Human Rights in China* consists of six paragraphs of the preface and 10 sections of the text. Classifying "human rights" as the "great term", the beginning paragraph of the preface is made clear that "It has been a long-cherished ideal of mankind to enjoy human rights in the full sense of the term". Those who strive for the cause of human rights are called "the people with lofty ideals", who has made unremitting efforts to let people enjoy their full human rights. The second paragraph compares briefly the human rights situations between old China and new China. The third paragraph shows the basic position regarding human rights by the Chinese government. While highly commending the *Universal Declaration of Human Rights* and affirming the universality of human rights , it points out that human rights, "an issue falling within the sovereignty of the country", cannot be separated from the fundamental realities. Thus, seeking truth from the facts is the attitude to follow in observing and measuring the human rights situations; neither history can be cut off nor the fundamental realities disregarded. The fourth paragraph introduces the three distinctive features human rights have in China; they are extensiveness, fairness and authenticity. The fifth paragraph evaluates objectively the great achievements and the areas of improvement in maintaining and developing human rights in China. With the full realization of human rights as a lofty goal, the Chinese people and government will boost proactively the development of human rights. The last paragraph is a transitional one, linking between the preceding and the following body of the white paper.

The body of the white paper has 10 sections. Section 1 makes it clear that "the right to subsistence is the foremost human rights". By quoting a large amount of data and hard facts, it argues that, in order to struggle for the right to subsistence, national independence must be won, and imperialism, feudalism and bureaucrat-capitalism eradicated. With regard to the history in the last hundred years, old China has been suffering foreign invasion and seizure, with the people leading a humiliating life. Numerous people with lofty ideals struggled dauntlessly to save the nation from subjugation and ensured its survival, finally overturning the "Three Mountains ". The CPC and the Chinese government, since the founding of the People's Republic of China, have been giving top priority to the guarantee of people's right to subsistence and basically solving the problem of food and clothing through strenuous efforts over decades of years. "As China's economic development is at a comparatively low level, people's living standard still has a long way to go compared with some developed Western countries. Moreover, the swell in population and relatively poor per-capita resources will restrict the development of society and economy and the improvement of people's life. The people's right to subsistence will still be threatened in the event of a social turmoil or other disasters. Thus, the most basic will and demand of the Chinese people, a long-term and pressing task for the Chinese government as well, is as follows: maintain national stability, concentrate efforts on productive force with the successful experience, persevere in reform and opening up, push national economy forward, enhance national strength, reach a well-off level based on a subsistent one, and finally avoid threatening people's right to subsistence" [8].

Section 2 expounds the view that "the Chinese people have gained extensive political rights". Since the very day of its founding, the Communist Party of China has been holding high the banner of democracy and human rights, and the Chinese people have gained real democratic rights after the founding of New China . The Constitution clearly defines the rights and duties of citizens, including equal rights for men and women, the right to equality before the law, the right to vote and stand for election, the right to free speech and a free press, the right to free assembly, association and procession, etc. It also provides that freedom of the person of citizens of the People's Republic of China is inviolable. Emphasizing the legal system construction, our country has done much work in legislation aspect. "It has promulgated and put into effect a series of major laws, including the

Constitution, the Criminal Law, the Law of Criminal Procedure, the General Provisions of the Civil Law, the Law of Civil Procedure and the Law of Administrative Procedure"[9]. The unity between rights and duties is a basic principle of China's legal system . Under the Constitution, "the exercise by citizens of the People's Republic of China of their freedoms and rights may not infringe upon the interests of the state, of society and of the collective, or upon the lawful freedoms and rights of other citizens"[10]. Therefore, the socialist democracy and legal system adopted by China are suited to the country's actual conditions. Nowadays, the country attaches great importance to the construction of democracy and building of its legal system, so as to lay better stress on ensuring that its citizens enjoy various civil and political rights.

Section 3 elaborates on the view that "citizens enjoy economic, cultural and social rights ". With regards to the protection of economic rights , the principle of socialist distribution is "from each according to his ability, to each according to his work", fully mobilizing the enthusiasm of the masses, and greatly improving the overall living standard of the Chinese people. As for property, the Constitution provides definite stipulations that the state protects the right of citizens to own the lawful property. Touching cultural rights, the rights of Chinese citizens to receive education has been further guaranteed; the government encourages students to study abroad and makes preferential policy to those who come back. As our citizens get legal protection in the field of scientific study, literary and artistic creation, intellectual property rights have been ensured. A lot has also been done concerning social rights. Health and medical undertakings have advanced greatly. Infectious and endemic diseases have come under control. The general level of the people's health has markedly improved. The Social Security System provides help to the old people. Old-age care becomes a reality. Respecting old folks fosters healthy social conduct. Moreover, China attaches great importance to safeguarding the rights of women, children and teenagers. As a developing country, China definitely has a long way to go in protecting the economic, social and cultural rights.

Section 4 gives a detailed account of "the guarantee of human rights in China's judicial work". China's public security and judicial organs follow the following principles in carrying out their duties:

> 1. All citizens are equal in regard to the applicability of law. In accordance with the law, each citizen's legal rights and interests shall be protected, and any citizen's offenses against the law and his criminal activities shall be looked into. 2. The judicial activities of China's public security and judicial organs shall base themselves on facts and take the law as the criterion. 3. The procuratorate and the court shall independently exercise their respective procuratorial and judicial authority. They shall only obey the law and not be interfered with by any administrative organ, social organization or person [11].

After that, seven strict regulations are introduced on the protection of human rights. 1. Detention and Arrest; 2. Search and the Obtaining of Evidence; 3. Prosecution and Judgment; 4. No "Political Prisoners" in China; 5. Prison Work and the Rights of Criminals; 6. Prison Labor; 7. Education through Labor and the Rights of Those Being Educated through Labor. The above-mentioned legal regulations show that the government emphasizes greatly the protection of human rights during judicial procedures, and the application of the judicial principles in judicial activities provide the legal guarantee for safeguarding human rights, such as prohibition of taking people into custody illegally, strict forbiddance of extorting confessions by torture, public trial system, the reprieve system of death penalty, the criminal human rights guarantee, the rights of those being educated through labor, etc.

Section 5 talks about "the guarantee of the right to work ". A citizen's right to work is the essential condition for his right to subsistence, while Old China has a high level of unemployment rate due to the overall collapse of the national economy. After the establishment of New China, the Chinese government adopted various effective measures to get unemployed people into employment and achieved remarkable success. The Chinese law guarantees women to enjoy equal labor rights with men, equal pay for equal work, so that women win independence politically and economically. "The Chinese government pays special attention to the protection of female workers. In July 1988, the State Council promulgated Regulations on Labor Protection of Female Workers, laying down specific guidelines" [12]. The government has also followed the policy of unified job assignment for all college graduates and has thus ensured that every one of them has the opportunity to work. Adopting the policy of "safety first and prevention first", China pays close attention to labor protection. With free medical service in the urban state institutions and undertakings and co-operative medical service in most rural areas, both urban and rural workers are assured of medical care. This section stresses the particularly important role the trade union plays in the protection of workers' right to work. Moreover, the Chinese government lays special emphasis on the legal construction in guaranteeing the right to work, issuing a series of laws and regulations together with the administrative department for labor.

Section 6 centers on "all citizens enjoy the freedom of religious belief". It firstly introduces the kinds and figures of religious relief in China, including Buddhism (no exact number), Daoism (no exact number), Islam (over 17 million), Catholicism (3.5 million), and Protestantism (4.5 million) etc. China's Constitution stipulates that citizens enjoy freedom of religious belief and departments of religious affairs are established just for this purpose. The government helps maintain the temples, monasteries and churches. Different religions may have their respective religious associations. There are 47 religious colleges, 10 religious periodicals and 200,000 professional religious personnel. The government supports the religious circles to actively carry out friendly exchanges with their counterpart abroad. It is also clarified that "the religious freedom that Chinese citizens enjoy under the Constitution and the law entails certain obligations stipulated by the same" [13]. That no one may make use of religion to engage in activities that disrupt public order, impair the health of other citizens or interfere with the state's educational system is made clear in the Constitution. Since no Chinese citizens are permitted to have privileges to transgress the law, those who are religious or pagan should be punished legally if they were involved in criminal activities.

Section 7 is about "the guarantee of the rights of the minority nationality". The first introduction goes to the national policy on ethnic affairs. China is a unitary multinational state. To realize equality, unity and common prosperity among the nationalities is China's basic principle guiding relationships between nationalities. Discrimination against and oppression of any nationality are prohibited; any acts that undermine the unity of the nationalities or instigate their secession are prohibited. Since New China establishes the system of regional autonomy for ethnic minorities, the right of the ethnic minorities is guaranteed, including civil rights, political rights, economic rights, cultural rights, social rights, and health rights of the minority nationality. The Chinese government is extremely mindful of the protection of cultural rights, making tremendous efforts to promote the culture and education of the minority nationalities, and giving them preferential treatment. Chinese law provides that all ethnic groups have the freedom to use and develop their own spoken and written languages.

> In the judicial activities, spoken and written languages of national minorities share equal status with Chinese language. Citizens of all nationalities have the right to use the spoken and written languages of their own nationalities in court proceedings. In an area where people of a minority nationality live in a compact community or where a number of nationalities live together, hearings should be conducted in the language or languages in common use in the locality; indictments, judgments, notices and other documents should be written, according to actual needs, in the language or languages in common use in the locality [14].

The Chinese government also fully respects the traditional cultures and customs of ethnic minorities. We, however, must be clear that the development in minority areas is extremely backward due to historical reasons, though the Chinese government has made strenuous efforts, and much has been accomplished in this regard.

Section 8 talks about "family planning and protection of human rights". Large population, little arable land, comparatively inadequate per-capita share of natural resources plus a relatively backward economy and culture—these features spell out China's basic national conditions. This section discusses the policy of birth control, illustrates the state's necessity to control population growth, and explains the family planning programs, including wide publicity to the advantage of family planning, birth-control measures, attitudes towards abortion, consultation and service for women of the child-bearing age, etc. The latter part discloses the attempt of the accuse that some Western countries censure China's family planning policy as "violating human rights" by invoking the article from *The World Population Plan of Action*, and advocating that the establishment and enforcement of the family planning policy falls by and large within the sovereignty of the country. By setting facts and reasoning things out in rhetoric questions, the last part fights back the censure about the family planning.

> China has only two alternatives in handling its population problem: to implement the family planning policy or to allow blind growth in births. The former choice enables children to be born and grow up healthily and live a better life, while the latter one leads to unrestrained expansion of population so that the majority of the people will be short of

food and clothing, while some will even tend to die young. Which of the two pays more attention to human rights and is more humane? The answer is obvious [15].

Section 9 elaborates on "the guarantee system of human rights for the disabled". The protection of human rights for the disabled has made great achievements which the Chinese government attaches great importance to. On account of that, UN Secretary-General awarded the "Peace Messengers Award" and "Special Award" to China's organizations of the disabled in 1988. In 1990, *the Law of the People's Republic of China on the Protection of Disabled*, a special law guaranteeing the human rights of the disabled, was adopted, which ensures human rights for the disabled legally. Many important department laws have special provisions guaranteeing the rights and interests of the handicapped and our government also lays down related policies, regulations and provisions. The citizen's rights, political rights, property rights, equality and non-discrimination rights have been effectively protected. In March 1988, the China Disabled Persons' Federation was established; hence China has a special organization guaranteeing the human rights of the disabled. With its local branches, this Federation plays a great role in the development of the cause of human rights for the disabled. The Chinese government also makes great efforts to develop education for disabled people and establishes many welfare enterprises employing the disabled, providing such welfare measures as aid, relief etc. In the meanwhile, China sets May 19 of each year as the legal "National Day for Helping the Handicapped", which creates the sound social environment for respecting and helping realize the various rights for the disabled. As social services are concerned, obstacle-free facilities are gradually set up to show the humanistic care to the disabled as well. China actively participates in the international community's efforts to secure the rights and interests of the handicapped and wins great admiration.

Section 10 centers around "the active participation in international human rights activities". It elaborates on the position that China has adopted on international cooperation in human rights, recalling the active participation in international human rights activities. That includes the scrutiny of human rights at the Economic and Social Council and the United Nations General Assembly, and the drafting and making the legal documents on international human rights. In drafting *the United Nations Convention on the Rights of the Child, the Protection of the Rights of All Migrant Workers and their Families, the Convention Against Torture and Other Cruel, Inhuman or Degrading Treatment or Punishment*, etc., the Chinese government adds valuable suggestions and amendments. From 1980 to the time when the white paper was released, the Chinese government signed and approved seven international conventions on human rights [16], an outstanding example in international human rights activities which laid the foundation for the international cooperation. China always conscientiously carries out its international obligations and makes unremitting efforts to safeguard the right of the third world countries to national self-determination and to stop massive infringements on human rights. With the premise of maintaining the fundamental principles of international law, China pays close attention to the issue of the right to development, standing firmly against the interference in other countries' domestic affairs on the pretext of human rights. China is also in favor of strengthening international cooperation in the realm of human rights on "the basis of mutual understanding and seeking a common ground while reserving differences". The end of this section makes clear the major tasks the international protection of human rights faces nowadays and indicates that the principal problem of realizing international peace and development lies in hegemonism and power politics. Moreover, the determination is made to make unremitting efforts to maintain and promote human rights and the fundamental freedoms together with the United Nations.

3.3 Basic Characteristics of the White Paper

The white paper has its own basic characteristics, which can be generalized into three aspects: 1. clear-cut stand and pointed reference; 2. adequate data and precise reasoning; 3. informative content and unexpected repercussion.

3.3.1 Clear-Cut Stand and Pointed Reference

Before the release of the white paper, "human rights" was once deemed to be the bourgeois class. Since people fail to understand the Marxist concept of human rights, it has always been regarded as the "forbidden area". Based on the positive summing up of China's socialist construction, the Chinese government studies the Marxist concept of human rights and makes clear the concept and connotation of "human right" in view of the existing conditions of China. For the first time, the white paper of *Human Right in China* holds high the banner of human rights. Human rights are no longer treated as the bourgeois slogan, instead, it is called "a great term", laying foundation for the timely and forceful counter-attack towards the Western countries represented by the US. The ten sections of the white paper counter the Western countries' attack on human rights in China, differentiate between right and wrong, newly clarify the human rights situation to the international community, make clear to the international community China's basic position and practice on human rights, and refute the indiscriminate attacks by the Western countries, such as the so-called "problems of religion, minority nationalities, family planning". Just like what Dong Yunhu pointed out, "it, historical comparison as the guideline, sticks to proceeding, from the history and the actual conditions of the country, winning people by facts and speaking with facts. While fully elaborating on the great efforts and historical achievements by the Chinese people, it not only describes objectively the mainstream in human rights of China, but also that of the practical situation. That strongly refutes the deliberate distortion and attack by the hostile forces at home and abroad, and answers the general questions that foreign countries care about with pointed reference, playing a major role in guiding the international community to understand properly the human rights in China "[2].

3.3.2 Adequate Data and Precise Reasoning

The white paper, quoting large bodies of data, shows the world the real situation of human rights protection in China by means of setting forth facts and reasoning things out. In the first place, the source of data is reliable. It is the ministries and commissions of the CPC Central Committee and the Institute of Law of Chinese Academy of Social Sciences (CASS) that provide the reliable and authentic data. The white paper leans heavily on data, for example, the imperialists massacred Chinese people in untold numbers during their aggressive wars.

> In 1900, the troops of the Eight Allied Powers—Germany, Japan, Britain, Russia, France, the United States, Italy and Austria—killed, burned and looted, razing Tanggu, a town of 50,000 residents, to utter ruins, reducing Tianjin's population from one million to 100,000, killing countless people when they entered Beijing, where more than 1,700 were slaughtered at Zhuangwangfu alone. During Japan's full-scale invasion of China which began in 1937, more than 21 million people were killed or wounded and 10 million people mutilated to death. In the 6 weeks beginning from December 13, 1937, the Japanese invaders killed 300,000 people in Nanjing [17].

Another example is the third section in the white paper where the correlating data on the overall standards of the Chinese people are analyzed in the same way. In the second place, the white paper adopts adequate data, and elaborates on the problems those data reflect as well. Such an empirical approach helps avoid hollowness and increase the sense of trust. With the brief preface and the text of the supported logic, each argument has both reasoning and data support, showing extremely rigorous logic of argument and high confidence level.

3.3.3 Informative Content and Unexpected Repercussion

The white paper is widely recognized with the informative content. Logical and well-organized, this magnificent piece of writing covers all areas of human rights, unfolding the grand picture of human rights protection in our country. It recalls, with splendid momentum, the humiliating history when old China was invaded and enslaved by various foreign powers over the last hundred years, unfolds, with superb language, the great achievements New China has made in human rights protection, explains sincerely the existing problems in human rights protection, and optimistically opens a prospect that human rights protection strives for lofty goals in China. The white paper wins wide acclaim since its very publication, deemed to be "the milestone in the history of human rights of China" [2] by Dong Yunhu.

Deng Xiaoping said, "This is a great article, and this is a well-written one" [7]. Liu Hainian put it this way, "The white paper on *Human Rights in China*, work of unusual power, summarizes history, exposes reality, looks into the future, sets forth facts and reasons things out. By its publication China is inspired and the world is shocked" [7].

3.4 Significance of the White Paper

The significance of the white paper can be summarized into three aspects: 1. break off the forbidden zone in human rights research and set the scope of human rights protection; 2. show the achievements in human rights protection and make clear the basic position and principle on human right in China; 3. maintain the Chinese international image and prepare the ground for the cause of human rights.

3.4.1 Break off the Forbidden Zone in Human Rights Research and Set the Scope of Human Rights Protection

Human rights, once a word with negative connotations, "used to be a forbidden area in the theoretical study and a vacancy in the theoretical construction due to the strong impact of the 'cultural revolution'. The white paper on *Human Rights in China* breaks off this theoretical forbidden zone, with the study of human rights theory springing up like mushrooms" [2]. As the study on human rights becomes a trend and research findings unfold one after another, an unprecedented new phase comes out in this field. Besides translating and publishing *Encyclopedia of Human Rights, General List of the World Conventions and Laws on Human Rights* and *General List of the World Conventions and Laws on Human Rights (continuation)*, such good-sized works as *Yearbook on Human Rights in China, Human Rights Encyclopedia of China,* etc., were published, coupled with a shower of research papers on human rights, human rights research presents a picture of prosperity.

Since the development of human rights research exerted great influence on the development practice of human rights cause and promoted its great progress, human rights protection, the ideas of which were established by the white paper and further developed in the later social practice, "systematic protection of human rights started to get on the right track" [6]. Obtaining the rights to subsistence and making a leap from having only adequate food and clothing to leading a well-off life, the Chinese people has achieved a lot not only in the aspects of civil and political rights but economic, social and cultural rights, not to mention the protection of the rights for women, children and the disabled.

3.4.2 Show the Achievements in Human Rights Protection and Make Clear the Basic Position and Principle on Human Right in China

Great achievements in human rights protection, by comparative analysis of old and new societies, are shown, and the system designing on and the practice of human rights protection analyzed in the eyes of laws and regulations. With the publication of such international concern as China's principled stand and view, understanding is strengthened in this field among the international community. As Professor Dong Yunhua points out as follows:

> Recognizing and respecting the universality of human rights, the white paper clearly puts forward the view that the right to subsistence is the foremost human right the Chinese people long fight for, and history cannot be cut off and the actual conditions can not be divorced in examining the situation of human rights of a certain country. China always advocates dialogue and cooperation and opposes creating confrontations in the field of human rights or interfering in the domestic affairs of another country. That systematically explains to the international community China's basic position and practice on human rights, thus taking the lead in setting up in the developing countries the view on human rights different from those in the Western ones, and holding in our hands the banner of human rights effectively [2].

3.4.3 Maintain the International Image of China and Prepare the Ground for the Cause of Human Rights

China has human rights and has done much work on human rights protection, making tremendous achievements. By faithful account and rigorous reasoning, the white paper not only explains the stand and principle of human rights in China, but repulses forcefully the anti-China "human rights attack" by the Western countries, which helps to project a good image and win wide acclaim in the international community. Professor Dong Yunhu believes:

> The white paper, for the first time, analyzes and summarizes the course and transformation that China has undergone from the semi-colonial and semi-feudal society to the modern society of people's democracy. Going through the revolution, reconstruction and reform, the CPC works to liberate and develop the productive forces, meet the growing material and cultural needs of the people and realize the human rights of the people. Building socialism with Chinese characteristics is the only road that can effectively promote human rights in China, thus pointing out the definite direction in which human rights construction in China proceeds from spontaneity to self-motivation, and laying down the important theoretical foundation [2].

In the meanwhile, the 10 sections in the white paper, while preparing the ground for human rights cause in China, open up a broad avenue for further development in those 10 fields.

In sum, the first white paper on *Human Rights in China* is not only a landmark event, but also an epoch-making one for the establishment of the human rights system in the history of human rights of China. Ever since the issue of the white paper, dozens of white papers on human rights have been published. The successive publications make clear profoundly and systematically China's basic position and practice on human rights, show the great progress and achievements in human rights cause of China, and increase the international community's understanding in this regard. Finding resonation with the international community, especially the developing countries and reaching broad agreement, China manages to maintain its international image with strong support, thus initially reversing the passive situation in human rights. The inclusion of "the state respects and guarantees human rights" in the Constitution in 2004 became a new milestone in the history of human rights system, and consequently the cause of human rights in China has taken a giant step forward.

References

1. Qu, X. (2009). Major theories on human rights in the 30 years of reform and opening-up. In X. Xu (Ed.), *Human Rights Research* (Vol. 8, pp. 1–66, p. 3). Jinan: Shandong People's Press.
2. Dong, Y. (2002). Major landmark in the history of China's human rights. *Human Rights, 1*, 24–29.
3. Hu, J. & Han, D. (1993). *Contemporary human rights protection system* (p. 299). Beijing: China University of Political Science and Law Press.
4. Hu, J. & Han, D. (1993). *Contemporary human rights protection system* (p. 300). Beijing: China University of Political Science and Law Press.
5. Speech at the meeting of the national Minister of Publicity Ministry, July 2, 1989.
6. Qu, X. (2009). Major theories on human rights in the 30 years of reform and opening-up. In X. Xu (Ed.), *Human Rights Research* (Vol. 8, pp. 1–66). Jinan: Shandong People's Press.
7. Liu, H. (2009). Establishment and development of rule of law of human rights in China. *Nandu Journal (College Social-Science Journal), 1*, 75–90.
8. The State Council Information Office. *Human Rights in China*. Issued on November 1, 1991. Section 1 of the text, last paragraph.
9. The State Council Information Office. *Human Rights in China*. Issued on November 1, 1991. Section 2 of the text, third paragraph from the bottom.
10. Article 51 of *Constitution of the People's Republic of China*, 1982.
11. The State Council Information Office. *Human Rights in China*. Issued on November 1, 1991. Section 4 of the text.
12. The State Council Information Office. *Human Rights in China*. Issued on November 1, 1991. Section 5 of the text.
13. The State Council Information Office. *Human Rights in China*. Issued on November 1, 1991. Section 6 of the text, paragraph 7.
14. The State Council Information Office. *Human Rights in China*. Issued on November 1, 1991. Section 7 of the text, paragraph 7, third paragraph from the bottom.

15. The State Council Information Office. *Human Rights in China*. Issued on November 1, 1991. Section 7 of the text, third paragraph from the bottom.
16. The seven International Conventions are: the Convention on the Reservation and Punishment of the Crime of Genocide; the International Convention on the Suppression and Punishment of the Crime of Apartheid; the Convention on the Elimination of All Forms of Discrimination Against Women; the International Convention on the Elimination of All Forms of Racial Discrimination; the Convention Relating to the Status of Refugees and the Convention Against Torture and Other Cruel, Inhuman or Degrading Treatment or Punishment.
17. The State Council Information Office. *Human Rights in China*. Issued on November 1, 1991. Section 8 of the text, last paragraph.

Chapter 4
"The State Respects and Guarantees Human Rights" Included in the Constitution

Abstract "The state respects and guarantees human rights" was included in the Constitution (human rights into the Constitution), and human rights became an important constitutional principle. "Human rights into the Constitution" provided not only the substantial rights but also obligations of the state's respecting and guaranteeing human rights, which became a new milestone for the development of human rights system in China. "Human rights into the Constitution" started a new era of human rights protection in China, which would benefit the further improvement of legal system, facilitate all-round development of our socialist human rights career, and benefit the international communication and cooperation of our country.

From a historical perspective, China's Constitution in 1982 is "a most complete one since the founding of the People's Republic of China" [1]. However, as time goes by, many changes have taken place in China's development, which demands the timely constitutional changes, hence the four constitutional amendments in 1988, 1993, 1999, and 2004. The four amendments gradually perfected the Constitution. However, although the previous three amendments modified the 1982 Constitution, they did not include laws on human rights. Then, in 2004, China wrote "the state respects and guarantees human rights" into the Constitution as a guiding principle, which is called "human rights into the Constitution". From then on, there have been explicit statements on human rights in the Constitution, which is the codified version of the Chinese Communist Party's ideas of governance, i.e., respecting and guaranteeing human rights, advanced in the 15 and 16th National Congress of CPC. And human rights became a constitutional principle and the will of both the people and the state. "The state respects and guarantees human rights" has substantive content and prescribes the state's obligations. Therefore, the inclusion of human rights in the Constitution is a new milestone in the history of China's human rights system.

P. Sun, *Human Rights Protection System in China*,
DOI: 10.1007/978-3-642-39663-2_4,

4.1 China's Constitutional Amendments

The Constitution which is implemented by China now was written in 1982. As has been mentioned above, it is the best one since the founding of the People's Republic of China (PRC). But with the development of China's socialist construction, the CPC and the state have accumulated more experience and gained deeper insights into the law of socialist construction, but situations kept changing and new problems kept coming up, all these made some contents in the Constitution seem divorced from the reality. Accordingly, there was the need for timely constitutional changes and reforms. Up to now, there have been four amendments to the Constitution respectively in 1988, 1993, 1999, and 2004. Altogether 31 articles have been amended. The Constitution is the state's fundamental law and has the supreme legal effect and power. According to the Constitution, the amendment to it must be proposed by the Standing Committee of the National People's Congress or by more than one-fifth of the deputies to the National People's Congress (NPC) and adopted by a vote of more than two-third of the deputies to the NPC.

After the promulgation of the 1982 Constitution, with the advance of China's reform of economic system, new situations and new problems emerged, among these were the issue of the legal status of private economy and the issue of land-use right. These two problems were a real trouble in China's socialist market economy and the overall development of the socialist cause. The law at that time was not enough to tackle them. Hence, amending the Constitution to meet the demand of the new situation was an inevitable choice. The first amendment to the Constitution was passed at the First Session of the Seventh National People's Congress on April 12, 1988. The major amendment is "The State permits the private sector of the economy to exist and develop within the limits prescribed by law" (article 11). This amendment established the legal status of the individual economy and notably promoted the development of the private sector of the economy. In addition, the 3rd item in article 10 was changed from "no organization or individual may appropriate, buy, sell or lease land, or unlawfully transfer land in other ways" to "no organization or individual may appropriate, buy, sell or otherwise engage in the transfer of land by unlawful means. The right to the use of the land may be transferred according to law." This change legalized compensated transfer of land-use rights.

The second amendment to the Constitution was passed at the First Session of the Eighth National People's Congress on March 29, 1993. it was made "under new circumstances when people were inspired by the talks given by Deng Xiaoping during his visit to the south and hence their ideas on the socialist economic system were significantly changed, and when great breakthroughs had taken place in the economic reform, and when the 14th National Congress of CPC formulated the theory of building socialism with Chinese characteristics as a longstanding guiding ideology for the reform and opening-up policy and for economic construction and the democratic political development" [2]. The main changes include: the legal terms like "the primary stage of socialism," "the theory of building socialism with Chinese characteristics" and "reform and opening-up" were officially written into the Constitution; "build China into a highly civilized and democratic socialist nation" was modified as "build China into a strong, prosperous, culturally advanced, democratic socialist nation"; the expression "the People's Communes" was replaced by "the household contract responsibility system" and "planned economy" was changed into "socialist market economy"; the amendment stated that "China's CPC-led multiparty cooperation and political consultation system will exist and develop for a long time to come." The above-mentioned changes not only established the guiding significance of the Deng Xiaoping Theory of building socialism with Chinese characteristics, but also completely described the basic line China was to follow. They also helped to strengthen China's CPC-led multiparty cooperation and political consultation system and clarify the target for the reform of socialist market economy. All these changes promoted the cause of reform and opening-up and the all-round development of our socialist cause.

The third amendment to the Constitution was adopted at the Second Session of the Ninth NPC on March 15, 1999. It was made in accordance with the report delivered at the 15th National Congress of CPC. The changes in the amendment were as follows: First, Deng Xiaoping Theory was written into the preamble of the Constitution, together with Marxism-Leninism, Mao Zedong Thought as the Great Banner of socialist modernization construction and as the guiding ideology for the nation. Second, "ruling the country in accordance with the law and building a socialist country ruled by law" was specifically laid down as a basic principle. Third, the amendment also stated that "China will stay in the primary stage of socialism for a long period of time" and it formulated China's basic economic system and distribution system, specifying: "During the primary stage of socialism, the State adheres to the basic economic system with the public ownership remaining dominant and diverse sectors of the economy developing side by side, and to the distribution system with the distribution according to work remaining dominant and the coexistence of a variety of modes of distribution." Fourth, the amendment also changed the production management system adopted in rural areas and emphasized the important role of the non-public sector in China's socialist market economy. Fifth, the expression in article 28 "counter-revolutionary activities" was changed into "criminal activities that endanger State security." The above-mentioned changes are of great historic and realistic significance to the cause of building socialism with Chinese characteristics. They not only established the guiding ideology for the construction of China's four modernizations and the basic principle of ruling the country by law, but also helped perfect China's economic system and distribution system and promote the advancement of collectively owned economy in rural areas.

The fourth amendment to the Constitution was promulgated in 2004. As China entered the twenty-first century, it began a new historic phase of building a well-off society in an all-round way and of socialist modernization. The important thought of "Three Represents," together with Marxism-Leninism, Mao Zedong

Thought, Deng Xiaoping Theory, was established as the guiding ideology for the Party's leadership in all causes. And the objectives and tasks for China's cross-century development were further specified. To meet the need of building a well-off society in an all-round way and to better create a new situation in building socialism with Chinese characteristics, it is necessary to improve the Constitution. Under these circumstances, the fourth amendment to the Constitution was adopted at the Second Session of the Tenth National People's Congress on March 14, 2004. It includes 14 changes, among which 12 concern human rights, especially the newly-added paragraph 3 to article 33 of the Constitution, that is "the state respects and guarantees human rights," and the original paragraph 3 was changed into paragraph 4 accordingly. The fourth amendment "raises human rights from being a political concept to being a legal concept and takes human rights as the central value of the Constitution, which signifies the constitutionality of the spirit of human rights and shows China enters a new epoch of human right protection. The amendment is of vital importance in China's constitutional reform and is a significant milestone in China's human rights history" [3].

4.2 Substantive Content of "The State Respects and Guarantees Human Rights"

To accurately understand the substantial content of "the state respects and guarantees human rights," it is necessary to start with understanding the concept of the state and the obligations imposed on the state by the principle of human rights. The concept of the state comes up frequently in the Constitution. To give a few examples, in article 5, "the state upholds the uniformity and dignity of the socialist legal system"; in article 7, "the state will ensure the consolidation and development to the state-owned economy"; in article 19, "the state popularizes the use of Mandarin Chinese nationwide"; in article 25, "the state promotes family planning." It can be seen that the concept of the state is very abstract and general. But "in terms of a specific constitutional law, the state in an abstract sense does not exist, as the rights and obligations of the state concern particular legislative, judicial and administrative organs of the government" [4]. The statement "the state respects and guarantees human rights" in the Constitution explicitly stipulates that the state is the subject of duty to respect and protect human rights and it is the state's constitutional duty to do so. It involves both the passive duty of respecting human rights and the positive duty of safeguarding human rights. "Respecting and protecting human rights is not only a political and moral requirement for state power, but also a normative requirement of checking state power. It's a constitutional responsibility" [5]. Below is a discussion on the state's responsibilities for human rights.

4.2.1 The State's Responsibilities for Respecting Human Rights

As mentioned above, the state is the subject of duty for respecting and protecting human rights; hence, its first responsibility is to respect human rights. It can be seen as a passive duty. That means by not interfering in people's lives or infringing upon human rights, i.e., by carrying out the duty of abstention, the state can ensure the respect for human rights. Professor Jiao Hongchang interprets the state's respect for human rights in two ways:

> First, the respect shows the state's standpoint on human rights and its enhanced constitutional sense, i.e., the guarantee of human rights becomes an orientation in value for state power instead of merely social stability as the top priority; second, the respect demonstrates that state power is restricted at a reasonable level so as to prevent human rights from being infringed upon by it. Thus infringement upon human rights by public power is constitutionally restricted. Some of citizens' fundamental rights, like freedom of person, freedom of religious belief, can be realized without the state's intervention. The state should not place restrictions on them except the restriction in accordance with the law for a justifiable reason. Here 'respect' means 'non-interference' or 'non-infringement' because the state has the passive duty of abstention [4].

But in fact, the state's responsibility for those passive human rights is more than merely non-interference or abstention. If someone infringes upon another's passive rights, the state still needs to intervene or correct the infringement on the basis of the individual's right transferred to the state.

4.2.2 The State's Responsibilities for the Guarantee of Human Rights

The state's responsibility for the guarantee of human rights is a positive duty. It requires the state to take effective measures to ensure the realization of human rights. When an individual's right is violated, the state needs to provide legal relief to protect his or her right. Professor Jiao Hongchang interprets the state's guarantee of human rights in this way:

> Guarantee of human rights means that the state endeavors to protect citizens' various human rights from being infringed upon or denied by government organs, other citizens, corporations and social organizations. For freedoms, like freedom of person, freedom of religious belief, the state should not only avoid infringing upon them, but also provide citizens with effective legal relief when their rights are violated; for those rights that require the state's intervention in order to be realized, like the right to education, the right to work, the state should avoid violating them and endeavor to take effective administrative measures to ensure the legal guarantee of them. Therefore, 'guarantee of human rights' is the state's positive duty [4].

Furthermore, the state's responsibility for guarantee of human rights involves both safeguarding them and promoting them. On the one hand, the realization of human rights involves both the state's passive non-interference and its positive intervention in the form of various measures. On the other hand, the development of human rights goes hand in hand with the changes in the economic pattern and socio-cultural context. Therefore, the state's duty to promote human rights is an integral and inseparable part of its responsibility for the guarantee of human rights. Inspired by the dichotomy between positive rights and passive rights, Yu Peilin proposes the dichotomy between positive duty and passive duty, which the state as the subject of duty has to perform, he suggests: "respecting human rights mainly refers to the state's attitude to passive rights, while the guarantee of human rights primarily refers to its attitude to positive rights. In other words, respecting human rights is the legal embodiment of the state's passive duty, while the guarantee of human rights is the legal embodiment of its positive duty" [6].

In conclusion, the state's respect for and guarantee of human rights sets limits to state power, with human rights used as the boundary marker. Any exercise of state power must be within the scope of the Constitution and laws. The legitimate source of state power is based upon the state's respect for and guarantee of human rights, i.e., the purpose of the existence of state power is to protect human rights. "When an individual's right is violated, he has the right to file a complaint to the government department concerned and get protection. After all, it is the state that takes responsibility for safeguarding human rights" [7]. As John Locke in seventeenth century pointed out, human rights are divine "natural rights," not endowed by the state or the law, and the legitimacy of a government lies in whether the government respects these rights [8]. Xu Xianming, a famous human rights expert in China, states:

> All of the restriction of state power by public opinion, the protection of the freedom of expression, the respect for the freedom of belief, the guarantee of the right to subsistence (the maintenance of the bottom line for subsistence) and the protection of citizens' individualistic development demonstrate fully China's strong sense of urgency to pursue a political civilization with human rights at the core. We have to admit, in developing human rights, that we can not wait and reap what our forefathers sowed, and human rights should be the bottom line for a government's political ethics. A government's promotion of human rights should not be a gradual process, but an urgent matter if the government aims to be a good one [9].

Another scholar points out: "from the perspective of constitutional science, the government (state organs) is the subject of duty for the state's respect for and guarantee of human rights, and the Congress, administrative organs, judicial organs and procuratorial organs are all part of it" [4].

4.3 Significance of "Human Rights into the Constitution"

The Constitution is the fundamental law of a country, which is the core of the entire legal system and has the supreme legal power. It stipulates state system, political institutions, basic policy of the state, the structure of the state, state organs and their functions and powers and other important matters. The Constitution is the basis on which all other laws and regulations are made, it is also the fundamental code of conduct for all state organs and social organizations and all citizens. Zhong Ruiyou discusses the significance of "the state respects and guarantees human rights" being written into the Constitution in the following ways:

> (1) From a legal perspective, the fact that respecting and guaranteeing human rights is constitutional will help to build a more complete system for the guarantee of human rights. On the one hand, theoretically, the concrete human rights can be presumed to form a better bill of rights. On the other hand, it will push the entire legal system to be perfected in the direction of guaranteeing human rights and more laws on human rights guarantee will be made. (2) From a cultural perspective, it will help bring about significant changes in values nationwide. Traditionally speaking, Chinese legal culture has placed more emphasis on obligations than on rights, more on group-based idea of law than on individual rights. Human rights becoming constitutional achieves the consistency between the ruling policy of the Party in power, i.e., serving the people, and the Constitution. It will enhance Chinese people's consciousness of human rights and make the people-oriented beliefs deeply ingrained in the public. Furthermore, it will gradually change the obligation-oriented and group/collective-oriented values, resulting in great cultural transformation. (3) From an academic perspective, human rights becoming constitutional will demystify and desensitize the issue of human rights and make it an everyday yet important theoretical theme. (4) From the perspective of diplomatic relations, it will help improve China's moral status in the international community and contribute to China's exchanges and cooperation with other countries in the realm of human rights [10].

The above-mentioned discussion provides an insightful analysis of the significance of human rights being constitutional from legal, cultural, academic, and diplomatic perspectives. Here are my own reflections on the same subject.

First, "human rights into the Constitution" establishes the principle of human rights and enhances the value of human rights and highlights the spirit of human rights, and it is an important milestone in the China's history of human rights. Professor Xu Xianming points out:

> In China's constitutional history, up to today, the framework for human rights established in the Constitution in 1982 provides the most types of citizen rights. It shows the legislator's strong consciousness of and devotion to human rights during that time. But after three constitutional amendments in 1988, 1993, 1999, there was still room for improvement, that is, the structural imperfection with the human rights law system needed to be addressed [11].

The constitutional amendment in 2004 helped fill the gap in human rights laws; hence it is a milestone in the history of China's constitution and human rights development. The significance of this milestone can be seen in the establishment of the principle of human rights, the enhancement of the value of human rights and the emphasis on human rights, among which, the establishment of the principle of human rights is the most important of all. Because the Constitution has the supreme authoritativeness in the state's legal system, hence the principle of human rights established by the Constitution also enjoys the highest authority, which will play a vital role in guaranteeing human rights.

> Respecting and safeguarding human rights is a fundamental objective and central principle of constitutional government. It is also the fundamental standard by which to judge whether a government truly follows the standard practice of a constitutional government. None of the Common Program and the four versions of the Constitution promulgated and enacted since the founding of the People's Republic of China introduced the concept of 'human rights'. They only used the concept of citizens' basic rights, which made the constitutional government of the people's democratic dictatorship seem incomplete [12].

Subsequently, the constitutional amendment in 2004 established the principle of the state respecting and protecting human rights, enhanced the value of human rights and fully represented the spirit of human rights. "Human rights into the Constitution" as a general principle not only makes laws on citizens' rights in article 33 more integrated and more accurate, but also provides central guidance for the concrete human rights laws in the entire Constitution, which will have far-reaching influence on the basic spirit and the development of the Constitution" [12].

Second, "human rights into the Constitution" represents the essential characteristic of socialism and is beneficial to the further perfection of China's legal system. The history of the Communist Party of China is the history of its struggle for human rights on behalf of Chinese people. And China's socialist construction led by the Party witnesses the real implementation of the Party's principle of assuming power for the people and serving the people. "Human rights into the Constitution" reflects the will and interests of the people and meets the essential requirements of the Constitution of a socialist constitutional government.

> Respecting and protecting human rights is the primary purpose and the supreme principle of a constitutional government. It is the prerequisite for, the basis of and the destination for the existence and improvement of the Constitution and the constitutional government. And it is also the fundamental standard by which to judge whether a government is truly a constitutional one [13].

The superiority of the socialist system over other political systems should be demonstrated by better guarantee of human rights, which means our legal system needs to be further improved. Therefore, "human rights into the Constitution" provides constitutional guarantee for the legislation on human rights matters and the perfection of existing human rights laws, which is extremely beneficial to the improvement of China's human rights legal system. Xin Chunying believes that the constitutional principle of the state respecting and safeguarding human rights will provide important guidance for human rights legislation. She points out:

> Human rights are embodied in concrete legal relations. Respecting and protecting human rights means when social relations are being readjusted, more emphasis should be placed on the balance between powers and rights, the balance between rights and responsibilities and the balance between rights and obligations in order to achieve the orderly and harmonious development of the whole society [14].

Because some stipulations in the Constitution are a little general, some concrete articles in it are not specific enough. But, the principle of human rights is consistent with the basic realities of our country and with the objective requirement of the guarantee of human rights. And as the Constitution is the fundamental law, the establishment of any new principle in it is bound to have profound and significant influence over other department laws.

> 'Human rights into the Constitution' establishes the supreme status of the principle of human rights in China's legal system and highlights the strategic importance of promoting China's human rights in the country's overall construction and social development. It not only reestablishes the reputation of China's human rights situation and redefines socialism with Chinese characteristics, but also reflects the urgent need for the promotion of human rights in the country's construction, social civilization and national progress and shows Chinese people's hope and demand for higher standard of living and better political life. It also demonstrates the consistency between the will of the Party and the state and that of the people, which will greatly promote the progress of human rights cause and its overall development in China [15].

A constitutional principle is ultimately embodied in concrete department laws; of course this will happen with the development and perfection of department laws.

Third, "human rights into the Constitution" ushers in a new era of human rights protection and provides guidance for state organs and all people working in them. Professor Dong Yunhua points out:

> Respecting and safeguarding human rights is the dynamic source for the harmonious development of the whole society, a fundamental principle on which social fairness and justice are guaranteed, a basic norm of a democratic society ruled by law, an important prerequisite for a stable and orderly society, the ideology basis for honesty and friendly love throughout society and an important means through which man lives in harmony with nature [16].

Just as Professor Xu Xianming points out, "human rights into the Constitution" increases the subject of human rights, opens up the human rights system; thus the standard and value of human rights are established and spread nationwide. Hence, the central purpose of the ruling party is to respect, protect, promote and realize human rights, law enforcement; judicial and legal supervision all should implement the principle of human rights protection [17]. Thanks to the universality of the subjects of human rights and the broadening of human rights system, the standard and value of human rights are commonly recognized, hence the arrival of a new era of human rights protection. From the perspectives of the Party's governance ideology and Chinese core values, it can be seen that respecting and protecting human rights is raised from the position of being a political governance policy to the standard of being a constitutional principle, meanwhile, "running the state in accordance with the law" will take respecting, protecting, promoting and realizing human rights as the sacred responsibilities and unshirkable obligations prescribed by the law for the government and all administrative organs.

The highest standard of a socialist country under the rule of law is to adhere to the principle of human rights, which is reflected in whether the departments of law enforcement, judicial and legal supervision uphold and apply the spirit of protecting human rights. According to the stipulations in the Constitution, all power in the PRC belongs to the people and the Chinese people are masters of the country and they should manage state and social affairs in accordance with the law. After "the state respects and guarantees human rights" became a constitutional principle, the government's administrative organs and the people working in them should all exercise their functions and powers lawfully. No organization or individual is privileged to be beyond the Constitution or the law. Xin Chunying believes that "the state respects and guarantees human rights" as a constitutional principle will serve as a guidance for state organs and their staff on their work, "'respecting and guaranteeing human rights' requires that government institutions and their staff members have a clear understanding of their positions and functions and fulfill their duties as devoted public servants. Any of their political decisions and administrative measures should take the best interests of the people into consideration" [14]. Only by adhering to the constitutional principle of respecting and safeguarding human rights, putting the people's interests first and taking the guarantee of human rights as the intent and purpose of all the work of the Party and state organs, can a new situation of human rights protection be created.

Fourth, "human rights into the Constitution" benefits the promotion of the overall cause of human rights. China has always put the people's rights to subsistence and development first, which is inseparable from the basic realities of our country, but China's protection of people's rights are not limited to the above-mentioned two rights. In 1997, China signed the International Covenant on Economic, Social, and Cultural Rights, which was approved by the National People's Congress on March 27, 2001 and came into effect in China on June 27 of the same year. China faithfully and meticulously fulfills its obligations in accordance with regulations in international law and submits regularly the implementation report. Up to now, two implementation reports have been completed and submitted to institutions concerned for judicial review [18]. Although China is a developing country and China's economy is comparatively weak and backward, the Chinese government attaches great importance to the rights to social security and education. On the other hand, citizens' civil and political rights are also well protected, particularly, the interests and rights of the disadvantaged groups, including the elderly, the ill, the vulnerable and the disabled, are well guaranteed, which fully demonstrates the characteristics of our socialist human rights cause. "Human rights into the Constitution" provides legal guarantee for the all-round and harmonious development of the socialist human rights cause and offers a promising future. China under the leadership of the Communist Party of China holds firmly to the principle of putting people first and putting human rights first, which provides a solid foundation for the guarantee and promotion of the overall development of human rights cause. The guiding ideologies, including adhering to the Four Cardinal Principles, upholding the important thought of "Three Represents," sticking to the Scientific Outlook on Development, together with the constitutional guarantee of human rights, all help China's cause of human rights achieve progress of world interest. A new situation for the overall and harmonious promotion of the human rights cause is emerging. Just as Liu Yuanfei points out, "'human rights into the Constitution' begins a new era of constitutional guarantee of human rights and lays a legal foundation for China's new image of respecting and safeguarding human rights and provides a prosperous future" [15]. Also, "'human rights into the Constitution' symbolizes the progress of our constitutional government and the perfection of the Constitution and starts a higher level of the guarantee of human rights" [19]. Thus, the subject of human rights becomes universal and the scope of the object of human rights is also further expanded, which greatly promotes the progress in China's cause of human rights.

Fifth, "human rights into the Constitution" helps promote China's exchanges and cooperation with other countries in the international human rights cause. The principle of human rights established by the Constitution provides constitutional foundation for China's international exchanges and cooperation. In today's world, the issue of human rights has become a focus of international dialogues. Human rights have gained increasing importance in communication among different countries, which is a historical trend in the international community. After the founding of the United Nations, thanks to its decades of untiring efforts, a comparatively complete system of international human rights laws has been established. The vast majority of countries have formulated their own views and interests, but because of the various differences in historical traditions, cultural background, economic development and political ideologies and convictions among them, international exchanges and cooperation in human rights become a necessity. And the cooperation must be based on the system of international human rights laws. China has written "the state respects and guarantees human rights" into its Constitution and presented a good and positive image in the realm of international human rights. In the international sphere of human rights, China has always upheld the principle of allowing differences among different countries, which reflects a realistic and objective attitude. Whether you admit it or not, it is undeniable that the differences are widespread, which means inevitably there are differences in the outlooks on human rights among different countries. The international community needs exchanges and cooperation to jointly promote the healthy, steady and continuous development of human rights in the whole world. But some countries use human rights as a tool to interfere with the internal affairs of other countries, and they try to pursue hegemonism and power politics and play antagonism in human rights, which will eventually make them lose the support of the people and become unpopular, as has been proven by historical experience. Exchanges and cooperation are the only correct ways to enhance human rights globally. However, we have to realize that the development of the cause of human rights is a long and difficult process and we have a long way to go. From the emergence of human rights conception to the formulation of human rights laws and to the full realization of human rights, every step of the way takes hard work and enormous efforts and is inseparable from international cooperation and communication. Historical facts have shown that China has carried out effective bilateral and multilateral dialogues and communication with the major Western countries, through which, mutual understanding concerning human rights has been enhanced and many consensuses have been reached. In the international field of human rights, China has long been actively involved in various endeavors and made its due share of contribution to the legislation of international human rights. Up to today, China has joined 25 international conventions on human rights. Furthermore, "human rights into the Constitution" in 2004 has greatly expanded the scope of our communication and cooperation with other countries in the realm of human rights.

References

1. Yu, Z. (Ed.). (2004). *Constitutional law*. Beijing: China University of Political Science and Law Press. p. 67.
2. Yu, Z. (Ed.). (2004). *Constitutional law*. Beijing: China University of Political Science and Law Press. pp. 68–69.
3. Qu, X. (2009). The main human rights theories in 30 years of reform and opening-up. In Xu, X. (Ed.), *Human Rights Research* (Vol 8, pp. 1–66). Jinan: Shandong People's Press.
4. Jiao, H. (2004). Constitutional analysis on "the state respects and guarantees human rights". *China Legal Science, 3*, 42–49.
5. Yan, H. (2006). The normative connotations of "the state respects and guarantees human rights". *Legal Studies, 4*, 141–143.
6. Yu, P. (2007). An interpretation of the legal relations "the state respects and guarantees human rights". *Legal Studies, 6*, 28–31.
7. Yang, Y. (2008). *Influence of international human rights law on China's Criminal and judicial reform*. (p. 2). Beijing: China Legal Publishing House.
8. Freeman, M. 2002. *Human rights: An interdisciplinary approach* (p. 7). Cambridge: Polity Press.
9. Xu, X. (2009). Preface. In Xu, X. (Ed.), *Human Rights Research* (Vol. 8, p. 1). Jinan: Shandong People's Press.
10. Zhong, R. (2005). From white paper to being constitutional: the development and choices of China's cause of human rights. *Henan Social Sciences, 1*, 10–15.
11. Xu, X. (2000). The system and categories of human rights. *China Social Sciences, 6*, 95–104.
12. China Society of Human Rights Studies. (2005). The significance of "the state respects and guarantees human rights" being written into the constitution. *China Daily*. August 3, p. 9.
13. Dong, Y. (2004). Human rights into the Constitution: An important milestone in China's human rights development. *Human Rights, 2*, 31–35.

14. Xin, C. (2004). The state respects and guarantees human rights: the significance of human rights becoming constitutional. *Seeking the Truth, 9*, 36–38.
15. Liu, Y. (2004). On the significance of human rights becoming constitutional. *Journal of the Party School of Wulumuqi, 4*, 61–63.
16. Dong, Y. (2006). Respecting and protecting human rights is the foundation for the construction of a harmonious socialist society. *The Forum of Party and Administrative Cadres, 9*, 53–54.
17. Xu, X. (2005). Human rights concepts in China in the past hundred years. *Social Sciences Forum, 3*, 26–32.
18. Information Office of the State Council. (2009). *National Human Rights Action Plan of China* (2009–2010). Issued on April 13. The second paragraph, Part 1, Section V of the text.
19. Gu, C. (2005). Constitution: The fundamental legal guarantee of human rights. In China Society for Human Rights Studies. (Ed.), *Human rights in China in the new century* (p. 207). Beijing: Unity Press.

Chapter 5
National Human Rights Action Plan as a Milestone

Abstract After "the state respects and guarantees human rights" was included in the Constitution, the constitutional principle of respecting and safeguarding human rights became conscious actions of our Party and the government. In recent years, the human rights career of China has continuously developed. Against this background, our government released the first National Human Rights Action Plan of China (NHRAP) in April, 2009, which puts forth practical requirements and clarifies the concrete measures of implementation, turning a new leaf for the development of human rights career in China. It serves as a significant milestone for human right protection in the Chinese context.

Since "the state respects and guarantees human rights" was included in the Constitution in 2004, the development of human rights cause has emerged new prospects both at home and abroad. At the international level, in March, 2006, the United Nation set up the Human Rights Council (HRC) affiliated with the United Nations (UN) General Assembly, taking the place of the Commission on Human Rights, and established a system of Universal Periodic Review (UPR). From then on, human rights, peace and security, development have become three themes of the work of the UN and all the activities in the UN seem to concentrate on safeguarding human rights and promoting the development of human rights cause. At home, after "the state respects and guarantees human rights" was included in the Constitution, the human rights cause of China has continuously developed. Human rights have become a significant component of economic and social development and the constitutional principle of respecting and safeguarding human rights has become conscious actions of our Party and the government.

5.1 The Background of the NHRAP

After "the state respects and guarantees human rights" became the constitutional principle, within a short span of 5 years, the Chinese government has successively released many white papers concerned with human rights, bringing "the state

P. Sun, *Human Rights Protection System in China*,
DOI: 10.1007/978-3-642-39663-2_5, © Springer-Verlag Berlin Heidelberg 2014

respects and guarantees human rights" into the *Guidelines of the Eleventh Five-Year Plan for National Economic and Social Development* and enabling the constitutional principle of respecting and safeguarding human rights to rise to an conscious action taken by the Communist Party and the government, which has set human rights as an integral part of China's socialist modernization. In particular, the release of *National Human Rights Action Plan of China (2009–2010)* (NHRAP) in April 2009 became a significant milestone marking China's transformation from legal human rights to actual human rights.

5.1.1 Five White Papers Concerning Human Rights Released in 2005

After "the state respects and guarantees human rights" was written into the Constitution in 2004, our government issued *China's Social Security and Its Policy* on September 7, 2004. In 2005, the Chinese government not only enacted many regulations and rules to protect human rights and positively developed human rights activities, such as the organization of large-scale seminars, the compilation and publication of human rights report—*China's Human Rights in Action* and so on, but also successively released five white papers concerning human rights: (1) On April 13, 2005, the Information Office of the State Council published *China's Progress in Human Rights in 2004*, which comprehensively and systematically summarized the efforts and important achievements in promoting and protecting the fundamental human rights of citizens; (2) On April 21, 2005, the Information Office of the State Council published *New Progress in China's Protection of Intellectual Property Rights*, which introduced the new achievements in details in protecting the intellectual property rights; (3) On August 24, 2005, the Information Office of the State Council published *Gender Equality and Women's Development in China*, which minutely explained the protection of women's fundamental human rights in China; (4) On October 19, 2005, the Information Office of the State Council published *Building of Political Democracy in China*, which interpreted the important aspect—"the state respects and guarantees human rights"; (5) On December 22, 2005, the Information Office of the State Council published *China's Peaceful Development Road*, which made peaceful development become Chinese people's serious choice and solemn promise and guided a new way to protecting human rights and exploring the road of peaceful development. On the one hand, the above publications on human rights proves that our government attaches great importance to the protection of human rights, on the other hand, it demonstrates the development achievements of our human rights cause, which lays solid foundations for setting up a good international image and made necessary preparations for the further promotion of China's great development in human rights cause.

5.1.2 Guidelines of the Eleventh Five-Year Plan for National Economic and Social Development in 2006

As early as on October 11, 2005, the Fifth Session of the Sixteenth Central Committee of the Communist Party of China (CPC) approved the *Proposal on the Eleventh Five-Year Plan for National Economic and Social Development*, which clearly put forward "respecting and safeguarding human rights and promoting the comprehensive development of human right causes." In March, 2006, the Fourth Session of the Tenth National People's Congress (NPC) approved the *Guidelines of the Eleventh Five-Year Plan for National Economic and Social Development*, which explicitly put forward "respecting and safeguarding human rights and promoting the comprehensive development of human right causes" [1] in Chapter 43. "It is for the first time that the development of China's human rights cause is considered as an important component of socialist modernization and brought into national development program" [2].

In terms of the specific contents of *Guidelines of the Eleventh Five-Year Plan for National Economic and Social Development*, human rights as a constitutional principle are carried on concretely. In Chapter 2 of Section 1, it suggests "strengthening the construction of harmonious society. We shall, in accordance with the requirements of human as fundamentality and starting from resolving the practical issues related to the people and masses' vital interests, pay more attention to the coordinated development of economy and society, accelerate the development of social cause and promote overall human development. Pay more attention to social equity and enable all people to share the achievements of reform and development. Pay more attention to democratic and legal system construction, correctly deal with the relations of reform, development, and stability and maintain social stability and solidarity" [3].

In Section 10 "Push forward the construction of harmonious socialist society", it clearly indicates that "according to the requirements of democracy and the government by law, equity and justice, good faith and friendship, full of ginger, stability and order and harmonious coexistence between man and nature, firmly push forward the construction of harmonious society proceeding from resolving the most direct and most realistic vital interest problem most cared by the people and the masses" [4]. With respect to correctly dealing with the contradictions among the people, we should "attach great importance to safeguarding the people and masses' fundamental interests, properly coordinate interest relations in various aspects and prevent and resolve the contradictions among the people from the sources" [5].

According to part 3 in Section 11 "strengthening the improvement of the Party's work style and building the honesty government", it clearly specifies "seriously investigating and prosecuting the cases of discipline and law breach and resolutely rectifying the unhealthy tendency that harms the masses' interests" [1]. The content above fully shows that the development of China's human rights cause has been formally brought into national development program.

5.1.3 *Confirming "the State Respects and Guarantees Human Rights" in the Report of the 17th National Congress of the Communist Party of China in October, 2007*

On October 15, 2007, the 17th National Congress of CPC was solemnly opened in the Great Hall of the People in Beijing. Hu Jintao delivered a report on behalf of the 16th Central Committee. The report of the 17th CPC National Congress, from the fundamental interests of the people of all ethnic groups, holding high the great banner of socialism with Chinese characteristics, carrying on matter-of-fact attitude and forging ahead with determination, objectively sums up the work and the glorious achievements of the past 5 years and soberly points out the existing outstanding problems. The report comprehensively summarizes the great historical course of reform and opening-up, makes a detailed description on the Scientific Outlook on Development and puts forward that "the Scientific Outlook on Development takes development as its essence, putting people first as its core, comprehensive, balanced and sustainable development as its basic requirement, and overall consideration as its fundamental approach" [6].

The report considers "serving the people wholeheartedly" as the fundamental purpose of the Party, stressing on "making sure that the aim and outcome of all the work of the Party and the state are to realize, safeguard and expand the fundamental interests of the overwhelming majority of the people" [6]. The report describes the realization of the goal to build a moderately prosperous society in all respects, and every included content is based on essential objectives of improving the livelihood of people and safeguarding all the rights of people, such as "everyone is assured of basic living standards", "everyone will have access to basic medical and health services" and so on. The various included measures for promoting the development of the national economy are basic to safeguard the fundamental human rights; while in terms of developing socialist democracy, it suggests "safeguarding the people's rights to be informed, to participate, to be heard, and to oversee" [7].

The report further stresses on "comprehensively implementing the rule of law as a fundamental principle and speeding up the building of a socialist country under the rule of law." It clearly points out "respecting and safeguarding human rights, protecting the right of all members of society to equal participation and development in accordance with the law" [7]. Besides, the report also takes the development and prosperity of socialist culture as the main measure to better guarantee the people's basic cultural rights and interests. It attaches much importance to accelerating social development with the focus on improving people's livelihood, and "we must do our best to ensure that all our people enjoy their rights to education, employment, medical and old-age care, and housing, so as to build a harmonious society" [8]. Moreover, the report also makes a comprehensive explanation and summarization of all respects, such as "modernization of the armed forces", "the great cause of peaceful national reunification", "the path of peaceful development", "party building" and so on, which requires the effective improvement of the work style of the Party, "putting into practice the principle of exercising power for the people, showing concern for them and working for their interests" [9].

On all accounts, the CPC, serving as a political party in power, plays an incomparably important role in the great practice of building socialism with Chinese characteristics. The report of the 17th CPC National Congress places the protection, promotion, and safeguarding of human rights on the prominent position of building a moderately prosperous society, and "the state respects and guarantees human rights" is further confirmed. It could be said that the report of the 17th CPC National Congress is a pioneering undertaking in reflecting the spirit of the time, grasping the regularity and being highly creative in the administrative concept of the Party, which lays a solid foundation for promoting greater victories in the cause of the Party and the people and points out the way forward for writing a new chapter of happy life for the people.

5.1.4 The White Paper: China's Efforts and Achievements in Promoting the Rule of Law in 2008

On February 28, 2008, the Information Office of the State Council published *China's Efforts and Achievements in Promoting the Rule of Law* [10], which was the first white paper on the rule of law released by the Chinese government. The white paper includes foreword, historical course of building a socialist country under the rule of law, legislation, and legal system with Chinese characteristics, legal systems of respecting and safeguarding human rights, legal systems regulating the order of the market economy, administration by law and building a government under the rule of law, judicial system and fair administration of justice, popularization and education of the law, international exchange and cooperation in legal construction, conclusion, and appendix.

The white paper comprehensively introduces that over almost 6 decades since its founding, especially during 30 years since the introduction of the reform and opening-up policy, China has made tremendous achievements in promoting the rule of law in its great task of building socialism with Chinese characteristics. It clearly points out: "A Constitution-centered socialist legal system with Chinese characteristics has basically taken shape" [10]. On the basis of the present Constitution, the state has enacted and improved a series of legal systems to safeguard human rights, "human rights have been better guaranteed in legislation, law enforcement, the judiciary and other aspects. The undertaking to protect human rights has been developing in a sound way, and citizens' political, economic, social and cultural rights are now fully respected and guaranteed in all aspects" [10].

Third part of the white paper specially discusses the "legal systems of respecting and safeguarding human rights", which explicitly demonstrates:

> China takes as its constant goal the elimination of poverty, enjoyment of human rights to the full by everyone and building of a prosperous, strong, democratic, culturally advanced and harmonious modern socialist country. China's basic stand on the development of human rights is: placing top priority on people's rights to subsistence and development, making development the principal task, and promoting citizens' political, economic, social and cultural rights to achieve their all-round development [10].

It also respectively expounds "legal safeguard of the right to life", "legal safeguard of the right to personal freedom and dignity", "legal safeguard of the right to equality", "legal safeguard of political rights", "legal safeguard of freedom of religious belief", "legal safeguard of the rights and interests of the working people" and "legal safeguard of economic, social, cultural and other rights." This part also indicates that China has joined international human rights conventions, and that "the Chinese government earnestly fulfills its obligations, submits implementation reports on its own initiative, and gives full play to the role of international human rights conventions in promoting and protecting human rights of the Chinese people" [10].

The sixth part of the white paper discusses the "judicial system and fair administration of justice", which clearly suggests that "China has established a sound judicial system, completed the adjudicative systems for civil, administrative and criminal cases, forming a modern judicial system in line with the requirements for building a socialist country under the rule of law, in a bid to safeguard judicial justice and social justice" [10]. Besides, the white paper introduces "the system of public trial", "the system of collegiate panels", "the system of people's assessors", "the system of defense", "the system of agent *ad litem*", "the system of challenge", "the system of mediation", "the system of judicial relief", "the system of judgment of the second instance as final" and "the system of review of death sentence". All the legal systems above ensure that human rights are respected and safeguarded and human rights cause of China is pushed forward.

5.1.5 Enactment and Release of the NHRAP (2009–2010) in 2009

As early as in 2008, the NHRAP [11] (2009–2010), headed by the Information Office of the State Council and the Ministry of Foreign Affairs, was enacted by over 50 state organs and institutions. According to Wang Chen, Director of the Information Office of the State Council, "in order to well enact the NHRAP and ensure the authority, effectiveness and feasibility, the Chinese government sets up the joint meeting mechanism of national human rights action plan of China, led by the Information Office of the State Council and the Ministry of Foreign Affairs, which includes 53 member institutions" [12].

In addition, a panel of experts invited from colleges and research organizations take part in drafting and developing the action plan. During the process of drafting and developing the action plan, the joint meeting mechanism and its organizations hold many conferences to carefully study and repeatedly negotiate the content of the action plan and the members of the joint meeting mechanism, so as to fully reflect the requirement of promoting the cause of human rights and sufficiently consider the practical situations of all sectors in China now and the opinions and demands of all related units. And it solicits opinions from all circles of society and nongovernmental organizations, as well as all public organizations, universities, research organizations, and all social sectors.

With the participation and efforts of more than 80 institutions, on the basis of repeated discussion and amendment for 10 times, the NHRAP took shape, which was approved by the State Council and published by the Information Office of the State Council with authorization on April 13, 2009. "It is observed that the action plan condenses the thoughts of all related state organs and every aspect of society, which is the crystallization of collective wisdom and reflects the consistency of the opinions of the Party, the will of the nation and the demands of citizens" [12]. Here is the analysis of the main content of the NHRAP.

5.2 Main Content of the NHRAP

Besides contents and introduction, the main text is divided into five parts. There are nine paragraphs in the introduction. The first paragraph gives a definition to full realization of human rights; the second paragraph explains the untiring efforts of a new China in realizing human rights; the third paragraph analyzes the basic national conditions; the fourth paragraph puts forward our fundamental position of human rights; the fifth paragraph introduces the basis of setting up the NHRAP; the sixth paragraph explains three major principles of enacting the action plan; the seventh paragraph introduces the broad participation by the relevant government departments and all social sectors; the eighth paragraph puts forward the demand of all government departments to implement the action plan and the mechanism of implementation, supervision and assessment; the ninth paragraph explains that this action plan has been approved by the State Council and authorized by its Information Office. The main text includes the following five parts: (1) guarantee of economic, social, and cultural rights; (2) guarantee of civil and political rights; (3) guarantee of the rights and interests of ethnic minorities, women, children, elderly people, and the disabled; (4) education in human rights; (5) performing international human rights duties, and conducting exchanges and cooperation in the field of international human rights. Here is the detailed introduction.

5.2.1 Guarantee of Economic, Social and Cultural Rights

Economic, social and cultural rights are the major rights admitted in the *Universal Declaration of Human Rights* (UDHR) in 1948 and stipulated in details in the *International Covenant on Economic, Social and Cultural Rights* (ICESCR) in 1966. By the end of May 6, 2013, the Covenant had 160 contracting countries. In October, 1997, China signed this Covenant, and it was officially approved by the NPC on March 27, 2001 and came into effect on June 27 of the same year. In order to positively undertake our obligations of international convention of human rights and progressively ensure the economic, social and cultural rights of all members of society, the NHRAP puts these rights in the first part, fully proving strong determination and confidence of the Chinese government in respecting and safeguarding human rights.

Moreover, the effective measures taken here are to safeguard the economic, social, and cultural rights of all members, which greatly extend the range of human rights subjects, from the civil rights protected by the Constitution to the rights of all members in society. These rights include the right to work, the right to basic living conditions, the right to social security, the right to health, the right to education, cultural rights, environmental rights, safeguarding farmers' rights and interests and guarantee of human rights in the reconstruction of areas hit by the devastating earthquake in Wenchuan, Sichuan Province.

In terms of the right to work, the core involves promoting employment, re-employment, and the protection of the workers' legitimate rights and interests. The realization of rights should be in accordance with the rule of law. It should keep a balance between the rural and urban employment situations, expand vocational training, guarantee production safety, and pay special attention to the employment problems of college graduates and rural migrant workers. With respect to the right to basic living standards, the country should gradually improve the incomes of rural and urban residents, make greater efforts in alleviating poverty, develop commodity housing as well as lost-cost housing, perfect the system of ensuring minimum living standards in the rural areas and accelerate the drafting of the *Regulations on the Rural Basic Living Allowances*.

In terms of the right to social security, the country should improve social security laws and regulations, expand the coverage of various types of social security, raise the pooling of social security funds to higher levels, improve the system of "Five Guarantees" and the system of aid to urban vagrants and beggars. In terms of the right to health, "the basic framework for a basic medical and health system covering the entire nation will be established so as to make China among the countries providing national basic health service" [13]. It come up with the main index of health, expedite the establishment of the basic medical care system, improve basic medical and health services, control the infectious diseases, enact the *Law on Food Safety*, pay attention to the safety of drinking water, and enhance the construction of sports facilities in communities.

In terms of the right to education, the country will give the priority to 9-year compulsory education and rural education, put great efforts into vocational education, enhance the quality of higher education, realize the equal right to education, and further improve the system of assistance to poor students. Regarding cultural rights, the country will promote cultural undertakings, establish a public cultural service system, fulfill the target of sharing the national cultural resources, promote the digitalization of films and broadcasting, and enhance the protection of intellectual property.

In terms of environmental rights, "upholding the principle of harmonious development between man and nature and the rational exploitation and utilization of natural resources, China will take an active part in international cooperation in an effort to create an environment favorable for human existence and sustainable development and build a resource-conserving and environment-friendly society to guarantee the public's environmental rights" [13].

In terms of safeguarding farmers' rights and interests, China will make great efforts to break the dual structure of urban and rural systems, safeguard farmers' legitimate rights and interests, guarantee farmers' land right, raising farmers' income level, improve farmers' health, strengthen the protection of the rights and interests of rural migrant workers, and construct a new socialist countryside. In addition, specific measures are put forward to guarantee human rights in the reconstruction of areas hit by the devastating earthquake in *Wenchuan*, Sichuan Province.

If we say that the economic, social and cultural rights prescribed in the UDHR are still abstract and macroscopical, the measures taken in the NHRAP are very specific. The measures are not only suitable to the national conditions, but also consistent with the requirements of the international human rights standards. Maybe in the eyes of Western countries our standards are still not high enough, but the development of human rights cannot be divorced from the fundamental national conditions. From the specific measures drawn up for the NHRAP, we can see that the release of the plan is not motivated by the need for foreign publicity; rather, it represents action of doing our own business in a down-to-earth way. It is a concrete measure to put into practice the constitutional principle of "the state respects and guarantees human rights" stipulated in the amendment to the Constitution of 2004. It does not only mark for the first time that China actively and systematically issued a human rights action plan, but all the measures set forth in the action plan also show strong feasibility and operability, thus making a great contribution to the improvement and development of our country's human rights.

5.2.2 Guarantee of Civil and Political Rights

The UDHR includes specific civil and political rights, and the *International Covenant on Civil and Political Rights* (ICCPR) makes detailed stipulations concerning these rights. China signed the Covenant in 1988. But it has not yet been officially approved by the NPC so far. The scholars are committing themselves to the linkage between this covenant and our domestic laws and have made many important achievements. Proceeding from eight aspects, the NHRAP has set forth a series of measures that our country will adopt, including administrative and judicial measures, to raise the level of ensuring people's civil and political rights. These eight aspects are: the rights of the person, the rights of detainees, the right to a fair trial, the freedom of religious belief, the right to be informed, the right to participate, the right to be heard, and the right to oversee.

In terms of the rights of the person, the NHRAP sets forth safeguarding measures in details, including two prohibitions, two strict regulations, and one measure involving establishment and improvement. The two prohibitions are: "The state prohibits the extortion of confessions by torture" and "The state prohibits illegal detention by law enforcement personnel" [14]. The two strict regulations are: "Death penalty shall be strictly controlled and prudently applied" and "The state implements stringent judicial procedures for death sentences, and improves such procedures for review" [14]. One measure is: "The state establishes and improves supervisory mechanisms for enforcement of law and administration of justice" [14]. All the judicial principles are strictly followed, and preventive measures are taken at every step to protect citizens' rights of the person. With respect to the rights of detainees, we should take positive measures of legislation and strictly carry out every procedure to improve supervision system, intensify real-time supervision conducted by the people's procuratorate on law enforcement in prisons and detention houses and effectively ensure detainees' rights and humanitarian treatment. Regarding the right to a fair trial, it prescribes the entities in the judicial process, as well as the specific procedures. Further, it also makes a detailed plan about the judicial assistance, the legal aid system and the *State Compensation Law*. As for the freedom of religious belief, China always stands on the policy of freedom of religious belief, namely, the freedom to believe in or not believe in any religion, which not only owns the "*Regulations on Religious Affairs*", but also stresses that the state respects ethnic minorities' religious beliefs, and protects their religious cultural heritage.

In addition, specific implementing measures are put forward for the enjoyment of the right to be informed, the right to participate, the right to be heard and the right to oversee. The actual enjoyment of the right to be informed is the basis to ensure the government administration in accordance with the law and ensure public information of government affairs; the government represents the people's will to manage national affairs and keeps the public informed of government affairs, which is important for self-discipline and a better image. The right to participate is a civil right, as well as a very significant political right. Under the current political systems, such as the people's congress system and the political consultation system, we should improve the system of people's self-governance at the grassroots level, promote democratic decision-making, and strengthen the construction and management of social organizations. The right to be heard is a political right of citizens, which is realized through the development of all industries, such as press and publication. The NHRAP not only safeguards "journalists' right to gathering materials, criticize, comment and publish" [14], but also stresses the role of social organizations in "guiding people to express their opinions in a reasonable way and participate in public affairs in an orderly way" [14]. "The channels for people to make complaints in the form of letters and visits will be broadened and remain unblocked" [14] to safeguard all the related rights of citizens. The right to oversee is an important right for people to supervise the work of the government, which on the one hand depends on the supervision by the people's congresses and people's political consultative conferences over administrative, trial and procuratorial organs, on the other hand depends on the people's supervision over state organs (administrative, trial, and procuratorial organs) and civil servants of all organs through the rights to criticize, give advice to, complain of, and accuse. Such supervision plays an important role in the prevention and punishment of corruption and the requirement for leading cadres to be clean and self-disciplined.

5.2.3 Guarantee of the Rights and Interests of Ethnic Minorities, Women, Children, Elderly People, and the Disabled

The guarantee of the rights and interests of ethnic minorities, women, children, elderly people, and the disabled has always been the stand of the Chinese government and these rights are also the main rights protected in our legal systems. The groups above are considered as the vulnerable groups, and the government not only protects them with improved laws and regulations, but also signs related international conventions on human rights. The Chinese government has already done lots of work in such a field, effectively promoting the development of the related work and strictly fulfilling international human rights obligations to draw up a new blueprint for the development of human rights cause of the vulnerable groups.

In terms of the rights of ethnic minorities, the Chinese Communist Party and the Chinese government have always attached much importance to the rights of minority groups. China is a unified country composed of 56 nationalities, and the biggest one is Han nationality. The other 55 nationalities, accounting for 8.41 percent of the total population of China, are called minority groups. The NHRAP provides specific measures in promoting the development of education for ethnic minorities, strengthening the training of personnel of ethnic minorities, guaranteeing ethnic minorities' rights, developing their own spoken and written languages, promoting the development of the cultures of ethnic minorities, promoting economic development in areas inhabited by ethnic minorities, and raising the standard of living of the ethnic minorities.

With respect to the guarantee of the women's rights, the action plan is set up to realize the goals stated in the *Program for the Development of Chinese Women (2001–2010)*, to achieve sexual equality, to eliminate the discrimination against women regarding the participation in the management of state and social affairs, and guarantee equal right for women in employment and women's right to education. Besides, the protection of women is also shown in safeguarding women's reproductive rights, improving maternity health care services, prohibiting all forms of domestic violence against women, preventing and cracking down on the crimes of trafficking in women.

In reference to the guarantee of children's rights, centering around the "children first" principle, China will endeavor to realize the goals set forth in the *Program for the Development of Children of China (2001–2010)*, and make every effort to guarantee all the rights of children in terms of the legal system of children protection, children's health, children's participation, prohibiting the employment of child labor, preventing and cracking down on the crimes of trafficking in children and reinforcing judicial protection for juveniles' rights. Concerning senior citizens' rights, "the government will continue to improve the social security system for the aged, pushing forward the establishment of a service system for the elderly and guaranteeing their legitimate rights and interests" [15]. Regarding the rights of the disabled, China not only safeguards and develops undertakings relating to the disabled, but also beefs up the building of the social security and service systems for the disabled and provides guarantees for the legitimate rights and interests of the disabled in terms of the disability prevention, rehabilitation and other services, education and employment, the construction of a barrier-free environment, and the cultural and sports rights of the disabled.

"Respecting the old and loving the young" has been a traditional virtue, and the state and society always pay special attention to the groups of ethnic minorities, women, children, and the disabled, which is manifested in the specific protection of all their rights. With the enhancement of national economic power, the guarantee of the rights of ethnic minorities, women, children, elderly people, and the disabled will be gradually carried out to promote the rapid development of our cause of human rights and make significant contributions to the development of human rights for the whole human race.

5.2.4 Education in Human Rights

Education in human rights is the content of the fourth part in the NHRAP. It is the foundation for spreading human rights knowledge, improving human rights awareness, respecting and safeguarding human rights. Education in human rights plays an essential role in the development of China's human rights cause. It is mainly achieved in relying on the current systems of education, as well as the media including radio, television, newspapers, magazines, and the Internet. Education in human rights first needs considerate plans and various ways of education to disseminate legal and human rights knowledge. It should be involved into the process of training all levels of talents by taking the characteristics of training objectives into considerations in order to cultivate human rights awareness of citizens.

Education in human rights is involved in the education of all levels, such as colleges, middle schools, and primary schools, which is a rather complex education system. According to characteristics of the talents at different levels, the NHRAP draws up the brief content of education and makes suggestions in the way of education in human rights. For example, human rights education in secondary and elementary schools should "be conducted in a flexible and vivid way" [16]:

> Through varied and vivid activities after class, students will receive education in human rights from first-hand experiences and build up a healthy personality. The reform of teaching and school management will be energetically pursued, and a democratic, equal, and interactive relationship will be advocated between teachers and students, encouraging students to participate in the democratic management of the class and school, so as to enhance their awareness of democracy, rule of law and human rights through experiencing an equal and democratic relationship [16].

While carrying out human rights education, the plan encourages institutions of higher education to conduct research on theories of human rights. The plan also sets forth new requirements for curriculum design, the compilation of textbooks, the development of teaching courseware, and the construction of education and training bases. In addition to the students in colleges, middle schools, and primary schools, civil servants are also the major groups to be educated, especially "focusing on people working in public security agencies, procuratorates, courts, prisons, urban management organs, and administrative law enforcement organs" [16]. The plan requires:

> The law enforcement departments will draw up their own plans for human rights education and training in line with their own work needs, highlighting publicity and education of regulations and laws on the protection of human rights, and give human rights education on a regular basis. The government will organize experts to compile special textbooks for human rights training. State agencies and cities with appropriate conditions will be selected as demonstration units for human rights education and training, and follow-up examinations will be conducted [16].

Additionally, the action plan calls for systematically carrying out human rights education activities targeting the general public, popularizing human rights knowledge and raising human rights awareness of the public. While carrying out the human rights education activities among the general public, the plan calls for "making good use of the media, including radio, television, newspapers, magazines and the Internet, to disseminate the knowledge of human rights among the general public" [16]. The plan calls for improving human rights awareness of Chinese citizens and promoting the development of the human rights cause in China by carrying out human rights education in different forms and through different ways. In the process of development, international human rights exchanges and cooperation should be launched by institutions of higher education, research organizations, and human rights organizations. Besides, the plan also points out:

> The state encourages and supports the China Society for Human Rights Studies, as well as human rights research organizations in institutions of higher learning and social science academies and institutes, to make good use of their teaching and scientific research platforms to engage in international exchanges and cooperation through various channels, and work hard to train senior professionals in human rights field with an international vision [16].

5.2.5 Performing International Human Rights Duties, and Conducting Exchanges and Cooperation in the Field of International Human Rights

The NHRAP clearly defines that "China will continue to fulfill its obligations to the international human rights conventions to which it has acceded, and initiate and actively participate in exchanges and cooperation in the field of international human rights" [17]. The Chinese government has always cherished the important role played by international instruments on human rights in promoting and protecting human rights and speaks highly of the value of international instruments on human rights under every circumstance. In the improvement of domestic legal systems, China strictly follows the requirement and spirit of international instruments on human rights and continuously promotes the safeguarding cause of human rights to a new higher level.

5.2.5.1 Fulfillment of International Human Rights Obligations

China not only actively participates in the draft and discussion of international instruments on human rights, but also actively joins many international human rights conventions. So far, China has joined 25 international human rights conventions. The action plan exemplifies the obligation conditions of some important international human rights conventions, namely, the *International Covenant on Economic, Social and Cultural Rights*, the *Convention on the Elimination of All Forms of Discrimination Against Women*, the *Convention on the Rights of the Child*, the *Optional Protocol to the Convention on the Rights of the Child on the Involvement of Children in Armed Conflict*, the *Optional Protocol to the Convention on the Rights of the Child on the Sale of Children, Child Prostitution and Child Pornography*, the *Convention on the Rights of Persons with Disabilities*, the *International Convention on the Elimination of All Forms of Racial Discrimination*, the *International Covenant on Civil and Political Rights (ICCPR)* ("China has signed the *ICCPR*, and will continue legislative, judicial and administrative reforms to make domestic laws better linked with this Covenant, and prepare the ground for approval of the *ICCPR*" [17].), and the *United Nations Anti-Corruption Convention*.

In view of the joined international human rights conventions, China always fulfills its obligations to the international human rights conventions to which it has acceded, holds constructive dialogues and cooperation with these treaty bodies, and submits reports on implementing the conventions in time to the treaty bodies concerned. In terms of the proposals raised by these treaty bodies, China attaches great importance, studies carefully and "adopts rational and feasible proposals in the light of China's actual conditions" [17]. Currently, the Chinese people are actively studying the linkage between the ICCPR and domestic laws and doing a large amount of work with respect to the legislative, judicial, and executive reforms. Concerning the commitment of the *United Nations Anti-Corruption Convention*, China is working hard to link the Convention to domestic laws. All of these fully show the positive cooperative spirit of the Chinese government, and the serious attitude and strong determination in carefully fulfilling the obligations of the international conventions.

5.2.5.2 Exchanges and Cooperation in the Field of International Human Rights

China not only fulfills its obligations to the international human rights conventions, but also holds exchanges and cooperation in the field of international human rights on the basis of equality and mutual respect, and becomes a great power in promoting the healthy development of international human rights. In the exchanges and cooperation of international human rights, China will further develop the exchanges and cooperation with all the United Nations human rights organs. As one of the first members of the UN Human Rights Council (HRC), China will take an active part in the work of the HRC and play an important role in dealing with international human rights issues. The exchanges and cooperation with the HRC are also shown in the participation in the HRC's first Universal Periodic Review (UPR) for China. In December, 2008, the Chinese government submitted the national reports and accepted the review of HRC. During the process of review, China held constructive dialogues with various sides and set up a good national image in the international community.

Additionally, the exchanges and cooperation in the field of international human rights are shown with respect to the exchanges and cooperation between the Chinese government and other UN human rights organizations, such as the Special Procedures of the UN HRC, the United Nations Office of the High Commissioner for Human Rights and other relevant international organizations, which includes the Food and Agriculture Organization (FAO) of the United Nations, the UN Educational, Scientific and Cultural Organization (UNESCO), World Health Organization (WHO), and International Labor Organization (ILO).

Furthermore, China holds bilateral exchanges and cooperation with various countries concerned on the basis of equality and mutual respect and actively carries on dialogues and exchanges on human rights to enhance mutual understanding and achieves general consensus. At the same time, the exchanges and cooperation in the field of human rights have also displayed China's scientific attitude and practical spirit in terms of international human rights issues and have played an important role in promoting the healthy and orderly development of international human rights cause.

5.3 Implementing Measures of the NHRAP

In order to implement the NHRAP, the Chinese government has taken a series of measures, including the joint meeting system and the principle of "each attending to its own duties" in particular.

5.3.1 Joint Meeting System and the Principle of "Each Attending to Its Own Duties"

It is not easy to set up a good action plan, and it is more difficult to implement it well. In order to implement the NHRAP well, China has established a joint meeting system, which is a specific measure in implementing and supervising the NHRAP. The system is in accordance with the constitutional principle, while the state is the subject of the obligation to "respect and guarantee human rights", and the state is in charge of the public authorities. The system was initiated by the Information Office of the State Council and the Ministry of Foreign Affairs, involving 53 national authoritative institutes:

> The General Office of the Standing Committee of the NPC, the Commission of Legislative Affairs of NPC Standing Committee, the Commission of Social and Legislative Affairs of Chinese People's Political Consultative Conference (CPPCC), the Supreme People's Court, the Supreme People's Procuratorate, the Ministry of Foreign Affairs, the National Development and Reform Commission, the Ministry of Education, the Ministry of Science and Technology, the Ministry of Industry and Information Technology, the State Ethnic Affairs Commission, the Ministry of Public Security, the Ministry of Supervision, the Ministry of Civil Affairs, the Ministry of Justice, the Ministry of Labor and Social Security, the Ministry of Land and Resources, the Ministry of Environmental Protection, the Ministry of Housing and Urban–Rural Development, the Ministry of Transport, the Ministry of Railways, the Ministry of Water Resources, the Ministry of Agriculture, the Ministry of Culture, the Ministry of Public Health, the State Family Planning Commission, the State Auditing Administration, the State Bureau of Quality and Technical Supervision, the State Administration of Radio, Film and Television, Press and Publication Administration, the State Physical Cultural Administration, the State Security Production Administration, the State Statistics Bureau, the State Forestry Bureau, the State Intellectual Property Office (SIPO), the State Bureau of Religious Affairs, the Office of Legislative Affairs, the Information Office of the State Council, the State Letters and Visits Office, the State Food and Drug Administration, the Women and Children Office of the State Council, the State Council Leading Group Office of Poverty Alleviation and Development, China National Committee on Aging, the State Council Three Gorges Project Construction

Committee, the Publicity Department of the CPC Central Committee, the United Front Work Department of the CPC Central Committee, the International Liaison Department of the CPC Central Committee, the Policy Research Department of the CPC Central Committee, All-China Federation of Trade Unions, All-China Women's Federation, China Disabled Person's Federation, All-China Youth Federation and China Society for Human Rights Studies [12].

All these departments jointly shoulder the responsibilities to "respect and guarantee human rights". They make work plans to improve the awareness of human rights and have the responsibility of implementing them. According to "each attending to its own duties," all the state authorities, administrative organs, and judicial organs and the related organizations will bring the NHRAP into their working obligations, and carry out the "state respects and guarantees human rights" with specific measures. The joint meeting mechanism adopts the methods to develop the assignment of the duties and obligations by negotiation and coordination with the relevant departments and units, the state organs undertake the main responsibility of the implementation of the action plan. The joint meeting mechanism not only takes responsibility for making work plans, but also coordinates the implementation of the plans and undertakes supervision and evaluation. The state will also carry out a series of publicity activities to make the NHRAP widely known to society as a whole, in an effort to invite all institutions, social organizations, nongovernmental organizations, news media, and the public to actively participate in publicizing and implementing the plan.

5.3.2 *Promote the Development of Human Rights Cause Legally, Comprehensively and Practically*

The NHRAP develops China's human rights cause legally, comprehensively and practically. When he was answering the questions of the journalists, Wang Chen, Director of the Information Office of the State Council, put forward three fundamental principles for the development of China's human rights cause [12], which are, promoting human rights according to law, promoting human rights comprehensively, and promoting human rights practically. Promoting human rights according to law means issuing and implementing the plan based on stipulations in the Constitutional and international human rights conventions. The constitutional principle "the state respects and guarantees human rights" and the related stipulations regarding "the fundamental rights and duties of citizens" should be implemented in the action plan. The principle of protecting human rights in the *Universal Declaration of Human Rights* and the basic spirits of safeguarding human rights in international conventions should be transformed into domestic practice of safeguarding human rights. The specific mechanism and objectives measures of "respecting and safeguarding human rights" should be systematically improved from all legislative, executive and judicial steps to promote the development of China's human rights cause.

Promoting human rights comprehensively means that China not only regards the rights to subsistence and development as the primary human rights to be protected and promoted, but also takes the Scientific Outlook on Development as a guide to action, putting people first and including all social members as the subjects of human rights.

According to the principle that all kinds of human rights are interdependent and undivided, the development of all human rights should be coordinated, arranged, promoted, and developed comprehensively, not only fully realizing the so-called "first-generation human rights", the citizen rights and political rights, but also gradually achieving the "second-generation human rights", the economic, social and cultural rights, as well as coordinating and developing the "third-generation human rights", such as the rights to development and environmental rights and so on.

Promoting human rights practically means:

> The plan not only reflects the general principles of human rights of the international community and absorbs relevant UN requirements and efficient measures taken by other countries in its content and formal specifications, but also always proceeds from basic national conditions, ponders problems and solves problems according to the practical situation of China, combining 'what should be done' with 'what can be done' to make our goals and measures feasible and obtainable and make sure that the human rights cause will be practically and scientifically promoted with a matter-of-fact attitude [12].

The UN requires that some basic human rights and freedom be realized immediately, while some other rights can be realized gradually by taking progressive measures, which require the state to act vigorously and shoulder the responsibility of respecting and safeguarding human rights in the process of implementing the obligation of protecting human rights. Due to differences in historical background, cultural tradition, and economic development, human rights development measures made by different countries cannot be the same. Taking a matter-of-fact attitude is the prerequisite for promoting the human rights cause, and the practical and feasible measures are the basic guarantees in promoting and safeguarding the full realization of human rights.

5.4 Significance of the NHRAP

The release of the NHRAP has great historical and practical significance. In terms of its historical significance, the action plan marks that China's human rights cause has developed into a new stage of plans and comprehensive promotion according to law and it becomes an eventful milestone in the history of the development of human rights; in terms of its practical significance, only by transforming the legitimate human rights into practical human rights can the idealism of human rights be turned into reality. The NHRAP has not only set a clear goal for China's human rights development, but also symbolizes that China's human rights cause has entered a new era.

5.4.1 *The Significant Milestone in the History of China's Human Rights Development*

If the openness of human rights or the banner of human rights held by China was characterized by releasing "*Human Rights in China*" in 1991 and "the state respects and guarantees human rights" included in the Constitution in 2004 was regarded as a symbol of human rights transforming from deserved rights to legitimate rights, the NHRAP would then be taken as a significant milestone in the transition from legitimate rights to practical rights. It is the first time for China to make an action plan on the subject of human rights, which is an important measure to carry out the constitutional principle of "the state respects and guarantees human rights". It is also a comprehensive plan for the development of China's human rights cause in the following two years. The extensive content and the specific measures involved will have profound influence on the all-round development of China's human rights cause. Although China, as a developing country, has become one of the several countries that have issued national human rights action plans, it still has not established a human rights protection system covering all members of society and its material conditions for human rights protection are still too weak. Therefore, the development of China's human rights cause still has a heavy responsibility to undertake and a long way to go.

With the improvement of civilization of all human beings, the demand for human rights will increase, and the connotations of human rights will gradually be expanded. The safeguarding level of human rights will be gradually improved and the ideal human rights will be increasingly transformed to legal human rights, which will become practical ones through specific implementation. However, there is an undeniable fact that the gap between ideal human rights and legal human rights, and the gap between legal and practical human rights will inevitably be long-standing. Bridging the gaps requires great effort to be made by the Communist Party and the government and a strong economic basis. In addition, effective measures should be taken to improve the safeguarding level of human rights. It is not easy for such a big developing country with a population of 1.3 billion to fully realize human rights safeguarding for all social members. The road ahead is also uneven, but China's human rights cause can only be improved by overcoming all kinds of difficulties. In this sense, the release of the NHRAP is a significant milestone marking the transformation from legal human rights to practical human rights.

5.4.2 *Clear Goals and a Guided Direction for the Development of China's Human Rights Cause*

The NHRAP is an effective measure in transforming legal human rights to practical human rights. It also makes clear the direction and the goals for the development of

China's human rights cause. The plan repeatedly uses words such as "safeguard," "improve," "perfect," "increase," "promote," "push," "strengthen," "expand," and so on. These words fully show the great determination and confidence of the Chinese government in promoting the cause of human rights. In order to achieve higher goals, the plan also takes the strategy of "orderly development" during the process of the implementation of human rights protection. That is an important measure that China is taking to gradually promote the development of the human rights cause, because the development of anything has to go through a process, and China's human rights cause is no exception.

Moreover, China is restricted by the fundamental state conditions, such as a large population, lack of resources, and a weak economic basis. Although the country has been rapidly developed during the past three decades, to fully realize human rights protection covering all members of society still requires going through a gradual process. During that process, the issuance of the NHRAP has set clear goals and a direction for the development of China's human rights cause. As long as the development measures of human rights action plan are fully implemented, the expected goals will be achieved.

5.4.3 Symbolize a New Phase of the Comprehensive Development of China's Human Rights Cause

The release of the NHRAP marks China's entrance into a new phase of the comprehensive development of human rights. The action plan has wide coverage including economic, social and cultural rights, civil rights and political rights, and the rights of minorities, women, children, the elderly, and the disabled. It has expanded the subjects of human rights to all members of society, and it has even adopted concrete measures to protect the legal rights of criminals. The measures it takes are legal, comprehensive, and practical. It also signifies that China is practically promoting its human rights cause according to law.

On April 14, 2009, Wang Chen, Director of the Information Office of the State Council, answered the questions of journalists from the *People's Daily* and *Xinhua News Agency* and pointed out:

> The release of the NHRAP has great importance in the history of the development of China's human rights cause. It signifies that China's human rights cause has become an important theme of national construction and social development, and it has entered a new phase of comprehensive promotion with plans. It has recorded the steps, determination and direction of the Chinese government in promoting and safeguarding human rights, which will definitely propel the governments of all levels, all walks of life and the whole society to establish the values of respecting and safeguarding human rights, and effectively promote the development of China's human rights cause [12].

On December 10, 2008, Hu Jintao wrote to the China Society for Human Rights Studies, congratulating on the 60th anniversary of the release of the UDHR. In the congratulatory letter, Hu Jintao penetratingly summarizes the great achievements

China has made after the founding and the reform and opening-up of the People's Republic of China (PRC). He points out:

> Since new China was founded, our society has achieved universally acknowledged progress. The destiny of Chinese people has dramatically been changed, and the historical development has also been realized in China's human rights cause. Especially after the 30 years' reform and opening-up, the Party and the government regard respecting and safeguarding human rights as an important principle of governing the country, and solemnly write it into the Constitution of CPC and the Constitution of PRC. Besides, the effective measures are taken to promote the development of human rights cause, to notably improve the material and cultural living standards of the people, to safeguard the political, economic, cultural and social rights of the people and compose a new chapter in the development of human rights cause in China [18].

The release of the NHRAP implements in details the constitutional principle "the state respects and guarantees human rights", which is a practical and effective measure to promote the development of human rights cause. The popularity of human rights subjects, the extensive content of human rights and the feasibility of safeguarding measures have opened a new chapter for the development of Chinese human rights cause. From then on, China's human rights cause has stepped into a new stage of legal, comprehensive and practical promotions.

References

1. *Guidelines of the Eleventh Five-Year Plan for National Economic and Social Development*, Chapter 43.
2. Qu, X. (2009). Major theories of human rights concepts in 30 years' reform and open door. In X. Xu (Ed.), *Human Rights Research* (Vol. 8, p. 4). Jinan: Shandong People's Press.
3. *Guidelines of the Eleventh Five-Year Plan for National Economic and Social Development*, Chapter 2.
4. *Guidelines of the Eleventh Five-Year Plan for National Economic and Social Development*, Chapter 37.
5. *Guidelines of the Eleventh Five-Year Plan for National Economic and Social Development*, Chapter 42.
6. Hu, J. (2007, October 15). *Hold high the great banner of socialism with Chinese characteristics and strive for new victories in building a moderately prosperous society in all respects*. Report to the Seventeenth National Congress of the Communist Party of China. Part III.
7. Hu, J. (2007, October 15). *Hold high the great banner of socialism with Chinese characteristics and strive for new victories in building a moderately prosperous society in all respects*. Report to the Seventeenth National Congress of the Communist Party of China. Part IV.
8. Hu, J. (2007, October 15). *Hold high the great banner of socialism with Chinese characteristics and strive for new victories in building a moderately prosperous society in all respects*. Report to the Seventeenth National Congress of the Communist Party of China. Part VIII.
9. Hu, J. (2007, October 15). *Hold high the great banner of socialism with Chinese characteristics and strive for new victories in building a moderately prosperous society in all respects*. Report to the Seventeenth National Congress of the Communist Party of China. Part XII.

10. Information Office of the State Council. (2008). *China's Efforts and Achievements in Promoting the Rule of Law*. Released on February 28./ Also refer to Appendix II
11. Information Office of the State Council. (2009). *National Human Rights Action Plan of China (2009–2010)*. Released on April 13.
12. Wang, C. (2009). Important measures to facilitate the development of Chinese human rights career in all aspects—Wang Chen's answering the journalists' questions regarding *National Human Rights Action Plan of China. People's Daily*. April 15. p. 8.
13. Information Office of the State Council. (2009). *National Human Rights Action Plan of China (2009–2010)*. Released on April 13, Part I.
14. Information Office of the State Council. (2009). *National Human Rights Action Plan of China (2009–2010)*. Released on April 13, Part II.
15. Information Office of the State Council. (2009). *National Human Rights Action Plan of China (2009–2010)*. Released on April 13, Part III.
16. Information Office of the State Council. (2009). *National Human Rights Action Plan of China (2009–2010)*. Released on April 13, Part IV.
17. Information Office of the State Council. (2009). *National Human Rights Action Plan of China (2009–2010)*. Released on April 13, Part V.
18. Hu, J. (2008). Congratulation letter to China Society for Human Rights Studies. *People's Daily* (Oversea Version). December 12. p. 1.

Chapter 6
Fundamental Principles for Achieving International Human-Rights Standards in China

Abstract Ten fundamental principles for the realization of international human-rights standards should be followed: (1) The universality of human rights must be integrated with country-specific situations. (2) Priority must be given to the right to subsistence and the right to development. (3) Human rights must be recognized for all members of society. (4) Human rights must be developed all around. (5) Rights must be balanced with obligations in promoting human rights. (6) Human rights are not divorced from social stability, economic development, and the legal construction. (7) Human rights are an essentially domestic affair of a sovereign state. (8) The international human-rights cause must be promoted through talks and cooperation. (9) Human-rights education is a basic measure for promoting human rights. (10) Peace, development, and human rights contribute to a harmonious world.

The new China faced a formidably tough situation from the outset: a longstanding sanction and blockade by Western countries, coupled with a century of colonization and despoliation by Western superpowers, led to the cruel reality that per capita resources were low nationwide and the economy and culture were extremely backward. In this laggard situation, the country experienced the wrongly staged Cultural Revolution and a consequent big setback in the development of human rights. For all that, "Chinese people have made unremitting effort to realize the ideals and goals of human rights prescribed in the *Universal Declaration of Human Rights* and scored notable achievements" [1]. Particularly, more than 30 years after the implementation of the "reform and opening-up policy," China has made universally acknowledged achievements in terms of human-rights protection, a notable contribution to the progress of mankind, and formed socialist human-rights theories and a rights-protection system with Chinese characteristics.

President Hu Jintao pointed out in a letter addressed to the China Society for Human-Rights Studies on December 10, 2008:

> In the process of building a moderately prosperous society in every respect and acceler ating socialist modernization, we will always insist on human-oriented approach. Not only respecting the universal principles of human rights but also considering the fundamental realities of the country, we will make sure that people's rights to subsistence and development remain top priorities in human-rights protection. In promoting the sound and quick

P. Sun, *Human Rights Protection System in China*,
DOI: 10.1007/978-3-642-39663-2_6, © Springer-Verlag Berlin Heidelberg 2014

development of economy and of society, we will ensure for all members of society equal rights to participation and development in accordance with the law. The Chinese people will strengthen international cooperation in human rights as they have always done, and are willing to join hands with people across the globe so as to do its part in promoting healthy development of the international human-rights cause and building a harmonious world with lasting peace and common prosperity [2].

Hu Jintao's concise explanation in this letter on our country's basic principles in implementing international human-rights standards is a succinct summary of the development of the country's human-rights cause. This chapter will mainly focus on 10 fundamental principles for achieving international human-rights standards in China.

6.1 Integrating the Universality of Human-Rights with Country-Specific Situations

Human rights feature both universality or popularity and peculiarity. An important principle in implementing international human-rights standards in China is that the universality of human rights must be integrated with specific national situations. Both the *Proclamation of Teheran* and the *Vienna Declaration and Program of Action* point out the universality of human rights as well as their peculiarity. Jiang Zemin said in a letter of congratulations to the China Society for Human-Rights Studies on December 10, 1998: "Ever since the founding of the People's Republic of China, and particularly after the reform and opening up, the Chinese government and people have combined the universality principle with China's specific national conditions and made universally acknowledged achievements in terms of promoting and safeguarding human rights" [3]. That the international community has managed to reach a consensus on dozens of international human-rights conventions is adequate in itself to prove the universality of human rights; at the same time, the contracting states were permitted to sign these conventions with reservations to certain provisions according to each state's specific national situations, and this shows that the peculiarity of human rights was also recognized and respected. But now we need to define both the universality and peculiarity of human rights.

The universality of human rights specifies that everyone enjoys universal rights and freedom, and in particular basic rights and freedom, just as is stated in the *Universal Declaration of Human Rights* (UDHR): "All human beings are born free and equal in dignity and rights" [4]. Human rights apply to the entire human race, to everyone in society. This concept is much different from that taken hold during the bourgeois revolution in the West. For instance, the human rights proclaimed in the American *Declaration of Independence* did not belong to colored people like black and native Americans, and the human rights in the French *Declaration of the Rights of Man and the Citizen* excluded the colored, women, and laborers. The principle of human-rights universality established under the UDHR adopted by the

UN General Assembly in 1948 entitled all people to rights and freedom, "without distinction of any kind, such as race, color, sex, language, religion, political or other opinion, national or social origin, property, birth or other status" [4]. The subject of human rights is thus maximized to include everyone.

Human rights are characteristic of generality, and the value of human rights is universal. The *International Bill of Human Rights* [5] covers more than one hundred rights, including the right to life, the right to self-determination, civil rights, political rights, economic rights, social rights, cultural rights, the right to development, the right to peace, and environmental rights, giving content to every right and generalizing each type. The human rights in the Western bourgeois revolution period only included the rights to life, health, freedom, property, security, and the right of resistance. These rights are neither concrete nor universal. Human rights are universal as a common goal and ideal by mankind. Human rights are not exclusive to bourgeois, but an ideal pursued by all human beings. Countries in both the East and the West are full of hope to realize the human-rights ideal and have made great efforts. No country or government has declared not to respect and protect human rights. In a certain sense, all countries, big or small, strong or weak, developed or developing, will make lasting efforts to achieve human rights, a common goal of mankind. All states in the international community attach great importance to the value of human rights. As pointed out in the UDHR, human rights will become "a common standard of achievement for all peoples and all nations," [6] recognized and observed by all member states.

However, Professor Milne at Durham University in Britain offers a minimum standard for human rights:

> A minimum moral standard which is applicable to all cultures and societies does not deny that every human being is largely made what he is by his particular cultural and social experience. It does not presuppose homogeneous desocialized and deculturized human beings. Rather it presupposes social and cultural diversity and sets minimum moral requirements to be met by all societies and cultures. Such requirements set moral limits to the scope of diversity but in no way deny its existence. The universal applicability to the minimum moral standard entails that the rights for which it requires respect should be universally recognized [7].

Milne doubts the universality of human rights, saying that the "idea of human rights as those which belong to all human beings at all times and in all places, ignores not only cultural diversity but also the social basis of personal identity. It presupposes homogeneous desocialized and deculturized human beings and there are no such beings" [8].

As the realization of human rights is closely bound up with the historical conditions, social structure, political system, cultural tradition, racial mentality, and religious beliefs of different countries, specific national conditions have to be considered in bringing into play the universality principle of human rights. Even for the realization of so-called "negative rights" [9], we should put into consideration such factors as a country's political system, cultural tradition, racial mentality, while the realization of the so-called "positive rights" [10] needs to be guaranteed by affluent economy of a country, as what Marx says, "rights can never transcend the economic structure of society and the cultural development of society restricted by the economic structure" [11]. Because of different levels of economic and social development, people in different countries are bound to have different needs to human rights. There is no use discussing the universality of human rights if the distinct characteristics and national conditions of different countries are disregarded, because the realization of human rights is not abstract but concrete.

> The exercise of human rights cannot be identical, and will be step by step, due to the differences in development levels in different countries. It is too much to ask for being once for ever or identical. In other words, different countries and races will always form their own human-rights concept and make human-rights policies and rules suitable for their own, according to their own political, economic, cultural conditions and specific regulations, and their own historic, religious and cultural backgrounds [12].

In developing countries with relatively weak economies, where poverty and underdevelopment still pose the biggest threat to human rights, the principle of universality should be integrated with their national situations, giving priority to the realization of the rights to subsistence and development for all.

By pursuing the principle of integrating the universality of human rights with country-specific situations, we can abandon the logic of cultural relativism and conceive the development of human rights as a dynamic process to be perfected over time. Professor Gu Chunlei thinks that there is a dialectic unity between the universality and the peculiarity of human rights, saying that "universality and peculiarity are relative rather than absolute. Universality is manifested through peculiarity, in that the universality of human rights can only be put into real play when the specific situations of different countries and nationalities are put into consideration" [13]. So it is concretely argued that integrating the universality of human rights with country-specific situations is a guiding principle for the gradual implementation of international human-rights standards.

6.2 Giving Priority to the Right to Subsistence and the Right to Development

The principle of integrating the universality of human rights with country-specific situations leads to another important principle, namely, the priority should be accorded to the rights to subsistence and development. In 1991, Chinese government officially stated in the white paper on *Human Rights in China* that the rights to subsistence and development are paramount human rights. The right to subsistence entitles people to the basic condition needed to maintain a normal life. It not only allows people to live, but to live with decency and dignity. It is not only a right to enable a person to live life biologically, "but also a right that guarantees a country, a race and its people to live" [14]. A person's right to subsistence guarantees life, inviolable personal freedom, personal dignity and freedom from insult, the right to basic living standard, and the right to health, and is even linked to the rights to food, housing, work that support a livelihood. Therefore, the right to subsistence should not be regarded as a human right at the lowest level, and the improvement of living conditions takes on richer and richer meanings. *On Theory and Practice of Human-Rights* groups the modern meanings of the right to subsistence under seven principles [15], namely, (i) life is the natural form of the right to subsistence; (ii) property is the material condition for realizing the right to subsistence; (iii) work is a common tool for realizing the right to subsistence; (iv) social security is the relief approach of the right to subsistence; (v) development is the necessary requirement of the right to subsistence; (vi) environmental rights and the rights to health and peace are contemporary meanings of the right to subsistence; and (vii) it is a country's function to provide guarantees for the right to subsistence.

The right to development was proclaimed as a basic right in the *Declaration on the Right to Development* adopted in 1986 at the forty-first UN General Assembly. It is both an individual right and a collective right. As an individual right, it designates the people's right to develop in politics, the economy, society, and culture. As a collective right, it designates "the right of peoples to self-determination, by virtue of which they have to exercise, subject to the relevant provisions of both *International Covenants on Human Rights*, full and complete sovereignty over all their natural wealth and resources" [16]. Article 11(1) of the *International Covenant on Economic, Social, and Cultural Rights* (ICESCR) "recognize[s] the rights of everyone to an adequate standard of living for himself and his family, including adequate food, clothing, and housing, and to the continuous improvement of living conditions." Article 12(1) "recognize[s] the right of everyone to the enjoyment of the highest attainable standard of physical and mental health."

The right to subsistence and the right to development are closely related because the right to subsistence is the precondition and basis of the right to development, while the right to development is the extension and guarantee of the right to subsistence. Without subsistence as the precondition and basis, other rights will lose their significance, and the right to development will be pointless. However, safeguarding the right to subsistence alone is far from sufficient for a holistic development of human rights. Development is of great importance for the realization of the right to subsistence, because only when a person is developed all around can the right to subsistence be fully realized.

The right to development is the extension of the right to subsistence. Living is the prerequisite for development, and it's pointless to talk about development without life; in the same way, development is a condition of living, and living without development would be of insignificance, which is a static "existing" leading only to decline or final elimination. Only with development can the quality of living be raised and improved [17]. In this way, the rights to subsistence and development are particularly significant to people in China. Therefore, making the right to subsistence and the right to development the foremost human rights is a pragmatic approach appropriate for our country's specific national situation.

Making the rights to subsistence and development the foremost human rights is a scientific conclusion drawn from our country's historical experiences and is at the same time a notable contribution to international human-rights theory. Looking back, that humiliating history of old China can not be forgotten. Since the Opium War of 1840, Western superpowers began to invade China in a large scale, plunging China into a semi-feudalist and semi-colonized society. In a hundred years that followed, "Imperialist countries like Britain, France, Russia, Japan, America alternatively started hundreds of aggressive wars in China, grabbing vast land of Chinese territory, slaughtering millions of Chinese civilians, forcing China into signing 1,100 unfair treaties, taking away up to 100 billion *Liangs* of silver in the name of warfare compensation and other causes" [18]. In 1900 when the Allied Forces of Eight Powers invaded China, they robbed and burned everything wherever they went. The county of Tanggu in Tianjin with 50,000 residents was turned to soulless wreckage overnight. In the Japanese invasion of China, more than 30 million Chinese lost their lives. In the notorious Nanjing massacre, Japanese solders brutally slaughtered more than 300,000 Chinese civilians. The above iron history shows explicitly that in the midst of the invasion and capturing by Western imperialists, China was on the edge of extinction, and the people were deeply humiliated and lost the least guarantee for security and dignity. Just because of the Western superpowers' excessive economic robbery and savage murdering of humanity, Chinese people suffered great losses in lives and property, the conditions for subsistence and development being greatly degraded. Therefore, to get state sovereignty and realize the rights to subsistence and development are the foremost pursuit of human rights in our country.

As a developing country, China is marked by some fundamental realities that include a large population, scarce resources, and low level of material life. Despite more than 30 years of economic development, China still falls far behind developed countries in the West in terms of per capita income. A prophet in the West once claimed that no country or government can solve the subsistence problem of 1.3 billion people. Our country, however, not only provides its people with adequate food and clothing but also sets them on the course to a moderately prosperous life. The miraculous achievements in China's human-rights endeavor are connected to the strategy of giving priority to the right of subsistence. Besides, only when the right to development is fully realized can other human rights be promoted and guaranteed in full. By adhering to the strategy of prioritizing the rights to subsistence and development, China can ensure that its human-rights cause continues in the right direction, having already made great progress, as has been acknowledged across the world. The priority strategy in human-rights practice breaks with the traditional concept of human-rights protection in such a way as to enrich the meaning of such protection. It is reasonable to say that taking the right to subsistence and development as the foremost human rights is our country's unique contribution to international human-rights theory.

6.3 Recognizing Human Rights for all Members of Society

As stated in the above mentioned American *Declaration of Independence* and French *Declaration of the Rights of Man and of the Citizen*, the human rights they advocate mainly refer to the rights of white males, thus excluding women and people of color. The American slave system was not abolished until the end of the American Civil War. It was also after a long process that women became the subjects of human rights. Only under the modern international human-rights system, with the UN General Assembly adopting the 1948 UDHR, was there a formal recognition that the first subject of human rights was "everyone", "without distinction of any kind, such as race, color, sex, language, religion, political or other opinion, national or social origin, property, birth or other status." (Article 2) This made the concept of person universal, greatly extending and expanding the concept of human-rights subject found in the *Declaration of Independence* and the *Declaration of the Rights of Man and of the Citizen.*

Early in the year 1985, Deng Xiaoping pointed out in a speech: "What are human rights? First of all, how many people have rights? Do they belong to the minority, to the majority or to all people in the country? Human rights in the western world is inherently different from ours" [19]. These words clearly convey how human-rights subjects are conceived differently in our country than they are in Western countries. The human rights China is trying to secure belong to *all* Chinese people, whereas human rights "from birth" in Western capitalist society are actually a privilege of the bourgeois. The socialist human rights with Chinese characteristics are explicitly set forth in the *Constitution of the People's Republic of China*: All power in the People's Republic of China belongs to the people. This can be appreciated under three headings: (i) The universality of the subject of human rights. This means, essentially, that the subjects enjoying human rights are all nationals, rather than a minority. Special protection is recognized for disadvantaged groups—including women, children, the elderly, the weak, the sick, and the disabled—and that gives full expression to the socialist conception of human-rights protection. (ii) The fairness of human-rights protection. The country has taken active and gradual measures in law, politics and the economy to make sure that its people equally enjoy the full range of human rights. Fairness is also evinced in the special protection afforded to the disadvantaged. (iii) The practicality of human-rights protection. Human rights in our country are not only grounded in the *Constitution*, protected by department laws, but are also supported by the political system and by economic conditions. This comes with the achievements of over 30 years after the adoption of the reform and opening-up policy, as economic conditions allow.

A well-known human-rights expert in our country, Professor Li Buyun, has pointed out in talking about universality:

> A person, as a human, should enjoy the right he is entitled to, regardless of race, color, gender, language and religion, political standpoint, property and education. In a country, at any historical era, everyone is born with fundamental human rights, including the rights to

life, security, freedom, thought, dignity, and minimum living necessities. This is a notable manifestation of the universality of human rights [20].

He mainly discusses the human rights that social members have, broadening the subject of human rights to include everyone in society.

In the new era, the subject of human rights is further expanded, when the concept of the right to development, especially sustainable development, makes its entry with the growth of international human-rights theory. "The Scientific Outlook on Development", proposed by our government, involves sustainable development, which requires environmental protection, coupled with resource- and energy-saving measures, and is aimed at benefiting descendents and sustaining human civilization. From the standpoint of the subject of rights, this is an extension to future generations, protecting the rights of offering. In this sense, human rights protect not only all members in present society but also those in future society, which refers to human rights of all human beings in the civilized society.

6.4 Realizing the Goal of all-around Development of Human Rights

Dealing with all kinds of human rights, our county takes a priority strategy, which is an inevitable result once the specific national conditions are taken into account, with a scientific attitude that is realistic and pragmatic. The rights to subsistence and development may be the foremost human rights, but this is not to say that they should upstage the development and realization of other kinds of human rights. The rights to subsistence and to development are taken as a basis in the effort to comprehensively promote and secure human rights, all the while realizing and protecting other kinds of human rights in tandem with economic development. In Western society, civil and political rights are always taken as human rights, and their respect and protection are highlighted. They are thought to be passive rights and need immediate realization. Unlike Eastern societies, Western societies do not attach importance to economic, social, and cultural rights, a case in point being that the United States' unwillingness to ratify the ICESCR. However, economic, social and cultural rights are programmatic, and thus need to be realized gradually. They can not be realized without developing material and economic conditions in the country and in society, and it is not practical to talk about realizing human rights without an existing economic foundation, since human rights are by nature part of superstructure.

Dong Yunhu argues that the "contents of fundamental human rights prescribed in the UDHR breaks the traditional concept of human rights in the West, enriching and fulfilling the connotation of human rights" [21]. The UDHR achieves two breakthroughs in the history of human rights, one consisting in expanding the range of *subjects* of rights, the other in expanding the range of *contents* of rights.

In terms of the contents, the UDHR for the first time declared economic, social, and cultural rights to be fundamental, a great breakthrough over the Western traditional narrow concept, limited to civil and political rights. The human rights listed in the UDHR are specified in the ICESCR and the *International Covenant on Civil and Political Rights* (ICCPR). These three documents on human rights form the core of the *International Bill of Human Rights*: They include one hundred human rights, greatly extending the range and contents of human-rights protection, and make such protection more specific and comprehensive. However, the different types of human rights stipulated in the aforementioned international documents are interrelated and interdependent. A point stated in the *Vienna Declaration and Program of Action*:

> All human rights are universal, indivisible and interdependent and interrelated. The international community must treat human rights globally in a fair and equal manner, on the same footing, and with the same emphasis. While the significance of national and regional particularities and various historical, cultural and religious backgrounds must be borne in mind, it is the duty of States, regardless of their political, economic and cultural systems, to promote and protect all human rights and fundamental freedoms [22].

China not only actively participates in the drafting of the core international treaties, but also signs and ratifies a good number of international human-rights documents. So far the Chinese government has acceded to twenty-five international human-rights conventions. Furthermore, China strictly observes its international obligations, vigorously promotes human-rights protection in the process of making and applying laws, and in 2009 launched on its own initiative a programmatic action plan laying out the future course of human rights in the country [23]. All of the country's administrative departments of the country are mobilized to promote the progress and development of our country's human-rights cause, working endlessly for the ideal that the entire human race should enjoy full human rights. Our country has made great efforts to protect individuals' civil, political, economic, social, and cultural rights and has given special care to underprivileged groups like the elderly, the weak, the sick, the disabled, and children, attesting to the advantage of our country's socialist system.

6.5 Balancing Rights and Obligations in Promoting the Development of Human Rights

In China's tradition, a profound influence is exercised by the Confucian idea of placing "righteousness" before "interest". A person's social duties and obligations are stressed, and personal rights and requirements follow. This obviously stands in stark contrast to the concept of rights in Western society, which lays emphasis on individual rights and limited government and regards self-interest as an important concept of Western capitalist countries. Therefore, the West concerns itself with the realization of individual rights but ignores the duties and obligations in the process of realizing individual rights.

Marx's concept of human rights emphasizes the correlative relationship between rights and obligations, saying "there is no right without obligation and no obligation without right" [24]. If we are to fully realize our own rights, we must each respect the rights of others and recognize their inviolability—a respect and recognition that becomes everyone's obligation. If one can not keep and enjoy rights without having to respect the rights of others, these others will have the right to do the same, and no one's rights will ever be fully realized. Therefore, "in order to turn human rights into universal rights enjoyed by everyone, everyone should perform relative obligations when exercising his rights" [25]. Professor Li Buyun once said that rights and obligations are compulsory components of human rights: "They are two basic ingredients of human rights, two important factors in deciding their nature and two important source of power in promoting their development" [26]. As to the dialectic relationship between rights and obligations, Professor Li Buyun thinks that "rights and obligations of human rights cannot be separated. To achieve a unity between the two, and deal with their relationship rationally and scientifically is an important feature of advanced human-rights system" [27].

Quite a few international human-rights instruments stipulate both rights and corresponding obligations that an individual has to society. Article 29.1 of the UDHR states: "Everyone has duties to the community in which alone the free and full development of his personality is possible." And Article 29.2 states: "In the exercise of his rights and freedoms, everyone shall be subject only to such limitations as are determined by law solely for the purpose of securing due recognition and respect for the rights and freedoms of others and of meeting the just requirements of morality, public order and the general welfare in a democratic society." This clarifies that the rights and freedom we enjoy are subject to an obligation to recognize and respect the rights and freedom of others. The ICCPR and the ICESCR—respectively setting out in detail civil and political rights, on the one hand, and economic, social, and cultural rights, on the other—clearly state in the preamble that individual has "duties to other individuals and to the community to which he belongs". This stipulation has become the international human-rights standards currently recognized across the world.

The Chinese *Constitution* clearly states that citizens are subjects of both rights and obligations: "Every citizen is entitled to the rights and at the same time must perform the duties prescribed by the Constitution and other laws". And: "Citizens of the People's Republic of China, in exercising their freedoms and rights, may not infringe upon the interests of the State, of society or of the collective, or upon the lawful freedoms and rights of other citizens". Therefore, our Constitution clearly stipulates both the rights and the obligations of citizens, who must faithfully meet their obligations when enjoying their rights: "Rights without obligations and obligations with rights are partial and wrong" [28]. Rights without obligations can only be privileges of some classes, and obligations without rights will only be slavery. Only when rights and obligations are balanced and united can we better carry on our human-rights cause and ensure human-rights protection, making a greater contribution to the cause of human rights for human race.

6.6 Human Rights and Social Stability, Economic Development, and the Legal Construction

China has never separated human rights from social stability, economic development, and the legal construction, thinking that "[s]tability is the precondition of realizing human rights, development the key, and the legal construction the guarantee" [29]. Our country experienced a century's wars and chaos in modern history. Because of the constant invasions by capitalist countries, China was plunged into extreme poverty, and owing to continual wars, people lived in agony. After its founding, China saw another chaotic decade of "cultural revolution", which added pain to disaster-loaded Chinese people. It is not at all easy to sufficiently realize all human rights in such a country as China with large population, weak economy and scarce resources.

Stability, to begin with, is a prevailing social order, the precondition for developing human rights and the basis for protecting them. As a developing country with weak economic basis, China needs to develop the economy to strengthen its power and protect human rights. Development can not be achieved without a stable social situation, since it is only in a stable social and political environment that people can settle down to produce more wealth for society and benefit humans. In more than 30 years since reform and opening up, China has kept society and politics stable, focused on economic construction, and marked other notable achievements.

Secondly, the realization of human rights depends on the economy, whose development in turn needs a stable social environment. Economic development should be focused and be on the top of the agenda in our party's strategy for governing and rejuvenating the country. As Deng Xiaoping has remarked, development is an absolute principle. Without economic development, human rights can not be protected, considering that they can not exist without a society's economic structure. Certain material conditions are needed in realizing and developing human rights: these conditions serve as a material guarantee, and in this sense it is fundamental to vigorously develop the economy in realizing human rights in our country.

Thirdly, human rights should be protected in keeping with the law, and so only when a socialist country is governed under the rule of law can human rights be properly guaranteed. If a country is to turn deserved rights into legitimate rights, it needs to makc an active effort. Our country's legal construction is aimed at governing the country and administrating in accordance with the laws. China's socialist Constitution and laws are a specific and centralized manifestation of the Party's idea and people's will, organizing and regulating all citizens and government officials. The principles framing the idea of rule by law—"There must be laws to go by, the laws must be observed and strictly enforced, and lawbreakers must be prosecuted."—provide a reliable guarantee for our country's human-rights protection. Our Constitution not only adds the provision of "the state respects and guarantees human rights" but also sets forth the specific rights of citizens.

In addition, *Criminal Procedure Law* was amended greatly in 1996, establishing the principle of protecting the innocent from legal prosecution, and abolishing the detained questioning system as a mandatory measure. *Criminal Law* amended in 1997 further established the three important human-rights principles of determining crimes according to law, matching crimes with penalty, and everyone being equal in front of law. In terms of human-rights legislation, a relatively complete legal system has been formed, with *Constitution* as guidelines, and department laws as aims. "In no more than 20 years since 1979, the central and local legislative authorities have made more than 6,000 laws and regulations, and basically established legal protecting system of human rights. The completion of legal system signifies that human-rights protection in our country is already legally ruled, scientific, and standardized" [30].

To sum up, China insists on social stability, economic development and the legal construction, and in this way the country has made universally acclaimed achievements over the past 30 years. These achievements contribute significantly to the development of human-rights cause. In our country's stable society, where people live happily, the creativity and initiative of individuals are greatly mobilized. Our country scientific policy of focusing on economic construction ensures a rapid development of the socialist economy, which provides a material foundation on which to develop the human-rights cause. In addition, a complete system of legal protection provides legal and regulatory guarantees for protecting both rights and people in our country.

6.7 Human Rights as an Essentially Domestic Affair of a Sovereign State

Human rights fall within a country's domestic affairs. International human-rights treaties can take effect at the national level in any country only once the country in question has ratified them. It mainly depends on the domestic legal system whether human rights can be respected, protected, promoted and realized. Every step forward on the way to realizing human rights as rights of the people involves a country's legal system, from moral rights to legitimate rights, and thence to practical rights exercised and secured. Human-rights legislation enforcement, as well as human-rights and relief efforts, are all conducted at the national level. Besides, the system that some international conventions provide for an individual to appeal can only be invoked when national relief efforts are exhausted and no solution is reached, and under the condition that the individual's country is a member state as a signatory of the convention in question. Therefore, human rights are jointly regulated by a country's social system, historical background, political system, cultural tradition and economic development. Different countries vary in the above aspects, and differences are big between Eastern and Western countries. As the factors regulating human-rights protection vary greatly from country to country, it is very hard to be same in human-rights protection: that is an objective and realistic attitude toward human rights.

Human rights are the province of a country's domestic affairs, without sovereignty, human-rights protection would be empty talk. As Forsythe has noted:

> For the foreseeable future, the primary issue about human rights in international relations is not whether we should acknowledge them as fundamental norms. Rather, the primary issue is when and how to implement human rights in particular situation. A central dilemma has always been, and remains, how to guarantee personal rights when the community itself is threatened. Thus, what is the proper protection of human rights when the order or security of the nation-*state is at risk?* [31]

These remarks are echoed by Ren Jiyu: "For developing countries, the individual right to subsistence can not be guaranteed without national sovereignty" [32]. So, from the point of view of international relationship, human rights are out of the question if a country loses its sovereignty.

In international human-rights communication, "national sovereignty" and "no interference in internal affairs" are core principles and values observed by international community. Despite the universality of human rights, they essentially belong to a state's domestic affairs. As to the nature of human rights, scholars abroad hold the same viewpoint. As Forsythe writes: "Despite the rhetoric of universality, however, human rights remained essentially a national matter, to be accepted or not, until 1945 when they were recognized in global international law" [33].

To insist that human rights essentially fall within the purview of a sovereign state's internal affairs is to observe the two traditional legal principles of international law, just stated: those of "national sovereignty" and "no interference in internal affairs." Only when human rights are regarded as a state's domestic affairs can we prevent some Western countries from using their mighty military power to bully and interfere in the internal affairs of weak countries, and better promote and protect human rights of the entire human race, moving away from hegemonism and power politics of Western superpowers.

6.8 Promoting the International Human-Rights Cause Through Talks and Cooperation

Our government has always insisted on cooperation and talks and the need to avoid confrontation. To this end we must follow the objectives and principles set out in the *Charter of the United Nations*. It is a cooperative and honest spirit that needs to be fostered, taking the greater interest into account and seeking common ground, which means setting our differences aside, with a view to communicating and working together in earnest to further mutual understanding, share experiences, and resolve disputes in a joint effort to pursue the progress and development of human-rights cause. In this kind of framework for cooperation and talks, one should not be stressing the human-rights understanding and model specific to one's own country, using that as a benchmark against which to evaluate and measure another country's human-rights situation, nor should one be striving to achieve one's own political and economic goals in the name of human rights. Cooperation and talks are the only proper way to go forward, in accordance with the *Charter of the United Nations* and basic principles of modern international law.

As has been pointed out by Huang Hua, a former vice premier of China and minister of foreign affairs:

> In international human-rights communication, China has always advocated the principles of equality, democracy and mutual respect, and encouraged dialogs rather than confrontation. Because of different historical development, social system, cultural traditions, religious beliefs, and different requirements and practice of human rights, it is natural and normal to have different human-rights attitudes in different countries. As long as communication and talks are made equally, sincerely, honestly and extensively, mutual understanding will be enhanced, misunderstanding dispelled, and common ground found. This is significant for the progress and development of human-rights cause in both China and the world [34].

The same line of thought can be appreciated in the words of Lin Bocheng, in charge of the China Foundation for Human-Rights Development, arguing that when it comes to "the issue of human rights, dialogs will reduce disputes, resolve conflicts, enlarge common grounds and enhance understanding. It is the only proper way in international human-rights contacts and has become an irresistible trend of global progress. Confrontation will increase disputes, alleviate conflicts, and further misunderstanding, which is a countercurrent in international human-rights contacts and has been cast aside by the world" [35]. China seeks common ground while setting aside differences in international human-rights affairs, with actions to engage in talks and reject confrontation in the human-rights arena—all of which has made it possible for the country to gain the esteem of the international community across the world.

China has unswervingly been committed to the United Nations' human-rights activities, and it will keep contributing to the development of human-rights cause and to the harmonious progress of the international community. A founding member of UN and a permanent member of the UN Security Council, China has actively participated in the UN human-rights activities and work as a responsible country, since its legitimate seat was restored at the United Nations in 1971. China not only took part in the work of several UN human-rights institutions, but was also involved in the drafting and ratification of several international legal documents on human rights. China has been a member state of the UN Human-Rights Commission since 1981, and a member of the first board meeting after the Human-Rights Council was founded in 2006. Representatives of the Chinese government play important roles in the UN human-rights institutions, and in these roles they expound viewpoints that enrich our understanding of human-rights concept.

China presents itself as a responsible nation with active and constructive attitude at the world human-rights conference held in Vienna in 1993.

> At the Asian Regional Preparatory Meeting China, along with other Asian countries, made an active effort to reach agreement on the Bangkok Declaration and systematically elaborate the basic position of the Asian countries on human rights. During the World Conference on Human Rights China actively made clear its position and frankly and sincerely exchanged opinions with the countries attending the conference. Together with other countries, China resolutely resisted and opposed the rude and unreasonable attitudes and actions of a small number of Western countries that provoked confrontation and forced their views on others, trying to hinder the smooth progress of the conference. During consultations over the conference's final documents the Chinese government delegation put forward many constructive plans and suggestions and handled and coordinated the problems and contradictions that occurred during the drafting of documents on the basis of adhering to principle and, with a flexible and cooperative attitude, taking the situation as a whole into account, thus helping all countries to reach unanimity through consultation and achieve the smooth adoption of the Vienna Declaration and Program of Action [36].

China successfully held the fourth United Nations World Conference on Women in September of 1995, and in the same year it also hosted the Nongovernmental Organizations Forum on Women, thus contributing to the progress of the world's women and the realization of women's human rights, and it won widespread applause from the international community. UN Under-Secretary-General Kitani said that the conference, which laid the foundation for a new era of relations between China and the United Nations, marked a milestone in women's history at the UN. What's more, China has held talks at various levels with many Western countries including the United States, Australia, and Canada and countries in the European Union. These talks help countries better understand one another, dispel misunderstandings, and reach agreement, playing active roles in promoting progress and development of human-rights cause.

As to the work done by human-rights organizations in our country, Lin Bocheng pointed out:

> Human-rights organizations in our country, with an open mind that transcends social system and ideological difference, under the social background when globalized economy, cultural pluralism and global multipolarization are developed with twists and turns, aim to promote democratization of international relationship and establish new order of international politics and economy, adhere to the principles of mutual respect, friendly consultation, seeking common points while reserving difference and enhancing understanding, and communicate frankly and talk equally with countries including major countries in the West, playing an active role in the communication and cooperation of international human rights [37].

Experiencc shows that confrontation in international human-rights affairs leads to nowhere and is unwelcome. Only talks and cooperation can promote the healthy and steady development of human-rights cause of the entire human race.

6.9 Human-Rights Education as a Basic Measure in Promoting Human Rights

Encyclopedia of Human Rights states in its "introduction by Chinese translators": "to enjoy sufficient human rights is a beautiful ideal that humans have long pursued. It is a complicated and systematic project to promote human rights. In the project, it is a crucial link to systematically carrying out theoretical researches, publicity and education in human rights, and popularizing fundamental knowledge of human rights, in order to enhance human-rights awareness of every social member" [38]. Here pointed out are the beautiful ideal of the sufficient realization of human rights, and the complicated realization process with human-rights studies and education as a crucial link.

A central conclusion on human-rights education to have come out of a UN human-rights teaching seminar held in Geneva from December 5 to 9, 1989, was as follows: "It was very important to confirm that everyone was aware of his or her own rights, as human rights and fundamental freedoms should be guaranteed to everyone. Human-rights teaching should thus be directed to every quarter" [39]. This conclusion also listed the classes of people who should receive human-rights education:

> First of all, those in a position to directly affect the basic human rights of the individual, such as law enforcement personnel, lawyers and judges, as well as the military when at war or when called upon to maintain security in times of emergency internal situations, should be well taught as regards human rights. It was also vital that legislators who are in charge of drafting laws should be educated about international human-rights standards so that their legislation would be in conformity with their country's international obligations. Persons, be they in medicine, engineering, technology, media, data processing, political parties, civil service, municipalities and other centers of power, such as village councils, trade unions, etc., also needed to be aware of human rights. Teaching and training of professionals should consist of not only the basic rules of the organization of their perspective profession, but also an ethical and legal code of conduct taking into account the impact of their activities on the basic human rights of others. School children and students at all institutions, be they civil, police or military, should also be the target of this process [39].

Section 4 of the *National Human-Rights Action Plan of China* set out detailed regulations regarding human-rights education:

> In the period 2009–2010, along with the dissemination of knowledge of the law among the general public, the state will actively rely on the present systems of compulsory education, secondary education, higher education, and vocational education, training organizations in state agencies, as well as the media, including radio, television, newspapers, magazines, and the Internet, to carry out education in human rights in various forms in a planned way, popularizing and spreading knowledge of the law and human rights [40].

More to the point:

> Human-rights education and training will be carried out especially among government employees, focusing on people working in public security agencies, procuratorates, courts, prisons, urban management organs, and administrative law enforcement organs. The law

> enforcement departments will draw up their own plans for human-rights education and training in line with their own work needs, highlighting publicity and education of regulations and laws on the protection of human rights, and give human-rights education on a regular basis. The government will organize experts to compile special textbooks for human-rights training. State agencies and cities with appropriate conditions will be selected as demonstration units for human-rights education and training, and follow-up examinations will be conducted [40].

The text thus grasps the crucial point of the issue. That is to say, human-rights protection in our country will benefit, and its level will be increased, by entrusting human-rights education the personnel who exercise public power.

The aim of human-rights education is quite clear, for it is "directed to the full development of the human personality and to the strengthening of respect for human rights and fundamental freedoms" [41]. Human-rights education includes not only a fair amount of theoretical knowledge but also abundant practical examples of application. One feature of human-rights education in our country consists in its emphasizing human-rights teaching to government employees. In fact, it is through such an educational approach that human-rights knowledge is disseminated, using media channels including radio, television, newspapers, magazines and the Internet: this makes it possible to meet the needs of the present information era, while ensuring that educational programs on human rights are effective. Thus, human-rights education has become a fundamental tool for promoting and protecting human rights in our country.

6.10 Peace, Development, and Human Rights Contributing to a Harmonious World

As early as on March 4, 1985 when Deng Xiaoping met the delegation of Japanese association of commerce and industry, he pointed out: "The real big issues of the present world, globalized strategic issues, are the issue of peace and the issue of economy or development. Peace is an issue of the East versus the West, while development is the issue of the South versus the North. Amidst the issue of the East, the West, the South and the North, the problem of the South versus the North is the core" [42]. The statement shows a great proletarian revolutionist's extraordinary vision and precise analysis and command of current international situation. He regarded the issue of the East versus the West, namely the relationship between the two supper powers of the United States and the Soviet Union, as an issue of peace; and the issue of the South versus the North, namely the relationship between developing countries and developed countries, as an issue of development. The profound analysis of relationship between the East and the West, the South and the North gave clear directory principles for the country to make development strategy and foreign policies.

Peace and development are two major subjects of current interest across the world. However, some Western countries have repeatedly enforced their own hegemonism and power politics in the name of human rights, attempting to use the issue of human rights to interfere in other country's politics, economy and culture. "Human-rights diplomacy" is widespread, and concerns should be shown by the international community with this phenomenon. As stated in the white paper *"Progress of Human Rights in China"*, "[w]ithout a peaceful and safe international environment and without a just and reasonable international economic order, it will be impossible to realize extensive human rights" [43]. The words clarify the relationship between peace, development, and human rights.

Human rights can not be separated from peace and development, which are the basis and prerequisites for the realization of human rights. Without peace and development, the issue of human rights can not be resolved completely. There are many occasions in international affairs on which the issue of human rights is unavoidable: this is so whenever the issues of peace or development come into play. Peace is required to protect the right to life and property, and development aims to promote the political, civil, economic, social, and cultural rights. The human-rights cause is a heavy political task undertaken by the current international community. Peace is a prerequisite for human-rights protection, and development a compulsory condition: the progress and development of human rights are therefore closely linked to world peace and development. Peace, development, and human rights thus figure as three major international trends in the current international community.

In the preface to the First Edition of *Encyclopedia of Human Rights*, the author Lawson makes a brief review of the development of international human-rights cause, and comments on the disparity between the stipulation and implementation of human-rights standards, and analyzes reasons of this disparity. He says:

> Formal international implementation of human-rights standards, unfortunately, has not kept pace with the promulgation and acceptance of these standards. Treaty-monitoring bodies such as the Human-Rights Committee, the Committee on Economic, Social, and Cultural Rights, the Committee on the Elimination of Racial Discrimination, the Committee on the Elimination of Discrimination against Women, and the Committee against Torture are just beginning to make progress in their work; and their functioning is hampered by a continuing backlog of reports on implementation from States parties to the relevant conventions, by a shortage of financial resources, and by some overlapping of the issues dealt with in those conventions [44].

Human rights became a major area of international concern—alongside security and social development—only after the United Nations undertook institutional reform and replaced the 60-year-old Human-Rights Commission with Human-Rights Council, which acts as the sole supervisory human-rights organization entrusted with putting out the Universal Periodic Review (UPR), and carrying out reviews at regular intervals in the UN member states. This has brought favorable changes to the work of human-rights supervisory organization. "The founding of Human-Rights Council puts human rights back to the central place in the United Nations, and places it along with peace and development to form the three pillars of the UN system" [45]. In terms of UN's institutional organization, the three central tasks are security, development and human rights:

> Peace development and human rights are common demands of all countries, a striving goal of Chinese people for more than a century. China is currently dedicated to building a prosperous, democratic and civilized country, a great cross-century cause that will extricate one fifth of the human population completely from poverty and sufficiently realize human rights, and an important component of the international cause of peace, development and human rights [46].

Here security serves to protect rights of humans, and development provides the material basis for improving human rights; as a major concern of the current world, the progress of human rights will also be beneficial for social stability and for the harmonious development of mankind.

As stated in the *National Human-Rights Action Plan of China* issued on April 13th, 2009, by the Information Office of the State Council:

> China cherishes the important role played by international instruments on human rights in promoting and protecting human rights. So far, China has acceded to 25 international conventions on human rights. China will earnestly fulfill its obligations to those conventions, submit timely reports on implementing the conventions to the treaty bodies concerned, hold constructive dialogues with these treaty bodies, take into full consideration the proposals raised by them, and adopt rational and feasible ones in the light of China's actual conditions [47].

This is the first time an active action plan was made for the protection of human rights, attesting to the Chinese government's confident determination to pursue human-rights protection. This undoubtedly stands as yet another example of how renewed and greater contribution to human-rights protection can be achieved through cooperation in the field of human rights.

6.11 Closing Remarks

The development of human rights is a gradual process, restricted by many relevant factors, particularly by economic foundation and by historical and cultural traditions. China respects the universal value of human rights, while at the same time believing in the need to prioritize different human rights according to specific national situations. Although, theoretically, different kinds of human rights are interdependent and inseparable, the actual construction of a human-rights system will not just have a single development pattern. This is a pragmatic attitude to human rights.

What it means to make the rights to subsistence and to development foremost human rights is to pay heed to our country's specific national situation. China is striving to ensure as well an all-round and harmonious development of other types of human rights, while laying emphasis on the rights to subsistence and development. But this is a long process. For one thing, the universal realization of human rights entails an ongoing struggle coupled with a continuous effort among human beings, and in this sense it is a never-ending cause. And, for another thing, all sorts of problems may arise in this endeavor. It therefore takes great energy and commitment to solve these problems, as well as a good deal of time, and so human rights cannot fully be realized until all these requirements are met.

So a feature to be borne uppermost in mind in constructing a distinctly Chinese human-rights system is continuity. This is evidenced by a constant and steady trend building toward an ever-stronger development of human rights, understood as a core value and aspect of our country's socialist political civilization. At every step of the way—from the moment the concepts are conceived to their translation into law and into specific social practices—the cause needs to be advanced by dint of committed and resolute work involving a menu of actions inclusive of education, legislation, and human-rights protection itself. The problems to be solved along the way are many and the difficulties great, and this only highlight how it is a long and tortuous path with formidable challenges that needs to be traveled on the way to a full realization of human rights in keeping with the principles set forth in our Constitution. As long as our country sticks to the ten previously outlined principles and will keep devoting an unwavering effort to their realization, the human-rights cause will continue to develop by yielding greater and greater achievements.

References

1. Zhao, Q. (2003). For the twenty-first century human rights in China. In China Foundation for Human Rights Development. (Ed.), *China's basic position and point on human rights* (p. 6). Beijing: New World Press.
2. Hu, Jintao's congratulation letter to China Society for Human Rights Studies. *People's Daily* (Oversea Version). (p. 1). December 12, 2008.
3. Letter of congratulation by Jiang Zemin for the annual convention commemorating the 50th anniversary of the *Universal Declaration of Human Rights. The convention was* hosted by China Society for Human Rights Studies, and the letter appeared in *People's Daily* on December 11, 1998. p. 1.
4. Quoted from *Universal Declaration of Human Rights* (Article 1). In Hu, Z. (Ed.), 2004. *International conventions on human rights* (p. 250). Beijing: China Translation and Publishing Corporation.
5. The International Bill of Human Rights consists of the Universal Declaration of Human Rights, the International Covenant on Economic, Social and Cultural Rights, and the International Covenant on Civil and Political Rights.
6. Quoted from *Universal Declaration of Human Rights* (Preamble). In Hu, Z. (Ed.), 2004. *International conventions on human rights* (p. 249). Beijing: China Translation and Publishing Corporation.
7. Milne, A. J. M. (1986). *Human rights and human diversity: An essay in the philosophy of human rights* (p. 6). New York: State University of New York Press.
8. Milne, A. J. M. (1986). *Human rights and human diversity: An essay in the philosophy of human rights* (p. 5). New York: State University of New York Press.
9. Negative right is the synonym for human rights of the first-generation human rights including civil rights and political rights which can be accomplished as a result of the respect and nonintervention from the state and the government.
10. Negative right corresponds with positive right which symbolizes the second-generation human rights. The rights covering economic, cultural and social aspects can simply be achieved relying on the energetic activities and great efforts by the state and the government.

11. Central Compilation & Translation Bureau for Works of Marx, Engels, Lenin and Stalin. (Ed.) (1972). *Selected works of Marx and Engels* (Vol. 3). (p. 12). Beijing: People's Publishing House.
12. Zheng, H. (2003). New China's cause of human rights and basic views. In China Foundation for Human Rights Development (Ed.), *Human rights in China's basic position and point* (p. 73). Beijing: New World Press.
13. Gu, C. (2004). *The cluster of democracy, human rights and rule of law* (p. 316). Beijing: China Procuratorial Press.
14. The national cadre training materials editing steering committee. (Ed.). 2006. *Cadre chrestomathy of knowledge of human rights* (p. 43). Beijing: People's Publishing House/Party Building Books Publishing House.
15. Han, D. & Li, L. (Eds.) (1995). *On theory and practice of human rights* (pp. 387–389). Wuhan: Wuhan University Press.
16. *Declaration on the Right to Development* (P1, A1), adopted by No. 41/128 resolution of the General Assembly of the United Nations. December 4th, 1986.
17. Gu, C. & Zheng, H. (Eds.) (1999). *Human rights: From the world to China—Theory and practice of human rights in contemporary China* (p. 387). Beijing: Party Building Books Publishing House.
18. Li, Y. (2005). China human rights development path and the basic experience. In China Society of Human Rights Studies. (Ed.), *Human rights in China in the new century* (p. 136). Beijing: Unity Press.
19. Deng, X. (1993). *Deng Xiaoping anthology* (Vol. 3). (p. 125). Beijing: People's Publishing House.
20. Li, B. (2003). Universality and particularity of human rights. In China Foundation for Human Rights Development. (Ed.), *Human rights in China's basic position and point* (p. 106). Beijing: New World Press.
21. Dong, Y. (1998). Universal Declaration of Human Rights—The important milepost in the world history of human rights. *People's Daily*. December 10th.
22. *The Vienna Declaration and Program of Action* (Paragraph 5, Part 1). In Hu, Z. (Ed.), 2004. *International conventions on human rights* (pp. 274–275). Beijing: China Translation and Publishing Corporation.
23. In April 13, 2009, the Information Office of the State Council issued the "National Human Rights Action Plan (2009–2010)". This is the first national human rights action plan of our government. It is an action plan at the national level to practice the principle of the *Constitution* "the state respects and guarantees human rights", which is a milestone in the development process of human rights in China.
24. Central Compilation & Translation Bureau for Works of Marx, Engels, Lenin and Stalin. (Ed.) (1972). *Selected works of Mark and Engels*. (Vol. 2). (p. 137). Beijing: People's Publishing House.
25. Zheng, H. (1993). *New theory of human rights* (p. 181). Beijing: China Youth Press.
26. Li, B. (2000). *Jurisprudence* (p. 459). Beijing: Economic Science Press.
27. Li, B. (2003). *Jurisprudential exploration* (p. 251). Changsha: Hunan People's Publishing House.
28. The national cadre training materials editing steering committee. (Ed.). (2006). *Cadre chrestomathy on human rights knowledge* (p. 47). Beijing: People's Publishing House/Party Building Books Publishing House.
29. The national cadre training materials editing steering committee. (Ed.). (2006). *Cadre chrestomathy on human rights knowledge* (p. 48). Beijing: People's Publishing House/Party Building Books Publishing House.
30. Zhang, X. (2003). On the socialist concept of human rights. In China Foundation for Human Rights Development. (Ed.), *Human rights in China's basic position and point* (p. 193). Beijing: New World Press.
31. Forsythe, D. P. 2006. *Human rights in international relations*. (2nd ed.). (p. 12). Cambridge: Cambridge University Press.

32. Ren, J. (2003). Safeguard and develop human rights. In China Foundation for Human Rights Development. (Ed.), *Human rights in China's basic position and point* (p. 10). Beijing: New World Press.
33. Forsythe, D. P. 2006. *Human rights in international relations.* (2nd ed.). (p. 3). Cambridge: Cambridge University Press.
34. Huang, H. (2003). Persist in using the 'Three Represents' important thought to guide the construction of contemporary China's human rights. In China Foundation for Human Rights Development. (Ed.), *Human rights in China's basic position and point* (p. 4). Beijing: New World Press.
35. Lin, B. (2003). The awareness of China's basic position on human rights". In China Foundation for Human Rights Development. (Ed.), *Human rights in China's basic position and point* (p. 235). Beijing: New World Press.
36. Information office of the State Council. (1995). "*Progress of human rights in China*". December.
37. Lin, B. (2003). The awareness of China's basic position on human rights. In China Foundation for Human Rights Development. (Ed.), *Human rights in China's basic position and point* (p. 235). Beijing: New World Press.
38. Lawson, E. (1997). *Encyclopedia of human rights.* (p. 7). Chengdu: Sichuan People's Publishing House. (This book is regarded as "the first relatively authoritative and objective encyclopedia of human rights"—see introduction by Chinese translators at page 9 of this book).
39. UN Doc. E/CN.4/1989/68, Paragraph 121.
40. Information office of the State Council. (2009). *National human rights action plan.* April 13.
41. *Universal Declaration of Human Rights* (Item 2, Article 26). In Hu, Z. (Ed.), 2004. *International conventions on human rights* (p. 254). Beijing: China Translation and Publishing Corporation.
42. Deng, X. (1993). *Deng Xiaoping anthology* (Vol. 3). (p. 105). Beijing: People's Publishing House.
43. Information office of the State Council. (1995). *Progress of human rights in China.* December.
44. Lawson, E. (1997). *Encyclopedia of human rights.* (p. 19). Chengdu: Sichuan People's Publishing House. / Lawson E. (1996). Encyclopedia of human rights (2nd ed., p. xvii). Washington: Taylor and Francis.
45. Chen, L. (2007). Reform of UN human rights institutions—On UN Human Rights Commission. *Commentary on human rights law* (Vol. 2). (p. 217). Beijing: Beijing University Press.
46. Zhao, Q. (2003). For the twenty-first century China human rights. In China Foundation for Human Rights Development. (Ed.), *China's basic position and point on human rights* (p. 8). Beijing: New World Press.
47. Information office of the State Council. (2009). *National Human Rights Action Plan of China.* April 13.

Chapter 7
Specific Measures to Improve Human Rights Protection Standards in China

Abstract The progress of human rights in China is a dynamic developmental process. In order to further increase the standards of Chinese human rights protection, practical measures should be taken: strengthening the legislation of human rights and improving the human rights protection system; carrying out the spirit of human rights completely and increasing state officials' governing ability according to law; establishing state human rights institutions and dealing with affairs relevant to human rights; showing more concern with human rights research and strengthening human rights education; making both mid-term and long-term human rights action plans, and realizing the human rights principles of the Constitution. The practical implementation of these measures will be significant for protection, promotion, and realization of human rights.

Historically, the *Constitution* of 1982 has been regarded as "the perfect constitution since the founding of the PRC" [1]. Due to the development and progress of our country over the time, China's process of modernization has entered a new stage. In order to adjust to changes in the new situation, the *Constitution* required amendments and modifications, leading to the four amendments of the *Constitution* in 1988, 1993, 1999, and 2004, respectively. The *Constitution* has been improved gradually through the four amendments, but the first three only modified partially on the basis of the *Constitution* of 1982 and failed to touch upon the content of human rights.

However, the amendment of the *Constitution* in 2004 included the general provision that "the state respects and guarantees human rights", which has been called "human rights into the Constitution". It was for the first time that the *Constitution* of China included a clear declaration about human rights, and it is the codification of the ruling idea of respecting and protecting human rights put forward in the 15th and 16th CPC National Congresses. Since then, respecting and safeguarding human rights has become an important principle in the *Constitution* and has been raised by the will of the Chinese people and the state.

The principle that "the state respects and guarantees human rights" not only prescribes substantive content, but also proposes obligations and requirements. Thus, "human rights into the Constitution" became a new milestone in the

P. Sun, *Human Rights Protection System in China*,
DOI: 10.1007/978-3-642-39663-2_7,

development of China's human rights system. The establishment of the principle of "respecting and guaranteeing human rights" puts forward higher requirements in the protection of human rights in the process of human rights legislation and judicial system perfection of China. To implement the human rights principle in the *Constitution*, the following specific measures must be taken.

7.1 Strengthen Human Rights Legislation and Improve the Human Rights Protection System

Before human rights entered the *Constitution*, though the protection of various rights had been regulated in different department laws, there was and still is no code concerning the concept of human rights. Based on the landmark "human rights into the Constitution", other department laws should be modified and adjusted so as to make a concrete embodiment of human rights principle in the *Constitution* and manifest the state's respect for and guarantee of human rights in the whole legal system [2], especially in human rights legislation and judicial procedures.

Legislation is a crucial step for both the transition from due rights to legal rights and the realization and practice of human rights protection. As the last line of defense for the realization of socialist justice, the judicial procedures are significant for human rights protection. Therefore, in the aspect of human rights legislation, human rights principles should be carried out and implemented well to underline its value.

> Through human rights legislation, rights-and-obligations relations between individuals and society, between individuals and community, and among individuals should be rationally allocated; the human rights principle of the Constitution should be concretized; and the human rights legal guarantee system should be further improved. Only in this way, can the principle of human rights be realized, and will the society develop harmoniously and orderly [3].

In addition, along with the increasing number of international human rights conventions China has joined, it needs to be put on the schedule that a scientific and rational implementation mechanism of international human rights conventions should be established. In the judicial process, human rights principles should be further implemented and measures of human rights protection should be improved. Through the establishment and perfection of the legal system, including an public trial system, panel discussion system, defense system, litigation system, challenge system, judicial mediation system, judicial aid system, two-tier trial system, and the system of reviewing the death penalty, and so on, the rights violated should be given impartial judicial remedy based on law, so as to safeguard the principles of fairness and justice in the socialist legal system.

Professor Xu Xianming, when talking about the five "obstacles" to a harmonious society, put the unfairness of society in the second place. He pointed out:

> Unfair distribution is the most salient social problem in China. The unfairness of gains without paying any effort and much gain with little effort are detested by society; the unfairness of much effort with little gain or even no gain at all is the gravest unfair problem; and as for the unfairness of equal effort without similar gain, people have no choice but to suffer [4].

As is mentioned in the preface of the first volume of *Yanhuang Chunqiu* in 2008, "there are still many problems in front of us though reform has undergone great achievement. The most serious problem is the unfairness of society" [5]. The preface continues like this:

> Technically speaking, the social rank which bears the lowest cost and risk of the reform should gain less from the profit of reform, and the rank which bears the highest cost and risk should gain more. However, the real situation in China is distorted: those who benefit the most from the reform are usually the people in power and their relatives, and those who benefit the least are the laborers, farmers and the middle and lower classes. But when it comes to the expenditure of the cost and risk, the latter group contributed far more than the former one [5].

An article was published in *Yanhuang Chunqiu* in 2008, entitled "Do Chinese farmers own their properties—Concurrently discussing the problem of compensation for contracted land of farmers" [6]. This article carried on the deep discussion concerning the value and compensation of contracted land, analyzed the current laws and regulations, and touched upon the deficiencies of them. The damages to the interests of the farmers in the process of land transfer were accounted for in great detail with abundant and accurate data. It also strongly questioned the profits gained by the government at all levels in the process of land transfer, and proposed reasonable policies for land compensation. This article reported on an outstanding problem existing in our society nowadays. Judging from the current situation of excess work from letters and calls, the problem of land compensation has become a major problem as suggested by the petitioners. Violation of farmers' rights frequently occurs, which is one of the focal problems reported in the letters and calls, as well as an outstanding issue in our country. To solve this problem, human rights legislation in China should be further improved, so as to ensure that the benefits brought about by the reform can be shared by everyone and to perfect the human rights protection system.

7.2 Implement the Spirit of Human Rights and Improve the State Officials' Governance Capability According to Law

In the discussion of the UN human rights teaching seminar held in Geneva from December 5th to 9th, 1989, a major conclusion for the issue of human rights education was drawn: "It was very important to confirm that everyone was aware of his or her own rights, as human rights and fundamental freedoms should be guaranteed to everyone. Human rights teaching should be directed to every quarter" [7]. This conclusion also listed in details the types of people that should receive human rights education:

> First of all, those in a position to directly affect the basic human rights of the individual, such as law enforcement personnel, lawyers and judges, as well as the military when at war or when called upon to maintain security in times of emergent internal situations, should be well taught as regards human rights. It was also vital that legislators who are in charge of drafting laws should be educated about international human rights standards so that their legislation would be in conformity with their country's international obligations. Persons, be they in medicine, engineering, technology, media, data processing, political parties, civil service, municipalities and other centers of power, such as village councils, trade unions, etc., also needed to be aware of human rights. Teaching and training of professionals should consist of not only the basic rules of the organization of their perspective profession, but also an ethical and legal code of conduct taking into account the impact of their activities on the basic human rights of others. School children and students at all institutions, be they civil, police or military, should also be the target of this process [7].

In order to implement the spirit of human right, specific work ought to be carried out in the administration of the state and government. This work includes: strengthening the construction of governance capability, cultivating such ruling ideas as respecting and safeguarding human rights, and ensuring that the power granted by the people is under correct management and application. We should also attempt to avoid corruption in the governing process and the abuse of power to seek personal interests. Instead, we shall always put the interest of the people in a prominent position, live up to the principle of "administrating according to law and governing for the people" and "exercise power for the people, showing concern for them and working for their interests." Thus, we should regard respecting and safeguarding human rights as a starting point and standpoint of all work. In order to satisfy and assure the people, we must do well in all the work concerning the administration of the state and government, which is entrusted by the people.

In order to improve the governance capacity, efforts must be made in the aspect of overall implementation of the spirit of human rights. Through a series of systematic human rights education and training programs, the party and government officials should improve their awareness of human rights and maintain a correct outlook on human rights. It is necessary to do so, and the explanation is as follows:

> The impact of feudal autocracy ideology has been far from being eliminated, and western decadent bourgeois ideology and culture keeps infiltrating. Various misperceptions still exist in the minds of the citizens, especially the officials. More intensive and in-depth education needs to be carried out, so as to improve their perception and solve their problems effectively [8].

We can promote unceasingly the progress and development of China's human rights cause, only by taking the following measures: overall implementation of the spirit of human rights and further strengthening the officials' awareness of human rights through education to enhance their consciousness on execution of duty and protection of human rights; "resolutely preventing such phenomena from happening as failure to observe the law, no strictness in enforcing the law, refraining from punishing law-breakers, unfairness in enforcing the law, and truly enforcing the law strictly, fairly, and courteously" [9].

7.3 Set Up a National Institution Specially for Human Rights Affairs

China has set up some nongovernmental human rights organizations, for example, the China Society for Human Rights Studies was founded in 1993 and the China Foundation for Human Rights Studies was founded in 2001. Such nongovernmental organizations have made contributions to the improvement and development of human rights causes in China. Overall, China has accessed and ratified 25 international human rights conventions. After adjustment of the UN's organizations for human rights and the UN Human Rights Council was founded in March 2006, the Universal Periodic Review was then established and responsible for supervision and review of the implementation of the internal human rights conventions in the world.

In view of the state report provided by the Chinese government, the implementation and preparation is mainly led by the Ministry of Foreign Affairs. So far there is not a special human right agency to manage and implement the work related to the human rights conventions. Thus, it is no wonder the work is passively carried out and unfavorable to exchange and cooperation of international human rights causes. With regard to certain meaning, the Chinese government's principle of "each attending to its own duties" involves human rights affairs.

However, work on human rights is very complicated and hard, and thus it is definitely necessary to assign a special state institution to coordinate all aspects of the work so as to promote complete and harmonious development of China's human rights causes. In view of practices in the protection of international human rights, establishment of a special human rights institution is also in line with requirements of cooperation on international human rights. Currently, most countries have their own human rights councils [10],[1] which are mainly

---

[1] France is the first country in the world to have set up national human rights institutions, and it set up a National Human Rights Advisory Committee in 1947; Japan also set up its Human Rights Protection Bureau under the Ministry of Justice as an exclusive national institution for protection of human rights (Refer to [11]); as of now, there are nearly 100 countries in the world that have already set up national human rights institutions. Main types of the national human rights institutions are: (1) Human Rights Committee (such as, Ireland, Canada, Mexico, India, Philippines, New Zealand, South Korea, Thailand, and South Africa, etc., and all of them have set up human rights committees); (2) Supervisory Commissioner (for instance, Spain and Portugal set up Supervisor Commissioner Offices in 1978 and 1991 respectively, and Russia set up Russian Federal Human Rights Commissioner Office): (3) Human Rights Center (countries such as Denmark, Norway and Germany etc., have set up their International Human Rights Institutions by

responsible for human rights affairs. In China, Professor Qi Yanping has performed a special investigation and discussion on the roles of the state human rights institution and tentative ideas of its establishment [11]. Here I would like to give my own opinions about it.

Establishment of a national human rights institution is not only a requirement of the UN, but also a general practice of the international community, as well as an important systematic assurance of human rights. On March 3, 1992, the UN Human Rights Council approved the "Principle on Improvement and Protection of Status of the State Human Rights Institution" (abbreviated as the Paris Principle) in the form of the attached resolution 1992/54 and then on December 20, 1993 the UN conference passed the principle by the resolution 48/134. The *Vienna Declaration and Program of Action* passed on June 25, 1993 reiterated the important role of the state institution for improving protection of human rights, and appealed the world to establish and strengthen the national human rights institution. To this end, the author believes that China's human rights institution (National Human Rights Commission) can be set up under the National People's Congress taking responsible for affairs of human rights.

Currently China uses several state organizations to assume responsibilities related to human rights and has not yet an integrated national human rights institution. According to the Paris Principle, the national human right institution shall be independent and staffed in diversity, which is in line with the functions and constitution of the National People's Congress. In addition to this, the national human rights institution is expected to be involved in the national human rights legislation and resolve human rights issues that fit the nature of the National People's Congress as a legislation division. Therefore, to set up the national human rights institution under the National People's Congress is the best choice for China. The national human rights institution can be staffed with one director and a few deputies, who are designated by the state government.

Official workers can be chosen from people with relevant experience. The state shall endow the national human rights institution with half jurisdiction, including the right to (1) receive individual appeal for human rights and handle domestic human rights issues; (2) participate in the formulation, implementation, supervision, and assessment of the national human rights action plans; (3) conduct research on the linking up of domestic laws to the international convention; (4) complete reports on the implementation of the international conventions based on the requirements of the UN treaty bodies; (5) engage in cooperation, exchange, and dialogue in the international human rights field; (6) perform studies on human rights legislation and improve domestic human rights legislation; (7) consider

---

(Footnote 1 continued)
means of establishment of Human Rights Research Center); (4) Human Rights Advisory Committee (for instance, the Human Rights Advisory Committee of France is the first national human rights institution in the world); (5) Specialised institutions (such as Canadian Human Rights Commission, Commission on Racial Equality (CRE) of the United Kingdom, the United Kingdom's Disability Rights Commission and Equal Opportunities Commission).

domestic situations, and periodically propose reports on major domestic human rights issues; (8) make overall plans for publication and education on human rights, as well as raise the national awareness and the whole status of protecting human rights in China.

As said by Professor Qi Yanping, "establishment of the national human rights institution is an important step toward normalization and systematization of improvement and security of human rights in China. After this step, it will provide a normal work platform and open up a new cause area for the development of China's human rights cause as well as China's involvement in the improvement and protection of international human rights" [11]. In a word, establishment and operation of the national human rights institution will not only play an important role in implementing the constitutional principle "the state respects and guarantees human rights", but also benefit the resolution of issues and conflicts as to make people safe and healthy, the society harmonious and the state stable forever as well as improving international exchange and cooperation in the field of human rights.

7.4 Emphasize Research on Human Rights and Strengthen Human Rights Education

As studies on human rights in China just cover a short amount of time, and many research fields are still quite weak as many blanks exist in the research of human rights theory and practice. Thus, it is necessary to deeply study the human rights theory and practice. Besides, in Chinese history "obligations" are traditionally more emphasized than "rights" and the conception of human rights has not yet been established into the whole society, people lack a sense of human rights and have little knowledge about human rights. Thus, it is urgent to strengthen publication and education of human rights knowledge. To strengthen human rights education, clear goals should be made and according to the need of the educated and set forth the content of systematic education. Detailed education plans should be prepared in order to establish the evaluation mechanism for the best results of education. Human rights education should be incorporated into the cultivation of talents at all levels, through the advantage of broadcast, television, newspapers, and journals, Internet and other public media in order to popularize the topic and educate the public.

Human rights education, especially to officials of state organizations, will raise every person's awareness of human rights, and effectively improve the overall progress and development of China's human rights cause. To strengthen human rights education, China needs to strengthen research work on human rights theory and practice, while popularization of human rights education will further improve the overall ability of research on human rights theory and practice. So in this way, strengthening human rights education and actually researching human rights theory and practice are mutually supplementary and harmonious. Harmonious unification of human rights education and research on human rights theory and practice will play a role that cannot be undervalued in improving people's awareness of human rights, respect for and protection of human rights as well.

The "*National Human Rights Action Plan*" set forth detailed regulations on human rights education in section IV:

> In the period 2009–2010, along with the dissemination of knowledge of the law among the general public, the state will actively rely on the present systems of compulsory education, secondary education, higher education and vocational education, training organizations in state agencies, as well as the media, including radio, television, newspapers, magazines and the Internet, to carry out education in human rights in various forms in a planned way, popularizing and spreading knowledge of the law and human rights [12].

This action plan further points out:

> Human rights education and training will be carried out especially among government employees, focusing on people working in public security agencies, procuratorates, courts, prisons, urban management organizations, and administrative law enforcement organizations. The law enforcement departments will draw up their own plans for human rights education and training in line with their own work needs, highlighting publicity and education of regulations and laws on the protection of human rights, and provide human rights education on a regular basis. The government will organize experts to compile special textbooks for human rights training. State agencies and cities with appropriate conditions will be selected as demonstration units for human rights education and training, and follow-up examinations will be conducted [12].

Such actions get the point of issues so as to provide human rights education to those executing the public rights which will be helpful in improving the protection of human rights in China and raise the whole level of human rights protection.

China has a very clear goal for human rights education, which aims at "fully developing the humane personality and strengthening respect for human rights and fundamental freedom" [13]. Human rights education is also rich in content, which can be seen when referring to the training textbook for national cadres—"*Cadre Chrestomathy on Human Rights Knowledge*" [14], which not only contains a lot of theories, but also describes abundant applications in practice. Regarding the people to be educated, human rights actions put emphasis on human rights education for public officials, reflecting the Chinese characteristics in the implementation of human rights education. In addition, education methods and channels are used by public media such as broadcast, television, newspapers, journals, and Internet to disseminate human rights knowledge, which adapts to the new information era occurring in modern society and is an effective measure to guarantee human rights education.

Therefore, human rights education has become the basic means to improve and protect human rights in China. However, to implement measures for human rights education listed in the human rights action plan, there would be a lot of problems in reality as there are many steps needed to carry out abstract regulation to specific implementation. Apart from the overall planning, there is a need to set specific numeric goals, and to list detailed implementation procedures and plans for various forms of human rights education. Only through careful work could these goals for human rights education be completely achieved.

Furthermore, the establishment of the National Site for Human Rights Education and Training is also an important measure that has been taken by the Chinese government. In China, three such national sites have been set up, including: the Institute for Human Rights, China University of Political Science and Law; the Center of Research for Human Rights, Nankai University; and the Research and Education Center for Human Rights, Guangzhou University. Though these national sites for human rights education and training have just been set up, I strongly believe that there remains a lot of work to do in human rights research and education, which will contribute to the cause of China's human rights protection.

7.5 Develop a Mid- to Long-Term Action Plan to Implement the Constitutional Principle of Human Rights

The cause of human rights along with human development has always been a crucial and national issue. Therefore, human rights plan should be implemented into an overall long-term goal. There should be a mid- to long-term plan, a 10-year or a 5-year plan. In order to develop the Chinese human rights cause continuously and healthily, specific implementation measures must be further detailed and more specific, and the evaluation system and a corrective mechanism should be established. The constitutional principle that "the state respects and guarantees human rights" should be implemented effectively by specific human rights plans. As Zhong Ruiyou points out, the Chinese human rights cause has developed tremendously, "from issuing the first 'white paper' to including human rights in the *Constitution*, the human rights cause in China launched a bud, encouraging development and prosperity of the era, and also brought the opportunity of a constant pursuit and full enjoyment of human rights" [15].

However, even though the *Constitution* provides that "the state respects and guarantees human rights", it does not mean that people can naturally enjoy the full benefits of human rights. The provision of the *Constitution* is only the first step toward protecting human rights, and in order to effectively implement the constitutional principle, we must take practical measures. As Professor Dong Yunhu points out:

> To implement the constitutional principles of human rights, the dignity and authority of the Constitution should first of all be upheld to strengthen the enforcement of the Constitution. The Constitution is the declaration and guarantee of rights belonging to the people, and is the highest criterion of human rights protection. A good constitution must be carefully implemented, and the provisions of the Constitution should be implemented, or, even the best constitution is a dead letter [16].

Professor Liu Jinguo also points out that even though "human rights were included in the Constitution, it is not a quick thing to implement human rights, and it takes time and requires a process. In this process we should change our ideas: the *Constitution* is the law, not God, but divine and inviolable. We need to make the two breakthroughs of the constitutional jurisdiction and the constitutional review" [17]. Only when the *Constitution* can be the direct basis of deciding a case by the court, can human rights be protected effectively. When human rights have been violated, especially in the absence of corresponding law, there is still a proper remedy to be provided for the violation. In aspect of concrete implementation of human rights, the Chinese government on April 13, 2009 issued the *National Human Rights Action Plan of China* (2009–2010) which provides details of measures to promote the development of Chinese human rights in the following 2 years. Professor Liu Hainian points out:

> As long as we insist on a 'people-oriented' scientific outlook on development, learning more about the importance of human rights in theory and continue working hard from the new starting point, it will take 1.3 billion Chinese individual human rights protection to a higher level, so as to make a greater contribution to international human rights protection [18].

The Human Rights Action Plan which is the first human rights plan provided by the Chinese government, is indeed a positive measure which will help change the constitutional principle of human rights into specific human rights. It will comprehensively promote the development of Chinese human rights, and create a new era of individual rights. As Professor Xu Xianming points out, "the essence of the legal system is human rights, and the ultimate goal of the legal system is to achieve human rights" [19]. Development of human rights is endless and of indefinite duration, and it should be a dynamic spiral development process, which includes the people's needs but also the nation's highest interests. Human rights protection should be the national ultimate goal and all systems should be designed to promote human rights and protect human rights. The constitutional principle of human rights protection should be the starting point, and respect for and guarantee human rights should be the basic principle and the ultimate goal of all state organs.

7.6 Conclusion

All in all, the development of human rights is a gradual process, limited by all kinds of relevant factors. The most direct and enormous influence on the development of human rights is by economic basis, historical and cultural traditions. Although in theory, all kinds of human rights are interrelated, interdependent, and indivisible, the construction of human rights protection cannot have only one development model due to the diversity of every country in the aspects of economic development level, social custom, and traditional culture along with many other factors and conditions. This is a realistic attitude toward human rights. China takes citizen rights to subsistence and development as the first right, which is suitable for the Chinese specific national conditions. Of course, China is extremely concerned about the rights to subsistence and development, at the same time it is also gradually attempting to ensure the comprehensive and coordinated development of other types of human rights, so as to enhance human rights protection and continually improve human rights conditions in the whole country.

However, it is a long process. On the one hand, the general realization of human rights demands all human beings to struggle and work hard continually, in one sense, which is endless; on the other hand, every process of realizing human rights will encounter different problems, and the solution of these problems also needs great efforts, much energy and time, so only when all the various conditions are well satisfied, the full realization can be possibly achieved. Therefore, the construction of a Chinese human rights protection system with socialist characteristics is a gradual process, seen in the dynamic spiral of the development of human rights, which is the core content of Chinese civilization of socialist politics. From idea generation to legal recognition, even to the specific social practice and so on, the development of every small part involves much dependable work, including human rights education, human rights legislation, and the specific actions of human rights protection, etc. Every step that we take is followed by a series of problems and countless difficulties. Therefore, the development of human rights is a complex and difficult task with a great challenge, and implementing the concept and the constitutional principle of human rights still has a long way to go. However, the development of China's human rights will make new and greater achievements as long as people continue with the unremitting efforts and struggle towards a greater sense of individual rights and freedoms.

References

1. Yu, Z. (2004). *Constitution.* (p. 67). Beijing: China University of Political Science and Law Press.
2. Wang, Z. (2010). Several issues on the formation of a socialist legal system with Chinese. *People's Daily*. November 15th. p. 6.
3. Gu, C. (2005). Constitution: The fundamental law of guarantee of human rights. In China Society for Human Rights Studies. (Ed.), *Human rights in China in the new century* (p. 211). Beijing: Unity Press.
4. Xu, X. (2006). The five "obstacles" to a harmonious society. *People's Daily*. August 9th.
5. The Editorial Section. (2008). A new year, new expectation. *Yanhuang Chunqiu, 1*, 1–2.
6. Gao, L. (2008). Do Chinese farmers own their properties—Concurrently discussing the problem of compensation for the contracted land of farmers. *Yanhuang Chunqiu, 9*, 4–12.
7. UN Doc. E/CN.4/1989/68, Para. 121.
8. Gu, C. (2005). Constitution: The fundamental law of guarantee of human rights. In China Society for Human Rights Studies. (Ed.), *Human rights in China in the new century* (p. 212). Beijing: Unity Press.
9. Gu, C. (2005). Constitution: The fundamental law of guarantee of human rights. In China Society for Human Rights Studies. (Ed.), *Human rights in China in the new century* (p. 213). Beijing: Unity Press.

10. Yuan, G. (2007). Introduction to national human rights institutions. In Xu, X. (Ed.), *Human Rights Research* (Vol. 7, pp. 253–350). Jinan: Shandong People's Press.
11. Qi, Y. (2005). The national responsibility for protection of human rights and establishment of National Human Rights Institutions. *Legal System and Social Development, 3*, 3–9.
12. Information Office of the State Council. (2009). *National Human Rights Action Plan of China (2009–2010)*. Released on April 13.
13. Refer to Item 2, Article 26 of the *Universal Declaration of Human Rights*.
14. The national cadre training materials editing steering committee. (Ed.). (2006). *Cadre chrestomathy on human rights knowledge*. Beijing: People's Publishing House/The Party Building Books Publishing House.
15. Zhong, R. (2005). From white paper to human right into the Constitution: Unfolding and choice of China's human rights undertaking. *Henan Social Sciences, 1*, 10–15.
16. Dong, Y. (2004). Human rights into the Constitution: An important milestone of China's human rights development. *Human Rights, 2*, 31–35.
17. Liu, J. (2004). Legal value of human rights into the Constitution. *Law Science Magazine, 2*, 6–8.
18. Liu, H. (2005). Construction and development of the rule of law of China's human rights. *Academic Forum of Nandu (Journal of Humanities and Social Sciences), 1*, 75–90.
19. Xiang, Y. (2005). Discussions by NPC representative Xu Xianming on the five major changes of the development of human rights in China. *Human Rights, 2*, 20–21.

Chapter 8
Foundations of Human Rights Guarantee in Contemporary China

Abstract Human rights guarantee has become a striking theme in contemporary China. For human rights guarantee, independent sovereignty means providing possibility of maximum human rights guarantee by dealing correctly with problems of regime, parties, economy, culture, and society. There were no human rights without property, and the realization of rights is restrained by economic development. Political civilization is the political foundation of human rights guarantee, while following the rule by law is a necessary approach for human rights guarantee in contemporary China.

Since the beginning of twenty-first century, China has entered into a new stage of institutional construction of human rights law. Human rights guarantee has become a striking theme of the establishment of human rights legality in contemporary China. However, by reviewing the theories and practice in human rights guarantee at all times and in all countries, human rights guarantee is not merely the thesis for law and rule by law, neither is the problem solved once for ever by politics-based declaration of human rights. Human rights guarantee is a colossal and complicated social and systematical project, the basis of which involves in many factors, such as national, economic and political factors, the factors of rule by law, etc. Without the development and suitable allocation of these factors, there cannot be a guarantee of human rights in reality.

8.1 National Foundation

Independent state sovereignty is the national base of human rights guarantee. Historical experiences prove that since modern times state's sovereignty was infringed and simultaneously human rights of Chinese were trampled for many times. Since Opium War, the modern history of China is both the history of humiliation in human rights guarantee and the history of humiliation in independence of Chinese sovereignty. The state sovereignty gradually lost led to a sharp change taking place ever before in the society of China. On the one hand, domestic

P. Sun, *Human Rights Protection System in China*,
DOI: 10.1007/978-3-642-39663-2_8,

political situations were turbulent without peace, people could not make their living and human rights could not be ensured. On the other hand, the sharp change in thought and social reform was urged to take place, risking human rights to buck for human rights guarantee. Declination of state sovereignty led to the crisis of Chinese human rights at modern times, causing the pursuit of human rights guarantee by Chinese society. In this sense, the declination of state sovereignty is the essential problem of all human rights at modern times in China. But this was not intensively understood by all the thinkers in modern China. For example, in the 1920s and 1930s, the bannerman of human rights, Mr. Hu Shi, lifted up his voice to pursue the human rights guarantee of Chinese society: "We shall have a provisional constitution to provide people with guarantee of 'person, freedom and property: Anyone who violates these legal human rights, whether he is company commander from brigade 152 or the chairman of the state government, will be charged by people and be tried by law" [1]. But in reality, his aims could not be achieved according to law before the nation won its independence and liberation, and before the problem of state sovereignty was completely solved. Therefore, it is necessary to win full independent sovereignty before solving the social problems of modern China. This was the problem that Hu Shi did not understand or would not solve. In his opinion, "Our real enemies are poverty, diseases, blindness, corruption and disorder. These five cacodemons are the real subjects to be removed, while they cannot be beaten down by revolution" [2].

The founding of the People's Republic of China was a turning point, serving as a milestone for Chinese social human rights guarantee since modern China. In the sense of human rights guarantee, the newness of new China lies in that new China is an independent state of sovereignty. For human rights guarantee, independent sovereignty means providing possibility of maximum human rights guarantee by dealing correctly with problems of regime, parties, economy, culture, and society. In this situation, it will become significant for human rights guarantee to deal with the problems of poverty, diseases, blindness, corruption, and disorder that Hu Shi ever put forth. We cannot deny that there have remained many problems since the founding of China. Serious trampling human rights during the "cultural revolution" supplied evidences. Emergence of this state was not caused by independent state sovereignty but the crisis of domestic management in the state of independent sovereignty. Independent sovereignty is a necessity of human rights guarantee in the existence of the state. Without independent sovereignty, it is impossible to ensure human rights to the greatest extent, which have been proved by Chinese modern history. Of course, this does not indicate that sovereignty is over human rights. We should treat with the relationship between sovereignty and human rights objectively, not generally believing that sovereignty is over human rights without analysis or that human rights are over sovereignty.

From the perspective of historical experiences in China, independent sovereignty of the state is the key element of human rights guarantee in China. Without independent sovereignty, there cannot be a complete guarantee of human rights. Therefore, countless Chinese people gave their lives to strive for the state independent sovereignty. However, this does not imply that sovereignty should be over human rights. Otherwise, it will deny the ultimate significance of endeavoring to win independent sovereignty. In reality, the relationship between human rights and sovereignty has the characteristics of relativity, at different periods of time, and their relationship has different connotations, but human rights are the most essential and at the highest level. For instance, in modern history, former generations would rather give up their right to life and the right to development so that they would win state sovereignty, by applying Petofi's poem mechanically: "Sovereignty and love, these two things I need. For love I sacrifice my life, for sovereignty I sacrifice my love." In this sense, we may say that countless people with lofty ideals would rather give up human rights for sovereignty. Nevertheless, the struggle for sovereignty in history can be significant only under the view of long-term humanity development and the pursuit of happiness. In the final analysis, the ultimate goal of struggling for sovereignty is to realize human rights of majority. State sovereignty is not a human right, but a kind of power. In a form of a country, this kind of independent sovereignty can show its value on the condition that it can provide service to human rights. Otherwise, it may possibly violate human rights. Human rights are ends, but sovereignty is the means to ensure and realize human rights. In the state society, this is the real meaning of laying an emphasis on independent sovereignty.

8.2 Economic Foundation

Emphasizing that there will be no human rights without property has great significance in contemporary China, which reveals the economic base of human rights guarantee. There exists this phenomenon of no human rights without property at different places such as homes, companies, schools and institutions or in different aspects such as clothing, food, housing, and actions. For example, in order to develop economy, many laws and regulations in the protection of subjects in market protect the interest of those representing capital too much, but protect the rights of labors insufficiently. Employed boys and girls "weak-spiritedly" transfer their human rights in order to gain their limited pay consciously or unconsciously. For another example, in the aspect of guarantee of the right to education, the students with stronger economic base can usually enjoy better and fuller education, while those students with weak economic base cannot usually enjoy the full realization of the right to education. Furthermore, the people with better economic base can receive better affirmation and appraisal of the society, and shall be respected, while the people with weaker economic base shall not be appraised high, and they cannot usually receive respect from the society.

The phenomenon of "no human rights without property" indicates that it is essential for "the State's respect and guarantee of human rights" to be based on solid material basis. Otherwise, "the State's respect and guarantee of human rights" is a beautiful nonsense, which has no significance for practical human rights. Some scholars have ever studied the political indicators both in 1960 and in

1965 from more than one hundred countries about their democratic regimes. Through this thorough correlative research, they found that "the level of economic development had a great effect on political democracy." Based on this understanding, scholars also recognize that the realization of rights "is restrained by regularity of economic development, which has its historic inevitability, and any country can exceed it" [3]. This is also the reflection of Mark's classical theory that "rights can never transcend the economic structure of society and the cultural development of society restricted by the economic structure" [4]. Analysis from the perspective of human rights guarantee and realization, this argument sounds reasonable because good economic environment and regime are conducive to the better realization of human rights.

Since the implementation of reform and opening-up policy, the most successful aspect lies in the establishment of market economy regime, which speeded up the accumulation of social wealth. Although this mode promoted the increase of social wealth, it has brought all kinds of problems, such as distribution of wealth, laboring and employment, flowage of population, freedom of speech, etc. However, this mode provided a material platform for human rights guarantee after all. The establishment of market economy system laid a solid foundation for continual accumulation of social wealth. Therefore, its value and significance cannot be evaluated in human rights guarantee. Market economy must bring changes of two social relations and five big conceptions. They are: the change of realization from status to contract, which to a great extent expands the freedom of individuals, enterprises and local freedom; the change of realization of state's functions, which changes "big country and small society" to "small country and big society," expanding space for social activities and the freedom beyond state's power. Meanwhile, market economy will change people's old opinions progressively, promoting the healthy development of self-consciousness, consciousness of rights, freedom of thoughts, conceptions of equality and thoughts of democracy. In this sense, market economy has brought not only the accumulation of social wealth, but also the stimulation of requirements for human rights from the people. And many kinds of requirements of human rights can be practical and realized.

8.3 Political Foundation

Political civilization is the political foundation of human rights guarantee. In the form of state, we should admit that on the one hand progress of production, development of material production to some extent of civilization indeed provide enjoyment of human rights at a certain stage and social civilization with a certain condition of materials. On the other hand, no democracy and no civilization of political regime would play a leading role in violating human rights. Both aspects consist of a new starting point for our modern human rights guarantee. Based on that point, material conditions play an essential role in the realization of human rights, it is reasonable and necessary for us to advocate material civilization in the past, now and in the future. But as for the essence of human rights, rights against power, this can only solve the problems of material conditions to realize human rights, and it cannot answer how to regulate the allocation and utilization of the power.

Human rights mainly belong to the language of public power rather than the language on material conditions. The realization of human rights to a great extent refers to how to regulate public power, making it work in order and avoiding the violation of human rights. The important intention of human rights lies in the mode and relevant regime of public power rather than material conditions. The mere principle of autocratic institution is to disregard humanity, making human inhuman, so we have to criticize the allocative system of public power in autocratic institution. Even though incomparable material wealth has been created, human rights cannot naturally be realized. In addition, any country or regime can not limit or boost human rights for the material conditional excuse. It is essential to create a good mode of regulating the public powers. With this mode, human rights can be fully embodied and developed. The author believes "that preventing individuals' rights from being violated by the state or government is the main characteristic on the basis of Western human rights of individualism" [5]. Also, it is the main feature of human rights guarantee of the state where there exist public powers. This requires that the mode of any state's power should be the one of a civilized power allocation, without violating human rights. As far as the present situation in China is concerned, this indicates the requirement for political civilizations.

Political civilization is the progressive status of humanity's political life and state's power circulation, the connotation of which is very abundant and complicated. Affirmation of the following two points is very important: firstly, political civilization is the progressive status of continuous development. On the one hand, political civilization is a continual progress from wildness to civilization, and this progress will never end. At a certain stage of development, the concrete content of political civilization may be civilized compared with former system and life relevant, but relative to the higher stage of development, it will become into uncivilized thing or phenomenon. The political civilization mentioned here refers to modern political civilization, such as democracy, rule by law and human rights, which are these three civilized factors relative to the archaic autarchy, rule by human beings, and people's no rights. Meanwhile, we should also see that at different stages and levels of development, democracy, the rule by law and human rights also have a progress of development, and we should watch and deal with problems according to practical situations of the country. On the other hand, the outcome of political civilization is the crystal of human's intelligence. With the continuous development of individuals and collective groups, political civilization must be sure to develop continuously. The highest ambit is the full realization of human rights and complete development of persons. This form of social existence is described by Marx as "social form of the basic principles for everyone's complete and free development" [6]. Secondly, political civilization is autochthonous. This characteristic refers to the differences in political conceptions, the mode of political system and political behaviors because of the different levels of economic development, and different historical and cultural traditions. That is to say, the existence of a country must have its special autochthonous political civilization to gather its people. If a country has no such political civilization differing from other countries, or a mixed civilization, this country cannot have its gathering force. Globalization is some outcome of political civilization and the crystal of human intelligence. Therefore, it can be borrowed and enjoyed by all the people from the world.

Based on the scientific connotations and important values of political civilization, political civilization in practice is the major standard for evaluating human civilization. Just like what some scholar says:

> The standard of political civilization is human rights. … The ultimate goal of all political combination is for human rights. The ultimate representation of all the political activities is to realize human rights. The ultimate content of political system is to show human rights. The ultimate standard of political civilization is judged from the human rights in practice. All the political judgments should be transferred into legal judgments. Furthermore, only being transferred into legal judgments can be significant judgments [7].

Therefore, political civilization is a good implemental status of a country's ensuring civilized human rights, viewing human rights guarantee as the ultimate gist. In this sense, there cannot be human rights guarantee without political civilization.

8.4 Foundation of the Rule by Law

The establishment of the rule by law is the base of rule by law in human rights guarantee. Where there is no rule by law, there is no adequate guarantee of human rights. Where there the rule by law is violated, there are human rights in the serious crisis. Following the rule by law is a necessary approach for human rights guarantee in contemporary China. By summarizing the rules and experiences of human rights guarantee in our country, on the historical condition that "the state respects and guarantees human rights" was written in our constitution, the present author believes that the most urgent things for us to do are as follows from four different aspects:

1. Enhancing legislation with the guidance of the conception in human rights guarantee.

In 1991, the Chinese government released a white paper on *Human Rights in China*, fully affirming and expatiating on human rights conceptions of China in a national instrument for the first time. In 1997, the 15th National Congress of the Communist Party of China put forth "respect and guarantee of human rights" at the highest level of the Party's instrument for the first time. After 15th National Congress, the 16th National Congress of the Communist Party of China put forth "respect and guarantee of human rights" once again. The 17th National Congress of the Communist Party of China pointed out that the career of human rights in China developed healthily. On 24 March 2004, "the state respects and guarantees human rights." was formally written into the Constitution, which consequently brought basic value of respecting and guaranteeing human rights into the legal field of our country. In addition, before human rights were written into the Constitution, though there was no clear term of human rights, and no legislation did not represent the spirit of human rights in amendments, such as Administrative Procedure Law of the People's Republic of China, Law of the People's Republic of China on State Compensation, Law of the People's Republic of China on the Protection of Minors, Law of the People's Republic of China on the Protection of Rights and Interests of Women, Law of the People's Republic of China on Protection of Consumer Rights and Interests, Law of the People's Republic of China on the Protection of Disabled Persons, Criminal Law of the People's Republic of China, the Criminal Procedure Law of the People's Republic of China. The amendments of these laws embodied the spirits of human rights conceptions and content. As for international conventions, after ratifying or accessing 18 conventions, China signed two Covenants (the Covenant A and the Covenant B) in 1998, and ratified Covenant A in 2001.

2. Judicial independence as a breakthrough to make the judicial mechanism of human rights guarantee improved.

When the reform of Chinese political regime cannot open the door, it is a rational choice to strengthen human rights guarantee by the approach of judicial reform to facilitate the establishment of the rule by law in China. One of the purposes in judicial reform is to find an approach for the reform of political regime. Through judicial reform, political issues are changed into legal ones, the focus of the State turns to court. With people's trust in court, political center turns to court and so does the national power. All the issues are decided on by court. But if the judicature would have universal beliefs and trust in realizing social justice, judicature must be independent. In the past, because our leaders paid insufficient attention to negative influence of no independent judicature and its serious results of violating human rights, which made it difficult for judicial independence to be actually realized. For example, in 1981, at the First National Congress of Politics and Law, one leader said:

> Judicial independent, does it need the leadership of the Party or not? … does it need the responsibility of the National People's Congress and the Standing Committee or not? Mutual restriction of public security, procuratorate and court is also a kind of interference. Isn't it impermissible? … Even individuals are independent without the leadership of the Trial Committee, the chief justice of the court and presiding judge, can it be all right? [8]

Judicature must be independent, because the power of judicature is the ultimate power of the state's restriction and is the final rights guarantee of rule by law. In this sense, judicial independence is the ultimate institutional remedy for all rights, powers and the right to judicature *per se* in society. If judicature *per se* is still caved in the relationship of other rights and powers, this kind of judicature has only left its "outer wear," and its functions to maintain social justice will exist no longer.

3. Administration strictly according to law with democratic political orientation.

The essence of human rights refers to the rights against powers. According to Chinese historical tradition, "power" mainly refers to the administrative power. Since the founding of the PRC, though various functions of power have been separated, the administrative power remains great influential. Therefore, in this sense, the exercise of the administrative power is always relevant to human rights protection, and it may violate human rights with little indiscretion. In the process of political civilization establishment, we must pay close attention to science and democracy of exercising the administrative power, avoiding the violation of human rights. Thus, in some sense, the government faces the greatest challenge in establishing political civilization. On the one hand, we must ensure that the government must be selected by people's votes through institutions. The government holds its power really in its own hand, administrating according to law with noninterference of any group, organization or individual. On the other hand, in order to ensure that the government does not interfere with legislation, judicial and other organs of public power, its administration according to law should be supervised by the people and the government should indeed shoulder the responsibilities for the people.

4. Strengthening the establishment of the Party's institutions following the spirits of the rule by law.

How to establish the socialist rule by law and to strengthen the guarantee of human rights is a challenging subject in this era under the leadership of the Party. It is under the leadership of the Party that socialist state of the rule by law will be established. The Party plays a key role in establishing socialist political civilization. Therefore, the 16th National Congress of the Communist Party of China emphasizes that managing state affairs must begin with the management of the Party's affairs, while managing the Party's affairs must be strict, which has been drawn from the history of the past 100 years. The practical rule of law since the Third Plenary Session of the 11th Central Committee of the Party has indicated that a word or an action of the Party is closely related to the establishment of the rule by law. The Party's policies and measures cannot surpass the law. If the Party acts beyond the range of law, it will weaken the leadership of the Party and will make no guarantee of human rights. If the Party actively obeys the law, it will get support from the people, thus, human rights will be safeguarded. Inseparation of the Party and government, or the Party instead of government, was a big disadvantage of our national political system in the past, which caused a lot of unfavorable consequences of the Party's career. Therefore, since the Third Plenary Session of the 11th Central Committee of the Party, leaders of the Party and country have summarized this lesson carefully, recognizing that the key factor to solve the problems lies in "no privilege is allowed for any one to surpass the law" [9]. The Third Plenary Session of the 11th Central Committee of the Party adopted *Resolution of the Party Historic Issues since the Founding of the PRC*, which clearly points out that "organizations of the Party at all levels, the same as other social organizations, must act within the range of the Constitution and the law."

Consequently, from the perspective of the content of law, the relationship between the Party and the establishment of the rule by law is already transparent. There exist no essential conflicts between the power of the Party and the power of legislative, judicial, administrative, and other public powers, which provides the establishment of the modern political party system with a solid theoretical base.

Acknowledgements This Chapter was originally written in Chinese by Chen Youwu, Associate Professor from Research Center for Human Rights at Guangzhou University. I am permitted by the original scholar to get it included here in the book as a chapter based on my translation, which was firstly published in *China Legal Science*. (Vol. 2007, pp. 11–15.).

References

1. Hu, S. (1998). Human rights and conventions. In W. Zhu (Ed.), *Self-reflection and trial* (p. 65). Shanghai: Shanghai Literature and Art Publishing House.
2. Hu, S. (1998). What way do we take? In W. Zhu (Ed.), *Self-reflection and trial* (p. 92). Shanghai: Shanghai Literature and Art Publishing House.
3. Hao, T. (2002). The pattern of difference in fulfillment of rights. *Social Sciences in China*, *5*, 112–124.
4. Central Compilation & Translation Bureau for Works of Marx, Engels, Lenin and Stalin. (Ed.) (1972). *Selected works of Marx and Engels* (Vol. 3, p. 12). Beijing: People's Publishing House.
5. Xu, X. (2002). Culture and subjects of human rights. In J. Wang (Ed.), *Human rights and 21st century* (p. 45). Beijing: China Legal Publishing House.
6. Central Compilation & Translation Bureau for Works of Marx, Engels, Lenin and Stalin. (Ed.) (1972). *Selected works of Marx and Engels* (Vol. 1, p. 273). Beijing: People's Publishing House.
7. Xu, X. (2003). Foreword. In X. Xu (Ed.), *Human Rights Research*. (Vol. 3). Jinan: Shandong People's Press.
8. Peng, Z. (1991). *Selected Works of Peng Zhen* (p. 416). Beijing: People's Publishing House.
9. Party Documents Research Office of the CPC Central Committee. (Ed.), 1982. *Selected from important documents since the Third Plenary Session*. (p. 11) Beijing: People's Publishing House.

Chapter 9
Human Rights, Culture and Their Reconstruction in the Chinese Context

Abstract The words human rights and culture have different understandings in different contexts. The contemporary argument about human rights universalism and cultural relativism has fundamental defects, so the Chinese theory of the human rights law should surpass the problematic visual field of both theories, oppose cultural nihilism and inaction of human rights, and reconsider our own modern cultural proposition of human rights.

In the field of contemporary international human rights, the discussion about the relationship between human rights and culture is becoming more and more popular, while this discussion is the main instrument for the non-Western countries to expatiate upon the characteristics of their own human rights. Different positions about the compatibility of the culture and rights mold the modern political and academic debates [1]. How should we on earth look at the complicated relationship between culture and human rights? How should we think about our own cultural proposition of human rights in the Chinese context? As far as the construction of contemporary Chinese human rights is concerned, it is of great significance to question these theoretical propositions closely without any doubt.

9.1 Understanding the Relationship Between Human Rights and Culture

Human right, as a universal moral right, is a cultural phenomenon from perspectives of its values and theories *per se*. Human rights have always been the product of a particular culture and can only be explained and understood within concrete cultural context. Therefore, human rights and culture are natural relatives. Unfortunately, the contemporary disputes about human rights and culture derive from the misunderstanding of the connotation to the great extent, which becomes ambiguous. Therefore, to explore the relationship between human rights and

P. Sun, *Human Rights Protection System in China*,
DOI: 10.1007/978-3-642-39663-2_9,

culture, different conversational contexts ought to be taken into account. Generally speaking, the understanding of the relationship between human rights and culture mainly includes the following three aspects:

9.1.1 Rights Versus Culture

This way of understanding puts human rights and culture into a dual-contrary position to perceive. Even from this same understanding viewpoint, the Western idea of human rights diverges greatly from the East. In some Western scholars' opinions, to admit rights is to deny, refuse, and overthrow culture, while to admit culture, in the contrary, is to prohibit the pursuit of individual rights in some situations at least potentially [2]. Therefore, the Western human rights' universalism almost takes the human rights' reasoning strategy of "cultural noninvolvement" or "cultural neutrality." For example, in Jack Donnelly's eyes, human rights are universal, that is, human rights are the rights of all the people in the world. Human rights mean that all human beings enjoy human rights [3].

Jack Donnelly's definition of human rights represents the common standpoint of the Western human rights' universalism. This standpoint insists the condition of universal human rights should be and only be the universal existence of human beings or the natural properties of human beings. The interior logic is that human is universal and human rights must be universal. The justice of human rights is only based on human's natural existence. As long as a person comes into the world, he should enjoy human rights in spite of whatever culture, country, and nation he belongs to [4]. However, in Eastern countries, based on the painful memory about the history of Western colonialism and the caution about the Western neocolonialism and cultural hegemony, some scholars insist on viewing national culture as the subject, associating human rights directly with Western culture. They believe that the essence of the value of human rights belongs to the Western culture, consequently contradicting human rights with culture in this way of understanding.

9.1.2 A Right to Culture

This way of understanding takes culture as the object or target of rights, that is, individuals belong to or enjoy the right to culture [5]. This kind of cultural right requirement mainly behaves at two levels:

At the domestic level, the cultural right mainly means that individuals enjoys the right to culture, education and so on, and together with the economic right and social right is the important content of the third world's idea of human rights. Otherwise, to the countries where minorities exist, cultural right sometimes means right requirement of the minorities to maintain their own cultural characteristics, like the cultural right requirement of the migrated people and native people in America and some European countries.

At the international level, some countries of the third world always hold kind of internal caution and antipathy to the Western human rights' culture, and sometimes they regard the maintenance of their native social living style as a requirement of the cultural right. For example, the Islamic conservatism considers that globalization or modernization is the trick of Western culture, the idea of human rights is one way of the Western cultural invasion, and the Islamic social paradigm ought not to submit to that of the global information society [6]. Under this understanding, cultural right becomes a powerful weapon against the Western cultural colonialism, which intends to use the language of rights against the Western cultural invasion and maintain the national culture's independence and self-autonomy.

9.1.3 Rights as Culture

Through the explanation of rights as culture we can see the different objectives and interest of the Western and the Eastern theories. The Western understanding is to view rights as a kind of modern culture, embodying the cultural features of constructivism. This understanding not only views human rights as a cultural phenomenon but also a cultural property to promote the social development. This way of understanding believes that human rights constitute a culture and the discourse of human rights has certain features to construct a culture as anthropologists think. Rights are usually understood as its discourse, concepts, and practice of human rights, and shoulder some kind of responsibility to construct certain given modes for individuals, society, and institutions [7]. According to this understanding, human rights, just like the law, reflect the world view in the modern cultural context. In this context of discourse, the Western understanding about the meaning of the modern world is actually hidden. As the cultural result of modernization, contemporary culture of human rights constitutes the core of the global culture, and both human rights and freedoms have become the roll booster to facilitate the process of globalization. Therefore, the globalization of the human rights culture is the universal construction of the Western individual and social mode.

However, the Eastern understanding is that human rights as cultural phenomena are not the result of modernization rather than cultural accumulation that any civilization has made in the social history. Different cultures of human rights actually reflect different world views and meanings of life, and there is no such question about which one has the universal justice for different cultures of human rights. The Eastern culture of human rights has its own system of cultural theories, its own traditions and modern problems, and its own reconstruction issue of the culture of human rights, but it does not rely on the Western culture of human rights to conduct the social reset. In a word, the difference of the human rights culture does not represent the nihilism of the Eastern culture of human rights, and the globalization and modernization of human rights do not only refer to westernization and liberalization, it should refer to independence and harmonization between different cultures of human rights.

9.2 Surpass Universalism and Cultural Relativism

The contemporary disputes about human rights and culture are usually submitted to the two groups of human rights universalism and cultural relativism. To discuss the relationship between human rights and culture needs to carefully clear and prudently analyze the controversial proposition of universalism and cultural relativism.

9.2.1 The Confusion of Universalism

Human rights universalism has many forms, here we mainly analyze and comment on the Western scholars' reasoning strategies. Western scholars, taking the position of human rights universalism, have their clear and Western reasoning manner, that is, to deduce this theory based on the definition of human rights. Their basic strategy is to place universality of human rights on the natural basis of the universal existence of human beings or certain properties of human beings to get the legitimacy of universal human rights. The legitimacy of the value of human rights in the West almost relies within the reason kingdom of abstract human beings. However, this kind of logic reasoning about "cultural noninvolved" or "historical wordless" have many problems:

9.2.1.1 The Problem of Universality of Human Beings or Humanity

The universality of human beings or humanity is the fundamental premise of the Western human rights universalism. The question is that the existence of human beings is concrete and historical rather than abstract or universal, and one cannot get rid of his historical and cultural context to achieve some kind of universal existence. The Western so-called universal existence of human is only their understanding of the human meaning schema and the world schema, that is, the universal existence of the meaning schema of "Westerners". "Westerner" is some kind of abstract person filtered and slides over the rich world of the presence meaning behind. Because the universal meaning of human beings diverges in different cultural contexts, and the assumption of universal human beings cannot get rid of the concrete historical conditions to receive some kind of unspoken rational self-evidence. As for the universality of humanity, the context is the same. Because any kind of abstract humanity is doubtable and certain human natural properties must be shown through concrete historical context. Universal and unchanged basis of humanity is just rational logic game not the real humanity in concrete social history. Thus, we can say that the logic proposition that the Western universalism of human rights relies on is false, because it forgets that human rights are the product of social and historical life.

9.2.1.2 The Rational Question of Universal Human Rights

The Western universal human rights have close relation with the moral philosophy. The Western moral philosophy, no matter the social contract, utility, or intuition, cannot part from the rationality of human, Archimedes basic point. Similarly, the Western universalism of human rights also relies on the hypothesis of the rational human. And the rational logic of universal human rights is that human beings should choose the value or principles of human rights because they have rationality or universal human rights can get the steady basis only through rational argument or choice. In the West, rationality not only regulates the possibility of universal human rights but also guarantee the conditions to realize the universal human rights. The hypothesis of rationality lies through the whole theory of universal human rights. First there is rationality, then follows the abstract, and then follows the question of universality: that is, the implied logic of the Western universalism. Nevertheless, the problem of rationality cannot be solved rationally, and Marxism had passed judgment on this earlier. Besides, from the view of the appearance of human rights, the birth of human rights is far beyond the control of rationality, and the different definitions of human rights in different cultures are not the logic results of the rational philosophy, either. Therefore, the Western universalism's reliance on the rationality must have many falsities. Moreover, even though people recognize the universal existence of human being on the basis of rationality and human rights do enjoy universality, we can still not solve what kind of human rights is universal rationally. Certain rational human rights proposed by some individuals or groups can hardly get recognized by other people's rationality. Therefore, the abstract rationality has to give place to the "historical rationality" or "cultural rationality" in the social life and practice.

9.2.1.3 The Question of Valid Reasoning

The reasoning of the Western universalism of human rights has the fundamental logic confusion. Ever after Hume brought forth the dichotomy of "fact" and "value", we know that the natural facts cannot deduce the justice of value. Similarly, the natural fact of human beings of universalism cannot prove the justice of universal human rights, which can only be proved in other values. However, regulative propositions have the logic paradox of the ultimate foundation, that is, if we admit the existence of the ultimate foundation, then the question of its justice comes up inevitably. Therefore, the reasoning of the moral justice will fall into an abyss of endless questions and the "Hume question" becomes the puzzle of Sphinx. Although the Western ethics has been pursuing industriously the ultimate logic basis for the regulative value, no one has ever got rid of the "Münchhausen dilemma". The contemporary Western universal human rights' reasoning also faces such problems, though someone tries to weaken the difficulty of the "Hume question." Thus, the International Covenants on Human Rights regards human dignity as the logic base for the justice of human rights, which cannot similarly deal with the argumentation and criticism of rationality and the cultural doubt of the non-Western countries. In brief, in the abstract sense, the human rights reasoning of the Western universalism not only leaves its disputes with cultural relativism unsolved but also let itself fall into theoretic difficulties.

9.2.2 The Misunderstandings of the Cultural Relativism

Cultural relativism is a very broad conception. In the context of human rights disputes, cultural relativism is regarded as the opposite theory against the universalism of human rights. Strictly speaking, cultural relativism is just a theoretic school of cultural anthropology and has reached its peak in anthropology in the beginning of twentieth century. The point of departure of the cultural relativism is the empirical facts which show the existence of the changeability of the uncertain culture. From this fact, anthropologists attribute to the lack of absoluteness. They believe that the principles to judge behaviors are effective only in the specific cultural context [8]. Generally speaking, cultural relativism at least contains two theoretic fields: one is the moral philosophy or the field of anthropology, where cultural relativism continues the theoretic argumentation between absolutism and relativism; the other is the field of human rights, where cultural relativism becomes the theoretical target that the universalism of human rights is against.

The particularity or "cultural specialism" of human rights in non-Western countries is an unsuccessful theory and also a dangerous strategy. It has the obvious mark of cultural relativism and utility of human rights political intentions. This kind of concepts of human rights which lacks strong theoretic supports cannot restraint the invasion and attack of the Western universalism of human rights effectively. Simply speaking, cultural relativism easily falls into the logic misunderstanding of dual-contrary: that is, "universal human rights = Western human rights", "particular human rights = non-Western human rights" or "universality of human rights = Western culture of human rights", "cultural relativity = non-Western culture of human rights". Or culture becomes an excuse to refuse any kind of human rights and a negative response to the theory of universal human rights. For the non-Western countries, to maintain the differences of the human rights cultural tradition means to insist on the particularity, locality, and limited modernization of the Western human rights; to insist on the universality of human rights means to accept the universality of the moral human rights in different cultures; to insist on the difference between the human rights knowledge and its practice also means to insist on the different families of human rights culture all over the world and the modernization of the non-West.

In a word, at the level of morality and wisdom, human rights culture of every country should take the equal place without any distinction. The human rights value of universalism can be realized only based on the admission of the justice and independence of different cultures of human rights. Culture should not be regarded as the fortress of human rights relativism and ought to become a strong support for the universal human rights. Therefore, the falsity of cultural relativism lies on that: on the one hand, it contributes to opposing any possibility of universal human rights, but it cannot put forward a vigorous theory of human rights; on the other hand, it can not effectively prove the falsity of the Western universalism of human rights and also let itself fall into the logic misunderstanding of criticism.

9.3 Cultural Nihilism and Cultural Inaction

In front of the uproar of the universality of human rights, recognition of the human rights value seems to be popular at home. "Fight for rights", "step into the era of rights" and other slogans are its representatives of discourse concerning the value of human rights at present. The questions are: what kind of human rights is to be believed in? Which value of human rights is to be advocated? Do the human rights belong to the West or China, if China, what are they? Through these questions we finally come to the initial question: what are the Chinese human rights? To answer this question, we have to construct China's own theory of human rights and the cultural problem becomes the central problem of the local human rights theory. Here, we are going to criticize two kinds of cultural tendencies.

First, to hackle and inherit the ancient tradition of human rights, cultural nihilism must be absolutely cleared out. There are strong and weak nihilism. Strong cultural nihilism completely denies Chinese traditional culture of human rights and admits that human rights are just the product of Western culture. In ancient China, there was no concept of human rights and no knowledge or theory of human rights, either. Chinese traditions are totally strange moral culture to human culture. And the weak cultural nihilism shows many situations, whose main ideas are: on the one hand, to admit the justice of the Western concepts and culture of human rights; on the other hand, to claim that Chinese cultures especially Confucian Culture have certain genes of modern human rights and the Confucian theoretic resources can be connected with the modern free liberalism, democracy, and human rights absolutely after alteration. Weak cultural nihilism has a big market in China and it also shows its appearance as a kind similarly local statement of utilitarianism. It is utilitarian because of the demand of human rights politics that it must accomplish the emergent work of Chinese human rights statement. This kind of seemingly "local" theory of human rights, however, does not show the interest in going deep into the ancient cultural resources or the willingness to inherit Chinese cultural traditions of human rights. In their eyes, the local culture of human rights is just an embellishment to the national characteristics, some kind of cultural conformation or a subterfuge against the Western theories of human rights. This kind of "local" theory of human rights can slightly show the differences between the Chinese and the Western human rights and quickly create the local theory of human rights, but it does not have profound basis of wisdom and knowledge compared with the true local tradition of human rights or give response to the Western theory of human rights appropriately.

Second, to promote the construction of human rights in China, cultural inaction must be abandoned. Cultural inaction is the logic result of the cultural nihilism. Oblivion of the traditional cultural groundwork, our own human rights are like water without a source and the local construction of human rights becomes the experimental field of the Western culture of human rights. As for the treatment to the domestic and Western culture of human rights, cultural inaction has the different theoretic presupposition. In the view of cultural inaction, Western theory of human rights has provided a completely systemic basis of wisdom and knowledge, so Chinese human rights construction does not need the cultural reconstruction of the theory of rights and it is completely possible to rebuild Chinese system of human rights and promote the cause of human rights relying on the Western theory of human rights. Therefore, to Chinese construction of human rights, local culture is neutral, value-uninvolved, or unimportant. Therefore, cultural inaction is not the exact cultural inaction but rather the Western culture's action and the local culture's inaction and it is another version of local culture uselessness. Cultural inaction exists in many hidden forms, and as for the theoretic research, it mainly shows that: whenever talking about the theory of human rights, talk about Western ones; the intellects of human rights are proud of the quotation of the Western theories of human rights; the consideration about our own theories is deserted just like worn shoes. As for China's true problems, they turn a deaf ear to them, or put them on the shelves or search the foundation in the old papers of Western human rights theories for China's human rights. In practice, cultural inaction is always busy with burying its head to work but never raises its heads to walk in the right direction. To recognize the value of human rights becomes just to recognize the Western understanding of human rights as good; though not even fully making clear the basic theories of human rights, they begin to construct the so-called complete system of human rights institutions in a hurry and judge the level of human rights conditions by the account of the institutions; as for the International Covenants of Human Rights, all kinds of system connection theories and institution reconstruction theories constitute the best annotations to cultural inaction. The inaction tropism to the local culture directly results in the lame process of China's human rights construction.

9.4 Transformation, Inheritance, and Reconstruction

In the contemporary conversation of different human rights and cultures, the theories and claims of the Eastern countries seem so pale and weak. Not only at the theoretic level or at the practical level, the Eastern countries do not have enough intellectual preparation to surpass the disputes between universalism and cultural relativism in order to truly defend the independent position of our own culture of human rights and response theoretically to the modern world schema of human rights. Therefore, for China, the ignorance of the culture of human rights and the temptation of cultural relativism seem to come to the end and to reconsider the way we have taken and we are going to take, which is not some kind of academic consideration but rather a moral responsibility. In a word, the future of Chinese human rights is: we must conduct the reconstruction of our local culture of human rights. Facing this historical mission, the East should think over the following propositions:

9.4.1 The Transformation of the Western Concept of Human Rights

Modern concept of human rights at first came from the West. It is the signal of human value in the Western cultural background and the product of the modern enlightening philosophy. Modern human rights exhibit individualism, liberalism, rationalism, and other innate characteristics of the Western modern culture. Modern concept of human rights signifies that the West has completely broken away from the traditional world and opened the modern world schema and conception schema of the Western capitalism. Therefore, modern concepts of human rights just reflect the meaning image of human in this concrete historical process, the concrete region and the concrete culture of the Western world. After Nietzsche's calling "God is dead", modern human rights and the concepts of these rights turned up on the Western stage and extended along with the Western modernization. We can say that the concept of human rights is a combination of all the Western modern ideas, which was already fully exposed by the enlightenment thinkers like Hobbes, Locke, Rousseau and Kant, and so on. For the non-West, the internationalization of the concept of human rights at least reflects some kind of impulse of the Western modernization. This kind of impulse is the pursuit final historical result of Western modernization or the maintenance of universal hegemony of Western rationalism. Therefore, the Western concept of human rights is not out of the moral consideration of all the human beings and it at least implies some kind of rational tricks of the Western culture. So, unless China takes the road of Western modernization, the transformation of the concept of human rights is inevitable, that is, the cultural transformation of the discourse of rights—to carry out the local cultural explanation of the theoretic connotation of the concept of human rights.

9.4.2 Inheritance of the Traditional Theory System

When facing the traditional culture of human rights, China lacks the necessary confidence and always doubts about the truth of our own culture of human rights. Generally speaking, for there is no such Western definition of rights and no clear concept corresponding to right, so we always lack confidence and feel short than others whenever talking about the ancient human rights. And there is another idea that though ancient China has no human rights we have a lot of theoretic resources that can be connected with the Western right and the future work is to join our ancient cultural resources into the main stream of Western human rights. Then, on the one hand, we can obtain some confidence, that is, it is a matter of time to achieve the Western human rights; on the other hand, the need of the human rights politics can be satisfied because all that is needed is a little modification and this idea can be used against the monologue of the Western universal human rights. However, if we look further into these two attitudes, they both hold tightly to the Western human rights and do not treat the tradition in a friendly way. If we do not erase these ideas out, it will be very harmful for China. Therefore, when facing the tradition, we should notice at first that culture of human rights is not the patent of the West and our the Eastern world has already had our own theory of human rights. Although there are no such concepts and statements of modern human rights in any school of human rights theory, these theories have certain propositions of human rights and their own thinking vision at that time. So, if we want to truly get into the ancient culture of human rights, we must break the shackles of the modern Western concept of rights and throw away the absolute antitradition deconstruction thinking and get into the Eastern culture of human rights with the idea containing the universal moral concept of right of the ancient and the modern and the Western and the Eastern. Only in this way can we avoid analyzing our ancestors' thinking and practice of human rights by modern system of human language and concepts. Therefore, China should not only treat our own ancient theory of human rights friendly but also need to get deep into our ancestors' context of human rights, reconsider their question consciousness, basic ideas and theoretic vision, and inherit the cultural traditions. Inherit the past to open the future and return to the root to open the new.

9.4.3 Reconstruction of the Modern Culture of Human Rights

As mentioned above, in order to solve the question whether human rights are Eastern or Western, China must complete the cultural transformation of human rights; in order to solve the question whether human rights are traditional or modern, China must inherit the already existing system of human rights. On the basis of the above questions, the reconstruction of modern human rights should combine the Western with the Eastern, inherit the local traditional culture of human rights, create a new theory of human rights, and form modern values of human rights and theoretic definitions. And the crux of the problem is to solve the question of the understanding of Chinese modernization. This question includes: is Chinese modernization a copy of Western modernization? If not, what kind of way of modernization should China take? What is the Eastern modernization question? To the Western meaning schema of the world and human after the enlightenment, what kind of attitude should China take? Facing the tidal wave of the Western neoliteralism derived from the globalization, how should China response to and explain? etc. For example, as for Chinese issue of modernization, Mr. Jin Yaoji has conducted valuable considerations. Considering that the world modernization movement fully develops and the antimodernization impulse is still in the ascendant, he thinks that Chinese modernization cannot be simply considered as China's being rich and strong and basically speaking, it is a historical process to find a new order of civilization. Therefore, China's problem is not the problem whether a new modern civilization is needed but the one how to construct what kind of new modern civilization [9]. And so does the modernization of Chinese culture of human rights. It needs embrace and also criticism; it needs deconstruction and also construction. In conclusion, China must stand on cultural independence and create new definitions of Chinese modern values of the world and life on this base. Only through this way can China truly provide a modern schema of life's meaning and image, reconstruct its own culture of human rights, and find the spiritual home of human rights.

Acknowledgments This chapter was originally written in Chinese by two scholars, including Xiao Junyong, Associate Professor from Department of Law at the University of International Relations and Tang Jianfei, Associate Professor from School of Law at Jiangxi University of Finance and Economics. I am permitted by original scholars to get it included here in this book as a chapter based on my translation, which was first published in *China Legal Science*. (Vol. 2008/1. pp. 51–57.).

References

1. Cowan, J. K., Dembour, M-B, & Wilson, R. A. (2001). *Culture and rights: Anthropological perspectives* (pp. 2–3). Cambridge: Cambridge University Press.
2. Cowan, J. K., Dembour, M-B, & Wilson, R. A. (2001). *Culture and rights: Anthropological perspectives* (p. 4). Cambridge: Cambridge University Press.
3. Donnelly, J. (1989). *Universal human rights in theory and practice* (p. 1). Ithaca: Cornell University Press.
4. Brems, E. (2001). *Human rights: university and diversity* (pp. 4–5). The Netherlands: Kluwer Law International.
5. Cowan, J. K., Dembour, M-B, & Wilson, R. A. (2001). *Culture and rights: Anthropological perspectives* (p. 8). Cambridge: Cambridge University Press.
6. Monshipouri, M. (2002). Islam and human rights in the age of globalization. In A. Mohammadi (Ed.), *Islamic encountering globalization* (pp. 100–101). London: Routledge Curzon.

7. Cowan, J. K., Dembour, M-B, & Wilson, R. A. (2001). *Culture and rights: Anthropological perspectives* (p. 11). Cambridge: Cambridge University Press.
8. Brems, E. (2001). *Human rights: University and diversity* (p. 23). The Netherlands: Kluwer Law International.
9. Jin, Y. (2002). On China's "modernization" and "modernity". In Y. Jin (Ed.), *Self-selections of Jin Yaoji* (p. 89). Shanghai: Shanghai Education Press.

Chapter 10
Several Issues on the Formation of a Socialist Legal System with Chinese Characteristics

Abstract This chapter studies the issues on the formation of a socialist legal system with Chinese characteristics, starting with the formation of a socialist legal system with Chinese characteristics, exploring the basic features and significance of the socialist legal system with Chinese characteristics, and ending with playing a further important role of local legislation.

Under the new situation of the Party and the country's thorough study and implementation of the spirit of the Fifth Plenary Session of the Seventeenth Session of the Party, we are here today holding the Sixteenth National Local Legislative Seminar, discussing in-depth the issues of a socialist legal system with Chinese characteristics. It is of great significance for the formation of a socialist legal system with Chinese characteristics, and for building a socialist country under the rule of law.

Now, I make a few comments, to explore with comrades.

10.1 The Formation of a Socialist Legal System with Chinese Characteristics

The 15th National Congress of Communist Party of China (CPC) proposed the goal of the formation of a socialist legal system with Chinese characteristics by 2010. The 16th National Congress of CPC reiterated this goal and the 17th National Congress of CPC set forth the task to perfect the socialist legal system

---

The Chinese version of this chapter is the speech of Comrade Wang Zhaoguo at the Sixteenth National Seminar of Local Legislation (November 11th), which was originally published in *People's Daily*/2010-11-15/Page 06/News.Wang Zhaoguo is the former Vice-Chairman of the Standing Committee of National People's Congress, who authorized me to translate his Chinese version into English and include the English translation in this book as a chapter.

P. Sun, *Human Rights Protection System in China*,
DOI: 10.1007/978-3-642-39663-2_10, © Springer-Verlag Berlin Heidelberg 2014

with Chinese characteristics. At the first meeting of the Eleventh Session of the Standing Committee of the National People's Congress, Wu Bangguo, Chairman of the National People's Congress, puts forth a clear goal for the legislative work, under the premise of improving the quality of legislation, ensuring the formation and continual improvement of the socialist legal system with Chinese characteristics by 2010.

Over 30 years of reform and opening-up, under the leadership of the Communist Party of China, after unremitting efforts in all areas, so far, China has developed 237 pieces of the Constitution and existing laws, more than 690 pieces of administrative regulations, and more than 8,600 pieces of local laws and regulations. China has laws to obey generally in all aspects of economic, political, cultural, social, and ecological civilization constructions. A multilevel and multisectoral legal system of socialism with Chinese characteristics having the Constitution as the commander will be formed based on China's national conditions, adapting to the requirements of the primary stage of socialism, reflecting the unification of the Party's views and the will of the people, and being in line with the reform and opening-up, and socialist modernization drive.

Viewed from the formation process, the socialist legal system with Chinese characteristics fully reflects three aspects of these "compatibilities." One is compatible with national conditions in the primary stage of socialism. China is and will be at the primary stage of socialism for a long time, which determines that the establishment of China's legal system must start from the characteristics of this stage, and cannot be divorced from these characteristics. Otherwise, it will become a river without water, and a tree without roots. The second one is compatible with the reform and opening-up and socialist modernization drive. The features of tasks for reform and opening-up and for modernization drive are different, which have different requirements of the law, and provide different conditions for development and implementation of laws. The legal system construction must firmly be based on the requirements for the reform and opening-up and for modernization drive, and firmly based on the requirements of building a socialist country ruled by law. It can be neither divorced from reality nor beyond it, nor to pursue the system *per se*. The third one is compatible with the formation of the legal system itself. The process of the formation and the continuous improvement of the legal system reflect not only economic and social development and constant changes, but also the rule of the legal system itself. The legal system must undergo a process from nonexistence to existence, from the initial formation to the general formation and then to the formation, and through continuous improvement until its state of being more mature.

Viewed from the legal system itself, in order to understand the formation of the legal system of socialism with Chinese characteristics, it is necessary to understand the following four aspects: First, the legal departments should be complete, covering all aspects of the social relations; second, the basic and major laws should be developed out in the various legal departments; third, the law acts as a backbone, and the corresponding administrative regulations, local regulations, autonomous regulations and specific regulations should be drawn up and match with the law;

fourth, the legal system should achieve the unity of science and harmony within itself. Measured by the above symbols, China has formed a socialist legal system with Chinese characteristics with the Constitution as commander in chief, the law as the backbone, including administrative regulations, local regulations, autonomous regulations, specific regulations, etc., and consisting of the Constitution-related laws, civil and commercial law, administrative law, economic law, social law, criminal law, litigation and nonlitigation procedure laws, and other legal departments as a unified whole. In the various legal departments, the basic and major laws, especially the laws as supportive frameworks, have been generally worked out, and the corresponding administrative regulations and local regulations have been more complete to match the law. Broadly speaking, there are a greater number of rules and regulations playing an important regulatory role in social life as well. In addition, after the concentrated clean-up of laws, administrative and local regulations, the legal system has basically united science and harmony from within itself.

Accurate understanding of the formation of the socialist legal system with Chinese characteristics also needs the understanding of the following points:

First, while looking at the formation of a legal system, we must judge it from its role it is going to play. Building a legal system is aiming to solve the problem so that there are laws to go by. Whether the legal system has been formed or not, cannot simply be judged by how many laws have been already made. The basic and major laws, especially the supporting laws as backbones, have been made in China's current economic, political, cultural, social, and other aspects. A socialist legal system with Chinese characteristics has generally been able to adapt to our country's current requirements of economic and social development. Of course, this is not to say, the existing laws are sufficient; after the formation of the legal system, we still need to develop new laws according to the changing circumstances, and amend the existing laws without delay.

Second, while looking at the formation of a legal system, we must look at it as a whole. We must look at not only laws but also the administrative regulations and local regulations, which are important components of China's legal system and play a coordinating part in regulating social relations. Some items are provided in the Constitution, some provisions should be made in law, and some may be provided by administrative regulations and local regulations. Legal norms at all levels play a role in their respective fields, carrying out their own duties. As for the conditions not fit to use the law to regulate, administrative regulations can be established by law, and after gaining experience, once the conditions are satisfied, the law can thus be made; for some of the local affairs, local regulations can be developed according to law.

Third, while looking at the formation of the legal system, we must start from China's national conditions and reality. The world docs not and cannot have a unified legal system criterion for evaluation. Due to different national conditions, the content and form of the legal system will be different in different countries. Building the legal system, at any time, must be based on national conditions. The laws that the foreign legal system has are not the ones that we must have. And the laws that the foreign legal system does not have are not the ones that we cannot develop. We do not make laws if they do not meet China's national conditions and practice. But to meet our real-life needs, we must formulate them promptly. We need to learn, but not copy from other countries' experience.

In addition, to understand the formation of the legal system, we also need to pay attention to the command of the relation between the legal norms and other social norms. Means of regulating social relations have always been varied, in addition to legal norms, there are national policies introduced in a certain period, policy measures in a particular area, as well as norms in professions, moral norms, social customs, and so on. Not all problems have to be resolved by legislation, nor are the more legal norms the better. Only if there is a real need to use legal means to regulate, we should consider the development of legal norms; if there can be adjustment through other means, there is no need for laws. We must not only give the legal system a full role to play, but also give other social norms a full role to play.

In short, an in-depth understanding of the formation of the socialist legal system with Chinese characteristics must start from the history and background of China, along with a comprehensive understanding of the historical mission and role of the socialist legal system with Chinese characteristics; starting from an objective reality and having always based on China's basic national conditions and practical needs of the primary stage of socialism.

10.2 Basic Features of the Socialist Legal System with Chinese Characteristics

The socialist legal system with Chinese characteristics is an important part of the great cause of socialism with Chinese characteristics. It is a foundation for the basic strategy to fully implement the rule of law, and for building a socialist country ruled by law, and it has been a concentrated reflection of institutionalization and legalization of practical experience of economic and social development since a new China was founded over 60 years ago, especially since reform and opening-up over 30 years ago, which has very distinctive characteristics.

10.2.1 This Legal System Reflects the Essential Requirements of Socialism with Chinese Characteristics

The nature of a country's legal system is determined by the nature of its social system. China is a socialist country led by the working class and based on the alliance of workers and peasants, the people's democratic dictatorship. In the primary stage of socialism, China implements a basic economic system with public ownership as the main body and is developing diverse forms of ownership. This determines that the nature of the legal system to be built must be a socialist system with Chinese characteristics. It takes Deng Xiaoping Theory and the important thinking of "Three Represents" as guidance, thoroughly implementing the Scientific Outlook on Development, upholding the Party's leadership with the people as the masters, administering the country according to law. All the legal norms included, the whole legal system established must be beneficial to the consolidation and development of the socialist system in order to reflect the common will of the people, safeguarding people's fundamental interests and the essential requirements of the people as masters of the country. These are the essential differences between the system based on public ownership of the socialist legal system with Chinese characteristics and the system based on private ownership of the legal system of capitalism. What laws need to be developed, what laws need not to be developed and what are the specific content of the legal system, which must start from the essential requirements of socialism, from the reality of the primary stage of the socialist system with Chinese characteristics, and from the fundamental will and long-term interests of the people.

10.2.2 This Legal System Reflects the Requirements of Our Times for Reform and Opening-Up and Socialist Modernization Drive

The most distinctive feature of the new era is reform and opening-up. China's reform and opening-up, as the great contemporary social practice, provides the establishment and improvement of the legal system with a magnificent stage. A socialist legal system with Chinese characteristics, which has distinctive characteristics of the era, is accompanied by reform and opening-up and modernization drive, promoting each other. On the one hand, the reform and opening-up and modernization drive provide the internal needs and motive for the establishment of the legal system, providing the basis of practice and experience. The more reform and opening-up and modernization drive move forward, the more profound changes in economic and social development will take place; the more urgent requirement is to improve and perfect the legal system, the more solid foundation of the legal system is to be laid. On the other hand, the construction of a legal system provides reform and opening-up and modernization drive with the legal environment, which will play an active role in promotion, norms, guidelines and guarantees, paying attention to properly handling the relationship between legal stability and reform variability, and confirming the existing success in time and consolidating the existing fruits of reform and opening-up, and leaving room for further reform and opening-up at the same time.

10.2.3 This Legal System Reflects the Unification of Internal Structure and Multilevel Scientific Requirements

After the founding of the People's Republic of China, a unified, multiethnic, unitary socialist country has been established. Due to historical reasons, economic and social development is very unbalanced all over our country. Correspondingly, under the premise of the highest organ of the state power concentrating in the exercise of legislative power, China has gradually established a unified and hierarchical system of legislation by following the constitutional principles with the central leadership and by giving full play to the local initiative and enthusiasm in order to enable the law both to come into force all over the country, to adapt to the needs of vastly different circumstances of each place, and to be workable in practice. Practice has shown that this legislative system is in line with China's national situations and it is effective. And corresponding to this legislative system, the socialist legal system with Chinese characteristics has shown a unified and multilevel feature in the structure. Not only the NPC and its Standing Committee have enacted laws, but also the State Council has enacted administrative rules and regulations, and the local people's congresses and their standing committees have developed local regulations based on statutory authority as well. This legislative system also determines the status and role of each component in the legal system. Generally speaking, the Constitution is the commander, the law is the backbone, administrative and local regulations are the refinement of and supplementation to the national law. They are developed by different legislative organs in accordance with the legislative authority prescribed by the Constitution and laws, distinguishing from different levels with different effects. They are an integral part of the socialist legal system with Chinese characteristics, constituting a complete unity in line with scientific requirements of being unified, systematic and hierarchical.

10.2.4 This Legal System Reflects the Cultural Requirements of Inheriting the Fine Traditions of the Chinese Legal Culture

The establishment of a socialist legal system with Chinese characteristics has always been based on the basic national situations, starting from the reality and insisting that inheriting and passing on the historical tradition, drawing on the achievements of civilization and undergoing the institutional innovation should be integrated in order to make the past serve the present and adapt foreign things to Chinese use, and incorporate things of a diverse nature, fully reflecting the advanced, compatible and universal cultural nature of this legal system. On the one hand, the Chinese legal system has inherited the fine ingredients of Chinese legal culture and adapted to the needs of reform and opening-up and modernization drive for institutional innovation. On the other hand, this legal system has fully absorbed the achievements of human's legal civilization, drawing on the useful experience of foreign countries, but it is not a simple copy. It has absorbed things beneficial for our own use according to China's national conditions and reality. Practice has proved that we can go on the socialist road of the rule of law with Chinese characteristics not only by carrying forward China's fine legal cultural traditions but also by learning from the achievements of human's legal civilization, which is in line with China's national conditions, adapting to the trend of the times.

10.2.5 This Legal System Reflects the Developmental Requirements of Being Dynamic, Open and Keeping Pace with the Times

After over 30 years of efforts, the country has laws to obey at present in all aspects of national economic, political, cultural, and social life in general. However, we must see that social practice serves as a foundation of the law, and that the law is the summary of the practical experience while the law continuously develops with the development of social practice. Practice is endless, and the legal system should keep pace with the times and should be constantly innovative. It must be dynamic, open, developing, rather than static, closed, and fixed. Our country is and will be in the primary stage of socialism for a long time. The whole country is still in the stage of institutional reform and social transformation, and the socialist system also requires constant self-improvement and development. There is also a process of improvement for the economic system of socialist market, and thus the socialist legal system with Chinese characteristics, reflecting and regulating the socialist and economic system, must integrate stability with volatility, phased features with forward-looking ones. The legal system, having to adapt to the practical needs of our national economic and social development and the process of the rule of law, will develop and improve continuously. Social reality has changed, and the legal system has to change and adapt to the changed social reality. With constant development of an economic society, we need make new legal norms in time, amend the existing legal norms, and repeal the outdated legal norms and the legal norms that do not meet the needs of social reality. Therefore, we cannot look at the legal system with a static and an isolated vision, but we should always preserve an attitude of development and openness.

10.3 Significance of Establishing the Socialist Legal System with Chinese Characteristics

The formation of the socialist legal system with Chinese characteristics is of great significance. It is an important milestone for our country's construction of socialist democracy and legal system, reflecting the significant achievements of reform and opening-up and reflecting the inherent requirements and practical needs to construct the socialism with Chinese characteristics.

10.3.1 It Is of Great Significance for Upholding the Political Development Path of Socialism with Chinese Characteristics, for the Development of Socialist Democracy, and for Promoting the Building of a Socialist Country Ruled by Law

A socialist legal system with Chinese characteristics, firmly based on the actual situation in China, established the people's congress system as the fundamental political system, and established the multiparty cooperation and political consultation system led by the Communist Party of China, and established a system of regional ethnic autonomy and a system of grassroots self-government and other democratic political systems. This will provide a solid legal foundation for the Party's leadership, for the masses' master status and the rule by law, and this will provide a legal guarantee to ensure that all the work of the State is done in accordance with the law, and ensure that the Party is leading the broad masses of the people as masters, managing state and social affairs and economic and cultural undertakings in accordance with the Constitution and the law through various channels and forms. The formation of socialist legal system with Chinese characteristics has an important role to play in ensuring the Party in governing and rejuvenating a nation, leading all peoples in building socialism with Chinese characteristics, and ensuring the national unity, peoples' solidarity, economic development, social progress, and long-term stability. It will comprehensively promote the administration in accordance with the law, constantly deepen the administrative system reform, speed up the transformation of government functions, and strive to build a government ruled by law. It will actively promote the judicial system reform, playing a full role of the judicial system and judiciary organs in achieving justice, improving judicial efficiency, and safeguarding social fairness and justice. It will protect national economic, political, cultural, and social life of the normal order to maintain the long-term social stability and fully implement the basic strategy of the rule of law, and accelerate the construction of a socialist country ruled by law.

10.3.2 It Is Important for Adhering to Reform and Opening-Up, for Establishing and Improving the Socialist Market Economy System, and for Promoting the Socialist Modernization Drive

Since reform and opening-up, according to the requirements of further emancipating and developing productive forces, and according to the objectives and requirements of establishing and perfecting the socialist market economy system reform, the state developed a series of laws and regulations to guide and regulate the market economy, to maintain the market economy order, and to ensure that national economic activity under the macro control and management. It will provide effective legal protection for the construction of a unified, open, competitive, and orderly modern market system, for improving macro-control system, and for promoting economic development rapidly, healthily, and sustainably. The formation of a socialist legal system with Chinese characteristics has a significant role to play in adhering to the reform and opening-up, in resolving deep-seated contradictions within the economic system with great efforts, in getting rid of all kinds of structural and institutional obstacles in the socialist modernization drive. It is of great significance for the efforts to build a dynamic, highly efficient and more open institutional mechanism conducive to scientific development. It is significant for the liberation and development of social productive forces, for greatly arousing the enthusiasm of the masses in building socialism with Chinese characteristics, and for further promoting the economic, political, cultural, social, and ecological civilization construction, and for substantially increasing the overall national strength and building a moderately prosperous society.

10.3.3 It Is Important for Adhering to Being People-Oriented, for Protecting and Improving People's Livelihood, and for Promoting a Socialist Harmonious Society

A socialist legal system with Chinese characteristics provides a legal guarantee, which will insist on people-orientation, respecting, and safeguarding human rights, safeguarding the legitimate rights and interests of citizens, and promoting the comprehensive development of the people. Since reform and opening-up, the state has specially focused on institutionally solving the safeguarding issues of citizens' rights and interests. China's Constitution stipulates that the state respects and guarantees human rights. Our legal system has made further specific provisions from different aspects of citizens' economic rights, political rights, cultural rights and social rights. It guarantees citizens' wide range of practical, full, true freedom and rights at both substantive and procedural levels, fully reflecting the superiority of the socialist system in safeguarding human rights, which is conducive to the realization, maintenance, and development of the fundamental interests of the overwhelming majority of people according to law. The formation of a socialist legal system with Chinese characteristics has an important role to play in the Party and the country's constantly expanding people's democracy and ensuring that people are the masters. It is important to stick to the path of prosperity, for the people to share the development results, to develop cultural and educational undertakings and increase investment and support in education, science and technology, culture, health, and other fields. It is also important to realize cultural, educational, and other rights of the citizens, to protect people's rights and interest according to law, to further protect and improve people's livelihood and to build a socialist harmonious society

10.3.4 It Is of Great Significance for the Realization of National Prosperity and the Great Rejuvenation of the Chinese Nation

In the world, China is an ancient civilized country with a long history, having created a splendid culture. Modern China gradually went downhill because of its slowly becoming a semi-colonial and semi-feudal country. The Communist Party of China led the Chinese people through a hard struggle to establish a new regime, and it has been making unremitting efforts to achieve national prosperity and national rejuvenation. Since the reform and opening-up, great achievements have been made in the cause of constructing socialism with Chinese characteristics. However, our country is still a large developing country. China, as an old large country, has 1.3 billion people with a unique history for thousands of years but with a late starting democracy and legal system, and it is an emerging power with a rapid economic development and rapid social transformation. In such conditions, it is difficult to carry out socialist modernization drive. To achieve national prosperity and the great rejuvenation of the Chinese nation, there must be a complete and modern legal system consistent with China's conditions as a support. The formation of a socialist legal system with Chinese characteristics has an important role to play. It is a historical achievement of the CPC's consciously using the concepts of governance ruled by law to guide legal practice, which is important for the people to change old ideas and to establish a socialist concept of the rule by law, to comprehensively promote governing the country ruled by law, to build a socialist country ruled by law, and ultimately realize the national prosperity and the great rejuvenation of the Chinese nation.

10.4 Playing a Further Important Role of Local Legislation in the Socialist Legal System with Chinese Characteristics

In order to adapt to the requirements of the new legislative work, as early as December 1978, Comrade Deng Xiaoping made an important speech of "Emancipating the mind, seeking truth from facts, and looking forward in the union": "Now the legislative workload is great ... some regulations can try at local level, and then after a summary for improvement, the law for the whole country is developed." According to this spirit, in 1979, the Organic Law of the People's Republic of China on the Local People's Congresses and Local People's Governments was revised at the Second Session of the Fifth NPC, which has experienced an important reform of China's legislative system, giving the power to the people's congresses of provinces, autonomous regions, municipalities and their standing committees to formulate local regulations. In 1982, the Constitution was clearly developed with these provisions contained within. The local organic law revised later also gave the power the people's congresses and their standing committees of the provinces, of the cities where the people's government of autonomous region is located, and of the large cities approved by the State Council to formulate local regulations. In addition, Legislation Law and other relevant laws and decisions also make provisions for the local legislative authority. The Constitution and the law give broad space for local legislation.

For over 30 years' reform and opening-up, local people's congresses and their standing committees have developed a large number of local regulations, based on the specific circumstances of the place, starting from the actual needs of local reform and opening-up and economic and social development, conscientiously fulfilling legislative mandates provided by the Constitution and the law, and carrying out legislative work according to local conditions. So far, the provinces, autonomous regions and municipalities directly under the Central Government have developed 5,079 pieces of regulations, which are currently in force; provincial capitals and large municipalities have developed 2,500 pieces of regulations currently in force; autonomous regions have developed 786 pieces of autonomous regulations and specific regulations currently in force; and special economic zones have developed 237 pieces of regulations currently in force. Local legislation has provided legal guarantees for local places to push forward reform and opening-up, to achieve fast economic and social development, to provide a strong support for national legislation, and make important contributions to ensuring that the legal system of socialism with Chinese characteristics is scheduled to form.

In the new situation, the local people's congresses and their standing committees are seizing the opportunity to face the challenges, carrying out legislative work, further playing the important role of the local legislation in the national legislation, and making new contributions to the formation and perfection of socialism with Chinese characteristics. Here, I make a few remarks for the working reference.

10.4.1 Pay Close Attention to Completing the Task and Ensure the Legal System of Socialism with Chinese Characteristics Scheduled to Be Formed

This year is an iconic year for the formation of the socialist legal system with Chinese characteristics. At present, time is very pressing, and the local people's congresses and their standing committees must pay close attention to all aspects of the work by comparing with main working points and plans drawn up at the beginning of the year. First, we must concentrate on completing the clean-up work of local regulations. Concentrating on the clean-up work of the laws, administrative regulations, local regulations are an important measure to ensure the scientific and harmonious unity of the socialist legal system with Chinese characteristics, and it is an important task to ensure the socialist legal system with Chinese characteristics as scheduled to be formed. Since last year, the local people's congresses and their standing committees have attached great importance to the clean-up work of local regulations, which is progressing smoothly. From a nationwide perspective, up to the end of October this year, 1,317 pieces of local regulations have been modified and 426 pieces of local regulations have been repealed, which better solves the problems of inconsistencies, the lack of adaptation and coordination existing in local regulations. At present, the clean-up work of local regulations is nearly ended and the localities should be in accordance with the requirements and time schedule, paying close attention to doing a good job and ensuring the timely completion of the clean-up task. Next, we would do a good follow-up work for cleaning up: Those regulations in need of an integration and modification must be included in the legislative plan for the future, and close attention must be paid to the modification. Based on the legal clean-up situations and the higher-level laws, for the supporting regulations in need of being formulated by the localities, we must lose no time in working them out. In the end of this clean-up work, each locality must make a timely summary and fix some of the successful practices as important experience for future clean-up work and other work. Through the clean-up work, we must constantly improve the consciousness and initiative of local legislation consistent with the central legislation, effectively ensuring the scientific and harmonious unity of the socialist legal system with Chinese characteristics throughout the local legislative work. Second, we must carry out the research work of the legal system. We must take this opportunity of the formation of the socialist legal system with Chinese characteristics, combined with the local legislative reality, to actively conduct the theoretical research, to deepen the understanding of the socialist legal system with Chinese characteristics, to deepen the understanding of the position and role of the local legislation in the socialist legal system with Chinese characteristics, to further deepen the understanding of the importance of the local legislative work in the new situation, to make the efforts to form the theoretical results, and effectively improve the theoretical level. Third, we must do well in the publicity work of the socialist legal system with Chinese characteristics. Through seminars, workshops, reports, and other media as well as a variety of media such as newspapers, radio, television, and network, we must actively publicize the great achievements in China's legislative work since the reform and opening-up, and publicize the significance of the formation of the socialist legal system with Chinese characteristics and the important contributions made by local legislation to local reform and opening-up and to local economic and social development, creating a favorable atmosphere of public opinion for the formation of the socialist legal system with Chinese characteristics.

10.4.2 Conscientiously Summarize Experience, and Continuously Improve the Ability and Levels to Carry Out the Local Legislative Work

The great practice of building the socialist legal system with Chinese characteristics is in an urgent need of our comprehensive, in-depth, and systematic summary. For over 30 years of reform and opening-up, the local people's congresses and their standing committees have carried out the vivid legislative practice by following the legislative authority conferred by the Constitution and laws, playing a full role of their initiative, enthusiasm, and creativity. They have carried out a large number of useful explorations and accumulated a lot of fresh experience either in the aspect of implementing legislation, or in the autonomous legislation, or in the first attempt of the legislation. Each locality should produce a better summary job, closely combined with the local reality and based on the last year's summary of 30 years' experience of the local standing committees in the legislative work since their establishment. Through summary, we must carefully review the developing path of the local legislation since the reform and opening-up, and have an in-depth understanding of the outstanding achievements of local legislative work and an important role to play in promoting local economic and social development, and constantly enhance the sense of accomplishment and pride engaged in legislative work. Through summary, we must systematically comb the valuable experience that local legislative work has accumulated, and have a better grasp of the characteristics and rules of the local legislative work, and constantly improve the ability and raise the level to carry out the local legislative work, and effectively improve the quality of local legislation. Through summary, we must have a deep understanding of the extreme importance to maintain the authority of the Constitution and the law, and further increase the initiative to ensure national uniformity of legal system, and more positively create the conditions and provide guarantees for the effective implementation of the Constitution and the law in their respective administrative areas. Through summary, we must fully be aware of the great achievements made in the construction of socialist democracy and legal system in our country since the reform and opening-up, and further strengthen the confidence and determination in building a socialist country ruled by law, and constantly enhance the consciousness of fully implementing the fundamental strategy of the rule by law.

10.4.3 Correctly Grasp the Situation and Plan the Next Tasks for Local Legislative Work as Soon as Possible

The formation of the socialist legal system with Chinese characteristics marks that China's legal construction has entered a new historical stage. With the in-depth development of the reform and the deepening of an economic society, the requirements of the legislative work will become increasingly high in all aspects, and the legislative work will be increasingly more difficult, and thus the task is still arduous for future legislative work. After the formation of the socialist legal system with Chinese characteristics, the main task of legislative work is to constantly improve this system and meanwhile actively promote and ensure the effective implementation of the Constitution and laws according to the changing needs of China's economic, political, cultural, and social development. The local people's congresses and their standing committees should have a profound understanding of new situations and new problems brought about by the changes in the international and domestic situations, comprehensively grasping the new issues and challenges for local legislative work, and further strengthen their sense of mission and responsibility of the local legislative work in the new situation. First, we should make an early plan to clarify the coming-period goals and direction of the local legislative work as early as possible, and be clear about them in mind. Especially in conjunction with the national "Twelfth Five-Year Plan" and the local plans of economic and social development, we should make good programs and plans of the local legislative work in advance. With the deepening of reform and opening-up and socialist modernization, and with fully implementing the basic strategy of governing the country by law, we should carry out the local legislative work according to law, more targeted according to local practice. Local legislation will be promising whether in the service of national reform, development and stability or in more effectively promoting local economic and social development. Second, we should give priority to serving scientific development and to giving prominence to local characteristics, strive to make the regulations more suitable to the actual needs of the region's economic and social development and effectively provide institutional support in order to promote mode transformation of economic development, to achieve sustainable economic and social development, and strengthen the construction of the resource-saving and an environmentally friendly society. Third, we should always adhere to people-orientation and actively adapt to the new requirements and new expectations of the broad masses based on local practice of economic and social development, having in-depth understanding of the masses' interests and concern, and make efforts to achieve, safeguard, and develop the fundamental interests of a good majority of the masses. Fourth, we should positively create working mechanisms, continuously explore new ways and methods of scientific and democratic legislation, and take active measures to provide more practical and effective ways for realizing the people's rights to know, to participate, to express and to supervise in the state and social affairs in the new situation.

It should be particularly emphasized here that the great achievements in the construction of democracy and legal system in China have been made under the leadership of the Communist Party of China since the reform and opening-up. They are the results of the organic unity of our adhering to the leadership of the Party for a long time, the people as the masters, and the state ruled by law. They are the results of our adhering to the political development road of socialism with Chinese characteristics for a long time. Practice has proved that China's current political system is in line with China's national conditions and the reality. Socialist Legal system with Chinese characteristics is gradually formed and constantly improved, reflecting steady reform and continuous improvement of China's political system, reflecting self-improvement and continual maturity of the socialist system with Chinese characteristics. The local people's congresses and their standing committees should fully play an important role as the organs of state power, and should always adhere to the political development road of socialism with Chinese characteristics and constant improvement of the people's congress system either in perfecting the socialist legal system with Chinese characteristics, or in the exercise of supervisory functions and other aspects.

Comrades, let us unite closely around the Party Central Committee with Comrade Hu Jintao as General Secretary, and always adhere to Deng Xiaoping Theory and the important thinking of the "Three Represents" as guidance, thoroughly implementing the unity of the Scientific Outlook on Development, adhering to the Party's leadership, people as the masters, and the country ruled by law. Forge ahead, do solid work, and strive to unswervingly push forward the formation and constant improvement of the socialist legal system with Chinese characteristics!

Chapter 11
Judicial Protection of Human Rights in China

Abstract This chapter discusses judicial protection of human rights in China, starting with the analysis of the characteristics of human-rights protection in China's criminal justice and focusing on human-rights protection of the victims, the suspects, the defendants and the criminals in order to discuss in detail the judicial protection of human rights in criminal justice.

Whether civil rights can be fully and effectively guaranteed in the field of justice or not reflects the status quo of human-rights protection, the degree of social civilization and progress, and the developing level of democracy and the rule of law in a country. China has always attached a great importance to the protection of civil rights, and has paid special attention to the protection of civil rights in the field of justice. After the founding of the People's Republic of China in 1949, especially since the reform and opening-up three decades ago, we have been regarding the judicial protection of human rights as an important task by constant improvement of legislation and by the reform and improvement of the judicial system and working mechanism, which provides for the judicial protection of human rights with the legal basis and institutional guarantees. We correct ideology of law enforcement through education and rectification, as well as the learning and great debate in order to have education of socialist legal concept, and continue to strengthen the ranks of public security and judicial organs to improve the political quality of law enforcement officers, to increase their legal knowledge and operation level, to strengthen the law enforcement capacity of the personnel of the public security and judicial organs, to investigate and punish violations of human rights in criminal cases, to promote the healthy development of the judicial

---

The Chinese version of this chapter was written by Li Zhongcheng, Deputy Director of Malfeasance Prosecutor's Office of Supreme People's Procuratorate, which was originally published in Dong Yunhu and Chang Jian (Eds.). (2009). *60 Years' Human Rights Construction in China* (pp. 122–156.). Nanchang: Jiangxi People's Press. I am permitted by the original author to include the English version as a chapter of this book based on my translation of his revised Chinese version.

P. Sun, *Human Rights Protection System in China*,
DOI: 10.1007/978-3-642-39663-2_11,

protection of human rights, and promote the healthy development of China's human-rights cause.

It should be pointed out that the rang of judicial protection of human rights is extensive, including the protection of human rights in the areas of civil litigation, administrative proceedings, criminal proceedings and the execution of punishment. Although the objectives of civil litigation is to resolve civil disputes between citizens, legal persons, and relevant organizations, to adjust the activities of civil legal relations between equal entities, it has the function to protect human rights because when citizen's civil rights have been violated, if the rights cannot be protected after consultation, seeking judicial relief, maintaining the civil rights, and resolving disputes are the most effective means to protect their own rights. The civil rights of citizens infringed are protected by the People's Court trial activities, which is a concrete manifestation of the protection of human rights. Moreover, in order to ensure that the citizens with economic difficulties and the citizens in special circumstances can afford the expenses of a lawsuit to protect their legitimate rights, the People's Court adopts the system of either exempting, or reducing or allowing deferral of the cost of litigation. If citizens believe that the specific administrative act of the state administrative organs violated their legitimate rights and interests and they need to seek judicial protection, they can bring an administrative lawsuit against the administrative organs of the state, asking the people's court to revoke the specific administrative acts of the administrative authorities to protect their legitimate rights and interests. As we all know, civil litigation and administrative proceedings are judicial activities of the People's Court, meanwhile the People's Procuratorate plays a role in supervising civil litigation and administrative proceedings in accordance with the law. Judicial protection of human rights should include human-rights protection in civil litigation and administrative proceedings. However, due to limited space, especially based on the general awareness of the people and the majority of criminal justice activities implemented in relatively closed conditions, more attention has been paid to the human-rights protection in the process, therefore, human-rights protection in the criminal justice should become the focus of our research.

11.1 The Characteristics of Human-Rights Protection in China's Criminal Justice

Human-rights protection in the criminal justice involves many aspects such as the protection of the rights of criminal victims, suspects, the defendant, and criminals. Since the founding of the People's Republic of China (PRC), especially after the reform and opening-up 30 years ago, China's protection of human rights in the criminal justice has made considerable progress and fruitful results, promoting the development of human rights. Generally speaking, human-rights protection in China's criminal justice has the following characteristics.

11.1.1 Human-Rights Protection in the Criminal Justice Has Criminal Justice Activities as the Carrier

Civil rights protection in the field of justice is to enter the judicial process and to be realized by judicial activities. If there are no criminal justice activities, we can never talk about human-rights protection in justice. Having criminal justice activities as the carrier manifests the following two aspects. On the one hand, when the rights of citizens are violated, crimes should be punished through criminal justice activities in order to safeguard their legitimate rights and interests, which is the protection of the rights of victims. Meanwhile, the crime has destructed the social order and punishment of the crime is not only to protect the social public but also to maintain the social order. On the other hand, the facts of the alleged crime involving the suspect and the defendant are to be found out through the judicial process, and criminal liability is recognized and investigated through the judicial process. In the investigation of criminal process, we have to protect the legitimate rights and interests of criminal suspects or defendants. Criminal justice activities should be conducted in accordance with the law, and the public security and judicial officers should respect and protect the legitimate rights and interests of the suspects and the defendants. In this sense, the criminal justice should become the carrier of human-rights protection both as procedures for a crime to be prosecuted and as an operating mechanism to protect the parties. Without the criminal justice, the extra-judicially investigating criminal responsibility of the suspects and defendants of the alleged crimes may not only infringe the civil rights, but also be not allowed in a country under the rule of law.

11.1.2 Human-Rights Protection in the Criminal Justice and the Rule of Law in China Developed Simultaneously

The protection of human rights in the criminal justice cannot be separated from the construction of the rule of law. After its founding, China focused on the rule of law for the protection of human rights in the criminal justice. In a nutshell, the legislation on the protection of human rights is mainly reflected in the following aspects:

First, the relevant developed rules of the organization emphasized the protection of human rights. On July 20, 1950, *Organic Principles on the People's Courts* promulgated by the Government Administration Council provides in Article 5 "After the county (city) people' courts and its sub-court accepts the case, they should seriously make an investigation for evidence, study the case, and strictly forbid the torture. In the process of trial, audience people can speak after the permission, but the order of the court must be kept." The Organic Principles clearly provide "torture strictly forbidden." On September 3, 1951, Article 9 of

Interim Organic Regulations on the People's Court of the People's Republic of China, adopted at the 12th meeting of the Central People's Government Council, provides: "Peoples of all nationalities have to use their national language for rights litigation; if necessary, the people's court should provide them with translators."

Second, legal norms were developed relating to citizens' personal freedom. On December 20, 1954, Article 2 of the *Regulations on Arrest and Detention of the People's Republic of China*, was adopted at the third meeting of the Standing Committee of the National People's Congress, which stipulates that "for the offender liable to arrest if there is a serious illness, or if they are pregnant women, or breast-feeding their babies, you can switch to the release on bail or under residential surveillance." It was then to focus on the protection of the rights of people with special circumstances who should be arrested.

Third, the content of the human-rights protection in the criminal justice was clearly provided in the Constitution. On September 20, 1954, at the first meeting of the first session of the National People's Congress, the *Constitution of the People's Republic of China* was adopted, and its Article 89 stipulates that "the personal freedom of citizens of the People's Republic of China is inviolable. Any citizen is free from arrest if not decided by the People's Court or not approved by the People's Procuratorate." In addition, Article 76 of the Constitution provides: "The accused has the right to defense."

Fourth, the protection of human rights was stressed by guidance document of judicial interpretation. Issue Seven of Judicial Work Communication (in 1955) records: *Notification and Answers about Convening a Mass Meeting on the Suppression of the Practice of the Arrest of an Offender* by the Supreme People's Court, Ministry of Justice stressed:

> Now our major social democratic reform has been basically completed, and the people's regime has significantly been strengthened, and the Constitution, the Organic Law of the People's Court, the Organic Law of the People's Procuratorate, and the Organic Law of Arrest and Detention Ordinance have been officially released, and it is apparently wrong to continue the way of arrest by the Arresting Assembly, or Big Criticism. … The problem is that the arrest of persons must comply with the law, cannot be arrested by the Arresting Assembly, which is illegal because it is against the law and wrong arrest would easily occur [1].

Fifth, not only is the focus on human-rights protection of its citizens in the criminal justice, but also on foreigners' human-rights protection in the criminal justice [1]. On June 22, 1956, the *People's Daily* published the "*Decisions on Handling the War Criminals of the Detained Japanese Invaders into China by the Standing Committee of the National People's Congress, People's Republic of China*", which provides:

> (c) The language and documents used in special military tribunals should be translated into the language understood by defendants. (d) The accused can defend themselves, or hire the lawyer registered in judicial organs of the People's Republic of China to defend him. When it deemed necessary, the special military court may also designate a defender to defend themselves. … (f) If their performance is good, the criminals sentenced to prison can be released earlier [2].

Through thc above introduction, we can see clearly that the protection of human rights in our criminal justice is based on the premise of the law, which is an important manifestation of the rule of law developed. Although we experienced a decade of the Cultural Revolution, and both the rule of law and the protection of human rights were also affected, after the smashing of the "Gang of Four," especially since the reform and opening-up, with the comprehensive economic and social development in China, the rule of law has been put to a further important position, and more attention has been paid to the protection of human rights in the criminal justice.

Legislative work has entered the fast lane, and some laws relevant to the protection of civil rights like the *Criminal Law*, the *Criminal Procedure Law*, the *Organic Law of the People's Court*, and the *Organic Law of the People's Procuratorate* were gradually promulgated. So far, China has enacted more than 200 laws and regulations in this regard. The important prerequisite of human-rights protection in the criminal justice is that the content of human-rights protection is confirmed in the law, which becomes the basis of public security and judicial protection of human rights. In this sense, the protection of human rights in the criminal justice must depend on the improvement of the legal norms. Laws alone are not sufficient to themselves, and law enforcement in accordance with the law is an important condition for the protection of human rights in the criminal justice. Exactly what we implement the idea of the protection of human rights to legal norms, the implementation in the actions of the law enforcement officers, makes the protection of human rights in the criminal justice be strengthened, improved, and sublimated in the process of the rule of law, and be implemented in criminal justice.

11.1.3 The Formation of the Concept of Human-Rights Protection in the Criminal Justice and System Design Are the Manifestation of the Achievements of China's Economic and Social Development

Law as an important part of the superstructure is determined by the economic base. Human-rights protection legislation in the criminal justice cannot be separated from economic and social development. Precisely because of the founding of New China, the Chinese people have stood up! People are the masters, and especially since the reform and opening-up, the leap of the economic and social development has promoted the smooth development of the work in our country. Legislation of human-rights protection in the criminal justice has been taken seriously and has continuously been strengthened, which provides human-rights protection in criminal justice with a legal basis. At the same time, economic development and social change have changed people's ideas. With the growing awareness of human-rights protection, the protection of human rights is not a tokenism slogan, but becomes a conscious action, and become a powerful weapon for the people to fight against the law enforcement officers with all kinds of abuse of state power and dereliction of duty. In this sense, the formation and development of the concept of human-rights protection cannot be separated from economic and social development, which is the so-called "full granaries contributing to people's observance of proprieties". Economic development and legal improvement makes human-rights protection in the criminal justice strengthened.

11.1.4 Human-Rights Protection in the Criminal Justice Has Experienced Several Shifts

Human-rights protection in the criminal justice has experienced a shift from thinking highly of punishment but belittling the protection to keeping balance between punishment and protection, a shift from thinking highly of substantial content and belittling the procedures to giving weight to both substantial content and procedures, and a shift from focusing on the protection of citizens' rights of society as a whole, in particular focusing on the protection of victims to giving equal weight both to human-rights protection of the suspects and the defendant and to all citizens' rights and victims' rights. Human-rights protection in the criminal justice is realized by law enforcement. It has been an important issue in the law enforcement on how to pay attention to the balance of law enforcement in criminal law in order to prevent deviations from stressing only one aspect and ignoring other aspects of the enforcement. It is especially the case in the area of human-rights protection. Human-rights protection in China's criminal justice has experienced a shift from focusing on the punishment of the crime to giving equal weight both to the punishment of the crime and to the protection of human rights. A crime is a serious act against the social order, and only to punish the crime according to law can maintain social harmony and stability, and can enable people to live peacefully and work happily. However, punishing criminals must be in accordance with the law in order to prevent injustice and wrong cases, which needs to safeguard the legitimate rights and interests of the suspects and the defendant, enhancing the right of defense. Thinking of rights protection after heavy punishment and attaching importance to rights protection in heavy punishment is an important manifestation of the protection of human rights in the criminal justice.

Giving equal weight to punishment and protection is achieved by focusing on both substantial content and procedures. Emphasis on punishment and focusing on substantial content are often concerned about the presence or absence of the suspect's and defendant's criminal responsibility, and ignore the importance of the procedures and their protective functions, which can easily violate human rights and lead to erroneous cases and irreparable loss. Therefore, the experience in the practice of criminal justice told us that if we would like to give equal weight to both crackdown and protection in the criminal justice we must realize this by giving equal weight to both entities and procedures. Only by adhering to both entities and procedures can we ensure proper investigation of criminal suspects and the accused for their criminal responsibility in accordance with legal procedures rather than ignoring legal procedures only to investigate their criminal responsibility, and even violating their human rights. Giving equal weight to entities and procedures and emphasizing protective functions of the procedures means investigating for criminal according to law, in which to extort confessions by torture and to collect evidence in a manner of enticement and deceit are strictly forbidden. The procedures are the operating agenda and procedural guarantees to ascertain the crime, and also the important barriers to guarantee the legitimate rights and interests of the persons prosecuted.

People have always been concerned about how to balance human-rights protection of the suspects, the accused and the protection of citizens, especially the victims in criminal justice. We have experienced a shift from stressing the maintenance of the people's interests of the whole society and emphasizing the protection of the collective human rights to respecting and protecting human rights of the suspects and the defendant. When we emphasize human-rights protection of criminal suspects or defendants, human-rights protection of the victims has also attracted more attention. It is because in the judicial practice after investigating the criminal responsibility for the crime, it is hard to gain the worthy compensation for the loss of the victim, and the loss of the victim will not be reduced because the crime has been prosecuted. In this case, how to protect the rights of the victims arouses more attention of the people. Therefore, the protection of human rights in our criminal justice also pays attention to the balance between the protection of human rights of the victims and the suspects, and the defendant.

In short, the protection of human rights in the criminal justice in China focuses on the balance of all kinds of interests, and the fulcrum of the balance is the law of the country.

11.1.5 The Protection of Human Rights in the Criminal Justice Reflects the Inheritance and Innovation, and the Combination of Localization and Use for Reference

Human-rights protection in our country's criminal justice has a historical tradition with the emphasis on the protection of human rights as early as the revolutionary regime in the liberated areas. In December 1942, Property Rights Regulations of Human-Rights Protection in the Shaanxi-Gansu-Ningxia Border Region provides in Article 10, "any arrest is not allowed to impose insults, beatings, forced confessions and forced surrendering, and trials are based on evidence rather than on oral confessions" [3]. Article 46 of current Criminal Procedure Law provides that "In the decision of all cases, stress shall be laid on evidence, investigation and study; credence shall not be readily given to oral statements." We can see the inheritance between the law for the liberated regions and the new Chinese law in the aspects of protecting human rights of the suspects and against forced confessions. The existing laws are a comprehensive reflection of the current social and political economy, the legislature is also based on the changing objective circumstances, and constantly enriching and improving the content of the protection of human rights in criminal justice. Protection of human rights in the criminal justice is not limited to only opposing to corporal punishment, and it also limits the behaviors of the mentally forced evidence. Article 43 of the Criminal Procedure Law currently in force provides: "It shall be strictly forbidden to extort confessions by torture and to collect evidence by threat, enticement, deceit or other unlawful means."

Human-rights protection in the criminal justice must be based on China's national conditions, and it cannot be divorced from China's reality. It is necessary to consider China's legal system and the legal culture, and also to learn from other countries with advanced legal system and legal culture. Especially in human-rights protection in the criminal justice, we also accelerated exchanges with the countries concerned in human-rights protection in the criminal justice including academic discussions and exchange between academia, mutual visit of the judicial department of practice, as well as learning and training on special topic. By personnel exchanges and exchanges in various forms, we publicize the achievements of human-rights protection in our country's criminal justice, expanding influence. Meanwhile, we also study and learn good methods and concepts in the protection of human rights in the countries concerned in the criminal justice system so that the theory about human-rights protection in the criminal justice becomes more profound, the concepts more updated, and the system construction more complete. It should be said, how to further strengthen the protection of human rights in the criminal justice is the subject faced by all countries in the world, therefore, based on the country's judicial system, and learning from the good experience and good practice of other countries, is one of the important methods to further promote the development of the work in human-rights protection of the criminal justice.

11.2 The Protection of Victims' Rights in the Criminal Justice

The victim, including the natural and legal persons, refers to the people who were violated by the crime. We here focus on the protection of the rights with natural persons as victims. The Criminal Procedure Law in China confirmed that the victim is the party to the court proceedings, which is of great significance for better protection of human rights in the criminal justice.

11.2.1 *Basic Content of the Protection of the Victims' Rights in the Criminal Justice*

According to China's law, the rights of victims in the criminal justice can be listed as follows:

(1) The right to use their native language in court proceedings. Article 9 of the Criminal Procedure Law of the People's Republic of China (PRC) provides:

> Citizens of all nationalities shall have the right to use their native spoken and written languages in court proceedings. The People's Courts, the People's Procuratorates and the public security organs shall provide translations for any party [4] to the court proceedings who is not familiar with the spoken or written language commonly used in the locality. Where people of a minority nationality live in a concentrated community or where a number of nationalities live together in one area, court hearings shall be conducted in the spoken language commonly used in the locality, and judgments, notices and other documents shall be issued in the written language commonly used in the locality.

China is a multiethnic country with 56 nationalities which generally have their own language and characters. This is not only the need for respect for and protection of minority language and characters but also the important guarantee of realization of the minorities as the masters. The protection of the rights of ethnic minorities in the criminal proceedings starts from the respect for their language. Our judiciary cases involving minority citizens in ethnic minority autonomous areas have been heard in the local minority language, as well as using ethnic minority languages and Chinese characters to make legal instruments. If the victim is not familiar with the local common language, translation will be provided. Thus, it will be conducive to ethnic minority victims' participating in the proceedings and defending their legitimate rights and interests.

(2) The right to charges. Article 14 of the Criminal Procedure Law of the PRC provides: "Participants in proceedings shall have the right to file charges against judges, procurators and investigators whose acts infringe on their citizen's procedural rights or subject their persons to indignities." If the acts of judges, procurators, and investigators infringe on the victims' personal rights or personal insults in criminal proceedings, the victims have the right to file charges to the discipline inspection and supervision departments of the unit where judicial officers work and to their leaders, and they can also file a complaint to the People's Procuratorate according to law, seeking the protection and investigating the responsibility of the perpetrator for infringement of their human rights.
(3) Apply for the right to withdrawal. Article 28 of the Criminal Procedure Law of the PRC provides: "In any of the following situations, a member of the judicial, procuratorial or investigatory personnel shall voluntarily withdraw, and the parties to the case and their legal representatives shall have the right to demand his withdrawal." The victims' right to withdrawal is conducive to the fairness of the trial, which can eliminate the victims' doubt about the litigation

process and the fairness of the outcome of the litigation, and reduce unnecessary complaints and petitions. However, according to the provisions of Article 30 of the Criminal Procedure Law, "An investigator may not suspend investigation of a case before a decision is made on his withdrawal. If a decision has been made to reject his application for withdrawal, the party or his legal representative may apply for reconsideration once."

(4) The right to entrust agents ad litem. Article 40 of the Criminal Procedure Law of the PRC provides:

> A victim in a case of public prosecution, his legal representatives or near relatives, and a party in an incidental civil action and his legal representatives shall, from the date on which the case is transferred for examination before prosecution, have the right to entrust agents ad litem. A private prosecutor in a case of private prosecution and his legal representatives, and a party in an incidental civil action and his legal representatives shall have the right to entrust agents ad litem at any time. The People's Procuratorate shall, within three days from the date of receiving the file record of a case transferred for examination before prosecution, notify the victim and his legal representatives or near relatives and the party in an incidental civil action and his legal representatives that they have the right to entrust agents ad litem.

Victims can not only customise to participate in the proceedings to safeguard their legitimate rights and interests, but also have the right to entrust agents ad litem to participate in the proceedings. The victims usually entrust lawyers to participate in the proceedings as an agent ad litem to safeguard their legitimate rights and interests.

(5) The right to file an incidental civil action. Article 77 of the Criminal Procedure Law of the PRC provides: "If a victim has suffered material losses as a result of the defendant's criminal act, he shall have the right to file an incidental civil action during the course of the criminal proceeding. When necessary, the People's Court may seal up or distrain upon the property of the defendant." When the infringed victims suffered material loss, they have the right to require the defendant committing the crime to make compensation in order to better protect the legitimate rights and interests of victims.

(6) The right to report. Article 84 of the Criminal Procedure Law of the PRC provides:

> When his personal or property rights are infringed upon, the victim shall have the right to report to a public security organ, a People's Procuratorate or a People's Court about the facts of the crime or bring a complaint to it against the criminal suspect. The public security organ, the People's Procuratorate or the People's Court shall accept all reports, complaints and information. If a case does not fall under its jurisdiction, it shall refer the case to the competent organ and notify the person who made the report, lodged the complaint or provided the information. If the case does not fall under its jurisdiction but calls for emergency measures, it shall take emergency measures before referring the case to the competent organ.

The right to report is the victims' important right, which requests the public security and judicial organs to start criminal proceedings prosecuting the crime in order to safeguard their legitimate rights and interests. To understand the victims' demands from the perspective of the right to report can enable the public security and judicial organs to seriously investigate for criminal filing from the angle of fulfilling their obligations. For those who have the case but do not place a case on file for investigation and prosecution and cause serious consequences should bear the criminal responsibility of dereliction of duty.

(7) The right to identity confidential in litigation. Item 3, Article 85 of the Criminal Procedure Law of the PRC provides:

> The public security organs, the People's Procuratorates and the People's Courts shall insure the safety of reporters, complainants and informants as well as their near relatives. If the reporters, complainants or informants wish not to make their names and acts of reporting, complaining or informing known to the public, these shall be kept confidential for them.

Victims as the informants, if wishing not to let the public know their own name and report behavior, the public security and judicial organs should keep them secret. The purpose of such provisions in the Criminal Procedure Law is to prevent the victims themselves and their families from being infringed, which is an important manifestation of the protection of the victims' rights and the modified content of the Criminal Procedure Law after its amendment. Before the amendment of the Criminal Procedure Law, the provision of confidentiality was only limited to the investigation stage, and after being amended, the requirements of confidentiality cover the whole process of the proceedings.

(8) The right to bring a suit directly in a case of private prosecution. Article 88 of the Criminal Procedure Law of the PRC provides: "As to a case of private prosecution [5], the victim shall have the right to bring a suit directly to a People's Court. If the victim is dead or has lost his ability of conduct, his legal representatives and near relatives shall have the right to bring a suit to a People's Court. The People's Court shall accept it according to law." In the case of private prosecution, the victim is the private prosecutor, who exercises the right to bring a suit under the law. In this case, a victim could make the decision whether or not to prosecute, or conciliate with the defendant according to the circumstances of less serious criminal cases, and the People's Court can play a function of mediation, so that the victim could master the effective way more flexibly to investigate for criminal and protect their own rights.
(9) The right to apply for a supplementary expert verification or another expert verification. Article 121 of the Criminal Procedure Law of the PRC provides: "The investigation organ shall notify the criminal suspect and the victim of the conclusion of the expert verification which will be used as evidence in his case. A supplementary expert verification or another expert verification may be conducted upon application submitted by the criminal suspect or the victim." The right to apply for a supplementary expert verification or another expert verification is very important for the protection of the legitimate rights

and interests of the victims. In judicial practice, conclusions of expert verification play a very important role in handling the case, while the expert conclusions verified are the conclusions made by expert about the special issues involved in the case by using scientific knowledge. The verifications, having darker subjective color, may affect the impartiality of the expert conclusions by outside interference. Entitling the victims the right to apply for a supplementary expert verification or another expert verification can prevent the deviations of the conclusions verified, which could cause undue harm to the rights of the victims.

(10) The right to petition or to bring a direct lawsuit for not initiating a prosecution. Article 145 of the Criminal Procedure Law of the PRC provides:

> If the People's Procuratorate decides not to initiate a prosecution with respect to a case that involves a victim, it shall send the decision in writing to the victim. If the victim refuses to accept the decision, he may, within seven days after receiving the written decision, present a petition to the People's Procuratorate at the next higher level and request the latter to initiate a public prosecution. The People's Procuratorate shall notify the victim of its decision made after reexamination. If the People's Procuratorate upholds the decision not to initiate a prosecution, the victim may bring a lawsuit to a People's Court. The victim may also bring a lawsuit directly to a People's Court without presenting a petition first. After the People's Court has accepted the case, the People's Procuratorate shall transfer the relevant case file to the People's Court.

Such a right is known as the transfer from public prosecution to self-prosecution in the criminal theory. The petitioner is the direct victim of the crime, having a strong desire to punish the criminals, and to investigate for criminal responsibility of the accused. If he thinks that there is an error in the decision of the People's Procuratorate not to prosecute, there will be no means of relief allowing the victim to understand the justice, which may lead to endless visits to the higher authority and even lead to aggressive behavior not conducive to social harmony. Therefore, the Criminal Procedure Law entitles the victim to present a petition to the People's Procuratorate at the next higher level and bring a lawsuit directly.

(11) The right to participate in the court investigation. Article 155 of the Criminal Procedure Law of the PRC provides: "After the public prosecutor has read out the bill of prosecution in court, the defendant and the victim may present statements regarding the crime accused in the bill of prosecution, and the public prosecutor may interrogate the defendant. The victim, the plaintiff and defender in an incidental civil action and the agents ad litem may, with the permission of the presiding judge, put questions to the defendant." It is very important to maintain the legitimate rights and interests of victims by letting them to participate in the court investigation, by directly exposing crime to prove the criminal, to understand the trial process and the results, and to oversee the activities of the trial.

(12) The right to receive a court judgment. Article 163 of the Criminal Procedure Law of the PRC stipulates: "In all cases, judgments shall be pronounced publicly. If the judgment on a case is pronounced in court, a written form of

the judgment shall be delivered within five days to the parties and the People's Procuratorate that initiated the public prosecution. In cases where the judgment is pronounced later on a fixed date, a written form of the judgment shall be delivered immediately after the pronouncement to the parties and the People's Procuratorate that indicated the public prosecution." The victims as a party, receiving the judgment of the case and knowing the verdict of the case may enable them to get spiritual comfort, and also can enable them to understand the seriousness and justice of the national laws. If there is any error in the judgment of the case, the realization of this right has made a preparation for their requesting the People's Procuratorate to present a protest.

(13) The right to make a request for a protest. Article 183 of the Criminal Procedure Law of the PRC stipulates:

> If the victim or his legal representative refuses to accept a judgment of first instance made by a local People's Court at any level, he shall, within five days from the date of receiving the written judgment, have the right to request the People's Procuratorate to present a protest. The People's Procuratorate shall, within five days from the date of receiving the request made by the victim or his legal representative, decide whether to present the protest or not and give him a reply.

When amending the Criminal Procedure Law, the right to make a request for a protest was confirmed, mainly on the basis of maintaining the legitimate rights and interests of victims. In the past, the task of maintaining the victims' rights used to be set entirely to the exercise of the public security and judicial organs. If the victims held some views about the judgment, although they could bring their views to the procuratorial organ, the procuratorial organ had no obligations to examine it and decide whether to present the protest. Now, as long as the victim is against the judgment of first instance, he can request the People's Procuratorate to protest, and the People's Procuratorate must study whether to present the protest and give a reply, which is conducive to safeguarding the legitimate rights and interests of victims.

(14) The right to present a petition regarding a legally effective judgment or order. Article 203 of the Criminal Procedure Law of the PRC stipulates: "A party or his legal representative or his near relative may present a petition to a People's Court or a People' Procuratorate regarding a legally effective judgment or order, however, execution of the judgment or order shall not be suspended." The petition of the party cannot directly lead to a retrial, but it can become the source materials for the retrial of the People's Court, and become the source materials for the People's Procuratorate to present a protest, which makes the protection of the rights of the victims form an interlocking safeguarding system in the criminal justice.

(15) The right to protect privacy. Article 152 of the Criminal Procedure Law of the PRC stipulates: "Cases of first instance in a People's Court shall be heard in public. However, cases involving State secrets or private affairs of individuals shall not be heard in public." Regarding personal privacy, it often

involves the victim's privacy. Such kind of cases shall not be heard in public, which is conducive to the protection of the victim's reputation, avoiding the second damage to his reputation.

(16) The right to obtain state assistance. With respect to those defendants who are indeed incapable of making compensation, or the compensation cannot be achieved, while the victims are in great need of help, the state should give aid to them, which is conducive to safeguarding the vital interests of the victims and to achievement of social harmony and stability. At present, the state aid to victims has been implemented in judicial practice. The People's Court began to explore aid methods of the criminal victims in 2006. According to the pilot work of ten Higher People's Courts, a total of 378 criminal victims and their relatives got 7,802,400 yuan from the state assistance, and these efforts have reduced the loss of the victims [6]. This shows that the victim is entitled to the right to obtain compensation from the State, and this also opens up a precedent for dealing with such cases, which will be conducive to the protection of the victims' rights.

11.2.2 The Realization of the Victims' Rights in the Criminal Justice

In accordance with the provisions of the Criminal Procedure Law of the PRC, we can summarize the following sixteen kinds of rights of criminal victims in the criminal justice. These rights are indispensable for the protection of the victims' rights in the criminal justice. The protection of the rights cannot be separated from the law, the rights recognized by law are the premise and foundation for the protection of the rights; the protection of human rights in the criminal justice cannot be separated from the law enforcement activities of the personnel of the Police and Justice, accurate and impartial law enforcement and respect for the rights of victims are the important guarantee to realize the rights of the victims.

In reality, what is the situation in the protection of the victims' rights in the criminal justice? Can the statutory right become actual rights? This is not only an important issue of the people's concern, but also the important subject for the protection of human rights. It should be said that the protection of the victims' rights in our criminal justice is effective. Sixteen types of rights of the victims in the criminal justice can be divided into two situations: One is concerned with the specific rights of the victims and the other is concerned with the rights shared by the victim and others, i.e., the victims enjoy this right, and other participants in the proceedings enjoy the same right.

(1) The special rights of the victim in the criminal justice. There are mainly seven kinds of rights as follows: ① the right to entrust agents ad litem; ② the right to file an incidental civil action; ③ the right of victims to direct prosecution in private prosecution; ④ the right to petition or to bring a direct lawsuit for not

initiating a prosecution; ⑤ the right to make a request for a protest; ⑥ the right to protect privacy; ⑦ the right to obtain state assistance.

The criminal victims also have four kinds of special rights in the criminal justice:

First, before the amendment, the Criminal Procedure Law of the PRC clearly provided the rights, further confirmed by the amended Criminal Procedure Law, which included the right to file an incidental civil action, the right to protect privacy, and the victims' right to a direct prosecution in private prosecution.

Second, before the amendment, the Criminal Procedure Law of the PRC clearly provided the rights, further improved and perfected by the amended Criminal Procedure Law, such as the right to petition or to bring a direct lawsuit for not initiating a prosecution. Before its amendment, the Criminal Procedure Law provided in Article 102: "If the victim does not accept the decision, he may present a petition to the People's Procuratorate within seven days after receiving the written decision. The People's Procuratorate shall notify the victim of the result of its re-examination." While the amended Criminal Procedure Law provides: "If the victim refuses to accept the decision, he may, within seven days after receiving the written decision, present a petition to the People's Procuratorate at the next higher level and request the latter to initiate a public prosecution. The People's Procuratorate shall notify the victim of its decision made after reexamination." By making a comparison between the original Criminal Procedure Law and the amended one, we found that the subject of the victim's presenting a petition for not initiating a prosecution has changed from the original Procuratorate to the People's Procurator at a higher level by amendment, which is conducive to the higher People's Procuratorate's strengthening the guidance and supervision to the lower People's Procuratorate, to correcting the wrong decision of not initiating a prosecution, and to protecting the legitimate rights and interests of the victim. At the same time, the requirements of initiating a prosecution are further clarified, i.e., initiating a public prosecution. Furthermore, in order to solve the problem that the higher People's Procuratorate cannot correct the issue of not initiating a prosecution, the Criminal Procedure Law was amended by adding the victim's right to directly initiate a prosecution, that is, when the higher People's Prosecuratoratorate did not support the victim's request to initiate a prosecution, or the victim believes that even if he presents a petition to the higher People's Procuratorate the problem can still not be solved. In this case, the victim can initiate a prosecution to the People's Court, asking for a fair trial of the People's Court. This right of the victim has reservations and improvement with the legislation focusing on the protection of the victim and its judicial practice is more conducive to the protection of the victim.

Third, the amended Criminal Procedure Law provides such rights as the right to entrust agents ad litem and the right to make a request for a protest. Victims, directly infringed by the crime, sometimes may be unable to appear in court due to health reasons, but the ideas of maintaining their rights have to be expressed. Although the public prosecutor may notice the interests of victims, but this may be less direct and concrete than the victims' own expressions or the expression of their agent ad litem. Therefore, the right to entrust agents ad litem was added to the amended Criminal Procedure Law. Safeguarding the victims' legitimate rights and interests is realized by entrusting agents ad litem to express the victims' demands and ideas. In addition, victims are more concerned about the outcome of the trial of the case, and concerned with the appropriateness of the defendant's conviction and penalty. If the victim believes that there are errors in the first-instance judgment, how to remedy it, whether to just wait passively or actively achieve something? The Criminal Procedure Law supports the victim to request the People's Procuratorate to present a protest in accordance with the law, so that the trial supervision of the People's Procuratorate shifts from its initiative implementation to both its own initiative and promotion of the victim. In this case, the protest is based not only on maintaining the legal justice, but also on giving due consideration to the request of the victim and accepting the supervision of the victim. The victim's right to present a protest has been fully and effectively guaranteed in the practice of criminal justice. For example, in 2006, there were 439 cases in which the victims request the procuratorial organs to present a protest, and there were 315 cases in which the procuratorial organs examine the cases and agree to the victims' protest. The adoption rate of the victims' request for the protest is 71.8 %, accounting for 11.5 % of the total number of 2,746 cases in which the procuratorate organs present the protest.

Fourth, the right to get the state compensation. Even though there is no provision in the Criminal Procedure Law, state compensation has been given to the victims and their family members in judicial practice as an individual case. Injuries and deaths caused by major accidents or emergencies, such as the innocent casualties of the Fifth of July Incident of 2009 in the Xinjiang Uygur Autonomous Region, have got the state compensation, which is a proof.

Viewed from the perspective of the realization of victims' rights in the criminal justice situation, we believe that the law has been continuously improved to protect the rights of victims, legal measures have been continuously increased, the level and ability of law enforcement have been improved, and victims' rights are fully protected. With respect to the special rights of the victims, the traditional right of prosecution has been strengthened, and the rights newly added have been more targeted entirely based on the perspective of maintaining the victims' rights, such as the right to entrust agent ad litem. The lawyers are usually entrusted, and they use legal knowledge and the skills and experience of participating in the proceedings, thinking about the issue from the perspective of the victim and putting forward opinions and suggestions to safeguard the rights of the victims in order to compensate for the omissions and deficiencies of the public security and judicial organs in the criminal process of investigating the crime.

(2) The rights of the victim and the rights shared by other participants in the proceedings. Some litigation rights of the victims in the criminal justice are shared by other participants in the proceedings, which are as follows: ① the right to use their native language in court proceedings; ② the right to present a

prosecution; ③ the right to apply for withdrawal; ④ the right to report the case; ⑤ the right to keep the identity confidential; ⑥ the right to apply for supplementary verification or reverification; ⑦ the right to participate in the court investigation; ⑧ the right to obtain a court verdict; ⑨ the right to appeal for effective judgment or decision.

These rights of the victims apply in the following situations:

First, these rights were clearly provided by the Criminal Procedure Law before its amendment, and reiterated by the amended Criminal Procedure Law, including the right to use their native language in court proceedings, the right to present a prosecution, the right to participate in the court investigation, the right to appeal for effective judgment or decision and so on. These rights in the long-term judicial practice were given the attention they deserve by public security organs, judicial organs, and public officials. Litigation documents are produced in both Han text and the text in minority language in the People's Court and the People's Procuratorate of the Inner Mongolia Autonomous Region, of Xinjiang Uygur Autonomous Region, and of Tibet Autonomous Region. With respect to the parties, who are not familiar with the local language, they are provided with translation by public security and judicial organs, which are powerful in protecting the legitimate right of the minority parties to prosecution.

Second, these rights were clearly provided by the Criminal Procedure Law before its amendment, and perfected and supplemented by the amended Criminal Procedure Law, including the victim's right to report the case, the right to keep the identity confidential in prosecution. Article 60 (3) of the Criminal Procedure Law before its amendent provides: "If the complainant or accuser wishes to remain anonymous, his name shall be kept confidential during the period of investigation."

There appears no term of a victim, but in fact, the complainants should include the victims. When their own rights have been infringed and they require the protection of the public security and judicial organs, the victims are also the complainants. Article 84 (2) of the amended Criminal Procedure Law stipulates: "When his personal or property rights are infringed upon, the victim shall have the right to report to a public security organ, a People's Procuratorate or a People's Court about the facts of the crime or bring a complaint to it against the criminal suspect." When the victim reports to a public security organ, a People's Procuratorate or a People's Court about the facts of the crime or bring a complaint to it against the criminal suspect, the victim is the reporter or complainant. Article 85 (3) of the amended Criminal Procedure Law stipulates: "The public security organs, the People's Procuratorates and the People's Courts shall insure the safety of reporters, complainants and informants as well as their near relatives. If the reporters, complainants or informants wish not to make their names and acts of reporting, complaining or informing known to the public, these shall be kept confidential for them." The protection of the reporters, complainants, and informants extends from the investigation stage throughout the whole litigation process, not disclosing their names and acts of reporting, complaining or informing. This will be conducive to protecting the legitimate rights and interests of the complainants, reporters, or informants.

Third, there are new rights in the amended Criminal Procedure Law, which were not provided in the Criminal Procedure Law before its amendment. These rights include the right to apply for withdrawal, the right to apply for supplementary identification or reidentification, and the right to obtain a court verdict, etc. These are the rights obtained by the victims because they are confirmed as the party's status. It is because the "parties" in the Criminal Procedure Law before its amendment refer only to the private prosecutor, the defendant, incidental civil plaintiff and defendant, not including victims. Though sometimes incidental civil plaintiff is the victim, but it is not always the case. When not suffering material losses, the victim cannot file an incidental civil action to participate in the trial activities, then he can only appear in the identity of the victim. In this case, the incidental civil plaintiff does not include the victim. The Criminal Procedure Law has elevated to a new level of protecting the rights of the victims by identifying the victims as the "parties", enabling the litigation action to be implemented, which is conducive to the exercise of their rights and safeguarding their legitimate rights and interests. Simply to say, the rights to prosecution enjoyed only by the parties become the rights enjoyed by the victims because the victims have become the parties. Therefore, the protection of human rights of the victims in the criminal justice has been strengthened.

As mentioned above, the laws relevant to the protection of the victims' rights and of the rights shared by other litigation participants are also being improved, while the level and the ability of law enforcement is continuously enhanced with increasing measures. The public security and judicial organs have established the discipline inspection organs, which are specifically in charge of investigating and punishing public security and judicial personnel violating the law and discipline. In addition, public security and judicial organs have established supervision system, which has played an important role in safeguarding the victim's right to prosecution in recent years. More and more attention has been paid to the protection of the victim's identity privacy rights in litigation.

(3) Developing space to strengthen the protection of the victims' rights in the criminal justice.

As mentioned above, both the specific rights of the victims and the rights shared with other participants in the proceedings are more fully guaranteed in the process of Chinese criminal justice. However, in order to further ensure the victims' rights, we can consider changing the victims' protest right into an independent right of appeal based on years of judicial practice; advancing the time of entrusting agent (after the case is placed on file for investigation by the public security and judicial organs, the victims have the right to entrust agents ad litem to participate in litigation so as to safeguard their legitimate rights and interests as early as possible); establishing the mental compensation system of the victims; and establishing a national assistance system for the victims. In this case, we can better the protection of the person, property, and other rights of the victims.

11.3 The Rights Guarantee of the Criminal Suspect/ Defendant in the Criminal Justice

It should be said that the protection of human rights in our criminal justice experienced a shift from focusing on the protection of the collective human rights of society as a whole to protecting the human rights of the criminal suspects and the defendants at the same time, and a transferring process from focusing on the protection of human rights of the criminal suspects and the defendants to focusing on the protection of human rights of the victims. It should be said that protecting human rights of the suspects and the defendants is an important focus of protecting human rights in the criminal justice. This is determined by the litigation status of the criminal suspects and the defendants. The criminal suspects and the defendants held the position of being prosecuted in criminal proceedings, facing national powerful machine of dictatorship. Therefore, more concerns have been shown to the protection of their human rights in the criminal proceedings, and the laws provide more clarified and concrete provisions with respect to protecting human rights of the criminal suspects and the defendants. In judicial practice, punishing the action of rights violations of the criminal suspects and the defendants in accordance with the law is beneficial to the protection of their human rights.

Meanwhile, there is a close relation between protecting the rights of the criminal suspects and the defendants and whether the public security and judicial organs and their personnel can properly perform their duties. The law requires the public security and judicial organs and their personnel to respect the objective facts and human rights of the criminal suspects and the defendants from the point of view of objectively and impartially handling the case in the process of the investigation, prosecution and trial in accordance with the law. In this sense, when we study the protection of human rights of the suspects and the defendants, we should pay attention to the requirements of the duties of the public security and judicial organs and to the requirements of the protection of the rights of the criminal suspects and the defendants. We should enhance the ability and level of protecting human rights of the criminal suspects and the defendants in the criminal justice by strengthening the duties of the public security and judicial organs and their personnel.

11.3.1 Fundamental Content of Human Rights of the Criminal Suspect and the Defendant in the Criminal Justice

(1) The right to use their native languages in court proceedings. This is the litigation right enjoyed by all the participants in the proceedings. Criminal suspects and defendants as parties naturally enjoy this right. Article 9 of the Criminal Procedure Law provides, "Citizens of all nationalities shall have the right to use their native spoken and written languages in court proceedings. The People's Courts, the People's Procuratorates and the public security organs shall provide translations for any party [4] to the court proceedings who is not familiar with the spoken or written language commonly used in the locality. Where people of a minority nationality live in a concentrated community or where a number of nationalities live together in one area, court hearings shall be conducted in the spoken language commonly used in the locality, and judgments, notices and other documents shall be issued in the written language commonly used in the locality."

(2) The right to file charges. Article 14 of the Criminal Procedure Law of the PRC provides, "Participants in proceedings shall have the right to file charges against judges, procurators and investigators whose acts infringe on their citizen's procedural rights or subject their persons to indignities." Criminal suspects and defendants in criminal proceedings are the object of the prosecution, and their personal rights are often vulnerably infringed. Therefore, in case of the police and justice personnel infringement of their personal rights or having personal insulting behavior, the victims can file a complaint to the discipline inspection and supervision departments or the leaders of the unit in which these police or judicial officers work, and can file a complaint to the People's Procuratorate in accordance with the law, seeking the protection of their right and investigating the criminal responsibility of the perpetrator who violates their human rights and constitutes a criminal action.

(3) The right to apply for withdrawal. Article 28 of the Criminal Procedure Law of the PRC provides, "In any of the following situations [7], a member of the judicial, procuratorial or investigatory personnel shall voluntarily withdraw, and the parties to the case and their legal representatives shall have the right to demand his withdrawal." The right to apply for withdrawal of the criminal suspects and the defendants is conducive to ensuring that some relevant members of the judicial, procuratorial, or investigatory personnel do not participate in case processing, eliminating the suspects and the defendants' concern about the fairness of the litigation process and the outcome of the proceedings, and reducing the unnecessary appeals and petitions. However, there is a limit about the suspects and the defendants applying for withdrawal. That is, before a decision about withdrawal of investigators is made, investigators cannot stop the investigation of a case. In dismissing the application

for withdrawal decision, the parties and their legal representatives can apply for withdrawal once more.

(4) The right to defense. In accordance with the provisions of Articles 32, 34, and 39 of the Criminal Procedure Law of the PRC, the suspects and the defendant's right to defense includes the following aspects:

① The right to self-defense. The criminal suspects and defendants can defend themselves and safeguard their legitimate rights and interests in criminal proceedings.

② The right to entrust the defense. Article 32 of the Criminal Procedure Law of the PRC provides, "In addition to exercising the right to defend himself a criminal suspect or a defendant may entrust one or two persons as his defenders. The following persons may be entrusted as defenders: (1) lawyers; (2) persons recommended by a public organization or the unit to which the criminal suspect or the defendant belongs; and (3) guardians or relatives and friends of the criminal suspect or the defendant. Persons who are under criminal punishment or whose personal freedom is deprived of or restricted according to law shall not serve as defenders." In judicial practice, in order to more effectively safeguard the legitimate rights and interests of the criminal suspects and the the defendants, lawyers are entrusted to the defense because of their proficient knowledge of the law and the defense business.

③ The right to designate a defense. Article 34 of the Criminal Procedure Law of the PRC provides, "If a case is to be brought in court by a public prosecutor and the defendant involved has not entrusted anyone to be his defender due to financial difficulties or other reasons, the People's Court may designate a lawyer that is obligated to provide legal aid to serve as a defender. If the defendant is blind, deaf or mute, or if he is a minor, and thus has not entrusted anyone to be his defender, the People's Court shall designate a lawyer that is obligated to provide legal aid to serve as a defender. If there is the possibility that the defendant may be sentenced to death and yet he has not entrusted anyone to be his defender, the People's Court shall designate a lawyer that is obligated to provide legal aid to serve as a defender." With respect to the defendant who has financial difficulties, who is handicapped, or who may be sentenced to death, a defender is designated, which is very necessary to safeguard the legitimate rights and interests of the defendant.

④ The right to refuse a defense. Article 39 of the Criminal Procedure Law of the PRC provides, "During a trial, the defendant may refuse to have his defender continue to defend him and may entrust his defense to another defender." Entitling the defendant with the right to refuse a defense is to better protect the defendant's right to defense.

(5) The right to apply for supplementary verification or reverification. This kind of right for the criminal suspects and the defendants is quite similar to the victims' right, detailed explanations have been given in section II, part 1 (9).
(6) The right to get a lawyer's help. Article 96 of the Criminal Procedure Law of the PRC provides:

> After the criminal suspect is interrogated by an investigation organ for the first time or from the day on which compulsory measures are adopted against him, he may appoint a lawyer to provide him with legal advice and to file petitions and complaints on his behalf. If the criminal suspect is arrested, the appointed lawyer may apply on his behalf for obtaining a guarantor pending trial. If a case involves State secrets, the criminal suspect shall have to obtain the approval of the investigation organ for appointing a lawyer. The appointed lawyer shall have the right to find out from the investigation organ about the crime suspected of, and may meet with the criminal suspect in custody to enquire about the case. When the lawyer meets with the criminal suspect in custody, the investigation organ may, in light of the seriousness of the crime and where it deems it necessary, send its people to be present at the meeting. If a case involves State secrets, before the lawyer meets with the criminal suspect, he shall have to obtain the approval of the investigation organ.

After the criminal suspect is interrogated for the first time or from the day on which compulsory measures are adopted against him, he may get a lawyer's help including providing him with legal advice, filing petitions, and complaints on his behalf, applying on his behalf for obtaining a guarantor pending trial, meeting and communication, which is very necessary to safeguard human rights of the criminal suspects.

(7) The right to refuse to answer the question irrelevant to the case. Article 93 of the Criminal Procedure Law of the PRC provides, "The criminal suspect shall answer the investigators' questions truthfully, but he shall have the right to refuse to answer any questions that are irrelevant to the case." Irrelevance to the case refers to the irrelevance to the investigators' investigation and handling of the criminal case, which may involve the suspects' personal privacy. Such legal provisions ensure that the investigation work is advancing in the right direction to protect the legitimate rights and interests of the criminal suspects on the one hand, and prevent them at the position of being prosecuted from investigators' unnecessary intrusion, inquiry into the privacy of the suspect, or inquiry into other irrelevant issues that the suspects know on the other hand. Thus, it contributes to the protection of the legitimate rights and interests of the suspects.

(8) The court cross-examination right. Article 47 of the Criminal Procedure Law of the PRC provides, "The testimony of a witness may be used as a basis in deciding a case only after the witness has been questioned and cross-examined in the courtroom by both sides, that is, the public prosecutor and victim as well as the defendant and defenders, and after the testimonies of the witnesses on all sides have been heard and verified. If a court discovers through investigation that a witness has intentionally given false testimony or concealed criminal evidence, it shall handle the matter in accordance with law." The defendant's cross-examination of the witness's testimony as basic evidence in deciding a case is conducive to exposing the witness's perjured testimony and to safeguarding the defendant's legitimate rights and interests.

(9) The right to present a final statement. Article 160 of the Criminal Procedure Law of the PRC provides, "After the presiding judge has declared conclusion

of the debate, the defendant shall have the right to present a final statement." Regarding trial of cases through summary procedure, Article 177 of the Criminal Procedure Law of the PRC provides, "Before the judgment is pronounced, the final statement of the defendant shall be heard." The right to present a final statement is the defendant's final views expressed to the court after the trial. The defendant may continue the defense for innocence, or may state the sincere repentance requesting the understanding of victims, or may ask the court to handle the case with leniency. No matter what the form or content, the right to present the final statement is a legal opportunity given to the defendant for the last speech, which is very necessary to safeguard the legitimate rights and interests of the defendant.

(10) The right to appeal. Article 180 of the Criminal Procedure Law of the PRC provides, "If the defendant, private prosecutor or their legal representatives refuse to accept a judgment or order of first instance made by a local People's Court at any level, they shall have the right to appeal in writing or orally to the People's Court at the next higher level. Defenders or near relatives of the defendant may, with the consent of the defendant, file appeals. A defendant shall not be deprived on any pretext of his right to appeal." The right to appeal is the important litigation rights of the defendant. Asking for the second trial and error correction through appeal is very important for safeguarding the legitimate rights and interests of the defendant. In order to protect the true realization of the defendant's right to appeal, Article 190 of the Criminal Procedure Law of the PRC provides, "In the trial of a case appealed by a defendant, or his legal representative, defender or near relative, the People's Court of second instance may not increase the criminal punishment on the defendant."

(11) The rights to present a petition regarding an effective judgment or order. Article 203 of the Criminal Procedure Law of the PRC provides, "A party or his legal representative or his near relative may present a petition to a People's Court or a People's Procuratorate regarding a legally effective judgment or order, however, execution of the judgment or order shall not be suspended." As the defendant's petition, although it does not directly cause a retrial, it can become material sources of the People's Court for retrial, and material sources of the People's Procuratorate to present a protest. The petition of the defendant has important significance for promoting a protest of the People's Procuratorate or a retrial of the People's Court.

(12) The right to compensation. When the criminal suspect and the defendant's right to person and to property have been violated, they have the right to compensation. Article 15 of the Law of the People's Republic of China on State Compensation provides:

> The victim shall have the right to compensation if an organ in charge of investigatory, procuratorial, judicial or prison administration work, or its functionaries, infringe upon his right of the person in the exercise of its functions and powers in any of the following circumstances: (1) Wrong detention of a person without incriminating facts or proof

substantiating a strong suspicion of the commission of a crime; (2) Wrong arrest of a person without incriminating facts; (3) Innocence is found in a retrial held in accordance with the procedure of trial supervision, but the original sentence has already been executed; (4) Extortion of a confession by torture or causing bodily injury or death to a citizen by using or instigating the use of violence such as beating one up; or (5) Causing bodily injury or death to a citizen by the unlawful use of weapons or police restraint implements.

Article 16 of the Law of the People's Republic of China on State Compensation provides:

The victim shall have the right to compensation if an organ in charge of investigatory, procuratorial, judicial or prison administration work, or its functionaries, infringe upon property rights in any of the following circumstances: (1) Unlawfully taking measures such as sealing up, distaining, freezing or recovering a property; or (2) Innocence is found in a retrial held in accordance with the procedure of trial supervision, but the fine or confiscation of property in the original sentence has already been executed.

If the criminal suspects and the defendants were wrongly detained, arrested, sentenced or tortured, injured or death caused by illegal use of a gun or by police apparatus, they have the right to compensation for the consequences of infringement of their right to person. If the measures taken such as sealing up, distaining, freezing, or recovering a property caused the damage or loss, they have right to compensation for the damage or loss. These provisions effectively protect the legitimate rights and interests of citizens and promote public security the judicial officers in law enforcement with standards, civilization, justice, and accuracy to reduce erroneous cases as many as possible. It should be pointed out that state compensation standards continue to increase with the development of the national economy and with the improvement of people's living standards. This change can be seen from national standards of compensation listing as follows (Table 11.1).

Table 11.1 National standards of compensation

Years	Average wage of workers	Annual working days	Compensation standards—Daily average wage (yuan)
1995	4,538	254	17.87
1996	5,500	254	21.65
1997	6,210	254	24.45
1998	6,470	254	25.47
1999	7,479	254	29.44
2000	8,346	254	32.86
2001	9,371	251	37.33
2002	10,870	251	43.3
2003	12,422	251	49.48
2004	14,040	251	55.95
2005	16,024	251	63.83
2006	18,405	251	73.3
2007	21,001	251	83.66
2008	24,932	251	99.31
2009	29,229	251	111.99

Table 11.2 The cases of state compensation heard by the People's Courts

Years	Cases requiring compensation	Concluded compensation cases	Compensation cases determined	Amount of compensation (yuan)
1995	197	154	64	
2000	2,447	2,430	925	
2004 [8]				31,670,000
2005	3,056	2,991	941	37,510,000
2006 [6]		2,323		34,840,700
2007	1,658	1,709	585	46,002,200
2008	1,535	1,634	543	

As can be seen from the above table, the daily amount of compensation from 17.87 yuan in 1995 to 111.99 yuan in 2009, 6.27 times increase in the past 15 years.

In order to guarantee the realization of citizens' rights to get the state compensation, since the implementation of the state compensation, the People's Courts have heard the cases of state compensation (Table 11.2).

As seen from the above table, the number of cases of application for compensation that the People's Courts accepted has been declining, but the amount of compensation has been increasing. It reflects the increasing standard of compensation of the People's Courts, the increasing compensation efforts in error correction, which is conducive to safeguarding citizens' legitimate rights and interests.

11.3.2 The Judicial Officers' Duty in the Criminal Justice and the Protection of Human Rights of the Criminal Suspects or Defendants

We analyze the legal rights of the criminal suspects or defendants, mainly introducing some of the specific provisions of the Criminal Procedure Law of the PRC. But enabling the legal right to become the actual enjoyment of rights depends on the objective, impartial and strict law enforcement in judicial practice. Regarding the protection of human rights in the criminal justice, the important part is fairness and accuracy in the enforcement of the law enforcement officers. Laws alone are insufficient to themselves. Even the best law also relies on law enforcement officers to enforce the law, if there is a problem on the part of law enforcement, the protection of human rights in the criminal justice would be an empty promise. Therefore, we must seriously study the duties requirements for law enforcement officers and investigate and prosecute job-related criminal acts of violation of duty, violation of civil rights according to law at the same time in order to really protect human rights.

(1) The duties of judicial officers to protect human rights. The judicial officers have duties to combat crime and safeguard citizens' rights from being violated. In judicial practice, if the judicial officers handle the cases only in strict accordance with the law, the cases can be ensured to be objectively and fairly treated, and the rights of citizens can be guaranteed.

① Torture and illegal methods to collect statements are strictly prohibited. China puts great emphasis on strictly forbidding extorting confessions by torture, and on the protection of human rights. Extorting confessions by torture was opposed by the revolutionary regime as early as in the liberated areas. Article 10 of Regulations of Protecting Human and Property Rights of the Shaanxi-Gansu-Ningxia Border Region stipulates that "Any arrest is not allowed to impose insults, beatings and forced confessions and forced surrender, and trial adopts evidence doctrine and does not lay emphasis on confessions." After liberation, our country's criminal justice firmly opposed to torture, and Article 43 of the Criminal Procedure Law stipulates that "It shall be strictly forbidden to extort confessions by torture and to collect evidence by threat, enticement, deceit or other unlawful means." Article 247 of the Criminal Law of the PRC clearly stipulates that extorting confessions by torture is a crime and it will impose the corresponding penalty. Judicial officers collect evidence in accordance with the law, focusing on the protection of human rights, which has played an important role in curbing forced confessions.

② Strict conditions of arrest to prevent the wrong arrest. Our country has always attached great importance to the review of the arrests, emphasizing the strict conditions of arrest, clearly separating arrest-approval organ from enforcement organ, and paying attention to prevent and correct the wrong arrests. In 1982, the country's Procuratorate organs concluded and approved 89.4 % of the arrest of the person who submitted for arrests by the public security organs, the arrest not approved accounted for 10.6 % [9]. In 1998, the procuratorial organs did not approve the arrest of 3,904 persons [10]. The five-year period from 2003 to 2007, the procuratorial organs of our country decided not to approve the arrest of 255,931 people which should not be investigated for criminal responsibility, or for the lack of evidence in accordance with the law. Thus, we have effectively protected human rights.

③ Strict conditions for prosecution to prevent the wrong prosecution. The procuratorial organs of our country have strict conditions of prosecution in the investigation and prosecution process by maintaining prosecution standards, and it makes the decision not to prosecute for those cases that should not be prosecuted in accordance with the law in order to prevent the wrong prosecution and to protect the rights of citizens. In 1998, the procuratorial organs made the decision not to prosecute 11,225 people [10]. The five-year period from 2003 to 2007, the procuratorial organs of our country decided not to prosecute 34,433 people [11] who should not be investigated for criminal responsibility in accordance with the law, or for the lack sufficient evidence.

④ Clean-up of extended detention. Cleaning up extended detention to improve the efficiency of the proceedings is one of the important measures to guarantee human rights. Since there appeared the problem of extended detention, the procuratorial organs have uninterruptedly corrected it. Especially in recent years, the procuratorial organs have carried out the clean-up activities of the extended detention on the basis of actively solving their own cases linking to extended detention. From 1998 to 2002, the extended detention of 308,182 people has been corrected [12]. In order to effectively protect the legitimate rights and interests of the suspect and the defendant, regarding the repeated case of extended detention in litigation activities, the Supreme People's Procuratorate carried out the special supervision activity to clean up extended detention in May 2003, strongly supported by the Standing Committee of the National People's Congress and the relevant specialised committees. The procuratorial organs started from their own work, correcting 555 people of extended detention relevant to procuratorial stage, and up to the end of July 2003, the goal of no extended detention has been realized. At the same time, the procuratorial organs conscientiously fulfilled the legal duties of supervision, supervising the investigating and judicial organs in carrying out the clean-up work. The Supreme People's Procuratorate in conjunction with the Supreme People's Court, the Ministry of Public Security issued "A Notice on the Strictly Implementing the Criminal Procedure Law and Effectively Correcting and Preventing Extended Detention", sending 18 inspection teams to check its implementation of the key areas. The procuratorial organs at all levels actively promote the network connection of the monitoring system in monitoring sites, conducting dynamic supervision, generally establishing time-countdown reminder system, publicizing to society the report telephone and e-mail for the extended detention, and supervising the handling of serious cases of extended detention. Through a case-by-case correction, the procuratorial organs corrected 25,181 people of extended detention at the stages of the investigation and trial. Through the efforts, 14 provinces had no extended detention at all stages of handling the case, and the extended detention in other provinces had also largely been corrected [13]. In 2004, the procuratorial organs continued to improve a long-term mechanism to prevent and correct the extended detention, implementing the systems of the on-site supervision, regular reporting and investigating responsibilities, and correcting 7,132 people of extended detention. By the end of 2004, the procuratorial organs continued to keep no extended detention at all handling stages, and the number of provinces with no extended detention at all handling stages rose from 14 to 29 [14]. Clean-up and correction of the extended detention have promoted litigation efficiency, accelerating the handling speed of cases, ensuring the timely processing of cases, and protecting the legitimate rights and interests of the suspect and the defendant.

⑤ Public trial. Public trial is a trial principle established by the Criminal Procedure Law of the PRC. Public trial can enable the trial activities of the People's Court to be placed under the supervision of the people and to be more open and transparent, which is conducive to the protection of the defendant's legitimate rights and interests. Since the founding of New China, the People's Court in China has always insisted on the principle of public trial, and constantly improved public trial mechanism as follows: First, the trial information is comprehensively make public. With respect to the public trial in accordance with the law, the People's Court makes public the brief summary of the case, the opening time and place three days before the public trial. As for the case not to be publicly tried, the People's Court needs to announce the reasons. Second, when the case is heard in public, the People's Court makes public evidence, cross-examination and debate, and publicly pronounces a judgement, and the citizens can observe with effective credentials. Third, the Court on conditions has recorded and video-recorded the courtroom activities and the relevant important trial activities, setting up audio and video files of the trial, and the parties may refer to them or replicate them as regulated. Fourth, the right of people's assessors to attend the trial is effectively protected in accordance with the law, and this ensures that people's assessor can independently exercise voting rights to fact-finding and law enforcement when they participate in the cases of collegiate bench trial. Fifth, the Higher People's Court is encouraged to make efforts to make public the instruments of judgement entering into force by publications, local area network and the Internet. Recently, Henan Province Higher People's Court has taken the initiative in requiring all the courts of the province to put the instruments of judgement on the Internet for the reference and evaluation of social communities, which fully implements the principle of public trial, playing an important role in legal publicity.

⑥ Withdraw the approval right to the death penalty, strict and careful application of the death penalty. Since the founding of New China, for a considerable period of time, death penalty cases are approved by the Supreme People's Court. In September 1983, the Standing Committee of the National People's Congress modified the Organic Law of the People's Court according to the prevailing social order, providing that for the cases in which criminals, causing serious harm to the social order, should be sentenced to death, the Supreme People's Court, if necessary, may authorize the Higher People's Court to exercise approval rights. In more than 20 years after that, the Higher People's Court exercised the approval rights over some death penalty cases in accordance with the authorization of the Supreme People's Court. This approach was consistent with the social security situation in this period. When the Higher People's Court review the trial of death-penalty cases, it, strictly according to law and the careful application of the death penalty, played an important role in timely punishing criminals seriously damaging public security, maintaining social stability, protecting the rights and interests of citizens, safeguarding reform and opening up, and promoting economic development. Since over three decades of reform and opening up, China's political, economic, and social situations have experienced the tremendous and profound changes. In order to adapt to new situations, to effectively implement China's death-penalty policy, and safeguard justice and the uniformity of law, according to the decision of the Standing Committee of the National People's Congress on Amending the Organic Law of the People's Court, the Supreme People's Court decided to unitarily exercise the approval right to death penalty by itself since January 1, 2007. The main purpose is to strictly enforce the law, to accurately punish the criminal, to strict control and carefully apply to death penalty, to unify the standards applicable to death penalty, to ensure the quality of the trial of death penalty cases, to maintain social stability, and promote social progress. The Supreme People's Court reviews death penalty cases with more than three singular judicial personnel forming a collegial panel to conduct a comprehensive review of the referee's factual findings, the application of law, and proceedings in cases of first instance and second instance. Review adheres to the principle of laying emphasis on evidence and not giving credence to confessions. If there is any doubt on the evidence, the investigation and verification of evidence is needed. If necessary, the crime scene may be visited for further investigation. During the review of death penalty cases, if the defenders entrusted by the accused propose requirements to hear their views, the collegial panel must listen to the views of the defenders and make a written record to be filed. Written comments made by the defenders should be docketed into the file. When the Supreme Court reviews death penalty cases, if the collegial panel considers it difficult to make a decision for complex cases, they can ask the Dean of the court according to law to submit the cases to the adjudication committee for its discussion and decision. In the process of review of death penalty cases, the Supreme People's Court performs its duties according to law, strictly implementing the criminal law and criminal procedure law, making strict checks on the facts, evidence, procedures and application of law in death penalty cases, avoiding deprivation or restriction of the legitimate rights of the suspect and the defendant and avoiding the occurrence of wrong cases, making efforts to enable every death penalty case to withstand the test of history, practice and people, and making efforts to enable the concept of the state's respecting and safeguarding human rights, especially the right to life, to be demonstrated and achieved.

(2) Investigating and dealing with cases of infringement. The duties of the procuratorial organs are to investigate and deal with cases of violation of citizens' right to person and democratic rights. The procuratorial organs' investigating and dealing with cases of violating the legitimate rights and interests of citizens including the suspect or the defendant will play an important role in safeguarding the rights of citizens, especially in safeguarding the legitimate rights and interests of the suspects or the defendant. China's criminal law provides that the violation of the criminal suspect or the defendant's legitimate rights and interests is defined as a criminal act.

The five-year period of 1998–2002, the national procuratorial organs investigated 7,760 criminal cases [12] in which staff of state organs used their powers to violate citizens' right to person and the democratic rights. Starting from May 2004, the Supreme People's Procuratorate conducted special activities nationwide to seriously investigate and deal with the criminal cases in which staff of state organs who used their powers to violate human rights, focusing on handling illegal detention, illegal searches, torture to extract confessions, violent evidence collection, abuse of detainees, destruction of elections, as well as a serious breach of duty resulting in significant loss of lives and property of the people, and investigating and dealing with 1,595 staff of state organs who were involved in suspected crimes, which enabled the criminal act of violation to be effectively curbed. The procuratorial organs placed cases on file for investigation of illegal detention, torture to extract confessions and other violations of citizens' right to person and democratic right by 930 staff of state organs in 2006 [15].

As seen in above discussions, we find that the infringement cases investigated and dealt with by the procuratorial organs tended to decrease year by year. On the one hand the criminal subjects under the jurisdiction of the procuratorial organs is shrinking, from general infringement cases by the citizens to the violation cases only by staff of state organs; on the other hand, because the procuratorial organs have increased the intensity of deterrence, while the state organs have also strengthened the team building and improved the ability and level of law enforcement, infringement cases have been curbed.

11.3.3 Realization of the Suspects or Defendants' Rights in Criminal Justice

Since the founding of the People's Republic of China, our country attached great importance to protecting the rights of the criminal suspects and the accused in criminal justice. Attention was paid to safeguarding the rights of the suspects or defendants in criminal justice by many laws and regulations, from the Constitution confirming the exercising powers of arrest to the formulation of arrest and detention regulations further standardizing the application of detention and arrest relevant to civil rights, and then to the formulation of the Criminal Procedure Law in 1979 and the amendments of the Criminal Procedure Law in 1996. Especially in criminal lawsuit, the accused people such as offenders, criminals, defendants, etc., are unitarily called the criminal suspects and defendants. To prosecute or not is as the demarcation line. Before the prosecution, we call them the criminal suspects, and after the prosecution we call them the defendants. This makes the accused people hold different litigation status in different litigation stages in the criminal proceedings, and enjoy different litigation rights, which is conducive to the protection of their litigation rights.

There are two main types of the legal rights of the suspects or the defendant: one is the defensive right, including the right to use the national language in prosecution, the right to apply for withdrawal, the right to apply for complementary identification or reidentification, the right to get assistance from a lawyer, the right to refuse to answer the questions irrelevant to the case, the court right of cross-examination, the right to give final statements and the right to defense. Another type is the relief rights, including the right of complaint, the right of appeal, and the right to get compensation. China has made clear legal provisions on the defensive right and the relief right of the criminal suspects and the defendants in the proceedings, which are fully guaranteed in judicial practice.

In 2012, the National People's Congress amended the Criminal Procedure Law, and the provisions of the amended Criminal Procedure Law have made new breakthroughs to protect the rights of the suspect or the defendant, especially in the protection of the right to get assistance from the lawyer and the right of defense. More clear and specific provisions have been made in terms of the principle of presumption of innocence and the right to silence as well as the investigation of the illegal evidence and the affirmation of misjudged cases.

11.4 Safeguarding the Rights of Criminals in the Criminal Justice

China has a population of 1.3 billion, and it is the most populous country in the world. Although the People's Government has taken a series of measures of economic development and maintaining social stability, and the incidence of criminal cases is far below the world average, but there are still a lot of criminal cases every year. There are tens of thousands of people convicted by the People's Court in accordance with the law. It is still a daunting task to punish and rehabilitate offenders in accordance with the laws in China. The basic goal of the rehabilitation of offenders in China is to transform criminals into law-abiding newcomers living by their own labor, enabling them to return to a society successfully as law-abiding citizens. Most offenders including the Last Emperor and war criminals have ever been transformed by the New China to law-abiding citizens, who were harmless to others and beneficial to society. This helps to maintain the stability of Chinese society, economic development and national security, which effectively protects the rights of the citizens.

Great achievements have been made in the work of transforming criminals in China. On the one hand, this is because we have the correct leadership of the Party and have a team of the people's justice, who are loyal to the Party and the people, faithful to the law, proficient with excellent style; on the other hand, it is because we adhere to the principle of protecting the offenders' deserved rights in the criminal rehabilitation work in accordance with the law, conscientiously implementing the humanitarian principles and the principle of transformation with education as a focus, especially paying attention to the protection of the criminals' rights in the execution of punishment, focusing on probation education of the offenders, developing knowledge and skills of the offenders in order to enable them to return to a society as newcomers living by their own labor. The recidivism rate of criminals has been maintained at the level of 6–8 % for many years in China, which is one of the lowest recidivism rates in the world.

11.4.1 Basic Content of the Offender's Human Rights in the Criminal Justice

The rights enjoyed under the law by the criminal prisoners in serving their sentences are protected and cannot be violated. Under current law, the criminal prisoners have the following rights while serving their sentences:

(1) The right to appeal. The criminals have the right to appeal for the judgment and decision rendered by the People's Court and entering into force. In 1990 and 1991, Chinese courts accepted about 40,000 such appeal cases.
(2) The right to defense when was accused of recidivism. The criminal in prison has the right to defend himself or appoint a defender to defend in the course of criminal proceedings when he is accused to have committed new crimes or have found the crime missed.
(3) Criminals in any case have the right to personality not insulted, and inviolable right to personal safety. For extorting confessions by torture, corporal punishment, and other illegal activities of supervisory staff, the criminals have the right to expose and accuse to the People's Procuratorate, People's Court, People's Government or other agencies.
(4) The right to vote. The offender, who has not been deprived of political rights, can exercise their electoral rights in accordance with the law.
(5) The right to give suggestions. Criminals have the right to make reasonable suggestions on the management, education, labor production, cultural entertainment, life and health of prisons, and reform-through-labor institutions.
(6) The right to livelihood security. The criminals have the right to maintain a normal life, their material living conditions including eating, wearing, living, and using are guaranteed by the state. The area of criminal living facilities per capita is more than 5 square meters, and their dormitory is sturdy, clean, warm, and ventilated. According to statistics, in 1990, the average prisoner actually consumed 22.75 kg of grain, 20–25 kg of vegetables, a considerable amount of pork, beef, mutton, fish, poultry, eggs, beans, and other nonstaple food per month. Daily intake of each criminal is 2,952 kilocalories from food. The average annual living expenses of a criminal are 650 yuan in different regions of the country, close to the average living standard of local residents.
(7) The right to health care. The criminals have the right to protect their own health, criminals enjoy free medical care and undergo regular health checks every year, and their sickness receives prompt medical treatment. Seriously sick criminals have the right to obtain medical parole by law. Female offenders pregnant or breast-feeding her own baby enjoy the treatment of severing a sentence out of prison. For offenders suffering from incurable diseases, prisons and reform-through-labor institutions invite medical experts for consultation or send them to the community hospital for treatment. So far,

the Chinese system of reform-through-labor has formed a three-level health care network composed of provincial center hospitals, hospitals of prisons and reform-through-labor institutions, grassroots clinics, having 2,944 various health institutions; and there are 3.54 doctors and 14.8 hospital beds for per thousand criminals, higher than the national average level.

(8) The right to communication. Criminals have the right to meet relatives on a regular basis and to communicate with friends and relatives. Prisons and reform-through-labor institutions have special interview rooms for criminals to use and meet the families. When the offender and his/her family have a misunderstanding or even family members do not come to visit or interrupt communication links, prison authorities try to mediate and clear up the contradiction as much as possible.

(9) The right to education. The criminals have the right to education. Chinese reform-through-labor institutions have created the necessary conditions for offenders to receive education. The offenders, based on the extent of their own culture, can receive formal education of the primary school and junior middle school, as well as senior high school or higher education if the conditions permit. At the same time, they can also receive vocational training, which lays the foundation for their return to the society, being self-reliant. Criminals can read newspapers, magazines and books, listen to the radio, watch TV, understand domestic and international events, and maintain some contact with the outside community.

(10) The right to religion. Criminals have the right to believe in religion. The Chinese government allows religious criminals in custody maintain their beliefs.

(11) Civil rights. Criminals have the rights to property and to inheritance and other civil rights. Criminals' legitimate property before imprisonment is protected by the law, and the criminals have the rights to the earnings and disposal. Criminals have the right to inheritance according to law. Criminals in prison have the rights to invention, copyrights, which are protected by the law. Prisoners also have the right to present a petition for divorce and have the right to defense for disagreement of divorce.

(12) The right to special treatment. For juvenile offenders, female prisoners, sick and elderly criminals, and minority criminals and foreign criminals, the Chinese government gives them special treatment in life, management and labor different from other criminals by taking full account of their physical, psychological and physical characteristics, and their life habits. Juvenile offenders are detained in a reformatory. The reformatory carries out the policy of "education and reform as a main method supplemented by minor labor," and labor belongs to a kind of vocational study. Prisons and reform-through-labor institutions have specialized food stove for minority offenders with special dietary habits.

(13) The right to commutation and parole. A prisoner may have his sentence reduced for good behavior or be released on parole according to law. Since the founding of our country, prisons have implemented the commutation

Table 11.3 List of the cases of the commutation and parole rendered by the People's Courts [16]

Years	Reduced penalty (cases)	Release on Probation (cases)	Reduce penalty + Release on Probation (persons)	Remark
1985			107,000	
1987			495,057	Five years' statistic data from 1983 to 1987
1988			151,538	
1991	201,893	21,461		
1992	932,542	104,237		Five years' statistic data from 1988 to 1992
1993	230,052	33,388		
1994	249,479	29,086		
1995	258,097	27,064		
1998	270,000	20,000		
2003	328,939	20,964		
2004	391,484	17,963		
2005	390,987	18,430		
2006	429,852	20,254		
2007	433,033	16,906		
2008	502,192	30,274		

and parole system in the execution of punishment in order to promote the rehabilitation of offenders, enabling the criminals to return to society as soon as possible, and get a new chance at life. Commutation and parole is outwardly the power of the judicial organs, but it is essentially the rights of criminals rewarded because the beneficiaries of this system are criminals. The following is the table of open data we can access to listing commutation and parole (Table 11.3).

Viewed from the data we can access to, there were a considerable number of criminals of commutation and parole. The number of offenders of commutation and parole reached 107,000 people in 1985. In the five-year period of 1983–1987, offenders of commutation and parole reached as many as 495,057 people, and there were as many as 99,011 people of commutation and parole on average every year. In the criminal cases of commutation and parole, cases of commutation were more than cases of parole. In the five-year period of 1988–1992, offenders of commutation reached as many as 932,542 people, and there were as many as 186,508 people of commutation on average every year; offenders of parole reached as many as 104,237 people and there were as many as 20,847 people of parole on average every year. In the five-year period of 2003–2007, offenders of commutation reached as many as 1,974,295 people, and there were as many as 394,859 people of commutation on average every year; offenders of parole reached as many as 94,517 people and there were as many as 18,903 people of parole on average every year. In recent years, the number of cases of commutation and parole reached as many as 400,000 per year. It should be said that this has played an important role in safeguarding the criminals' right to commutation and parole in accordance with the law.

(14) The right to rest. The criminals have the right to rest, the provisions of Article 43 of our Constitution, "Working people in the People's Republic of China have the right to rest." Criminals should enjoy the right to rest.
(15) Criminals have the right to work. Labor is one of the means of reforming criminals. For those who want to transform themselves through participation in the labor and to increase the skills and abilities of the return to society, the criminals have the right to participate in the work. This point was stipulated by Article 42 of the Constitution, "Citizens of the People's Republic of China have the right as well as the duty to work." Criminals are also citizens, and their right to work cannot be denied.

Criminals also undertake corresponding obligations in the enjoyment of rights, which is the inevitable requirement of the equivalent principle of rights. The criminals must fulfill the obligations prescribed by law, and these obligations are: complying with laws and regulations and the prison regulations and disciplines unitarily developed by the reform-through-labor institutions; obeying management and education by the staff of supervision and management; actively participating in productive labor; accepting the ideological, cultural, and technical education; taking good care of state property and protecting public facilities; being civilized and polite, and abiding by social morality; reporting illegal and criminal activities; strengthening the organic disciplines, and participating in group activities; bearing in mind the nature of the crime, and accepting the reform, etc.

11.4.2 The Realization of Protecting Offenders' Rights in Criminal Justice

In order to safeguard the legitimate rights of criminals, the legislature and the government of China have formulated laws and regulations; regulatory staff must go through the training of specialised legal and business knowledge to be certified before taking up a post; it is strictly forbidden to torture, insult, or otherwise maltreat prisoners. If corporal punishment occurs to the criminal, the violations should be dealt with severely, until investigating the criminal responsibility. In other words, in accordance with the provisions of the criminal law of China, a serious case of illegal corporal punishment of a prisoner which constitutes administering unauthorized corporal punishment to a detainee is tried in the People's Court. In 1990 and 1991, a total of 24 supervisory staff was sentenced because of corporal punishment. The People's Procuratorate has sent permanent prosecuting agencies in prisons and institutions to supervise the law-enforcement activities of these reform-through-labor institutions and protect, according to law, the prisoners' right to appeal, right to complain, and right to make accusation. Representatives from all levels of the people's congresses and the committee members from all levels of Chinese People's Political Consultative Committee (CPPCC) inspect prisons and reform-through-labor institutions from time to time in order to check the law enforcement situations. For example, in 1991, a total of more than 30 members of the National People's Political Consultative Committee and Beijing CPPCC had four inspections of Beijing First Prison, checking the law enforcement work there. It should be said that the overall status of the protection of the rights of the offenders in the criminal justice is good, criminals have effectively been reformed, and the recidivism rate is quite low, which has been maintained at the level of 6–8 % over the years [17].

The rights of criminals are mainly derived from the Constitution and the law, from the authorization in management of the judicial and administrative authorities, such as meeting and homoclinic rights. Viewed from the forms of offender's right and the realization approaches of the right, after the founding of our country, because of the continuously strengthening education and reform of offenders and of focusing on the protection of the rights of criminals, the rights of criminals have been gradually expanded, the conditions of the realization of the rights of offenders have been improved, and the extent of criminals' realization of rights have been constantly improved. In the early stage after the founding of our country, the construction of the national economy was in a recovery period. The rehabilitation of offenders was also linked with the economic situation at the time, prison management adhered to the working policy of "reform the first, production the second," but due to a single method in the management and economic backwardness, labor became the primary means of reform. During the "Cultural Revolution", prison management education emphasized strict management, tending to attach importance to the function of the prison punishment, the protection work of the offender's rights was not placed in the proper location. Since the reform and opening-up, because of China's economic revitalization, and the continuous development of democracy and the legal system, the rights of offenders have comprehensively been safeguarded.

In order to make the prisoners' human rights protected more effectively, the Chinese government has taken effective measures for the improvement on the various problems existing in the management of the prison. In order to prevent the prison from deviating from the principle of "combining punishment with reform, and keeping reform of people as its purpose," the Ministry of Justice conducted an investigation of the national prison situations in 2001. In 2002, the Central Committee put forward the goal of prison reform: "full protection, separation of enterprise from prison, separation of income and expenditure, standardized operation". On January 31, 2003, the State Council issued the "Notice of the working guidelines on the prison, deciding from the beginning of 2003 to carry out the prison system reform pilot work in 6 provinces (cities) of Heilongjiang, Shanghai, Jiangxi, Hubei, Chongqing, Shaanxi."

On August 19, 2009, the National Prison Reform Working Symposium was held in Yantai. Minister of the Ministry of Justice Wu Aiying stressed in the meeting that the prison system should adhere to the Deng Xiaoping Theory and the important thought of "Three Represents" as guidance, thoroughly implement the Scientific Outlook on Development, conscientiously implement the policy decisions of both the Party Central Committee and the State Council, and further deepening understanding, unifying thoughts, strengthening measures, intensifying efforts and strengthening leadership to accelerate the reform of the prison system, to making efforts to complete the task for the prison system reform and establish a new reform of the prison system of being just, honest, civilized, and efficient in accordance with the requirements of "full protection, separation of enterprise from prison, separation of income and expenditure, standardized operation," The reform of the prison system not only provides opportunities and creates the conditions for innovation and development of the prison, but also provides the system safeguard for the protection of criminals.

Outstanding achievements have been made by China in protecting the criminals' rights. At the same time, the specific measures for protecting the criminals' human right need continuous improvement according to the changes of the reality. Especially in normalizing the check rights of the police, the commutation of the criminal, the right to parole, the rights of the criminals to get labor remuneration and labor protection and so on, China needs to further strengthen the legislation, to strengthen the construction of judicial and police teams, to establish an effective mechanism for the criminals to claim for and maintain their rights and strengthen supervision of the procuratorial organs.

References

1. Beijing Institute of Political Science and Law (Ed.), 1956. Reference collection of the Law of the People's Republic of China on trial. (5): 72–73.
2. Beijing Institute of Political Science and Law (Ed.), 1956. Reference collection of the Law of the People's Republic of China on trial. (2): 339.
3. History Teaching Group of the State and Law of Marxism and Leninism, East China Institute of Political Science and Law (Ed.), 1956. *History Reference Materials on Chinese Nation and Law* (3). P.237.
4. According to Article 82: "Parties" means victims, private prosecutors, criminal suspects, defendants and the plaintiffs and defendants in incidental civil actions. "Participants in the proceedings" means the parties, legal representatives, agents ad litem, defenders, witnesses, expert witnesses and interpreters.
5. According to the provision of Article 170 of the Criminal Procedure Law of the PRC: "Cases of private prosecution include the following: (1) cases to be handled only upon complaint; (2) cases for which the victims have evidence to prove that those are minor criminal cases; and (3) cases for which the victims have evidence to prove that the defendants should be investigated for criminal responsibility according to law because their acts have infringed upon the victims' personal or property rights, whereas, the public security organs or the People's Procuratorates do not investigate the criminal responsibility of the accused."

6. Refer to Report on the Work of the Supreme People's Court made by the President of the Supreme People's Court Xiao Yang at the Fifth Meeting of the 10th Session of National People's Congress on March 13, 2007.
7. Here situations refer to the following: (1) if he is a party or a near relative of a party to the case; (2) if he or a near relative of his has an interest in the case; (3) if he has served as a witness, expert witness, defender or agent ad litem in the current case; or (4) if he has any other relations with a party to the case that could affect the impartial handling of the case.
8. Amount of compensation has only appeared since 2004.
9. Refer to Report on the Work of the Supreme People's Procuratorate made by Chief Prosecutor Huang Huoqing at the First Meeting of the 6th Session of National People's Congress on June 7, 1983.
10. Refer to Report on the Work of the Supreme People's Procuratorate made by Chief Prosecutor Han Zhubin at the Second Meeting of the 9th Session of National People's Congress on March 10, 1999.
11. Refer to Report on the Work of the Supreme People's Procuratorate made by Chief Prosecutor Jia Chunwang at the First Meeting of the 11th Session of National People's Congress on March 10, 2008.
12. Refer to Report on the Work of the Supreme People's Procuratorate made by Chief Prosecutor Han Zhubin at the First Meeting of the 10th Session of National People's Congress on March 11, 2003.
13. Refer to Report on the Work of the Supreme People's Procuratorate made by Chief Prosecutor Jia Chunwang at the Second Meeting of the 10th Session of National People's Congress on March 10, 2004.
14. Refer to Report on the Work of the Supreme People's Procuratorate made by Chief Prosecutor Jia Chunwang at the Third Meeting of the 10th Session of National People's Congress on March 9, 2005.
15. Refer to Report on the Work of the Supreme People's Procuratorate made by Chief Prosecutor Jia Chunwang at the Fifth Meeting of the 10th Session of National People's Congress on March 13, 2007.
16. Refer to the statistics in public report of the Supreme People's Court.
17. Refer to *Criminal Reform in China* released by the Information Office of the State Council, the People's Republic of China, in August, 1992.

Appendix I
Teaching Module: Human Rights in China (LAWM706)

I am very glad to have this opportunity to introduce my course called Human Rights in China. Before my introduction to the course, I would like to make a self-introduction to all of you.

Tutor: Associate Professor SUN Pinghua

Self-Introduction

Pinghua, Sun, MAs (Beijing Normal University; the University of Warwick), Ph.D. in human rights law (China University of Political Science and Law—CUPL), Associate Professor (CUPL) and MA Supervisor, Visiting Scholar to the University of Exeter. My research interests include: human rights law and applied linguistics. My research projects include, "National Social Science Foundation Post-funded Project" (*The Study of the Universal Declaration of Human Rights* published by Peking University Press in August 2012) and "National Social Science Fund, China Academic Translation Project" (*Human Rights Protection System in China*—to be published by Springer in August 2013) besides dozen of provincial and ministerial scientific research programs. More than 80 journal articles have been published, 8 of which are included in "*Politics of China*", "*International Law*", and "*Constitutional Law, Administrative Law*" by Information Center for Social Sciences, Renmin University of China.

In 2011, I was a visiting scholar in the United Kingdom and ran a postgraduate course "Human Rights in China" (LAWM706) for the Law School, the University of Exeter; and I was invited to participate in the 47th Session of the United Nations Committee on Economic, Social and Cultural Rights in Geneva. In May 2012, I was invited to attend the International Conference of the China-EU Fundamental Rights at the University of Bologna, Italy, and delivered a speech entitled "*Fundamental Principles for Achieving International Human Rights Standards in China*", which is included in Rossi, L. S. and Federico, G. D. (Eds.),

P. Sun, *Human Rights Protection System in China*,
DOI: 10.1007/978-3-642-39663-2,

Fundamental Rights in Europe and China: Regional identities and universalism published by Editoriale Scientifica in Italy (2013). In February 2013, I accepted the invitation to be a panelist of the International Human Rights Symposium—"Human Trafficking and Sex Slavery in the Modern Era" held in Albany, New York, the United States, attending two panels including both "International perspectives on human trafficking" and "Issues in domestic law enforcement of human trafficking" as a panelist, and making two speeches. Based on the panel speeches, I wrote an article entitled "Human Trafficking and Sex Slavery in the Modern World", which will be published in the journal *Albany Government Law Review* in 2013. During my stay in New York, I was invited to pay a visit to both the Columbia Law School and Albany Law School of the Union University, meeting with Professors and students there for further communication. At Albany Law School, I was invited to give a speech entitled "The development of human rights in China" to the law students.

I am now committed to "Chinese Wisdom in Establishing the International Human Rights System—Viewed from the perspective of P. C. Chang's contributions to the drafting of the UDHR", which was appraised by Michael K. Addo, the global leading human rights expert: "This is an original research to fill the gaps in the academic research field of international human rights". The draft based on this research has been included in the publishing agenda of Springer.

What Is the Course (Human Rights in China) about?

Human rights refer to basic rights and freedoms that all people enjoy regardless of nationality, sex, age, national or ethnic origin, race, religion, language, or other status. Human rights are conceived as universal and egalitarian, with all people having equal rights by virtue of being human. Human rights originate from human dignity, while human dignity comes from human beings' reason and conscience, which distinguish human beings from animals. These rights may exist as natural rights or as legal rights, in both national and international law.

The first article on the Universal Declaration of Human Rights: "All human beings are born free and equal in dignity and rights. They are endowed with reason and conscience and should act towards one another in a spirit of brotherhood."

The doctrine of human rights in international practice, within international law, global and regional institutions, in the policies of states and the activities of non-governmental organizations has been a cornerstone of public policy around the world. Human rights have become a common moral language for the international community. Despite this, the strong claims made by the doctrine of human rights continue to provoke considerable skepticism, debates about the content, nature, and justifications of human rights continue to this day. Issues relevant to human rights are still controversial problems, which are worthy of further studies.

Why Do We Choose "Human Rights in China"?

China is a big country with a long history, a brilliant culture, and a large population. China is one of the four civilized countries with more than a 5,000-year-long civilization. Does anyone know the Four Great Inventions of ancient China? (Compass—was invented in the fourth century B.C; Papermaking—was invented in AD 105; Gunpowder—was invented in the ninth century; Printing—was invented in AD 868). What roles do these inventions play in our modern education system? Can we have a library without papermaking and printing? Yeah, China is a big country with a large population. For example, the number of official residents in Beijing is 20 million excluding about 10 million moving people. China is no doubt an influential country in the world, and it is playing an important part in the international community. Human rights in China have become an important foci both in the academic area and in the international politics.

What Are the Aims and Intended Learning Outcomes?

The course of "Human rights in China" (LAWM706) is specially designed for postgraduate students of the Law School. This module aims at introducing students to the human rights protection system in China from different perspectives including theoretical contributions, legislative system, judicial protection system, and some milestones indicating the new progress of human rights protection in China.

This module places a particular emphasis on the emerging regime for the protection of human rights in China, and will enable students to know the key developments in human rights protection in the Chinese context. In addition, the module will enable students to make informed career decisions in human rights in China.

This module is designed to broaden your horizons to view things from different cultural perspectives. Through the course, you are expected to make a better achievement by taking advantage of eastern wisdom and philosophy. It will make it much easier to open the window to the Chinese culture and Chinese human rights protection system as well. Human rights research in China is a stimulating and exciting area, and a promising field.

Currently, I am working on the Chinese contributions to the drafting of the Universal Declaration of Human Rights. I really hope some of you can get involved in this promising research project. Relevant to my research project, I really hope that all students of this course can apply for attending the Geneva Human Rights Conference, which is a very beneficial experience for your whole life and your future career, particularly for Chinese students, it is the only good opportunity for all the students to go further in the field of human rights law research. In addition, you can learn to conduct a scientific research by getting involved in the research process.

What Should Students Be Able to Do on Successful Completion of This Module?

On successful completion of this module, students should be able to:

Module Specific Skills

1. critically contrast theories and practice of human rights in China;
2. reflect on and assess the nature of human rights in China;
3. analyze the relevant issues to human rights protection in China;

Discipline Specific Skills

4. have general knowledge of human rights protection system in China;
5. objectively evaluate some aspects relevant to human rights in China;

Personal and Key Skills

6. conduct autonomous study and group work including the ability to present material developed through the course of learning for group discussion;
7. research, study, identify, categorize, and organize materials for purposes of producing a coherent and analytical account of the results of the research.

Details of Learning and Teaching Methods

Lectures/seminars/attending Geneva Human Rights Conference (5 × 3 h): encouraging students' active involvement, independent or group research on specific topics. (ILOs 1–7)

Assignments (Formative Assessment)

Clarifying an interested area in human rights protection system in China in a few passages with a clear outline including major references based on reading in the course of this module. This assignment (20 %, 1,000-word Literature Review) will encourage students to read extensively on the system for the protection of human rights protection in China. (ILOs 1–5) It is easy for everyone to finish it in the course of this module.

Assessment (Summative Assessment)

Assessment (80 %) will be by assessed essay of 3,500 words. (ILOs 1–7) It may be a little challenging, but it will be beneficial and helpful for you to develop your skills of writing your final MA dissertation.

Syllabus Plan

Week 2: Nature and development of human rights in China
Week 4: Socialist legal system with Chinese characteristics
Week 6: Judicial protection system with Chinese characteristics
Week 8: Human rights education and research in the Chinese context
Week 10: New development of human rights protection in China

Reading Materials

1. **Baehr,P. R.** et al. (Eds.), 1996. *Human Rights: Chinese and Dutch perspectives*. The Hague/London/Boston: Martinus Nijhoff Publishers.
2. **Bell, D. A.** 1996. The East Asian challenge to human rights: Reflections on an East West dialogue. *Human Rights Quarterly* 18/3: 641–667.
3. **Dong, Yunhu** and **Chang, Jian.** 2009. *60 Years' Human Rights Construction in China*. Jiangxi People's Press. (董云虎, 常健主编, 《中国人权建设60年》, 江西人民出版社2009年版。)
4. **Han, Yanlong.** 1996. Legal protection of human rights in China. In P. R. Baehr et al. (Eds.), *Human Rights: Chinese and Dutch perspectives*. The Hague/London/Boston: Martinus Nijhoff Publishers.
5. **Kolodner, E.** 1994. Religious Rights in China: A Comparison of International Human Rights Law and Chinese Domestic Legislation. *Human Rights Quarterly* 16/3: 455–490.
6. **Li, Buyun.** 1996. On individual and collective human rights. In P. R. Baehr et al. (Eds.), *Human Rights: Chinese and Dutch perspectives*. The Hague/London/Boston: Martinus Nijhoff Publishers.
7. **Liu, Nanlai.** 1996. Developing countries and human rights. In P. R. Baehr et al. (Eds.), *Human Rights: Chinese and Dutch perspectives*. The Hague/London/Boston: Martinus Nijhoff Publishers.
8. **Lo, Chung Shu.** 1949. Human Rights in the Chinese Tradition. In UNESCO (Ed.), *Human Rights: Comments and Interpretation* (pp. 186–187). London & New York: Allan Wingate.
9. **Peerenboom, R. P.** 2005. Assessing Human Rights in China: Why the Double Standard? *Cornell International Law Journal* 38: 71–172.
10. **Qi, Yanping** and **Zang, Zhen.** 2008. Progress and reflection: China's human rights in the past 30 years. *Human Rights* 3: 19–26.
11. **Tu, Weiming.** 1996. Confucian traditions in East Asian modernity. *Bulletin of the American Academy of Arts and Sciences* 50/2: 12–39.
12. **Twiss, S. B.** 2009. Confucian contributions to the Universal Declaration of Human Rights: A historical and philosophical perspective. In A. Sharma (Ed.), *The World's Religions after September 11*: Volume 2 Religion and human rights (Chapter 14, pp. 153–173). Westport, CT and London: Praeger.
13. **Twiss, S. B.** 2007. Confucian ethics, concept-clusters, and human rights. In M. Chandler and R. Littlejohn (Eds.), *Polishing the Chinese Mirror: Essays*

in Honor of Henry Rosemont, Jr (pp. 50–67). New York: Global Scholarly Publications.

14. **Wan, Ming.** 2007. Human rights lawmaking in China: Domestic politics, international law, and international politics. *Human Rights Quarterly* 29/3: 727–753.
15. **Wang, Qifu** and **Liu, Jinguo.** 2003. *Judicial Protection of Human Rights in China*. Xiamen University Press. (王启富, 刘金国主编, 《中国人权的司法保障》, 厦门大学出版社2003年版。)
16. **Wang, Zhaoguo.** 2010. Several Issues on the Formation of Socialist Legal System with Chinese Characteristics. *People's Daily*, November 15th, p. 6.
17. **Wu, Bangguo.** 2011. The formation of a socialist legal system with Chinese characteristics, the significance and basic experience. *People's Daily*, March 10th.
18. **Xia, Yong.** 1996. Human rights and Chinese tradition. In P. R. Baehr et al. (Eds.), *Human rights: Chinese and Dutch perspectives*. The Hague/London/Boston: Martinus Nijhoff Publishers.
19. **Xu, Xianming**. 2009. On the formation and improvement of socialist legal system with Chinese characteristics. *People's Daily*, March 12th.
20. **Zhang, Jiliang.** 2004. *CPC Human Rights Theory and Chinese Human Rights Legislation*. Chinese Social Science Press. (张继良著, 《中共人权理论与中国人权立法》, 中国社会科学出版社2004年版。)

Timetable for Module LAWM706 (Human Rights in China)

Time: Tuesday 14:00–16:00
Place: Amory Building/Room B106
Report start date 03 October 2011, covering weeks: T1:02, T1:04, T1:06, T1:08, T1:10
(*This brief Introduction was made in Newman Lecture Theatre at Peter Chalk Centre on Tuesday afternoon, September 27, 2011.* The first section—"Self-Introduction" was updated in August 2013.)

Appendix II
China's Efforts and Achievements in Promoting the Rule of Law

Foreword

The rule of law signifies that a political civilization has developed to a certain historic stage. As the crystallization of human wisdom, it is desired and pursued by people of all countries.

The Chinese people have made protracted and unremitting struggles for democracy, freedom, equality, and the building of a country under the rule of law. They know well the significance and value of the rule of law, and thus cherish the fruits they have achieved in building China into a country under the rule of law.

The rule of law in a country is determined by and conforms to its national conditions and social system. To govern the country according to law and build a socialist country under the rule of law is the Chinese people's demand, pursuit and practice.

The Communist Party of China (CPC) has led the Chinese people in successfully opening up the road of socialism with Chinese characteristics. Along this road, China, in line with the objective requirements arising in the course of continuous economic, political, cultural, and social development, has upheld the organic unity of the CPC's leadership, the position of the people as masters of the country and law-based governance, stuck to the principle of people first, advocated the spirit of the rule of law, fostered the idea of democracy and rule of law, freedom and equality, fairness and justice, developed and improved the socialist legal system with Chinese characteristics, promoted the exercise of administrative functions in accordance with the law in all respects, deepened the reform of the judicial system, perfected the mechanism of restraint of and supervision over the use of power, guaranteed the citizens' lawful rights and interests, maintained social harmony and stability, and continuously promoted institutionalization of all work.

Information Office of the State Council of the People's Republic of China
February 28, 2008

P. Sun, *Human Rights Protection System in China*,
DOI: 10.1007/978-3-642-39663-2, © Springer-Verlag Berlin Heidelberg 2014

The Chinese people are comprehensively implementing the rule of law as a fundamental principle, and speeding up the building of a socialist country under the rule of law. This is a great, unprecedented social practice involving 1.3 billion Chinese people under the leadership of the CPC. The Chinese nation, with a long history and splendid civilization, is striding ahead on the road of democracy and the rule of law, and opening up a new realm in the development of human political civilization.

Historical Course of Building a Socialist Country Under the Rule of Law

China has a 5,000-year history of civilization. The Chinese legal system goes back to ancient times. As early as in the twenty-first century BC, consuetudinary law appeared in China's slave society. In the Spring and Autumn and Warring States periods (770–221 BC), written law was promulgated in China, and a systematic written code of laws appeared. In the Tang Dynasty (618–907), China had a fairly complete code of feudal laws, which was passed on and developed in the following feudal dynasties. The Chinese system of law emerged as a unique one in the world. Ancient China made significant contributions to the legal civilization of mankind.

After the Opium War broke out in 1840, China was reduced to a semi-colonial and semi-feudal society. To obliterate the sufferings of the country and rejuvenate the Chinese nation, people with lofty ideals tried to transplant to China modes of the rule of law from modern Western countries, but failed for various historical reasons.

Under the leadership of the CPC, the Chinese people, after revolution, construction, reform, and development, gradually took the road of building a socialist country under the rule of law.

The founding of the People's Republic of China in 1949 ushered in a new era for China's promotion of the rule of law. The period from 1949 to the mid-1950s was the period when China's socialist legal system was first set up. In this period, China promulgated the Common Program of the Chinese People's Political Consultative Conference, in the character of an interim constitution, and some other laws and decrees, which played an important role in consolidating the new-born political power, maintaining social order and reviving the national economy. In 1954, at the First Session of the First National People's Congress (NPC), the Constitution of the People's Republic of China was promulgated. The Constitution and other laws enacted later defined China's political and economic systems, citizen's rights and freedom, set the standards for the organizational structure, functions and powers of state organs, and established the basic principles for China's legal system, thus initially laying the foundation for the rule of law in China. From the late 1950s, and especially during the chaotic period of the "cultural revolution" (1966–1976), China's socialist legal system was severely damaged.

At the end of the 1970s, the CPC, after summarizing historical experiences, and especially learning painful lessons from the "cultural revolution," made an important decision to shift the focus of national work to socialist modernization, and adopted the policies of reform and opening-up. It also made clear the importance of the principle of governing the country by law. To guarantee democracy for the people, it is necessary to strengthen the socialist legal system, institutionalize democracy and make laws to ensure democracy. The goal was to make the system and laws stable, consistent and authoritative—not changing with changes of state leaders or state leaders' opinions or attention—and achieve the goal of having laws to go by, laws that must be observed and strictly enforced, and lawbreakers prosecuted. This was set up as the basic idea for the rule of law in the new era of reform and opening-up. Under the guidance of the basic principle of developing socialist democracy and improving the socialist legal system, China promulgated the present Constitution and basic laws, such as the Criminal Law, Criminal Procedure Law, Civil Procedure Law, General Principles of the Civil Law and Administrative Procedure Law, ushering in a new development stage of the rule of law.

In the 1990s, China started to promote the development of a socialist market economy in an all-round way, further laying the economic foundation and putting forward higher demands for the rule of law. In 1997, the 15th CPC National Congress decided to make "the rule of law" a basic strategy and "building a socialist country under the rule of law" an important goal for socialist modernization, and put forward the significant task of building a socialist legal system with Chinese characteristics. In 1999, "the People's Republic of China exercises the rule of law, building a socialist country governed according to law" was added to the Constitution, ushering in a new chapter in China's efforts to promote the rule of law.

Entering the twenty-first century, China is continuing this undertaking. In 2002, the 16th CPC National Congress decided to take further improvement of the socialist democracy and socialist legal system, comprehensive implementation of the rule of law as important goals for building a moderately prosperous society in all respects. In 2004, "the state respects and guarantees human rights" was included in the Constitution. In 2007, the 17th CPC National Congress expressly called for comprehensively implementing the fundamental principle of rule of the country by law and speeding up the building of a socialist country under the rule of law, and made arrangements for strengthening the rule of law in an all-round way.

Over almost six decades since its founding, especially during 30 years since the introduction of the reform and opening-up policies, China has made tremendous achievements in promoting the rule of law in its great task of building socialism with Chinese characteristics.

- The rule of law has been established as a fundamental principle. It is a fundamental state principle as well as the common understanding of all sectors of society to govern the country according to law and build a socialist country under the rule of law. Moreover, the socialist idea of the rule of law has been gradually established, with the rule of law at the core, law enforcement for the people as an essential requirement, fairness and justice as a value to be pursued, serving the overall interests as an important mission, and with the leadership of the CPC as a fundamental guarantee. The awareness of law and the rule of law has been generally strengthened in all sectors of society, and a social atmosphere of consciously learning, observing and employing law is coming into being.

- The CPC has markedly improved its governance capability. The Party has constantly enhanced its consciousness and firmness in governing the country in a scientific and democratic way, and by law. It has led the people in making the Constitution and laws. Meanwhile, it has carried out activities within the scope prescribed by the Constitution and the law, with the Constitution as the fundamental criterion; it upholds the Constitution and persists in the rule of law, and takes the lead in safeguarding the authority of the Constitution and the law; and it has mobilized and organized the people to the maximum extent to manage state and social affairs, the economy and cultural undertakings. By leading the people in making and abiding by laws and guaranteeing law enforcement, the Party has continuously consolidated its ruling position.
- A Constitution-centered socialist legal system with Chinese characteristics has basically taken shape. On the basis of the present Constitution, the state has enacted and improved a large number of laws, administrative regulations, local regulations, autonomous regulations, and separate regulations, making the legal system more complete and providing the state with laws to go by in economic, political and cultural sectors, as well as in social life. Legislation has become more scientific and democratic, and its quality has been improved. Laws now play an increasingly greater role in promoting economic and social development, ensuring social fairness and justice, and guaranteeing the people's rights and the proper exercise of the state power.
- Human rights are under reliable legal protection. While improving the people's rights to subsistence and development through economic and social development, the state attaches great importance to protecting citizens' basic rights and freedom in accordance with the Constitution and the law. It protects in accordance with the law the right of all members of society to equal participation and development. With the continuous improvement of laws, regulations, the judicial system and the mechanism for safeguarding rights and interests, human rights have been better guaranteed in legislation, law enforcement, the judiciary and other aspects. The undertaking to protect human rights has been developing in a sound way, and citizens' political, economic, social, and cultural rights are now fully respected and guaranteed in all aspects.
- The environment for the rule of law, which promotes economic development and social harmony, has been constantly improved. In response to the demands of building a socialist market economy, the state has been strengthening

economic legislation and improving macro-control. It prohibits any organization or individual from disrupting the economic and social order in accordance with the law. China has enacted and improved a series of laws and systems promoting economic development, safeguarding market order and achieving social fairness and justice, established an initial law regime for the socialist market economy. The social security system has been continuously improved, with social insurance, social relief and social welfare as the bases, with basic endowment insurance, basic medical insurance and the subsistence allowance system as focuses and supplemented by charities and commercial insurance.

- Administration by law and fair administration of justice have been constantly improved. By establishing and improving the organizational and working mechanisms for administrative law enforcement and the judiciary, China guarantees that the administrative and judicial organs exercise their power and perform their duties in accordance with their legitimate authorization and legal procedures. Administrative legislation and institutional improvement have been further strengthened, the system of keeping the public informed of matters being handled is being constantly improved, and government administration based on the rule of law is being furthered. Public security organs fulfill their duties in accordance with the law, safeguarding state security and public order, and guaranteeing that people can live and work in peace and contentment. Courts and procuratorates exercise their powers independently in accordance with the law, make judgments based on facts and with the law as the sole benchmark, and insist on the principle that all citizens are equal before the law, thereby safeguarding and enforcing judicial justice and authoritativeness.
- Restraint of and supervision over the use of power have been strengthened. A power structure and a power operating mechanism featuring decision-making authority, enforcement power and supervision right restraining and coordinating each other have been set up and improved continuously; fairly complete supervision systems and rules have been established; and the composite force and effectiveness of supervision have been constantly strengthened. The people's congresses at all levels and their standing committees exercise supervision over the governments, people's courts and people's procuratorates of the same level. The people's political consultative conferences at different levels give full scope to their role of democratic supervision, and such supervision has been gradually institutionalized and standardized. The general public and news media have more and more ways and means to supervise government and judicial work. The constantly improved systems of inquiry, accountability, economic accountability audit, resignation and recall guarantee that the supervision over government functionaries is powerful and effective.

Legislation and Legal System with Chinese Characteristics

The People's Republic of China is a united, multi-ethnic, and unitary socialist country. To guarantee the uniformity of the legal system of the state and reflect the common will and overall interests of the people, China exercises uniform yet multi-tiered legislation.

The Constitution prescribes that the NPC and its Standing Committee exercise the legislative power of the state. The NPC enacts and amends basic laws, such as the criminal law and civil law as well as organic laws on state organs and other matters. The Standing Committee of the NPC enacts and amends laws other than those that should be enacted by the NPC, and it can partially supplement and amend, when the NPC is not in session, laws enacted by the NPC, provided that the basic principles of these laws are not contravened.

In accordance with the Legislation Law of the People's Republic of China, laws on the following affairs must be made exclusively by the NPC and its Standing Committee: affairs involving state sovereignty, the formation, organization as well as the functions and powers of state organs, the system of regional ethnic autonomy, the system of special administrative regions, the system of self-government of people at the grassroots level, criminal offences and their punishment, deprivation of citizens' political rights, mandatory measures and penalties involving restriction of the freedom of the person, expropriation of non-state-owned property, basic civil system, basic economic system and basic systems of finance, taxation, customs, banking and foreign trade, and systems of litigation and arbitration.

With a vast land, China faces complicated conditions and imbalanced development among different regions. To guarantee the uniformity of the state's legal system and yet adapt to different conditions in different regions, the Constitution and Legislation Law both prescribe that, in addition to the NPC and its Standing Committee, the State Council may enact administrative regulations in accordance with the Constitution and the law; the people's congresses or their standing committees of the provinces, autonomous regions and municipalities directly under the central government may enact local regulations, provided that such regulations do not contradict the Constitution, the laws and administrative regulations, and approve local regulations formulated by people's congresses or their standing committees of the larger cities; the people's congresses of the ethnic autonomous areas have the power to enact autonomous regulations and separate regulations on the basis of the political, economic and cultural conditions of the local ethnic group(s). Moreover, the ministries and commissions of the State Council and the other organs endowed with administrative functions directly under the State Council may, in accordance with the laws and administrative regulations, enact rules within the limits of their power; and the people's governments of the provinces, autonomous regions, municipalities directly under the central government and the larger cities may, in accordance with laws, administrative regulations and local regulations of their respective province, autonomous region or municipality, enact rules.

To conform to the fundamental interests of the public and the overall interests of the state, and at the same time take into consideration all types of specific interests and guarantee scientific and democratic legislation, the Chinese legal system prescribes the legislative procedures of the NPC and its Standing Committee, procedures for the State Council in making administrative regulations, and procedures for local people's congresses and their standing committees at various levels in enacting local regulations. The Standing Committee of the NPC follows the "system of three deliberations" in making laws, which means that a legal bill should be deliberated at three meetings of the Standing Committee of the NPC before it is voted on; and in the case of an important or controversial legal bill, it may undergo more than three deliberations. For instance, the bill of the Property Rights Law went through seven rounds of deliberation at the meetings of the Standing Committee of the NPC before being submitted to the Fifth Session of the Tenth NPC for discussion and adoption. A legal bill submitted to the NPC should be repeatedly deliberated at the plenary meetings, delegation sessions, and group discussions of the Congress; and a legal bill submitted to the Standing Committee of the NPC should go through deliberations at the plenary sessions and group discussions of the Standing Committee. Before being promulgated, each law must go through repeated deliberations until a consensus is reached, and then be submitted to the NPC or its Standing Committee for final voting at a plenary meeting. This process, involving many rounds of deliberation, is precisely aimed at giving full expression to all kinds of interests through consultation, and adjusting and balancing relations between different interests. This democratic process, focusing on full consultation before a bill is submitted for final voting, displays a distinctive feature of the system of the NPC of China.

In the legislative process, we uphold democracy, pool the people's wisdom and reflect the people's will. To propose legal bills and bills concerning administrative regulations and local regulations, the legislation authorities listen to opinions from all sectors of society through various ways, such as holding forums, feasibility study meetings, hearings, so as to enhance transparency and public participation. Bills of laws, regulations, and rules concerning vital public interests or dictating the obligations of citizens are published in full in the news media to ask for comments from the people. After being adopted, the laws and regulations are published in a timely way in gazettes of the people's congresses and governments at all levels, government websites and the mass media. In recent years, the Standing Committee of the NPC and the State Council have sought advice from all sectors of society regarding draft laws and administrative regulations, including the Property Rights Law, Law on Labor Contracts, Law on the Promotion of Employment and Regulations on the Administration of Properties. The Standing Committee of the NPC has held feasibility study meetings and hearings regarding revisions of the Law on the Protection of Cultural Relics, Law on Individual Income Tax, and others.

To guarantee the uniformity of the state's legal system and coordination of various laws and regulations, the Chinese legal system prescribes the validity of laws or regulations at different levels: The Constitution has the supreme legal authority, and no laws, administrative regulations, local regulations, autonomous regulations, separate regulations, or rules may contravene the Constitution. The authority of laws is higher than that of administrative regulations, local regulations, and rules. The authority of administrative regulations is higher than that of local regulations and rules; and the authority of local regulations is higher than that of the rules of local governments at and below the corresponding level. The legal system also prescribes a system of record and examination for regulations and rules: Administrative regulations shall be filed to the Standing Committee of the NPC for the record; local regulations shall be filed to the Standing Committee of the NPC and the State Council for the record; and the rules of a department and of a local government shall be filed to the State Council for the record. The NPC has the power to alter or annul any inappropriate laws enacted by its Standing Committee; the Standing Committee of the NPC has the power to annul any administrative regulations that contradict the Constitution and the law, and to annul any local regulations that contradict the Constitution, laws or administrative regulations; and the State Council has the power to alter or annul any inappropriate rules of the government departments and of local governments. The NPC gives the Hong Kong and Macao special administrative regions (SAR) the power of legislation in accordance with their respective Basic Law, and no laws of the SAR may contradict the Basic Law of the SAR.

The legal system of China also prescribes the procedure of examination of administrative regulations, local regulations, autonomous regulations and separate regulations on whether they contradict the Constitution or the law: When the State Council, the Central Military Commission, the Supreme People's Court, the Supreme People's Procuratorate and the standing committees of the people's congresses of the provinces, autonomous regions and municipalities directly under the central government consider that any administrative regulation, local regulation, autonomous regulation or separate regulation contradicts the Constitution or any law, they may submit to the Standing Committee of the NPC written requests for examination; and when other state organs, public organizations, enterprises, and public institutions or citizens consider that any administrative regulation, local regulation, autonomous regulation or separate regulation contradicts the Constitution or any law, they may also submit to the Standing Committee of the NPC written requests for examination.

The precondition for building a socialist country under the rule of law is that there must be laws to go by. Unremitting efforts over many years have seen the establishment of a socialist legal framework with Chinese characteristics and with the Constitution at the core. The modern Chinese legal system, with complete branches, distinctive levels, a balanced structure, and scientific style, mainly consists of seven branches of legislation and three levels. The seven branches of legislation are: the Constitution and the Constitution-related laws; civil and commercial laws; administrative laws; economic laws; laws on society; criminal law; and litigation and non-litigation procedural laws. The three levels are: laws; administrative regulations; and local regulations, autonomous regulations, and separate regulations. The NPC and its Standing Committee have enacted 229 laws currently in effect, covering all the above seven branches; and have made most of each branch, including basic laws as the framework of the socialist legal system with Chinese characteristics and laws urgently demanded by reform, development, and stability. As supplements, the State Council has enacted nearly 600 administrative regulations currently in effect; local people's congresses and their standing committees at various levels have enacted over 7,000 local regulations currently in effect; and the people's congresses of the ethnic autonomous areas have enacted over 600 autonomous regulations and separate regulations currently in effect. The departments under the State Council, the people's governments of the provinces, autonomous regions, municipalities directly under the central government, and the larger cities have also enacted numerous rules.

In the socialist legal system with Chinese characteristics, the Constitution is at the core and dominant. The present Constitution, on the basis of the 1954 Constitution, was adopted at the Fifth Session of the Fifth NPC in 1982 after public discussion. The Constitution, as the fundamental law of the state, has supreme legal authority. The people of all ethnic groups, all state organs, the armed forces, all political parties and public organizations and all enterprises and public institutions in the country must take the Constitution as the basic standard of conduct, and they have the duty to uphold the dignity of the Constitution and ensure its implementation. To implement the basic principle of governing the country by law, it is first of all necessary to implement the Constitution in an all-round and thorough way.

The present Constitution of China, summarizing historical experiences and taking lessons from the "cultural revolution," has not only prescribed the fundamental rights and duties of citizens, but also included specific provisions guaranteeing the inviolability of the personal dignity and freedom of the person of Chinese citizens, and that Chinese citizens enjoy freedom of religious belief. The Constitution, based on the principle of democratic centralism for the state organs and experience in building political power since the founding of New China, has comprehensive stipulations on the state organs: The state strengthens the system of the People's Congress as the basic political system of China; part of the NPC's functions and powers are delegated to and exercised by its Standing Committee; the state has the president and vice-president; the 'state establishes the Central Military Commission to lead all the armed forces of China; under the uniform leadership of the Central Authorities, the state strengthens the building of local organs of state power, and people's congresses at and above the county level have their standing committees; and the president and vice-president of the state, chairman and vice-chairmen of the Standing Committee of the NPC, premier, vice-premiers and state councilors, president of the Supreme People's Court and procurator-general of the Supreme People's Procuratorate shall serve no more than two consecutive terms each. The Constitution also stipulates that regional autonomy is practiced in areas where people of ethnic minorities live in compact communities, where organs of self-government are established to exercise the power of autonomy; grassroots autonomy is practiced in both urban and rural areas in the form of residents committees and villagers committees, respectively; and the state may establish special administrative regions when necessary, and the systems to be instituted in the special administrative regions shall be prescribed by law enacted by the NPC in the light of the specific conditions there.

After the present Constitution was adopted in 1982, the NPC, to adapt to the changes in Chinese society, made amendments as many as four times to its content and some articles. The Amendments to the Constitution made in 1988 prescribes: The state permits the private sector of the economy to exist and develop within the limits prescribed by law; and the right to the use of land may be transferred in accordance with the law. The Amendments to the Constitution made in 1993 prescribes: The state practices socialist market economy; and the system of multi-party cooperation and the political consultation under the leadership of the Communist Party of China shall exist and develop for a long time to come. The Amendments to the Constitution made in 1999 prescribes: The People's Republic of China exercises the rule of law, building a socialist country governed according to law; and in the primary stage of socialism, the state upholds the basic economic system with the dominance of the public ownership and the simultaneous development of an economy of diverse forms of ownership, and upholds the distribution system with the dominance of distribution according to work and the coexistence of diverse modes of distribution. The Amendments to the Constitution made in 2004 prescribes: The state encourages, supports, and guides the development of the non-public sectors of the economy, and exercises supervision and control over the non-public sectors in accordance with the law; the lawful private property of citizens may not be encroached upon, and the state protects by law the right of citizens to own and inherit private property; and the state respects and protects human rights.

The legal system of China accords with the principle of universality for the development of human political civilization, and conforms to the basic conditions of the primary stage of socialism in China. It is in line with the basic tasks of socialism, and has distinctive Chinese characteristics. The essence of this legal system is to put people first, reflects the common will of the people and guarantees the fundamental interests of the people. It is in line with the economic development and social progress of China, and provides legal safeguards for scientific, harmonious, and peaceful development of the country.

China's socialist legal system with Chinese characteristics is open and developing. As China is at a stage of social transformation, its legal system is phased, and forward-looking. It will continue to promulgate new laws and revise present ones, so as to develop and improve the legal system.

Legal Systems of Respecting and Safeguarding Human Rights

China takes as its constant goal the elimination of poverty, enjoyment of human rights to the full by everyone and building of a prosperous, strong, democratic, culturally advanced, and harmonious modern socialist country. China's basic stand on the development of human rights is: placing top priority on people's rights to subsistence and development, making development the principal task, and promoting citizens' political, economic, social, and cultural rights to achieve their all-round development.

Based on its Constitution, China has formulated and improved a series of legal systems to codify and institutionalize the safeguarding of human rights.

- Legal safeguard of the right to life. China attaches great importance to safeguarding its citizens' right to life. The Constitution, Criminal Law, and General Principles of the Civil Law all include fundamental stipulations on protecting citizens' right to life. The Production Safety Law, the Law on the Prevention and Treatment of Occupational Diseases, and other laws and regulation slay down provisions for the protection of working people's life and health. In view of the country's situation, China retains the death penalty in the law, but upholds the policy of "killing fewer and with caution" and exercises strict and cautious control over the use of the death penalty to ensure that it is applied only in the most serious cases. The death penalty shall not be imposed on persons who have not reached the age of 18 at the time the crime is committed or on women who are pregnant at the time of adjudication. The Criminal Law also prescribes the system of a 2-year probation of execution, which is conducive to rigorously controlling the death penalty and reducing the actual number being executed.
- Legal safeguard of the right to personal freedom and dignity. The Constitution rules that freedom of the person of citizens of the People's Republic of China is inviolable. No citizen may be arrested without the approval or decision of a people's procuratorate or a decision of a people's court, and any arrest must be made by a public security organ. Unlawful detention and deprivation or restriction of citizens' freedom of the person by other means is prohibited. The residences of citizens are inviolable, and unlawful search of, or intrusion into, a citizen's residence is prohibited. The freedom and privacy of correspondence of citizens are protected by law, and unlawful censorship of citizens' correspondence is prohibited. The Criminal Procedure Law expressly outlaws extortion of confessions by torture, and prescribes strict legal procedures for compulsory measures and means, including detention, execution of arrests, investigation and gathering of evidence, related to personal freedom and safety. The Criminal Law lays down a special provision on the crime of extorting confessions by torture by judicial functionaries. Both the Legislation Law and Law on Administrative Punishment provide too that no administrative regulation or local regulation may impose any penalties restricting personal freedom. Any compulsory measures or penalties restricting personal freedom

shall only be enacted by law. In 2003 the State Council annulled the Measures for Taking in and Sending back Vagrants and Beggars in Cities and, at the same time, enacted the Measures for Assisting Vagrants and Beggars with No Means of Support in Cities. The Constitution stipulates that the personal dignity of citizens is inviolable, and that insult, libel, false accusation, or false incrimination directed against citizens by any means is prohibited. The General Principles of the Civil Law protects citizens' right to personal name, honor, and portrait.

- Legal safeguard of the right to equality. The Constitution establishes the principle that all citizens of the People's Republic of China are equal before the law. Every citizen is entitled to the rights and, at the same time, must perform the duties prescribed by the Constitution and the law. Protection or punishment is applied equally to everyone regardless of personal differences. No organization or individual is privileged to be beyond the Constitution or the law, and all acts in violation of the Constitution or the law must be investigated. The Constitution and the Law on Regional Ethnic Autonomy prescribe that all ethnic groups in the People's Republic of China are equal, and that the state protects the lawful rights and interests of ethnic minorities, and discrimination against and oppression of any ethnic group are prohibited. All ethnic groups have the freedom to use and develop their own spoken and written languages, as well as the freedom to preserve or reform their own folkways and customs. The Constitution, the Law on the Protection of Rights, and Interests of Women and other laws stipulate that women enjoy equal rights with men in all spheres of life —political, economic, cultural, social, and family.
- Legal safeguard of political rights. It is stated in the Constitution that all power in the People's Republic of China belongs to the people. The Legislation Law prescribes that deprivation of any citizen's political rights can only be done in accordance with the law. The right to election is an important political right for citizens. It is stipulated by the Constitution and the law that all citizens of the People's Republic of China who have reached the age of 18 have the right to vote and stand for election, regardless of ethnic status, race, sex, occupation, family background, religious belief, education, property status or length of residence, except for persons deprived of political rights in accordance with the law. The Electoral Law and the Organic Law of the Local People's Congresses and People's Governments prescribe that a group of ten or more voters or deputies may recommend candidates, who enjoy equal legal status with those nominated by political parties and social organizations. Deputies to the people's congresses at all levels, vice-chairmen of the standing committees of local people's congresses and deputy heads of the local people's governments must all be selected through competitive election. The chairmen of the standing committees of local people's congresses, heads of the local people's governments, presidents of local people's courts, and chief procurators of local people's procuratorates must also be selected through competitive election, although a non-competitive election may be conducted if only one candidate is nominated. Citizens' freedom of speech, of the press, of assembly,

of association, of procession, and of demonstration is also guaranteed by the Constitution and the law. The Electoral Law, Law on Assemblies, Processions and Demonstrations, and administrative regulations regarding publication and registration and management of social organizations provide legal guarantees for the political rights and freedom of citizens. The Regulations on Written and Personal Petitions promulgated by the State Council protects citizens' rights to criticism, suggestion, petition, accusation, and impeachment through strengthening governments' responsibility for handling people's letters and visits regarding petitions.

- Legal safeguard of freedom of religious belief. The Constitution stipulates that citizens of the People's Republic of China enjoy freedom of religious belief. No state organ, public organization or individual may compel citizens to believe in or not believe in any religion; nor may they discriminate against citizens who believe in or do not believe in any religion. The state protects normal religious activities. No one may make use of religion to engage in activities that disrupt public order, impair the health of citizens or interfere with the educational system of the state. Religious bodies and religious affairs are not subject to any foreign domination. The Regulations on Religious Affairs promulgated by the State Council prescribes that the state, in accordance with the law, protects the lawful rights and interests of religious bodies, venues of religious activities and religious believers, and their normal religious activities. Since the adoption of the reform and opening-up policies in 1978, Chinese citizens' freedom of religious belief has been fully respected and protected. In 1994 the State Council enacted the Provisions on the Administration of Religious Activities of Aliens within the Territory of the People's Republic of China to respect freedom of religious belief of aliens within Chinese territory, protect and administer their religious activities in accordance with the law and safeguard friendly contacts and cultural and academic exchanges of aliens with Chinese religious circles in respect of religion.
- Legal safeguard of the rights and interests of the working people. The Labor Law, Law on Labor Contracts, Law on Labor Disputes Mediation and Arbitration, Law on the Promotion of Employment, Regulations on Paid Annual Leave of Employees, Regulations on Labor Security Supervision, and other regulations and laws regulate and promote employment, rationally define the rights and obligations of employers and employees, and protect the lawful rights of employees. The Regulations on Work-related Injury Insurance, Regulations on Unemployment Insurance, Provisional Regulations on Collection and Payment of Social Insurance Premiums, Interim Measures on Maternity Insurance for Enterprise Employees and other regulations and rules guarantee necessary material assistance to the working people in regard to old age, unemployment, illness, work-related injury and childbearing. The Regulations on the Employment of the Disabled, Provisions on the Labor Protection of Female Employees, Provisions on the Prohibition of Child Labor and other regulations and rules provide special protection for the physical and psychological health and lawful rights of all underprivileged groups.

- Legal safeguard of economic, social, cultural, and other rights. The Constitution rules that the lawful private property of citizens is inviolable. The Property Rights Law stipulates that the property rights of the state, collective, individual, and any other holder of such rights shall be protected by law, and may not be encroached upon by any entity or individual. The Law on the Protection of the Rights and Interests of the Elderly, Law on Maternal and Infant Health Care, Law on the Protection of Minors, Law on the Protection of the Disabled, and other laws reinforce the protection of special groups. The Regulations on the Minimum Standard of Living of Urban Residents, Regulations on Rural "Five-Guarantee" Work and other regulations prescribe basic living security for urban poverty-stricken people and farmers without labor ability, sources of income, or any supporter, provider or fosterer. The Regulations on Special Care and Preferential Treatment for Servicepersons, Regulations on the Placement of Demobilized Compulsory Servicepersons, and other regulations lay down the state's special care and preferential treatment system for demobilized, injured or dead servicepersons and their families. Citizens' right to education is protected by the Constitution and the law. The Compulsory Education Law intensifies the state's responsibility for guaranteeing the implementation of compulsory education, brings compulsory education completely under the coverage of national financial guarantee, and ensures the equal right of all school-aged children and other teenagers to compulsory education. The Constitution also prescribes that citizens of the People's Republic of China have freedom to engage in scientific research, literary and artistic creation, and other cultural pursuits.

China has joined 22 international human rights conventions, including the International Convention on the Elimination of All Forms of Racial Discrimination, Convention on the Elimination of All Forms of Discrimination against Women, Convention against Torture, and Other Cruel, Inhuman or Degrading Treatment or Punishment, Convention on the Rights of the Child, International Covenant on Economic, Social and Cultural Rights, and other key international conventions in this respect. The Chinese government earnestly fulfills its obligations, submits implementation reports on its own initiative, and gives full play to the role of international human rights conventions in promoting and protecting human rights of the Chinese people.

Legal Systems Regulating the Order of the Market Economy

During the transition from a planned economy to a market economy since the adoption of the reform and opening-up policies in 1978, China has continuously strengthened its legislation in economic and related fields. A legal system compatible with the socialist market economy has basically taken shape.

- Civil law system. China makes the confirmation, alteration, exercise, circulation, termination, and protection rules of property ownership the core of its civil law system compatible with the building of a socialist market economy. A series of laws, such as the General Principles of the Civil Law, Contract Law, Security Law, and Property Rights Law, have set up and improved the system of creditor's rights and property rights system that covers ownership, usufructuary right and property right for security of realty or chattel, established the principle of freedom of contract and the principle that property rights of the state, collective, individual or any other rights holder are equally protected by law, and formed a new pattern that all economic entities with different types of ownership lawfully coexist, equally compete, and mutually enhance each other.

- Legal systems for market entities. China's legal systems for market entities have been accommodated to the basic requirements of a market economy for market entities after the transformation from ownership-oriented legislation to one oriented toward the forms of organization and liabilities. The Company Law, Partnership Law, Sole Proprietorship Enterprise Law, Law on Commercial Banks, Law on Farmers Specialized Cooperatives, and other laws guarantee the legitimacy of various market entities and their equitable participation in market competition. The Company Law establishes basic systems, such as the limited liability company system and the system of company limited by shares, and improves corporate governance structure, laying an institutional foundation for building a modern enterprise system and safeguarding the lawful rights and interests of corporate investors and stakeholders. The Law on Enterprise Bankruptcy set up the bankruptcy system, regulating the withdrawal from the market of market entities. China has also set up a great number of organizations offering legal, financial, and information consultation services, and actively improve legal systems concerning market agents.
- Legal systems for market management. The Anti-monopoly Law and Law on Countering Unfair Competition regulate market competition behavior, facilitate the reform of monopolized industries, intensify government and public supervision, and accordingly establish a legal remedy system combining civil and administrative compensation. The Law on the Protection of the Rights and Interests of Consumers and Product Quality Law have established a legal system for protecting the interests of consumers and for ensuring product quality. The Law on the Administration of Urban Real Estate has set up a system conducive to administering urban real estate, safeguarding the order of the real estate market, and guaranteeing the lawful rights and interests of real estate owners. The Insurance Law, Securities Law, Law on Regulation of and Supervision over the Banking Industry, Regulations on Foreign Exchange Control, and other laws and regulations have set up a financial supervision and regulation system with open, fair and just value orientation, to effectively prevent and dissolve financial risks. The Regulations on Direct Selling Administration, Regulations on Commercial Franchise Administration, and other regulations effectively regulate market behavior.
- Legal systems for macro-control. Exercising macro-control over the economy by means of law is a major characteristic of China's socialist market economy.

While giving full play to the role of the market mechanism in optimizing resource allocation, and for the sake of expediting the sound and rapid development of the national economy, the Budget Law, Audit Law, Government Procurement Law, Pricing Law, Individual Income Tax Law, Enterprise Income Tax Law, Law on the Administration of Tax Collection, Law on the Promotion of Small and Medium-sized Enterprises, and other laws put forth provisions on macro-control in their corresponding fields. The Law on the People's Bank of China and other laws provide an institutional guarantee for maintaining currency value, dissolving financial risks and ensuring financial security. The Statistics Law forms the legal foundation for scientific decision-making regarding national economic and social development. The construction of legal systems for macro-control effectively gives full scope to the guiding role of national development plans and industrial policies, and thus elevates the level of macro-control.

- Legal systems for the protection of intellectual property rights. The enactment of laws such as the Patent Law, Trademark Law, Copyright Law and Law on Countering Unfair Competition, and the promulgation of a series of administrative regulations, including the Regulations on the Protection of Computer Software, Regulations on the Protection of Layout-design of Integrated Circuits, Regulations on the Collective Management of Copyrights, Regulations on the Protection of Dissemination of Information Through Internet, Regulations on Customs Protection of Intellectual Property Rights and Regulations on the Protection of New Varieties of Plants, have established relatively complete legal systems for the protection of intellectual property rights in their corresponding aspects. China adopts a law enforcement and protection mechanism for intellectual property rights through the coordinated implementation of judicial justice and administrative execution. Judicial justice has a fundamental status and plays a guiding role in the law enforcement and protection of intellectual property rights. The combination of investigation by law enforcement agencies in accordance with the law on their own initiative with mediation at the request of the parties concerned offers optional channels for the latter. The Interpretation of Issues Regarding the Specific Application of Laws in the Handling of Criminal Cases of Intellectual Property Right Infringement (I) and (II) enacted by the Supreme People's Court and Supreme People's Procuratorate of the People's Republic of China serve to crack down on crimes infringing intellectual property rights.
- Legal systems for resource conservation and environmental protection. China regards resource conservation and environmental protection as two basic state policies, and continuously strengthens the building of the legal systems in these two aspects. China has enacted nine laws concerning environmental protection, including the Environmental Protection Law, Law on Environmental Impact Assessment, Law on the Prevention and Control of Atmospheric Pollution, Law on the Prevention and Control of Water Pollution, Law on the Prevention and Control of Environmental Noise Pollution, Law on the Prevention and Control

of Environmental Pollution by Solid Waste and Law on the Prevention and Control of Radioactive Pollution, and 17 laws with regard to resource conservation and protection, such as the Renewable Energy Law, Energy Conservation Law, Land Administration Law, Water Law, Forest Law, Grassland Law, Mineral Resources Law, Coal Law, Electric Power Law and Clean Production Promotion Law. The state has also promulgated over 50 administrative regulations, more than 660 local and sectoral regulations as well as government rules, and over 800 national standards related to environmental and resource protection. It has established and improved legal systems by establishing environmental impact assessment, synchronous project design, construction and completion of safety and sanitation facilities, pollution discharge declaration and registration, pollution discharge fee, elimination or control of pollution within a prescribed period of time, control of levels of pollution and pollution discharge permission, and legal systems concerning the planning, ownership, permission, paid use, and energy conservation assessment of natural resources. At the same time, China sets great store by international cooperation in resource conservation and environmental protection. It has acceded or joined over 30 international conventions on environmental and resource protection, including the United Nations Framework Convention on Climate Change, Kyoto Protocol on Global Warming, Convention on Biological Diversity and United Nations Convention to Combat Desertification, and actively performs its obligations under these conventions.

- Legal systems for foreign economic and trade cooperation. A series of laws, such as the Law on Chinese-Foreign Equity Joint Ventures, Law on Chinese-Foreign Cooperative Joint Ventures, Law on Foreign-Capital Enterprises and Foreign Trade Law, provide multiple modes or organizational forms for foreigners to invest in China, and fully guarantee the lawful rights and interests of foreigners who invest and conduct economic and trade activities in China. Following its accession to the World Trade Organization (WTO) in 2001, China, by revising its Foreign Trade Law, has further standardized the rights and interests of foreign trade operators, improved the trade administration systems of import and export of goods and technologies, and international services, established foreign trade investigation and promotion systems suited to Chinese conditions, perfected the trade remedy system and improved the systems of customs supervision and inspection and quarantine of imported and exported commodities, to form a unified, transparent foreign trade system pursuant to the WTO rules. In light of the requirements for developing its socialist market economy and its commitments to the WTO, China has comprehensively straightened out laws and regulations concerning the utilization of foreign capital. Over the past 6 years, the state has sorted out a total of 887 sectoral regulations and other regulatory documents in the field of foreign economy and trade.

Administration by Law and Building a Government Under the Rule of Law

Administration by law and building a government under the rule of law are essential for the overall implementation of the fundamental principle of governing the country by law. They are basic norms of the Chinese government for its administration. For many years the Chinese government has taken a series of measures to promote the work in a down-to-earth way in this regard. After promulgating the Decision of the State Council on Promoting Law-based Administration in an All-round Way in 1999, the Chinese government issued the Outline for the Implementation of Promoting Law-based Administration in an All-round Way in 2004, specifying the goal of building a government under the rule of law, and setting forth the guidelines and specific targets, basic principles and requirements, as well as major tasks and measures for the full-scale promotion of administration by law in the ensuing 10 years. Currently, the administrative powers of the people's governments at various levels have been gradually guided along the track of a legal system; the legal system that regulates the acquisition and operation of government power has taken shape; and significant improvement has been achieved in administration based on the law.

- Legal systems for subjects of administration. In accordance with the stipulations of the Constitution, Organic Law of the State Council, Organic Law of the Local People's Congresses and Local People's Governments, the Chinese government has five administrative levels: namely, the State Council; the people's governments of provinces, autonomous regions and municipalities directly under the central government; the people's governments of autonomous prefectures and cities that have districts; the people's governments of counties, autonomous counties, cities that have no districts, and districts under cities; and the people's governments of townships, townships of ethnic minorities and towns. The Constitution stipulates that the State Council is the central people's government, and is the executive body of the NPC and the highest state administrative organ; local people's governments at different levels are the executive organs of local people's congresses and local state administrative bodies at different levels and local people's governments at all levels are state administrative organs subject to the unified leadership of the State Council.
- Legal systems for administrative acts. First, the administrative licensing system. The Law on Administrative Licensing sets strict limitations and stipulations on the matters and procedures of administrative licensing: Administrative licenses are not required for matters that can be decided by citizens, legal persons or other organizations themselves; that can be effectively regulated by the market competition mechanism; that may be subject to the self-discipline management of trade organizations or intermediary institutions; that can be handled by the administrative organs by means of supervision afterwards or through other

administrative methods. The Law on Administrative Licensing also stipulates that the administrative licensing work conducted by administrative organs must be legitimate, open, impartial and convenient for the people, and must not contradict the trust protection principle by altering an effective administrative license without authorization.

Second, the system of administrative expropriation and administrative requisition for use. According to the Constitution and the Property Rights Law, in order to meet the demands of public interest, the state may expropriate collectively owned land, housing properties and other immovable properties owned by entities and individuals according to authorization and procedures prescribed by law. Adequate amount of land compensation fee, relocation subsidy, and compensation for attachments on the ground and young crops, etc., shall be paid for expropriation of collectively owned land; social security fees shall be arranged for farmers affected by the land expropriation, so that the livelihood of farmers affected by the land expropriation shall be assured and the legitimate rights and interests of farmers affected by the land expropriation shall be safeguarded. Compensation for relocation shall be made according to law for expropriation of housing properties and other immovable properties of entities and individuals, so that the legitimate rights and interests of the persons affected by the expropriation shall be safeguarded. In the case of expropriation of residential property of individuals, the living conditions of the persons affected by the expropriation shall be assured.

Third, the administrative penalty system. The Law on Administrative Penalties prescribes that where administrative penalties need to be imposed for violations of the order of administration, they shall be prescribed by laws, regulations or rules, and enforced by administrative organs according to the procedures prescribed by relevant laws, regulations, or rules. Any administrative penalty that is not imposed in accordance with the law or legal procedures shall be invalid. Administrative organs, upon discovering that citizens, legal persons or other organizations have committed acts for which administrative penalties should be imposed according to law, shall conduct investigation in a comprehensive, objective and fair manner to collect relevant evidence. After an administrative penalty has been decided on, the penalized party shall have the right to apply for administrative review, lodge administrative litigation, or demand compensation in accordance with the law.

- Legal systems for administrative supervision and remedy. First, the system of administrative review. The Law on Administrative Review stipulates that a citizen, legal person or any other organization considering that his/her or its lawful rights and interests have been infringed upon by a specific administrative act may apply for administrative review to an administrative organ. After the administrative review organ has examined the specific administrative act, it may annul, alter, or confirm the act as illegal in accordance with the law, and order the administrative organ concerned to perform its statutory duty and undertake a new specific administrative act within a time limit.

Second, the administrative procedure system. The Administrative Procedure Law stipulates that citizens, legal persons or other organizations refusing to accept a disposition imposed by an administrative organ or administrative official have the right to institute proceedings to a people's court. After hearing the case, the people's court shall make the judgment to annul or partially annul the disposition, or to require the defendant to undertake a new specific administrative act, if the specific administrative act has been found to have inadequacy of essential evidence, erroneously applied the law or regulations, violated legal procedure, exceeded authorization or abused power.

Third, the system of administrative compensation. The Law on State Compensation prescribes that the aggrieved person shall have the right to demand compensation when an administrative organ or its personnel has infringed upon his/her right of the person or property right in violation of the law when exercising administrative functions and powers. The law also contains provisions covering claimants for administrative compensation, organs having obligation for administrative compensation, compensation procedures, methods of compensation, and calculation standards.

Fourth, the administrative supervision and auditing systems. The Law on Administrative Supervision stipulates that the supervisory organs shall exercise supervision over state administrative organs' problems in their observation and enforcement of laws, regulations, decisions, and orders of the people's government. In accordance with the Auditing Law, audit institutions shall audit revenues and expenditures of departments of the State Council and the local people's governments at different levels, as well as revenues and expenditures of state-owned financial institutions, enterprises, and public institutions.

– Legal systems concerning civil servants. Administrative acts are mainly performed by civil servants. The Law on Civil Servants and the Regulations on Punishment of Civil Servants of Administrative Organs have defined the civil servants' qualifications, obligations and rights, posts and ranks, recruitment, assessment, appointment and removal, promotion and demotion, rewards and penalties, training, exchange of posts and withdrawal, salary and welfare benefits, resignation and dismissal, retirement, complaint and accusation, post appointment, and legal liability. The law and the regulations have prescribed administration of civil servants by classification and a post appointment system, as well as a penalty system for civil servants in administrative organs.

In recent years, the Chinese government has further transformed its functions and stepped up the building of a government under the rule of law by strengthening its self-improvement. First, it has expedited the establishment of a public emergency response mechanism to enhance its capability to handle emergencies, and strives to build a government of service. The Standing Committee of the NPC has promulgated the Law on Emergency Response, and the State Council has issued the National Overall Emergency Response Program for Unexpected Public Emergency Incidents. Based on this overall program, relevant government departments have enacted 25 specialized emergency response plans, 80 sectoral emergency response plans, and 31 provinces, autonomous regions and municipalities directly under the central government have worked out their regional overall emergency response plans, thus basically bringing into being a nationwide system of emergency response programs. Second, further efforts have been made to build a government in "sunshine" by making government information more open and available to the public. The State Council has deliberated and adopted the Regulations on Open Government Information. In 2006, the central government launched its official web portal, and so far over 80 % of the governments and their departments at and above county level have established their own official web portals. Seventy-four State Council departments and institutions, governments of 31 provinces, autonomous regions and municipalities directly under the central government have established the news release system and have their own spokespersons. Third, greater efforts have been made to enforce the administrative accountability system in order to establish a government of accountability. Governments at all levels and their departments have gradually adopted the administrative accountability system. According to the principle of whoever has made the decision is responsible for its consequences, where serious losses have resulted from decisions made by going beyond authorized power or violating the established procedures, liabilities of decision-makers shall be strictly investigated.

Pressing on with the accountability system of administrative law enforcement and continuously improving the government's capacity in this regard are inevitable requirements for building a government under the rule of law. The Chinese government sets great store by the reform of the administrative law enforcement system, requires its administrative organs at all levels to exercise their power within authorization and legal procedures, promotes the accountability system for administrative law enforcement in all aspects, and implements the accountability system in a stringent manner. As required by the Several Opinions on Pushing Forward the Administrative Law Enforcement Accountability System issued by the General Office of the State Council in July 2005, all regions and all departments have focused on promoting the administrative law enforcement accountability system by defining law enforcement duties and responsibilities according to law, setting up law enforcement posts in a scientific way, standardizing law enforcement procedures, clarifying the duties and powers of law enforcement bodies, and removing illegal law enforcement bodies. According to incomplete statistics, since the adoption of the said accountability system, over 280,000 cases of irregularities of administrative law enforcement have been dealt with by administrative organs of various levels throughout the country.

In the process of building a law-based government, the Chinese government has been strengthening its responsibility for administrative supervision and taking an active approach to solving administrative disputes. More efforts have been made to supervise abstract administrative acts such as the formulation of regulations, rules, and regulatory documents. On January 15, 2008, the premier of the State Council signed the order to issue the Decision of the State Council on the Annulment of Some Administrative Regulations. A total of 655 administrative regulations in force that had been promulgated before the end of 2006 have been reexamined, of which 49 have been repealed since the main content of these regulations have been replaced by new laws or administrative regulations; 43 declared invalid because their effective validity period had expired or they had lost their validity with the disappearance of their objects of regulation. While strengthening examination on regulations and rules filed for the record, the State Council has further improved the filing system concerning regulations and regulatory documents formulated by the governments of provinces, cities, counties, and townships, and three lower levels of governments should file such regulations and regulatory documents to the next-higher levels for the record so as to promote law-based administration of local governments at different levels. From March 2003 to the end of 2007, the State Council examined 8,402 local regulations, autonomous regulations, separate regulations, local governments' rules and rules enacted by the departments of the State Council, which had been filed for the record by local governments and the departments under the State Council with legislative power, and addressed 323 problematic regulations and rules in accordance with the law. The State Council has enacted the Regulations on the Implementation of the Law on Administrative Review, and has made active attempts to reform the system of administrative review in order to enhance the ability of all personnel involving in the administrative review work. Since the Law on Administrative Review came into force in 1999, over 80,000 administrative disputes have been settled through administrative review each year.

Judicial System and Fair Administration of Justice

The people's court is the judicial organ in China and the people's procuratorate is the supervisory organ for law enforcement. The people's court and the people's procuratorate, in accordance with the Constitution, Organic Law of the People's Courts, Organic Law of the People's Procuratorates, Civil Procedure Law, Administrative Procedure Law, and Criminal Procedure Law, independently exercise their adjudicative power and supervisory power, respectively, free from any interference of administrative organs, public organizations and individuals.

Judicial organs in China include the Supreme People's Court, local people's courts at different levels and special people's courts such as military courts. Local people's courts are classified into primary people's courts, intermediate people's courts and higher people's courts. As the highest judicial organ, the Supreme People's Court supervises the judicial work of all local people's courts and special people's courts. The people's court at a higher level supervises the judicial work of the people's court at the next-lower level.

China has established a sound judicial system, completed the adjudicative systems for civil, administrative and criminal cases, forming a modern judicial system in line with the requirements for building a socialist country under the rule of law, in a bid to safeguard judicial justice and social justice.

- The system of public trial. The people's court follows the principle of openness according to law and timely openness in adjudication of cases. Some civil cases, such as divorce cases or cases involving commercial secrets, may be heard in private sessions if the parties concerned so request. Except for cases involving state secrets, individual privacy and minors, all other cases are heard and decided by the people's court in an open manner. A public notice is issued about a forthcoming public trial, allowing citizens and the media to observe the trial. The people's court often invites deputies to the people's congresses and members of the Chinese People's Political Consultative Conference and their local branches to observe the trial process. In the course of adjudication of a case, evidences are given, cross-examination is carried out, and the trial is conducted in an open way. All effective information relating to the protection of the rights of the parties concerned, such as the filing of the case, its trial and enforcement of judgment, is publicized promptly and completely within the time frame provided by the law.
- The system of collegiate panels. When a people's court hears and decides a case of first instance, unless it is a simple civil case, or a minor criminal case or other cases that may use the summary procedure as provided by the law and in which case a single judicial officer will hear and decide the case, the case will be heard and decided by a collegiate panel composed of several judicial officers or by a collegiate panel composed of judicial officers and people's assessors. A collegiate panel of judicial officers is formed when adjudicating cases on appeal or protested cases. The number of a collegiate panel must be an odd number.
- The system of people's assessors. To guarantee all citizens' lawful right to participate in trials and promote justice, except for cases suitable for summary procedure or cases provided otherwise by the law, all civil, administrative and criminal cases, including all cases of first instance in which the defendant in a criminal case, the plaintiff or defendant in a civil case or the plaintiff in an administrative case, has requested to have people's assessors participate in the trial, will be heard and decided by a collegiate panel composed of people's assessors and judges. People's assessors hear and decide cases as members of the collegiate panel in accordance with provisions of the law. They are entitled to the same rights and shoulder the same duties as other members of the collegiate panel, and independently exercise their voting right, together with other members of the collegiate panel, when it comes to the confirmation of evidence and application of law. However, they cannot serve as chief judges.
- The system of defense. In order to guarantee the human rights of criminal suspects and defendants, and ensure the fairness of the criminal proceedings, criminal suspects and defendants have the right to defense according to law and the people's court has the obligation to ensure that all defendants are entitled to defense. Criminal suspects and defendants may defend themselves or ask one or two people to serve as their counsels. Based on facts and the law, the counsels provide the court with their own materials and give their views. They may claim that the criminal suspect or the defendant is not guilty, or has committed a lighter crime than he/she is accused of, or ask the court to lessen or relieve his/

her criminal liabilities in a bid to safeguard the legitimate rights and interests of the criminal suspect or the defendant.

- The system of agent ad litem. In a civil or administrative procedure, if a person has no capacity for an act of procedure, his/her guardian will undertake the litigation as the legal representative. If he/she has more than one guardian and they all refuse to serve as his/her legal representative, the people's court will designate one of them as his/her legal representative in the case. The party to the lawsuit or his/her legal representative may ask one or two persons to serve as agent ad litem on his/her behalf. If it is a criminal procedure, the victim and his/her legal representative or close relative in the case of a public prosecution, the voluntary prosecutor and his/her legal representative in the case of a private prosecution, the party concerned in incidental civil action and his/her legal representative, are all entitled to entrust someone as agent ad litem. Attorneys, close relatives of the person concerned, people recommended by relevant organizations or their employers, or any citizen approved by the people's court can serve as agent ad litem for others. The agent ad litem takes part in the litigation on behalf of the person concerned to materialize and safeguard the legitimate rights and interests of the person concerned.
- The system of challenge. Any party concerned in a case is entitled to apply to the court to remove anyone from the adjudication personnel whom he/she believes has an interest in the case or is otherwise related to the party concerned in the case and may endanger the defendant's right to a fair trial. If any of the adjudication personnel is a party concerned in the case, a close relative of a litigating party, or when he/she believes he/she has an interest in the case, he/she must withdraw from the case.
- The system of mediation. When a people's court hears a civil case, it follows the principle of "doing all it can to mediate first, adjudicating when so doing is proper, and combining mediation with adjudication to close the case." According to the requirements of voluntaries, legitimacy, and democracy, judicial personnel will try, through mediation, to persuade the opposing parties to reach a compromise to solve their dispute about civil rights and interests. In 2006, about 56 % of civil cases of first instance in China were solved through mediation.
- The system of judicial relief. The judicial relief system issued by the people's court when financially straitened litigants take legal action in a civil or administrative case, in order to safeguard their legitimate rights and interests. The people's court may allow such litigants to postpone paying, reduce or even waive their legal expenses. The Provisions on Judicial Relief for Financially Straitened Litigants was enacted by the Supreme People's Court for the purpose of guaranteeing the procedural rights of underprivileged people.
- The system of judgment of the second instance as final. The party concerned has the right to appeal to the people's court at a higher level, within the time period prescribed by the law, against the ruling or judgment made by a local people's court in a case of first instance. If the party concerned does not appeal against the ruling or judgment, the ruling or judgment will come into force once the time period expires. Regarding rulings and judgments in cases on appeal or

protested cases, the rulings and judgments made by a higher people's court are final, except for cases involving the death penalty, which need to be reviewed by the Supreme People's Court. All rulings and judgments made by the Supreme People's Court in cases of first instance it hears are final.

- The system of review of death sentence. The system of review of death sentences is independent of the system whereby the judgment of the second instance is final. This is important because it requires that all death sentences be reexamined and approved. Apart from the death sentences given by the Supreme People's Court according to law, all death sentences must be reported to the Supreme People's Court for review and approval. The Supreme People's Court has enacted the Decisions on Several Issues Regarding the Review of Death Sentences. This document contains strict and uniform criteria on the use of the death sentence. It also contains uniform criteria on evidences for death sentences, and strictly standardizes the procedure for review of death sentences, in a bid to ensure that capital punishments are given sparingly and fairly. Starting from the latter part of 2006, all death penalty cases of second instance are tried publicly.

The procuratorial organs in China include the Supreme People's Procuratorate, local people's procuratorates at different levels and special procuratorates, such as military procuratorates. The Supreme People's Procuratorate is the highest procuratorial organ. It directs the work of local people's procuratorates and special procuratorates. A people's procuratorate at a higher level directs the work of a people's procuratorate at the next-lower level.

It is the duty of the people's procuratorates to ensure justice and the proper enforcement of law. Provisions in laws stipulate that the people's procuratorates shall use their procuratorial power to deal with treason, attempts to split the country, and other serious criminal cases that sabotage the implementation of state policies, laws, and administrative orders; that they shall investigate criminal cases directly by themselves involving personnel of state agencies, such as cases of embezzlement, taking bribes, dereliction of duty and infringement of others' rights; that they shall decide, in accordance with the law, whether to approve proposals for arrest put forth by the organs of public security; that they shall, upon examination of cases transferred to them from the organs of public security for action, decide, in accordance with the law, whether to bring the cases to court or not; and that they shall bring criminal cases to court or support legal action in such cases. The law also stipulates that procuratorial organs shall supervise legitimacy of the trials of the people's courts, the investigatory activities of the organs of public security and state security, as well as law enforcement in prisons. People's procuratorates at all levels establish procuratorial committees to discuss and decide major cases and other issues of importance under the guidance of the chief procurator.

China has enacted the Arbitration Law, the Lawyers Law, the Notarization Law, and the Law on Labor Dispute Mediation and Arbitration, and established an arbitration system, attorney system, notary system, legal aid system, and judicial examination system.

The Arbitration Law stipulates that on the principle of voluntariness, contractual disputes or other property right disputes arising between the citizens, legal persons, and other organizations can be submitted for arbitration; disputes arising from marriage, adoption, guardianship, fosterage and inheritance, and administrative disputes that should be handled by administrative organs may not be submitted for arbitration. In China, all arbitration awards are final. Unless a people's court revokes an arbitration award or makes a ruling that the arbitration award shall not be implemented, the parties concerned may not request a second arbitration on the same dispute or bring the case again to a people's court.

The Law on Labor Dispute Mediation and Arbitration stipulates that where a labor dispute arises, if a party does not desire consultation, the parties fail to settle the dispute through consultation, or a party does not execute a reached settlement agreement, any of the parties may apply to a mediation organization for mediation; if a party does not desire mediation, the parties fail to settle the dispute through mediation, or a party does not execute a reached mediation agreement, any of the parties may apply to a labor dispute arbitration commission for arbitration; and a party disagreeing with the award may bring an action in a people's court except as otherwise provided for by the law.

The Lawyers Law stipulates that anyone who applies to become a professional practitioner must first of all pass the state's standard judicial examination, must endorse the Constitution, must work as an intern in a law firm for 12 months and demonstrate that he/she is a person of integrity before receiving a certificate to practice. Professional practitioners can serve as legal counsels or agent ad litem for others. They can provide legal aid to criminal suspects in criminal cases, serving as defenders for criminal suspects and defendants in criminal cases. Their practice according to law is protected by the law. By the end of 2006 there were over 13,000 law firms in China with more than 130,000 professional practitioners. In China law firms can be established as a partnership or by an individual. They can also be set up with the funds of the state.

The Notarization Law stipulates that notaries must pass the state's judicial examination before they can practice. Notary agencies can, at the request of their clients, verify the truthfulness and legitimacy of civil juristic acts, or of facts and documents with legal significance. Notarial deeds have legal effect, mainly including evidentiary effect, compulsory execution effect, effect of major factors for a juristic act, public notification effect, against-third-party effect, and irreversibility effect. The number of notarial deeds issued by notary agencies across China in the past few years has remained at about 10 million each year, of which 3 million are foreign-related and have involved over 100 countries and regions. By the end of 2006, there were more than 3,000 notary agencies in China, employing close to 12,000 notaries.

China set up a legal aid system in 1994. Financially straitened citizens can apply for legal aid according to state stipulations when they demand state compensation, social security or subsistence allowance, or when they demand that pension (for the disabled or for the family of a deceased person), relief payment, alimony, maintenance, child support, or remuneration of labor be paid, or when they claim civil rights or interests arising from offering assistance in a just cause. In criminal procedures, financially straitened citizens may apply for legal aid according to state stipulations for commissioning lawyers, agent ad litem, or defenders. If the defendant is blind or deaf-mute, or is a minor, and has not entrusted someone to serve as his/her defender, or if the defendant is likely to be sentenced to death but has not entrusted someone as his/her defender, the people's court should designate a lawyer who is responsible for providing legal aid to serve as the defender. Legal aid departments have been established by the governments at all levels and equipped with specialized staff.

The state adopts a standard judicial examination system for those who want to be judges, prosecutors and those who want to acquire the qualification of the lawyer. The best of the examinees who pass the state judicial examination are employed as junior judges and prosecutors. The first nationwide uniform examination for the qualification of the lawyer was held in China in 1986. In order to establish and standardize a uniform state judicial examination system, the Measures for the Implementation of State Judicial Examination (Trial) contains provisions on the content, manner, and organization of the examination, and for the conditions for entering the examination and the conferring of qualifications. From 2002 to 2007, China successively held six state uniform judicial examinations, which promoted the building of the professional ranks of judges, prosecutors, lawyers, and notaries.

China has quickened the pace of judicial system reform in recent years. It has carried out the reform based on national conditions while drawing on the sound practices of other countries. The purpose of the reform is to maintain justice in the judicial field. By first tackling problems of particular concern to the people, with focuses on how to restrain and supervise power more effectively, the reform is aimed to optimize the allocation of judicial responsibilities and functions, standardize judicial acts, and promote democracy and openness in the judicial field. China is working hard to establish a socialist judicial system featuring fairness, efficiency and authority, to ensure that judicial organs and procuratorial organs can exercise judicial power and procuratorial power fairly, independently and according to law.

- As restraint and supervision of judicial powers are tightened, some prominent problems affecting judicial fairness are being solved. A system of openness has been improved in relation to trials, procuratorial work, police work, and prison work. The rights of the general public to participate, to know and to sue are better protected. The mechanism of procuratorial supervision of litigation, particularly the mechanism of supervision of malfeasance among judicial personnel, has been further improved. The pilot work of instituting people's supervisors is proceeding smoothly. The focus of their supervision will be on cases in which the arrests are not accepted, or cases that are expected to be canceled or no action to be taken. Complaints about uncivilized, non-standardized handling of cases by procuratorial personnel have been reduced significantly.

- New progress has been made in respecting and guaranteeing human rights through the improvement of the criminal justice system. The procedures for handling capital punishment cases have been further improved. The judicial system with respect to minors has also been improved, with the gradual adoption of methods for investigation, arresting, charging, and trial suitable to the situation of minors. There has been an obvious drop in the number of overdue detainees. Legal supervision of the execution of punishment has become more standard. Pilot programs in the reform of the prison system are proceeding smoothly. The quality of education and reformation in prisons has been improved, and the legitimate rights and interests of those incarcerated protected according to law. There has been a big drop in escapes and crimes committed in prisons. Pilot programs featuring reform of criminals in communities and the system of people's supervisors have yielded good results. Pilot work for the reform of criminals in communities has been carried out in 25 provinces, autonomous regions and municipalities directly under the central government throughout China. Less than one percent of the convicted criminals who serve their time in such communities re-offend.
- The efficiency of judicial work has been raised by reforming and improving the working mechanism. At present, 38.87 % of the criminal cases and 71.26 % of the civil and commercial cases heard by people's courts are adjudicated using the summary procedure. Cases can be put on file for investigation directly in an overwhelming majority of the people's courts throughout the country. The mediation mechanism for settling conflicts of varied nature, such as people's mediation, administrative mediation and judicial mediation, has been improved. In 2006, mediation organizations in China conducted mediation for over 4 million civil disputes, and more than 95 % of the disputes were settled. In order to improve and standardize the management system of judicial expertise, the Standing Committee of the NPC adopted the Decision on the Management of Judicial Expertise. Efficiency has been raised with case-filing for investigation through the Internet and from a distance, and the creation of "digital courts."
- By strengthening judicial relief and legal aid, the difficulties of filing a lawsuit and of enforcing a court's judgment have been eased. The newly promulgated Measures on the Payment of Litigation Fees has reduced litigation fees by 60 % on average. The newly adopted Measures on the Administration of Lawyers' Service Fees has strict provisions on the procedures for the fees charged by lawyers, as well as provisions specifying severe punishment for violations. In recent years, the state has increased, year by year, the expenditure on legal aid. The transfer payment system for legal aid in poverty-stricken areas has been established by the central treasury and some provincial treasuries. In 2006, the number of cases handled with legal aid totaled 318,514, and law consultancy services were provided to 3,193,801 person-times across the country, up 25.6 % and 19.9 %, respectively, over the previous year.
- Justice is further guaranteed through reforming and improving the management system of personnel and the mechanism that ensures the availability of working funds. The management system that separates administrative work from judicial

and procuratorial work has also been improved. Systems such as public recruitment and testing of judicial personnel, competition for posts and exchange of judicial personnel have been established and improved. In recent years the state and local financial departments have all greatly increased spending in the judicial field, providing a solid material guarantee for law-enforcing departments to carry out their duties.

Popularization and Education of the Law

China has actively promoted the awareness of the rule of law among the public. For many years, the state has unremittingly carried out education and publicity of the legal system, promoting the spirit of law, and enhancing public awareness. It strives to develop the fine tradition of studying, observing and applying the law.

Since 1985, the Standing Committee of the NPC has adopted five decisions to popularize the knowledge of law among the people, and has successively implemented four 5-year plans for the dissemination of general knowledge of the law. During the first 5-year plan for popularization of knowledge of the law (1986–1990), over 700 million citizens studied elementary knowledge of the law; during the second 5-year plan for popularization of knowledge of the law (1991–1995), 96 industries made plans for the dissemination of general knowledge of the law, organizing study programs for more than 200 laws and regulations; and during the third 5-year plan (1996–2000), 30 provinces, autonomous regions, and municipalities directly under the central government dealt with irregularities according to law, accompanied by activities to popularize knowledge of the law. Some 95 % of prefecture-level cities, 87 % of counties (districts, cities) and 75 % of grassroots units joined efforts in this regard. During the fourth 5-year plan for popularization of knowledge of the law (2001–2005), 850 million citizens received various forms of education in law. At the moment, the fifth 5-year plan for popularization of knowledge of the law is being vigorously implemented.

The target of popularizing the knowledge of law is every citizen, and the focus is civil servants. For ordinary citizens, popularizing the knowledge of law not only aims to make them know the laws and abide by them, more importantly, is to enable them to use the laws as a weapon to protect their lawful rights and interests. For civil servants, popularizing the knowledge of law aims to make them develop a clear understanding of the rule of law, and act according to law more consciously. China has all along insisted on combining the popularization of knowledge of the law with governance according to law. Activities, including "Governing the Province According to the Law" and "Governing the City According to Law," are widely carried out to promote the construction of the rule of law in daily work of different regions, departments and units, as well as the production and life of the citizens, so as to strive to enhance the level of the rule of law of the whole society and promote the combination of studying the law and practicing the law.

Today, disseminating the general knowledge of law has become a common act of the whole society. Since the 16th National Congress of the CPC was held in 2002, the Political Bureau of the CPC Central Committee has held more than 20 study sessions in relation to the rule of law, which have played an exemplary role for the whole society, especially for civil servants, in studying the law and fostering the concept of the rule of law. The Standing Committee of the NPC, the executive meeting of the State Council and the Standing Committee of the National Committee of the Chinese People's Political Consultative Conference have held a number of meetings to study the law. It has become a system for Party and government organizations at all levels to organize collective law study sessions. Various activities for popularizing the knowledge of law have been organized by the state. December 14, the day when the present Constitution was promulgated, is celebrated as Chinese law publicity day. Legal publicity has also become a focus on the March 15 International Day for Protecting Consumers' Rights, the June 5 World Environment Day, the June 26 International Day against Drug Abuse and Illicit Trafficking, as well as on days marking the promulgation of important laws and regulations. Schools of different types at all levels have brought law education into required courses. The media, including radio, television, newspapers, and the net, have all enhanced their efforts in law publicity. At present, over 300 TV stations at provincial and municipal levels have started programs on the law. Some places have also launched websites for law publicity and education.

The state attaches great importance to law education. In the early years of the People's Republic of China, the central government established the Beijing Institute of Political Science and Law, the East China Institute of Political Science and Law, the South Central Institute of Political Science and Law, the Southwest Institute of Political Science and Law, and the Northwest Institute of Political Science and Law, as well as departments of law in such comprehensive universities as the Renmin University of China, Northeast People's University, Peking University and Fudan University in line with a uniform national plan. Thus, law education in China developed into a considerable scale. Since the introduction of the reform and opening-up policies in 1978, law education in China has entered a period of rapid development. By the end of 2006, some 603 institutions of higher learning had offered bachelor's degrees in law, with nearly 300,000 students majoring in law. In addition, some 333 institutions of higher learning and scientific research institutes were entitled to confer master's degrees in law, 29 were entitled to confer doctorates in law, and 13 law education institutions had launched mobile stations for postdoctoral law studies. After nearly 30 years' restoring, rebuilding, reforming, and developing efforts, a law education system has taken shape and it focuses on bachelor, master, and doctorate education and combines the education of law majors and vocational education in law, basically satisfying the needs to build a modern socialist country.

International Exchange and Cooperation in Legal Construction

China upholds that the practice in regard to the rule of law should proceed from the country's actual conditions. At the same time, it pays attention to draw on other countries' valuable experience in legal construction and the achievements in legal civilization made by mankind to enrich and improve the socialist legal civilization with Chinese characteristics.

China pays attention to making reference to and learning from other countries' experience in legislation. In the field of civil and commercial legislation, the General Principles of the Civil Law, Property Rights Law, and Contract Law have adopted the basic systems of both common law countries and continental law countries, used the spirit of the private law and legislation principles applicable throughout the world, confirmed the liberty of contract, autonomy of the will and subject equality, and safeguarded both public property and legitimate private property of citizens. In the field of administrative legislation, China has adopted the principle of trust protection and the principle of proportionality applicable in modern administrative law. In the field of criminal legislation, the Criminal Law, and the Criminal Procedure Law have consulted and adopted the basic principles and spirits of other countries, including punishments determined by law and public trials. In recent years, in view of the new development in criminal offences and consulting foreign experience in criminal legislation, China has prescribed new charges in its criminal laws, such as the crime of financially aiding terrorist activities, the crime of money laundering, the crime of insider trading, the crime of manipulating trading prices of futures and securities, and the crime of impairing credit card administration. Regarding legislation for the protection of intellectual property rights and environmental protection, China has also learned much from foreign experience.

China has established relations of equal and mutually beneficial judicial cooperation with many countries and international organizations, accepting and adopting judicial cooperation regulations common throughout the world. Up to October 2007, China had signed 98 bilateral treaties and agreements on international judicial cooperation with 53 countries, and joined over 20 multilateral international conventions that include provisions of judicial cooperation. In 2001, China signed the Shanghai Convention against Terrorism, Separatism and Extremism with other member countries of the Shanghai Cooperation Organization. China joined the UN Convention against Transnational Organized Crime and UN Anti-corruption Convention in 2003 and 2005, respectively, thus enhancing judicial cooperation in combating crimes. China also promotes international exchange in the enforcement of law in various forms, including international meetings. In 1990 and 2005, it hosted the 14th and 22nd International Law Congress, respectively. In 2006, the International Anti-corruption Conference was held in China.

China pays great attention to turning international judicial cooperation into concrete operational rules by way of domestic legislation. The Civil Procedure Law rules that, when there is discrepancy between domestic laws and regulations and international treaties acceded or joined by China, the people's court gives priority to the stipulations of international treaties in handling foreign-related civil cases. It also prescribes the principles, conditions, and procedures for judicial administration and assistance in foreign-related cases. The Civil Procedure Law sets the principles of international treaty relationships and mutual benefit as the base for Chinese judicial organs to conduct judicial assistance in foreign-related cases. The Extradition Law draws on the universally applicable principles of the world for extradition cooperation to decide the concrete rules, conditions and procedures for extradition cooperation between China and other countries. At present, a growing trend has appeared in the number of judicial assistance cases handled by the competent Chinese authorities in accordance with bilateral treaties and multilateral conventions, and large numbers of requests for civil and commercial judicial assistance have been implemented effectively, safeguarding the rights, and interests of both foreign and domestic litigants. In the field of criminal litigation, international judicial cooperation has been playing a more and more important role. In the last decade, China has carried out effective criminal judicial cooperation with some countries and international organizations, focusing on the crimes of murder, embezzlement, bribery, terrorism, infringement of intellectual property rights and money laundering, in offering mutual help to gather evidence, freeze, seize, and recover illegally transferred proceeds of crime, and extradite and repatriate suspects on the run. These have effectively safeguarded the judicial justice.

In recent years, China has held dialogues on the rule of law regularly with the United Nations, international human rights organizations and the WTO, and launched multilateral and bilateral legal exchange mechanisms with the European Union, the Association of Southeast Asian Nations, the League of Arab States, and the Shanghai Cooperation Organization, as well as the United States, the United Kingdom, Germany, France and Australia, greatly enhancing mutual understanding and trust.

Conclusion

China is the largest developing country in the world. It is, and will be, in the primary stage of socialism for a long time to come. China's legal construction is still facing some problems: The development of democracy and the rule of law still falls short of the needs of economic and social development; the legal framework shows certain characteristics of the current stage and calls for further improvement; in some regions and departments, laws are not observed, or strictly enforced, violators are not brought to justice; local protectionism, departmental protectionism and difficulties in law enforcement occur from time to time; some government functionaries take bribes and bend the law, abuse their power when executing the law, abuse their authority to override the law, and substitute their words for the law, thus bringing damage to the socialist rule of law; and the task still remains onerous to strengthen education in the rule of law, and enhance the awareness of law and the concept of the rule of law among the public.

The great practice of socialist legal construction has made the Chinese people realize that the following principles must be observed to carry out the fundamental policy of governing the country by law: adhering to the leadership of the CPC, the people as the masters and ruling the country by law, ensuring that the CPC always plays the role as the core of leadership in directing the overall situation and coordinating the efforts of all quarters in legal construction, ensuring the people's position as masters of the country according to prescriptions of the Constitution and the law, and making sure that all work is carried on according to law; persevering in focusing on both construction and the rule of law, continuously improving the legal system in the light of the objective needs of economic and social development, and making legal construction serve economic and social development as well as the construction of a harmonious society; striving for rooting the legal construction in the reality of Chinese society, drawing on valuable foreign experience for reference while basing our efforts on China's actual conditions without copying indiscriminately other countries' legal systems or political mechanisms; and persisting in basing legal construction on institutional building and enhancing the public's awareness of the rule of law, and unremittingly enhancing the level of legal civilization of the whole society.

In this new century, China will uphold the scientific outlook on development, focus on perfecting legislation, strict enforcement of the law, impartial administration of justice, and conscious observation of the law to implement the fundamental policy of governing the country by law in an all-round way and quicken the tempo of building a socialist country under the rule of law. By strengthening and improving legislation work, we will further improve the quality of legislation to form as soon as possible a more comprehensive socialist legal system with Chinese characteristics. By strengthening the implementation of the Constitution and the law, we will safeguard people's legitimate rights and interests and social justice, and defend the uniformity, dignity and authority of the socialist legal system. By enhancing the supervision over law enforcement, we will guarantee the proper operation of power, ensure that power must be linked to responsibility and under supervision, and offenders must be prosecuted. By carrying out intensive publicity of the law and education in the law, we will further enhance the awareness of law and the concept of the rule of law among the public, and develop asocial atmosphere of consciously studying, observing and applying the law.

The Chinese people are now going all out to build a well-off society in all aspects. Along with the sound and rapid development of the economy and society, the rights and interests of the Chinese people will certainly enjoy better protection, the construction of a socialist country under the rule of law will certainly witness more fruitful results, and China will surely make more contributions to the development and advancement of human society.

Appendix

List of Current Effective Laws of the People's Republic of China (229)

Constitution and the Constitution-Related Legislation (39)

1. Constitution of the People's Republic of China (1982)

   Amendments to the Constitution of the People's Republic of China (1988)
   Amendments to the Constitution of the People's Republic of China (1993)
   Amendments to the Constitution of the People's Republic of China (1999)
   Amendments to the Constitution of the People's Republic of China (2004)

2. Organic Regulations of Urban Sub-district Offices (1954)
3. Organic Law of the People's Republic of China on the Local People's Congresses and Local People's Governments (1979, revised respectively in 1982, 1986, 1995 and 2004)
4. Electoral Law of the People's Republic of China on the National People's Congress and the Local People's Congresses (1979, revised respectively in 1982, 1986, 1995 and 2004)
5. Organic Law of the People's Courts of the People's Republic of China (1979, revised respectively in 1983, 1986 and 2006)
6. Organic Law of the People's Procuratorates of the People's Republic of China (1979, revised respectively in 1983 and 1986)
7. Nationality Law of the People's Republic of China (1980)
8. Organic Law of the People's Republic of China on the National People's Congress (1982)
9. Organic Law of the People's Republic of China on the State Council (1982)
10. Provisions of the Standing Committee of the National People's Congress on the Direct Election of Deputies to People's Congresses at or below the County Level (1983)
11. Law of the People's Republic of China on Regional Ethnic Autonomy (1984, revised in 2001)
12. Decision of the Standing Committee of the National People's Congress on the Establishment of Maritime Courts in Coastal Port Cities (1984)
13. Regulations of the People's Republic of China on Diplomatic Privileges and Immunities (1986)
14. Rules of Procedures of the Standing Committee of the National People's Congress of the People's Republic of China (1987)
15. Decision of the Standing Committee of the National People's Congress Approving the "Provisions on Conferring Honorary Medals of the People's Liberation Army on Retired Officers Who Joined the Army before the Founding of New China for Their Meritorious Service" (1988)

Annex: Provisions on Conferring Honorary Medals of the People's Liberation Army on Retired Officers Who Joined the Army before the Founding of New China for Their Meritorious Service

16. Rules of Procedures of the National People's Congress of the People's Republic of China (1989)
17. Law of the People's Republic of China on Assemblies, Processions and Demonstrations (1989)
18. Organic Law of the People's Republic of China on Urban Neighborhood Committees (1989)
19. The Basic Law of the Hong Kong Special Administrative Region of the People's Republic of China (1990)

    Annex I: Method for the Selection of the Chief Executive of the Hong Kong Special Administrative Region
    Annex II: Method for the Formation of the Legislative Council of the Hong Kong Special Administrative Region and Its Voting Procedures
    Annex III: National Laws to Be Applied in the Hong Kong Special Administrative Region

20. Law of the People's Republic of China on the National Flag (1990)
21. Regulations of the People's Republic of China on Consular Privileges and Immunities (1990)
22. Law of the People's Republic of China on the Procedure of the Conclusion of Treaties (1990)
23. Law of the People's Republic of China on the National Emblem (1991)
24. Law of the People's Republic of China on the Territorial Sea and the Contiguous Zones (1992)
25. Law of the People's Republic of China on Deputation to the National People's Congress and the Local People's Congresses at Various Levels (1992)
26. The Basic Law of the Macao Special Administrative Region of the People's Republic of China (1993)

    Annex I: Method for the Selection of the Chief Executive of the Macao Special Administrative Region
    Annex II: Method for the Formation of the Legislative Council of the Macao Special Administrative Region
    Annex III: National Laws to Be Applied in the Macao Special Administrative Region

27. State Compensation Law of the People's Republic of China (1994)
28. Judges Law of the People's Republic of China (1995, revised in 2001)
29. Public Procurators Law of the People's Republic of China (1995, revised in 2001)
30. Martial Law of the People's Republic of China (1996)

31. Electoral Measures on Deputation of the People's Liberation Army to the National People's Congress and the Local People's Congresses at the County and Above Levels (1981, revised and changed to the current title in 1996)
32. Law of the People's Republic of China on the Garrisoning of the Hong Kong Special Administrative Region (1996)
33. Law of the People's Republic of China on Exclusive Economic Zones and Continental Shelves (1998)
34. Organic Law of the People's Republic of China on Villagers Committees (1998)
35. Law of the People's Republic of China on the Garrisoning of the Macao Special Administrative Region (1999)
36. Legislation Law of the People's Republic of China (2000)
37. Anti-secession Law (2005)
38. Law of the People's Republic of China on Immunity of Judicial Enforcement of Assets of Central Banks of Foreign Countries (2005)
39. Supervision Law of the Standing Committees of the People's Congresses at All Levels of the People's Republic of China (2006)

Civil and Commercial Legislation (32)

1. Law of the People's Republic of China on Chinese-Foreign Equity Joint Ventures (1979, revised respectively in 1990 and 2001)
2. Marriage Law of the People's Republic of China (1980, revised in 2001)
3. Trademark Law of the People's Republic of China (1982, revised respectively in 1993 and 2001)
4. Patent Law of the People's Republic of China (1984, revised respectively in 1992 and 2000)
5. Succession Law of the People's Republic of China (1985)
6. General Principles of the Civil Law of the People's Republic of China (1986)
7. Law of the People's Republic of China on Enterprises with Foreign Investment (1986, revised in 2000)
8. Law of the People's Republic of China on Industrial Enterprises Owned by the Whole People (1988)
9. Law of the People's Republic of China on Chinese-Foreign Cooperative Joint Ventures (1988, revised in 2002)
10. Copyright Law of the People's Republic of China (1990, revised in 2001)
11. Adoption Law of the People's Republic of China (1991, revised in 1998)
12. Maritime Law of the People's Republic of China (1992)
13. Law of the People's Republic of China for Countering Unfair Competition (1993)
14. Law of the People's Republic of China on the Protection of Rights and Interests of Consumers (1993)
15. Company Law of the People's Republic of China (1993, revised respectively in 1999, 2004 and 2005)
16. Law of the People's Republic of China on Commercial Banks (1995, revised in 2003)

17. Law of the People's Republic of China on Negotiable Instruments (1995, revised in 2004)
18. Security Law of the People's Republic of China (1995)
19. Insurance Law of the People's Republic of China (1995, revised in 2002)
20. Auction Law of the People's Republic of China (1996, revised in 2004)
21. Partnership Law of the People's Republic of China (1997, revised in 2006)
22. Securities Law of the People's Republic of China (1998, revised respectively in 2004 and 2005)
23. Contract Law of the People's Republic of China (1999)
24. Law of the People's Republic of China on Enterprises Wholly Owned by Individuals (1999)
25. Law of the People's Republic of China on Invitation and Submission of Bids (1999)
26. Trust Law of the People's Republic of China (2001)
27. Law of the People's Republic of China on Land Contracting in Rural Areas (2002)
28. Law of the People's Republic of China on Securities Investment Funds (2003)
29. Law of the People's Republic of China on Electronic Signature (2004)
30. Law of the People's Republic of China on Enterprise Bankruptcy (2006)
31. Law of the People's Republic of China on Farmers Specialized Cooperatives (2006)
32. Property Rights Law of the People's Republic of China (2007)

Administrative Legislation (79)

1. Organic Regulations on Police Stations (1954)
2. Resolution of the Standing Committee of the National People's Congress Approving the "Decision of the State Council on the Issue of Rehabilitation Through Labor" (1957)

   Annex: Decision of the State Council on the Issue of Rehabilitation Through Labor

3. Resolution of the Standing Committee of the National People's Congress Approving the "Measures of the State Council on the Establishment of Schools with Donations of Overseas Chinese" (1957)

   Annex: Measures of the State Council on the Establishment of Schools with Donations of Overseas Chinese

4. Regulations of the People's Republic of China on Residence Registration (1958)
5. Resolution of the Standing Committee of the National People's Congress Approving the "Interim Measures of the State Council on Settlement of Cadres Who Are Old, Weak, Sick or Disabled" (1978)

   Annex: Interim Measures of the State Council on Settlement of Cadres Who Are Old, Weak, Sick or Disabled

6. Resolution of the Standing Committee of the National People's Congress Approving the "Supplementary Provisions of the State Council on Rehabilitation Through Labor" (1979)

   Annex: Supplementary Provisions of the State Council on Rehabilitation Through Labor

7. Regulations of the People's Republic of China on Academic Degrees (1980, revised in 2004)
8. Resolution of the Standing Committee of the National People's Congress Approving the "Interim Provisions of the State Council for Veteran Cadres to Leave Their Posts for Retirement" (1980)

   Annex: Interim Provisions of the State Council for Veteran Cadres to Leave Their Posts for Retirement

9. Law of the People's Republic of China on the Protection of Maritime Environment (1982, revised in 1999)
10. Law of the People's Republic of China on the Protection of Cultural Relics (1982, revised respectively in 1991, 2002 and 2007)
11. Law of the People's Republic of China on the Prevention and Control of Water Pollution (1984, revised respectively in 1996 and 2008)
12. Military Service Law of the People's Republic of China (1984, revised in 1998)
13. Law of the People's Republic of China on the Administration of Pharmaceuticals (1984, revised in 2001)
14. Law of the People's Republic of China on the Control of the Entry and Exit of Aliens (1985)
15. Law of the People's Republic of China on the Control of the Entry and Exit of Citizens (1985)
16. Law of the People's Republic of China on Compulsory Education (1986, revised in 2006)
17. Law of the People's Republic of China on Frontier Health and Quarantine (1986, revised in 2007)
18. Customs Law of the People's Republic of China (1987, revised in 2000)
19. Law of the People's Republic of China on the Prevention and Control of Atmospheric Pollution (1987, revised respectively in 1995 and 2000)
20. Archives Law of the People's Republic of China (1987, revised in 1996)
21. Regulations of the Military Ranks of Officers of the People's Liberation Army (1988, revised in 1994)
22. Law of the People's Republic of China on Keeping Confidentiality of State Secrets (1988)
23. Law of the People's Republic of China on the Protection of Wildlife (1988, revised in 2004)
24. Law of the People's Republic of China on the Prevention and Treatment of Infectious Diseases (1989, revised in 2004)

25. Law of the People's Republic of China on Environmental Protection (1989)
26. Law of the People's Republic of China on the Protection of Military Installations (1990)
27. Law of the People's Republic of China on the Protection of Rights and Interests of Returned Overseas Chinese and Their Relatives (1990, revised in 2000)
28. Regulations of the People's Republic of China on the Policemen Ranks of the People's Police (1992)
29. Law of the People's Republic of China on Surveying and Mapping (1992, revised in 2002)
30. Law of the People's Republic of China on State Security (1993)
31. Law of the People's Republic of China on the Progress of Science and Technology (1993, revised in 2007)
32. Teachers Law of the People's Republic of China (1993)
33. Law of the People's Republic of China on the Administration of Urban Real Estate (1994, revised in 2007)
34. Law of the People's Republic of China on Maternal and Infant Health Care (1994)
35. Prison Law of the People's Republic of China (1994)
36. Law of the People's Republic of China on People's Police (1995)
37. Education Law of the People's Republic of China (1995)
38. Law of the People's Republic of China on Military Officers on Reserve Service (1995)
39. Law of the People's Republic of China on Physical Culture and Sports (1995)
40. Law of the People's Republic of China on the Prevention and Control of Solid Waste Pollution (1995, revised in 2004)
41. Law of the People's Republic of China on Food Hygiene (1995)
42. Law of the People's Republic of China on Administrative Penalties (1996)
43. Lawyers Law of the People's Republic of China (1996, revised respectively in 2001 and 2007)
44. Law of the People's Republic of China on the Promotion of Application of Scientific and Technological Achievements (1996)
45. Law of the People's Republic of China on Vocational Education (1996)
46. Law of the People's Republic of China on the Control of Firearms (1996)
47. Law of the People's Republic of China on the Prevention and Control of Ambient Noise Pollution (1996)
48. Law of the People's Republic of China on People's Air Defense (1996)
49. Law of the People's Republic of China on National Defense (1997)
50. Law of the People's Republic of China on Administrative Supervision (1997)
51. Construction Law of the People's Republic of China (1997)
52. Law of the People's Republic of China on Blood Donation (1997)
53. Law of the People's Republic of China on Precautions Against Earthquake and Relief of Disaster (1997)

54. Law of the People's Republic of China on Fire Prevention and Control (1998)
55. Law of the People's Republic of China on Medical Practitioners (1998)
56. Law of the People's Republic of China on Higher Education (1998)
57. Law of the People's Republic of China on Administrative Review (1999)
58. Meteorology Law of the People's Republic of China (1999)
59. Law of the People's Republic of China on the Standard Spoken and Written Chinese Language (2000)
60. Law of the People's Republic of China on Military Officers on Service (1988, revised respectively in 1994 and 2000, and changed to the current title)
61. Law of the People's Republic of China on the Education of National Defense (2001)
62. Law of the People's Republic of China on the Prevention and Control of Desertification (2001)
63. Law of the People's Republic of China on Population and Family Planning (2001)
64. Law of the People's Republic of China on the Popularization of Science and Technology (2002)
65. Law of the People's Republic of China on the Promotion of Clean Production (2002)
66. Law of the People's Republic of China on the Assessment of Environmental Affects (2002)
67. Law of the People's Republic of China on the Promotion of Education Run by Non-governmental Entities and Individuals (2002)
68. Law of the People's Republic of China on Ranks of Customs Officers (2003)
69. Law of the People's Republic of China on Residents' Identification Cards (2003)
70. Law of the People's Republic of China on the Prevention and Control of Radioactive Pollution (2003)
71. Law of the People's Republic of China on Administrative Licensing (2003)
72. Law of the People's Republic of China on Road Traffic Safety (2003, revised in 2007)
73. Law of the People's Republic of China on Civil Servants (2005)
74. Law of the People's Republic of China on Punishments in Public Order and Security Administration (2005)
75. Notarization Law of the People's Republic of China (2005)
76. Passport Law of the People's Republic of China (2006)
77. Law of the People's Republic of China on Emergency Responses (2007)
78. Law of the People's Republic of China on Urban and Rural Planning (2007)
79. Law of the People's Republic of China on the Prohibition of Narcotics (2007)

Economic Legislation (54)

1. Regulations on Application for Use of the State-owned Wasteland and Barren Hills by Overseas Chinese (1955)
2. Resolution of the Standing Committee of the National People's Congress Approving the "Regulations on Special Economic Zones in Guangdong Province" (1980)

   Annex: Regulations on Special Economic Zones in Guangdong Province
3. Law of the People's Republic of China on Individual Income Tax (1980, revised respectively in 1993, 1999, 2005 and twice in 2007)
4. Law of the People's Republic of China on Maritime Traffic Safety (1983)
5. Statistics Law of the People's Republic of China (1983, revised in 1996)
6. Forestry Law of the People's Republic of China (1984, revised in 1998)
7. Accounting Law of the People's Republic of China (1985, revised respectively in 1993 and 1999)
8. Grassland Law of the People's Republic of China (1985, revised in 2002)
9. Metrology Law of the People's Republic of China (1985)
10. Fishery Law of the People's Republic of China (1986, revised respectively in 2000 and 2004)
11. Law of the People's Republic of China on Mineral Resources (1986, revised in 1996)
12. Law of the People's Republic of China on Land Administration (1986, revised respectively in 1988, 1998 and 2004)
13. Postal Law of the People's Republic of China (1986)
14. Water Law of the People's Republic of China (1988, revised in 2002)
15. Standardization Law of the People's Republic of China (1988)
16. Law of the People's Republic of China on the Inspection of Import and Export Commodities (1989, revised in 2002)
17. Railway Law of the People's Republic of China (1990)
18. Law of the People's Republic of China on Tobacco Monopoly (1991)
19. Law of the People's Republic of China on the Conservation of Water and Top Soil (1991)
20. Law of the People's Republic of China on the Entry and Exit Animal and Plant Quarantine (1991)
21. Law of the People's Republic of China on the Administration of Tax Collection (1992, revised respectively in 1995 and 2001)
22. Law of the People's Republic of China on Product Quality (1993, revised in 2000)
23. Law of the People's Republic of China on the Popularization of Agricultural Technology (1993)
24. Agriculture Law of the People's Republic of China (1993, revised in 2002)
25. Law of the People's Republic of China on Certified Public Accountants (1993)

26. Decision of the Standing Committee of the National People's Congress Regarding the Application of Provisional Regulations on Such Taxes as Value-added Tax, Consumption Tax and Business Tax to Enterprises with Foreign Investment and Foreign Enterprises (1993)
27. Law of the People's Republic of China on the Protection of Investment by Taiwan Compatriots (1994)
28. Budget Law of the People's Republic of China (1994)
29. Law of the People's Republic of China on Foreign Trade (1994, revised in 2004)
30. Auditing Law of the People's Republic of China (1994, revised in 2006)
31. Advertisement Law of the People's Republic of China (1994)
32. Law of the People's Republic of China on the People's Bank of China (1995, revised in 2003)
33. Law of the People's Republic of China on Civil Aviation (1995)
34. Law of the People's Republic of China on Electric Power (1995)
35. Coal Law of the People's Republic of China (1996)
36. Law of the People's Republic of China on Township Enterprises (1996)
37. Highway Law of the People's Republic of China (1997, revised respectively in 1999 and 2004)
38. Law of the People's Republic of China on the Epidemic Prevention of Animals (1997, revised in 2007)
39. Law of the People's Republic of China on Flood Control (1997)
40. Law of the People's Republic of China on the Conservation of Energy Resources (1997, revised in 2007)
41. Pricing Law of the People's Republic of China (1997)
42. Seeds Law of the People's Republic of China (2000, revised in 2004)
43. Law of the People's Republic of China on the Administration of Use of Sea Areas (2001)
44. Law of the People's Republic of China on Government Procurement (2002)
45. Law of the People's Republic of China on the Promotion of Small and Medium-sized Enterprises (2002)
46. Port Law of the People's Republic of China (2003)
47. Law of the People's Republic of China on the Administration of Banking Supervision (2003, revised in 2006)
48. Law of the People's Republic of China on the Promotion of Agricultural Mechanization (2004)
49. Law of the People's Republic of China on Renewable Energy (2005)
50. Law of the People's Republic of China on Animal Husbandry (2005)
51. Law of the People's Republic of China on the Quality and Safety of Agricultural Products (2006)
52. Law of the People's Republic of China on Anti-money Laundering (2006)
53. Law of the People's Republic of China on Enterprise Income Tax (2007)
54. Anti-monopoly Law of the People's Republic of China (2007)

Legislation for the Public (17)

1. Resolution of the Standing Committee of the National People's Congress Approving the "Interim Measures of the State Council on the Workers' Retirement and Leaving of Posts" (1978)

   Annex: Interim Measures of the State Council on the Workers' Retirement and Leaving of Posts

2. Resolution of the Standing Committee of the National People's Congress Approving the "Provisions of the State Council on Home Visit Subsidies" (1981)

   Annex: Provisions of the State Council on Home Visit Subsidies

3. Law of the People's Republic of China on the Protection of the Disabled (1990)
4. Law of the People's Republic of China on the Protection of Minors (1991, revised in 2006)
5. Law of the People's Republic of China on the Trade Union (1992, revised in 2001)
6. Law of the People's Republic of China on the Guarantee of the Rights and Interests of Women (1992, revised in 2005)
7. Law of the People's Republic of China on Safety in Mines (1992)
8. Law of the People's Republic of China on the Red Cross (1993)
9. Labor Law of the People's Republic of China (1994)
10. Law of the People's Republic of China on the Guarantee of the Rights and Interests of the Elderly (1996)
11. Law of the People's Republic of China on the Prevention of Crimes Committed by Minors (1999)
12. Law of the People's Republic of China on Donations for the Public Good (1999)
13. Law of the People's Republic of China on the Prevention and Treatment of Occupational Diseases (2001)
14. Law of the People's Republic of China on Production Safety (2002)
15. Law of the People's Republic of China on Labor Contracts (2007)
16. Law of the People's Republic of China on the Promotion of Employment (2007)
17. Law of the People's Republic of China on Labor Dispute Mediation and Arbitration (2007)

Criminal Legislation (1)

Criminal Law of the People's Republic of China (1979, revised in 1997)

Decision of the Standing Committee of the National People's Congress Regarding the Punishment of Fraudulent Purchase of Foreign Exchanges, Evasion of Foreign Exchange Control and Illegal Purchase and Sale of Foreign Exchanges (1998)

Amendments to the Criminal Law of the People's Republic of China (1999)
Amendments to the Criminal Law of the People's Republic of China (2) (2001)
Amendments to the Criminal Law of the People's Republic of China (3) (2001)
Amendments to the Criminal Law of the People's Republic of China (4) (2002)
Amendments to the Criminal Law of the People's Republic of China (5) (2005)
Amendments to the Criminal Law of the People's Republic of China (6) (2006)

Litigation and Non-litigation Procedural Legislation (7)

1. Criminal Procedure Law of the People's Republic of China (1979, revised in 1996)
2. Decision of the Standing Committee of the National People's Congress Regarding Exercising Criminal Jurisdiction over the Crimes Prescribed in the International Treaties to Which the People's Republic of China Has Acceded or Is a Party (1987)
3. Administrative Procedure Law of the People's Republic of China (1989)
4. Civil Procedure Law of the People's Republic of China (1991, revised in 2007)
5. Arbitration Law of the People's Republic of China (1994)
6. Law of the People's Republic of China on Special Procedures Concerning Maritime Litigations (1999)
7. Extradition Law of the People's Republic of China (2000)

Appendix III
The Socialist System of Laws with Chinese Characteristics

Foreword

Governing the country by law and building a socialist country under the rule of law is a fundamental principle for the Communist Party of China (CPC) to lead the people and effectively govern the country. We need to bring into being a socialist system of laws with Chinese characteristics so as to ensure there are laws to abide by for the carrying on of state affairs and social life; this is a precondition and foundation for us to implement the fundamental principle of the rule of law in all respects, and an institutional guarantee for China's development and progress.

In 1949 the People's Republic of China was founded, marking the great transition from the centuries-old dictatorial system of feudalism to the system of people's democracy, putting an end to the period of semi-colonialism and semi-feudalism in China, and enabling the people to become masters of the country, society and their own life. For over 62 years, particularly since the policy of reform and opening up was adopted in 1978, the CPC has led the Chinese people in making the Constitution and laws. With concerted and unremitting efforts, by the end of 2010 we had put in place a socialist system of laws with Chinese characteristics, which is based on the conditions and reality of China, meets the needs of reform, opening up and the socialist modernization drive, and reflects the will of the CPC and the Chinese people. This legal system, headed by the Constitution, with laws related to the Constitution, civil and commercial laws and several other branches as the mainstay, and consisting of laws, administrative regulations, local regulations and other tiers of legal provisions, ensures that there are laws to abide by in economic, political, cultural and social development, as well as in ecological civilization building.

Information Office of the State Council of the People's Republic of China
October 27, 2011

P. Sun, *Human Rights Protection System in China*,
DOI: 10.1007/978-3-642-39663-2, © Springer-Verlag Berlin Heidelberg 2014

The socialist system of laws with Chinese characteristics is a legal foundation for socialism with Chinese characteristics to retain its nature, a legal reflection of the innovative practice of socialism with Chinese characteristics, and a legal guarantee for the prosperity of socialism with Chinese characteristics. Its establishment is an important milestone in China's development of socialist democracy and the legal system, and showcases the great achievements of reform, opening up and the socialist modernization drive. It is of great realistic and far-reaching historic significance.

Establishment of the Socialist System of Laws with Chinese Characteristics

The socialist system of laws with Chinese characteristics was formed gradually under the leadership of the CPC in the course of adapting itself to the cause of building socialism with Chinese characteristics.

When the People's Republic of China was founded, it was confronted with the difficult tasks of organizing and consolidating the new political power, restoring, and developing the national economy, and realizing and guaranteeing the people's right to be masters of the country. To meet the needs of construction of the political power, from 1949 to 1954, before the convening of the First National People's Congress (NPC), China promulgated and implemented the Common Program of the Chinese People's Political Consultative Conference, which acted as a temporary constitution, and enacted the Organic Law of the Central People's Government, Trade Union Law, Marriage Law, Land Reform Law, Interim Regulations on the Organization of the People's Courts, Interim Regulations on the Organization of the Supreme People's Procuratorate, Regulations on Punishment of Counter-revolutionaries, Interim Regulations on Punishment for Impairment of the State Currency, Regulations on Punishment for Embezzlement, Electoral Law of the National People's Congress and Local People's Congresses, and laws and regulations on the organization of local people's governments and local judicial organs, on regional ethnic autonomy, on the management of public and private enterprises, and on labor protection. With these laws and regulations, New China embarked on its course of development of democracy and the legal system.

In 1954 the First Session of the First NPC was held. The session adopted the first Constitution of New China, which established the principles for people's democracy and socialism, established the people's congress system as a fundamental political system, and provided for the basic rights and obligations of Chinese citizens. The session also adopted organic laws of the NPC, the State Council, local people's congresses and local people's committees, people's courts, and people's procuratorates, thus establishing the basic principles for state affairs. In 1956 the Eighth National Congress of the CPC proposed that "the state must make a complete legal system gradually and systematically according to its needs." Before the "cultural revolution" broke out in 1966, China's legislature had enacted over 130 laws and decrees. The building of democracy and the legal system in this period provided valuable experiences for building a socialist system of laws with Chinese characteristics. During the "cultural revolution," China suffered grave setbacks in its work to improve democracy and the legal system, and its legislation almost came to a standstill.

In 1978 the Third Plenary Session of the 11th Central Committee of the CPC summarized the experience and lessons since the founding of New China, made a historic decision to shift the focus of the work of the Party and the state to economic development and to adopt the policy of reform and opening up, and stated, "To ensure people's democracy, we must strengthen our socialist legal system, which will enable democracy to be institutionalized and codified, and ensure that such system and laws are stable, continuous, and authoritative. All this will ensure that there are laws to go by, that they are observed and strictly enforced, and that violators are brought to book." This session ushered in a new chapter in China's history of reform and opening up, and the building of the socialist democracy and legal system. Legislation in this period focused on restoring and re-establishing state order, and carrying out and advancing reform and opening up. In 1979 the Second Session of the Fifth NPC passed a resolution concerning the amendment to several provisions of the Constitution, which provided that local people's congresses at and above the county level established standing committees, and deputies to the people's congresses of counties were to be elected directly by their constituencies. The meeting also enacted the Electoral Law of the National People's Congress and Local People's Congresses, Organic Law of the Local People's Congresses and Local People's Governments, Organic Law of the People's Courts, Organic Law of the People's Procuratorates, Criminal Law, Criminal Procedure Law, and Law on Chinese-Foreign Equity Joint Ventures, marking the beginning of large-scale legislation work in the new period.

In 1982, to adapt to the great changes in the economic, political, cultural, and social life of China, the Fifth Session of the Fifth NPC adopted the present Constitution, establishing the fundamental system of the country and fundamental principles for state affairs, and setting basic tasks for the country, providing basic guarantees for reform and opening up, and the socialist modernization drive in the new period and symbolizing that China's efforts to improve democracy and the legal system had entered a new era. As reform and opening up deepened, and profound changes took place in China's economy and society, China made amendments to the Constitution in 1988, 1993, 1999, and 2004, respectively. These amendments affirmed the important status of the non-public sector of the economy, and wrote into the Constitution that the state "practices a socialist market economy," "exercises the rule of law, building a socialist country governed according to law," and "respects and protects human rights," that "citizens' lawful private property is inviolable," and that "the system of multi-party cooperation and political consultation led by the Communist Party of China will exist and develop in China for a long time to come." These amendments contributed to China's economic, political, cultural, and social development and progress. During this period, to meet the needs for centering on economic development and promoting reform and opening up, the legislature enacted the General Principles of the Civil Law, Law on Industrial Enterprises Owned by the Whole People, Law on Chinese-Foreign Cooperative Joint Ventures, Law on Foreign-funded Enterprises, Patent Law, Trademark Law, Copyright Law, Economic Contract Law, Law on Enterprise Bankruptcy, and some other laws. To carry out the policy of "one country, two systems," the legislature enacted the Basic Law of the Hong Kong Special Administrative Region and the Basic Law of the Macao Special Administrative Region. To strengthen ethnic unity, develop socialist democracy and safeguard citizens' legitimate rights and interests, the legislature enacted the Law on Regional Ethnic Autonomy, Organic Law of the Villagers' Committees, Criminal Procedure Law, Civil Procedure Law, Administrative Procedure Law, and some other laws. To protect and improve the living and ecological environment, the legislature enacted the Environmental Protection Law, Law on the Prevention and Control of Water Pollution, Law on the Prevention and Control of Atmospheric Pollution, and some other laws. To promote education and culture, the legislature enacted the Compulsory Education Law, Law on the Protection of Cultural Relics, and some other laws. These great achievements in legislation laid an important foundation for the establishment of the socialist system of laws with Chinese characteristics.

In 1992 the 14th National Congress of the CPC made an important strategic decision to establish a socialist market economy. It expressly stated that the establishment and improvement of this socialist market economy must be regulated and guaranteed by a complete legal regime. To meet the requirements for establishing a socialist market economy, the Chinese legislature accelerated the pace of enacting economic laws; to regulate market players, maintain market order, strengthen macro-control and promote opening to the outside world, the legislature enacted the Company Law, Partnership Enterprise Law, Law on Commercial Banks, Law on Township Enterprises, Anti-Unfair Competition Law, Law on the Protection of Consumers' Rights and Interests, Product Quality Law, Auction Law, Guaranty Law, Maritime Code, Insurance Law, Negotiable Instruments Law, Law on Urban Real Estate Administration, Advertising Law, Law on Certified Public Accountants, Arbitration Law, Audit Law, Budget Law, Law on the People's Bank of China, Foreign Trade Law, Labor Law, and some other laws. To improve criminal laws, the legislature revised the Criminal Law, making it unified and complete, and revised the Criminal Procedure Law, improving criminal procedure. To regulate and supervise the use of power, the legislature enacted the Law on Administrative Penalty, Law on State Compensation, Judges Law, Public Procurators Law, Law on Lawyers, and some other laws. To strengthen the protection of the environment and resources, the legislature enacted the Law on the Prevention and Control of Environmental Pollution by Solid Waste, and some other laws while revising the Mineral Resources Law and some other laws.

In 1997 as the socialist market economy was gradually put in place, the level of opening up was constantly enhanced, the efforts to improve democracy and the legal system were advanced, and all undertakings were developing, to advance the cause of building socialism with Chinese characteristics in all aspects in the twenty-first century, the CPC, at its 15th National Congress, set the first 10-year target for the national economic and social development for the new century, established a basic strategy of "governing the country according to law and building a socialist country ruled by law" and set the goal of completing the socialist system of laws with Chinese characteristics by the year 2010. To achieve this goal, to guarantee and promote the socialist market economy, and to meet the requirements of joining the World Trade Organization (WTO), the Chinese legislature kept on making new economic laws. It enacted the Securities Law, Contract Law, Law on Bid Invitation and Bidding, Trust Law, Law on Individual Proprietorship Enterprises, Law on the Contracting of Rural Land, Government Procurement Law, and some other laws, while revising the Foreign Trade Law, Law on Chinese-Foreign Equity Joint Ventures, Law on Chinese-Foreign Cooperative Joint Ventures, Law on Foreign-funded Enterprises, Patent Law, Trademark Law, Copyright Law, and some other laws. To regulate legislative activities and improve the legislation system, the NPC enacted the Law on Legislation, systematizing and codifying the principles, mechanism, extent of power and procedure of legislation, and the systems of legal interpretation, application of law, and registration and other systems. To develop socialist democracy, foster socialist culture, protect the ecological environment, and develop social undertakings, the legislature enacted the Administrative Reconsideration Law, Higher Education Law, Law on Prevention and Control of Occupational Diseases, and some other laws; revised the Trade Union Law, Law on the Protection of Cultural Relics, Marine Environmental Protection Law, Pharmaceuticals Administration Law, and some other laws. And to ensure that the laws are effectively carried out, the NPC Standing Committee made legal interpretations of articles in the Criminal Law, Basic Law of the Hong Kong Special Administrative Region and some other laws. These efforts enabled a socialist system of laws with Chinese characteristics to take shape.

Entering the new century, the CPC set the goal of building a moderately prosperous society of a higher level in all aspects for the benefit of over one billion people by 2020 at its 16th and 17th national congresses. To meet this goal, and to improve socialist democracy and the socialist legal system, fully carry out the basic strategy of governing the country by law, better safeguard the people's rights and interests, social fairness and justice, and promote social harmony, the Chinese legislature strengthened legislation work and constantly improved the quality of legislation. To safeguard China's sovereignty and territorial integrity, and promote the peaceful reunification of the country, the legislature enacted the Anti-Secession Law. To develop socialist democracy, it enacted the Law on the Supervision of Standing Committees of People's Congresses at All Levels, Administrative Licensing Law, Administrative Coercion Law, and some other laws. To protect the lawful rights and interests of the citizens, legal persons and other organizations, and guarantee and promote the healthy development of the socialist market economy, the legislature enacted the Property Law, Tort Law, Law on Enterprise Bankruptcy, Anti-monopoly Law, Law on Anti-money Laundering, Enterprise

Income Tax Law, Law on Vehicle and Vessel Taxation, Law on the State-owned Assets of Enterprises, Banking Supervision Law, and some other laws. To improve the social security system, and ensure and improve the people's livelihood, the legislature enacted the Social Insurance Law, Labor Contract Law, Employment Promotion Law, People's Mediation Law, Law on Labor Dispute Mediation and Arbitration, Food Safety Law, and some other laws. To conserve resources, protect the environment and build a resource-conserving and environmentally-friendly society, the legislature enacted the Law on Renewable Energy, Circular Economy Promotion Law, Law on Environmental Impact Assessment, and some other laws. In addition, the Chinese legislature also promulgated and revised a group of laws to strengthen social management, and safeguard social order.

As the NPC and its Standing Committee enact laws, the State Council and local people's congresses and their standing committees, based on their scope of legislative power as prescribed in the Constitution and related laws, have adopted many administrative regulations and local regulations, which play an important role in improving China's socialist democracy and legal system, and promoting the establishment of the socialist system of laws with Chinese characteristics.

To ensure a unified legal system and make it more scientific and consistent, legislative bodies at different levels sorted out laws and regulations on several occasions. From 2009, the NPC Standing Committee, the State Council, and local people's congresses and their standing committees started to sort out laws and regulations in an all-round way. The NPC Standing Committee annulled eight laws and decisions about legal issues, and revised 59 laws. The State Council annulled seven administrative regulations and revised 107 administrative regulations. Local people's congresses and their standing committees annulled 455 local regulations, and revised 1,417 local regulations. Such work has helped to solve the problem of incompatibility among laws and regulations.

Since New China was founded, and particularly since the policy of reform and opening up was introduced in 1978, China has made remarkable achievements in its legislation work. By the end of August 2011, the Chinese legislature had enacted 240 effective laws including the current Constitution, 706 administrative regulations, and over 8,600 local regulations. As a result, all legal branches have been set up, covering all aspects of social relations; basic and major laws of each branch have been made; related administrative regulations and local regulations are fairly complete; and the whole legal system is scientific and consistent. A socialist system of laws with Chinese characteristics has been solidly put into place.

Composition of the Socialist System of Laws with Chinese Characteristics

The socialist system of laws with Chinese characteristics is an organic integration of the related laws of the Constitution, civil and commercial laws, administrative laws, economic laws, social laws, criminal laws, litigation and non-litigation procedural laws, and other legal branches, with the Constitution in the supreme place, the laws as the main body, and administrative and local regulations as the major components.

1. *Tiers of the socialist system of laws with Chinese characteristics*

The Constitution is the paramount law of the socialist system of laws with Chinese characteristics. As China's fundamental law, the Constitution assumes the commanding position in the socialist system of laws with Chinese characteristics and is the fundamental guarantee of lasting stability and security, unity of ethnic groups, economic development and social progress. In China, people of all ethnic groups, all state organs, the armed forces, all political parties and public organizations, and all enterprises and institutions in the country must take the Constitution as the basic standard of conduct, and they have the duty to uphold the dignity of the Constitution and ensure its implementation.

China's present Constitution is one with Chinese characteristics and geared to the needs of socialist modernization, and is the general charter for governance of the country and good order of the nation. It was passed by the NPC in 1982 after nationwide discussion. Later, in accordance with the national economic and social development, the NPC passed four Amendments to the Constitution. China's Constitution defines the basic system and basic tasks of the state, affirms the leadership of the CPC, establishes the guiding role of Marxism-Leninism, Mao Zedong Thought, Deng Xiaoping Theory and the important thought of the Three Represents, determines the state system as a people's democratic dictatorship led by the working class and based on the alliance of workers and peasants, and takes the system of people's congresses as the form of administration. It rules that all state power belongs to the people and that the citizens enjoy extensive rights and freedom in accordance with the law, establishes the system of multi-party cooperation and political consultation led by the CPC, the system of regional ethnic autonomy and the system of primary-level self-governance, and specifies the basic economic system in which public ownership is dominant and diverse forms of ownership develop side-by-side and the distribution system in which distribution according to work is dominant and diverse modes of distribution coexist. While maintaining its stability, China's Constitution is constantly improving and advancing with the times, along with the reform and opening up and the progress of the cause of socialist modernization. Promptly written into the Constitution are important experience, principles and systems that have been proven mature by practice, which fully reflects the outstanding achievements of China's reform and opening up, the great achievements of the cause of socialist construction with Chinese characteristics and the self-improvement and constant development of the socialist system, providing a fundamental guarantee for the progress of the reform and opening up, and socialist modernization.

The Constitution has supreme legal authority in the socialist system of laws with Chinese characteristics. All laws, administrative and local regulations must be made in accordance with the Constitution and follow its basic principles, and must not contravene the Constitution.

The laws are the main body of the socialist system of laws with Chinese characteristics. The Constitution stipulates that the NPC and its Standing Committee exercise the legislative power of the state. The laws formulated by the NPC and its Standing Committee are the main body of the socialist system of laws with Chinese characteristics, and deal with matters of fundamental and overall importance to national development and those which affect the country's stability and long-term development. The laws are the basis of the nation's legal system, and must not be contravened by administrative or local regulations.

The Law on Legislation ensures exclusive legislative power to the NPC and its Standing Committee. The NPC enacts and amends basic laws governing criminal offences, civil affairs, state organs and other matters; the Standing Committee of the NPC enacts and amends laws other than the ones to be enacted by the NPC. When the NPC is not in session, it may supplement and amend laws enacted by the NPC, but must not contradict the basic principles of such laws. The Law on Legislation also stipulates that the following must be governed by law: affairs concerning state sovereignty; formation, organization, and functions and powers of state organs; the system of regional ethnic autonomy; the system of special administrative regions; the system of primary-level self-governance; criminal offences and their punishment; mandatory measures and penalties involving deprivation of citizens' political rights or restriction of the freedom of the person; requisition of non-state-owned property; basic civil system; basic economic system; basic systems of fiscal administration, taxation, customs, finance and foreign trade; systems of litigation and arbitration; and other affairs.

The laws enacted by the NPC and its Standing Committee establish the important and basic legal systems in the nation's economic, political, cultural, social, and ecological civilization construction, are the main body of the socialist system of laws with Chinese characteristics and provide an important basis for the formulation of administrative and local regulations.

Administrative regulations are an important component of the socialist system of laws with Chinese characteristics. The State Council formulates administrative regulations in accordance with the Constitution and laws, which is an important form of the State Council's implementation of its responsibility endowed by the Constitution and laws. The administrative regulations may regulate matters concerning the implementation of the provisions of the laws and performance of the administrative functions and powers of the State Council. For matters that shall be governed by laws to be formulated by the NPC and its Standing Committee, the State Council may enact administrative regulations first in its place with authorization from the NPC and its Standing Committee. The administrative regulations occupy an important position in the socialist system of laws with

Chinese characteristics by detailing the related systems stipulated by laws, elaborating and supplementing the laws.

The State Council, in accordance with the actual needs of socioeconomic development and administrative work, has enacted—within its statutory power limits and conforming to legal procedures—a large number of administrative regulations which cover all areas of administration, concerning the nation's economic, political, cultural, and social matters. They play an important role in the implementation of the Constitution and laws, the guaranteeing of the reform and opening up and socialist modernization, the promotion of comprehensive, balanced and sustainable economic and social development and the advancement of administration in accordance with law of the people's governments at all levels.

Local regulations are another important component of the socialist system of laws with Chinese characteristics. The people's congresses and their standing committees of the provinces, autonomous regions, municipalities directly under the central government, and the larger cities may, in accordance with the Constitution and laws, formulate local regulations, which is an important channel and form of the people's participation in the administration of state affairs and promotion of local economic and social development by law. The people's congresses and their standing committees of the provinces, autonomous regions and municipalities directly under the central government may, in the light of the specific local conditions and actual needs, formulate local regulations, provided that they do not contradict the Constitution, the laws and the administrative regulations. The people's congresses and their standing committees of the larger cities may, in the light of the specific local conditions and actual needs, formulate local regulations, provided that they do not contradict the Constitution, laws, administrative regulations and local regulations of their respective provinces or autonomous regions. Moreover, they shall submit such regulations to the standing committees of the people's congresses of the provinces or autonomous regions for approval before implementation. The people's congresses of the ethnic autonomous areas have the power to formulate autonomous regulations and separate regulations on the basis of the political, economic, and cultural characteristics of the local ethnic group(s). Where certain provisions of the laws and administrative regulations are concerned, adaptation may be made in autonomous regulations and separate regulations, but such adaptation may not contradict the basic principles of the laws and administrative regulations. However, no adaptation may be made to the provisions of the Constitution and the Law on Regional Ethnic Autonomy, or the provisions in other laws and administrative regulations that are specially formulated to govern the ethnic autonomous areas. The autonomous regulations and separate regulations of the autonomous regions shall be submitted to the Standing Committee of the NPC for approval before they go into effect. The autonomous regulations and separate regulations of the autonomous prefectures or counties shall be submitted to the standing committees of the people's congresses of the relevant provinces, autonomous regions or municipalities directly under the central government for approval before they go into effect. The people's congresses and their standing committees of the provinces and cities where special economic zones are located may, upon authorization by the NPC and its Standing Committee and in the light of specific local conditions and actual needs, formulate regulations in accordance with provisions of the Constitution and basic principles of the laws and administrative regulations, and enforce them within the limits of the special economic zones. Local regulations may be formulated to govern matters requiring the formulation of rules to implement the provisions of laws and administrative regulations, and matters pertaining to local affairs. Except for matters governed by laws exclusively formulated by the NPC and its Standing Committee, local regulations can also be made on other matters which are not yet covered by existing laws and administrative regulations. The local regulations also occupy an important position in the socialist system of laws with Chinese characteristics. They elaborate and supplement the laws and administrative regulations, extend, and improve national legislation and accumulate useful experience for national legislation.

Local people's congresses and their standing committees, which actively exercise local legislative functions and powers, have enacted a large number of local regulations in the light of the actual conditions of local economic and social development, playing an important role in guaranteeing the effective implementation of the Constitution, laws and administrative regulations within their respective administrative regions, and promoting the reform and opening up and socialist modernization drive.

2. *Branches of the socialist system of laws with Chinese characteristics*

Laws related to the Constitution. The laws related to the Constitution are the collection of legal norms supporting the Constitution and directly guaranteeing its enforcement and the operation of state power. They regulate the political relationships of the state and mainly consist of laws in relation to the establishment, organization, functions, powers, and basic working principles of state organs; laws on the system of regional ethnic autonomy, the system of special administrative regions and the primary-level self-governance; laws in relation to maintaining state sovereignty, territorial integrity, national security, and national symbols; and laws in relation to guaranteeing the basic political rights of citizens. By the end of August 2011 China had enacted 38 laws related to the Constitution, as well as a number of administrative and local regulations.

China has formulated electoral laws related to the NPC and local people's congresses at all levels, organic laws of local people's congresses and people's governments at all levels, and developed mechanisms for the election of deputies of the people's congresses and the leadership of state organs, providing an institutional guarantee for the people's exercise of state power and a legal basis for the formation of state organs. It has enacted organic laws of the NPC, the State Council, the People's Courts and the People's Procuratorates, and established systems concerning the organization, function and power, and limits of related state organs. To implement the "one country, two systems" policy and realize national reunification, it has promulgated the basic laws of the Hong Kong and Macao special administrative regions and established the system of special administrative region which has ensured the long-term prosperity and stability of Hong Kong and Macao. It has formulated organic laws governing urban residents' committees and villagers' committees for the establishment of urban and rural primary-level self-governance. In this way, citizens directly exercise the rights of democratic election, decision, administration and supervision by law, and implement democratic self-government of public and welfare affairs at the grassroots level, which have become the most direct and extensive democratic practices in the country. China has promulgated the Law on the Procedure for the Conclusion of Treaties, Law on Territorial Waters and the Contiguous Zones, Law on Exclusive Economic Zones and the Continental Shelf, Anti-Secession Law, Law on the National Flag, Law on the National Emblem, and other laws, and established a legal system which maintains state sovereignty and territorial integrity while safeguarding the fundamental interests of the country. It has enacted the Law on Assemblies, Processions and Demonstrations, Law on State Compensation, and other laws, as well as administrative regulations concerning ethnic group, religion, petition, and publication and registration of mass organizations, which guarantee the basic political rights of the citizens.

China fully protects its citizens' right to vote and stand for election. Elections follow the principles of universal suffrage and equality, and are carried out in the forms of direct, indirect and competitive elections. The Constitution stipulates that all citizens of the People's Republic of China who have reached the age of 18, except persons who have been deprived of their political rights in accordance with the law, shall have the right to vote and stand for election, regardless of ethnic status, race, sex, occupation, family background, religious belief, education, property status, or length of residence. To guarantee its citizens' right to vote and stand for election, China is constantly modifying and improving the electoral system in accordance with the country's actual conditions, and has gradually realized the election of deputies to the people's congresses consonant with the proportion of the populations in urban and rural areas, and ensured that an appropriate number of representatives can appear at the NPC from all regions, ethnic groups and walks of life, realizing complete equality of the voting right of urban and rural residents.

China has enacted the Law on Regional Ethnic Autonomy, which ensures the implementation of the system of regional ethnic autonomy, fully respects and guarantees the right of ethnic minorities to administer their own affairs, and protects the legitimate rights and interests of the ethnic minorities by law. According to the Constitution and laws, China has currently 155 ethnic autonomous areas, i.e., five autonomous regions, 30 autonomous prefectures and 120 autonomous counties (banners). In addition, there are over 1,100 villages where ethnic minorities live in concentrated communities. According to the Constitution and the Law on Regional Ethnic Autonomy, ethnic autonomous areas have extensive autonomous power. First, they have the exclusive right to govern the local affairs of their ethnic groups and other affairs within their respective administrative regions. The chairman or vice-chairmen of the standing committee of the people's congress of an ethnic autonomous area must be a member of the ethnic group exercising regional autonomy in the area, and the head of an autonomous region, autonomous prefecture or autonomous county must be a citizen of the ethnic group exercising regional autonomy in the area concerned. Secondly, the people's congresses of ethnic autonomous areas have the power to enact regulations on the exercise of autonomy and separate regulations in the light of the political, economic, and cultural characteristics of the ethnic group or groups in the areas concerned, and by law may also make adaptations to the provisions of laws and administrative regulations in the light of the characteristics of the ethnic group(s) in the areas concerned. By the end of August 2011, the ethnic autonomous areas had enacted more than 780 regulations on the exercise of autonomy, as well as separate regulations, which are currently in force. Thirdly, ethnic autonomous areas use and develop their own spoken and written languages. Fifty-three of the 55 minority groups have their own languages, and there are altogether 72 languages; 29 minority groups have their own scripts. The system of regional ethnic autonomy established by the Constitution and the Law on Regional Ethnic Autonomy is consistent with the common interests and development needs of all China's ethnic groups. It guarantees the minority groups' self-government of their own affairs by law, their democratic participation in the administration of state and social affairs, and their equal entitlement to economic, political, social and cultural rights, and maintains relations of equality, solidarity, mutual assistance, and harmony among ethnic groups.

China respects and upholds human rights. The Constitution has comprehensive stipulations on the fundamental rights and freedoms of the citizens. The state has promulgated a series of laws and regulations and has developed a comparatively complete legal system to protect human rights, and ensures the citizens' right to subsistence and development, personal rights and property rights, freedom of religious belief, of speech, of the press, of the assembly, of association, of procession and of demonstration, the right to social security and education, as well as other economic, political, social and cultural rights. The Constitution stipulates that citizens of the People's Republic of China enjoy the freedom of religious belief. No state organ, public organization or individual may compel citizens to believe in, or not to believe in, any religion; nor may they discriminate against citizens who believe in, or do not believe in, any religion. The State Council has also promulgated the Regulations on Religious Affairs. Currently China has a total of more than 100 million believers in various religions, and the state fully protects its citizens' freedom of religious belief. The Constitution also provides that citizens who have suffered losses as a result of infringement of their civic rights by any state organ or functionary have the right to compensation in accordance with the provisions of the law. The state has enacted the Law on State Compensation and established the system of state compensation to effectively guarantee the right to state compensation of all citizens, legal persons, and other organizations in accordance with the law.

Civil and commercial laws. Civil laws adjust property and personal relationships between civil subjects with equal status, that is, between citizens, between legal persons and between citizens and legal persons, and follow the principles of equal status between civil subjects, autonomy of will, fairness, honesty and credibility, and other basic principles. Commercial laws adjust commercial relationships between business subjects, and follow the basic principles of Civil Law and the principles of the freedom of commercial transaction, compensation of equal value and convenience and safety, among other principles. By the end of August 2011 China had promulgated 33 civil and commercial laws, as well as a large number of administrative and local regulations concerning commercial activities.

The state enacted the General Principles of the Civil Law, which establishes the basic principles that shall be followed in civil and commercial activities, and defines the target of regulation and basic principles of civil laws, as well as the systems concerning civil subjects, civil activities, civil rights and civil liability. With the development of the market economy, China gradually formulated the Contract Law, Property Law, Law on the Contracting of Rural Land and other laws, and established and improved the system of creditors' rights and the system of property rights including the proprietary rights, usufructuary rights and collateral rights; enacted the Tort Law and improved the tort responsibility system; promulgated the Marriage Law, Adoption Law, Succession Law and other laws and established and improved the marriage and family system; formulated the Law of the Application of Law in Foreign-related Civil Relations and improved the legal system of civil relations with foreigners; made the Company Law, Partnership Enterprise Law, Law on Individual Proprietorship Enterprises, Law on Commercial Banks, Law on Securities Investment Fund, Law on Specialized Farmers' Cooperatives, and other laws, and established and improved the system of business subjects. It also promulgated Securities Law, Maritime Code, Negotiable Instruments Law, Insurance Law and other laws, and established and improved the system of commercial activities. The systems of maritime trade, negotiable instruments, insurance, securities and other market economy activities gradually took form and quickly developed.

China attaches great importance to the protection of intellectual property rights, and has promulgated a large number of laws and regulations, including the Patent Law, Trademark Law, Copyright Law, Regulations on the Protection of Computer Software, Regulations on the Protection of Integrated Circuit Layout Design, Regulations on the Collective Administration of Copyright, Regulations on the Protection of the Right to Network Dissemination of Information, Regulations on the Protection of New Varieties of Plants, Regulations on the Customs Protection of Intellectual Property Rights, Regulations on the Administration of Special Signs, Regulations on the Protection of Olympic Symbols, and other laws and regulations, centered on the protection of intellectual property rights. The promulgation of the Trademark Law in 1982 marked the beginning of China's systematic development of a modern legal system covering intellectual property rights. To further enhance the protection of intellectual property rights in China and meet the requirements for joining the WTO, China has been constantly improving the legal system of intellectual property rights, and has made a number of amendments to the Patent Law, Trademark Law, Copyright Law and other laws to highlight legal protection of the promotion of scientific and technological advancement and innovation from the perspectives of the principles of legislation, the contents of rights, the standard of protection and the means of legal remedy, among others. By the end of 2010, the state had approved over 3,890,000 patents of various types, and effectively registered over 4,600,000 trademarks, including 670,000 trademarks from 177 countries and regions. According to incomplete statistics, during the period 2001–2010 copyright administration organs at various levels confiscated 707 million pirated copies, delivered 93,000 administrative penalties and transferred 2,500 cases to judicial organs.

To promote the reform and opening up, and expand international economic cooperation and technical exchanges, China enacted Law on Chinese-Foreign Equity Joint Ventures, Law on Foreign-funded Enterprises and Law on Chinese-Foreign Cooperative Joint Ventures, with provisions on the investment conditions, procedures, operation, supervision, administration, and the protection of legitimate rights and interests of foreign investors in China. The state has established the principle that foreign investors should respect China's sovereignty when investing in China and other principles, including the protection of investors' legitimate rights and interests, equality and mutual benefit, extending of preferential policies and conforming to international prevailing norms, creating a favorable environment for foreign investors in China. To better implement the principles of equality and mutual benefit and conforming to international prevailing norms, China has made several amendments to the above three laws, and fully guarantees the legitimate rights and interests of foreign investors in their investment and commercial activities in China. By the end of 2010 China had approved the establishment of 710,747 foreign-funded enterprises with an actual investment of US$1.107858 trillion, which fully demonstrates the constant improvement of China's legal system regarding the protection of foreign investors.

Administrative laws. Administrative laws are the collection of legal norms on the granting, execution and supervision of administrative power. They regulate the relationships between administrative authorities and subjects of administration because of administrative activities, follow the principles of statutory remit, statutory procedure, fairness and openness, and effective supervision, and guarantee the discharge of the functions and powers of administrative organs, as well as the rights of citizens, legal persons and other organizations. By the end of August 2011 China had enacted 79 administrative laws and a large number of administrative and local regulations regulating administrative power.

China attaches great importance to the regulation of the administrative organs' execution of their power, strengthens the supervision of the execution of administrative power in accordance with the law, and ensures the correct execution of administrative power by administrative organs. China has formulated the Law on Administrative Penalties, established the basic principles of penalty by law, fairness and openness, corresponding penalty for offence and combination of penalty and education, standardized the enactment rights of administrative penalties, developed fairly complete procedures of the decision and execution of administrative penalties, and established the hearing system of administrative penalties, by which an administrative organ, before making a decision on administrative penalty that may have a significance influence on the production and life of the party concerned, shall notify the party the right to request a hearing. The state has promulgated the Administrative Reconsideration Law, established the self-correction mechanism within administrative organs, and provided remedies to citizens, legal persons and other organizations for the protection of their legitimate rights and interests. Under this law, about 80,000 cases of administrative dispute are handled each year. The state has enacted the Administrative Licensing Law, which regulates the institution, executive organs and procedures of administrative licensing, standardizes the system of administrative licensing, and, in order to reduce the number of administrative licensing, defines the matters involved in the application for administrative licensing. It also stipulates that administrative licensing will not be used for matters in which citizens, legal persons and other organizations can make decisions themselves, matters which can be effectively regulated by the competitive mechanism of the market, matters which the organizations of trades or intermediary bodies can manage through self-discipline, and matters which administrative departments can solve by other administrative means such as subsequent supervision. In order to thoroughly implement the Administrative Licensing Law, the 11th meeting of the Standing Committee of the 10th NPC passed nine amendments, removing 11 types of administrative licensing. The State Council canceled 1,749 matters of administrative licensing at the central level, changed the administrative method for 121 matters and transferred 46 matters to lower administrative levels. The state has promulgated the Administrative Coercion Law, which clearly defines the principles of the institution and execution of administrative enforcement, standardizes the types, statutory limits, executive bodies and procedures of administrative enforcement, providing a legal basis for the guarantee and supervision of the administrative organs' performance of administrative functions and powers in accordance with the law, and the protection of the legitimate rights and interests of citizens, legal persons and other organizations.

China attaches great importance to the protection of the ecological environment for mankind's survival and sustainable development. The state has promulgated the Environmental Protection Law, which lays down the basic principle of coordinated development of economic construction, social development, and environmental protection, and dictates that governments at all levels, all organizations and individuals have the right and duty to protect the environment. To prevent negative impact on the environment in the course of project construction, the state has enacted the Law on Environmental Impact Assessment. The state has enacted laws for specific targets in environmental protection, such as those on prevention and control of water pollution, marine environment, atmospheric pollution, environmental noise pollution, environmental pollution by solid waste, radioactive pollution, and other laws. The State Council has formulated the Regulations on the Administration of Environmental Protection of Project Construction, Regulations on the Safe Management of Hazardous Chemicals, Regulations on the Collection and Use of Pollutant Discharge Fees, Measures on the Administration of Permits for Operations Involving Hazardous Waste, and other administrative regulations. The local people's congresses, in the light of the specific local conditions in their respective areas, have drawn up a large number of local regulations on environmental protection. China has established a system of national environmental protection standards, and had implemented over 1,300 national environmental protection standards by the end of 2010. China is also constantly strengthening the administrative enforcement of environmental protection laws. Over the past 5 years the state has investigated over 80,000 cases of violation of environmental protection laws, and has closed down 7,293 offending operations in accordance with the law.

China has also enacted the Education Law, Compulsory Education Law, Higher Education Law, Vocational Education Law, Teachers Law, Regulations on the Administration of Kindergartens, Regulations on the Qualifications of Teachers, and Regulations on Chinese-Foreign Cooperation in Running Schools to establish and improve its national education system. It has enacted the Drug Administration Law, Law on Maternal and Infant Health Care, Blood Donation Law, Law on the Prevention and Treatment of Infectious Diseases, Law on Physical Culture and Sport, Frontier Health and Quarantine Law, Food Safety Law, Regulations on the Supervision and Administration of Medical Devices, Regulations on Traditional Chinese Medicine and Anti-Doping Regulations to establish and improve the medical health system to ensure the people's health and safety. It has enacted the Law on Residents' Identity Cards, Law on the Control of Frontier Exit and Entry of Citizens, Law on the Control of Guns, Fire Prevention Law, Law on the Control of Narcotics, Law on Public Security Penalties, Emergency Response Law, Regulations on Detention Centers, Regulations on Safety Management of Large-Scale Mass Activities, and Regulations on the Safety Administration of Fireworks and Firecrackers to establish and improve systems aimed at maintaining social order and stability, promoting social harmony and ensuring public security. China has enacted the Civil Servants Law, People's Police Law, Law on Diplomatic Personnel, and Punishment Ordinance for Civil Servants Working in Administrative Organs to set up and improve the system of public service. China has enacted the National Defense Mobilization Law, Law on the Protection of Military Installations, Civil Air Defense Law, Military Service Law, Law on National Defense Education, Regulations on the Recruitment of Soldiers, and Militia Work Regulations to establish and improve the system of national defense and armed forces building. It has formulated the Law on Science and Technology Progress, Law on Popularization of Science and Technology, Law on the Protection of Cultural Relics, Law on the Intangible Cultural Heritage, Regulations on the Protection of Fossils, Regulations on the Protection of the Great Wall, and Regulations on the Administration of Films to establish and improve the system to promote scientific and technological progress, and protect and nourish culture.

Economic laws. Economic laws are a collection of laws and regulations which adjust social and economic relations arising from the state's intervening in, managing and regulating economic activities for the society's overall interests. They provide legal devices and an institutional framework for the state to conduct appropriate intervention in, and macro control of the market economy, thereby preventing malpractices resulting from spontaneous and blind operation of the market economy. By the end of August 2011 China had formulated 60 economic laws and a large number of related administrative and local regulations.

China has enacted the Budget Law, Price Law, and Law on the People's Bank of China to exercise macro-control and management over economic activities. It has formulated the Law on Corporate Income Tax, Individual Income Tax Law, Law on Vehicle and Vessel Taxation, Law on the Administration of Tax Collection, Provisional Regulations on Value-Added Tax, Provisional Regulations on Business Tax, and Provisional Regulations on City Maintenance and Construction Tax to improve the taxation system. It has enacted the Law on Regulation and Supervision of the Banking Industry, and Law on Anti-Money Laundering to supervise and regulate the banking industry to ensure its safe operation. It has enacted the Agriculture Law, Seed Law, and Law on Agricultural Product Quality and Safety to guarantee agricultural development and food safety of the country. It has formulated the Railway Law, Highway Law, Civil Aviation Law, and Electric Power Law to supervise and administer key industries and promote their development. It has formulated the Land Administration Law, Forest Law, Water Law, and Mineral Resources Law to regulate the rational exploitation and utilization of important natural resources. It has enacted the Energy Conservation Law, Renewable Energy Law, Circular Economy Promotion Law, and Law on the Promotion of Clean Production to promote the effective utilization of energy and development of renewable energy.

China stresses the use of laws to safeguard fair and orderly competition among market players. The Anti-Unfair Competition Law is an important law formulated by China during its transition from the planned economy to the market economy. By drawing lessons from other countries, it makes provisions to forbid counterfeiting, commercial bribery, false publicity, infringement on trade secrets, unfair lottery-attached sales and vilifying competitors to safeguard the rights and interests of commercial operators and enable them to compete fairly and justly. The Price Law stipulates that the state institutes and gradually improves a mechanism under which prices are formed mainly by the market under the state's macro-economic control. The prices of most commodities and services shall be regulated by the market while the prices of a very small number of commodities and services shall be guided or fixed by the government. The Anti-Monopoly Law has prohibitive provisions on monopolistic agreements, abuse of dominant market positions, and concentration of business operators that eliminates or restricts competition. China has carried out reforms to its fiscal, taxation, banking, foreign exchange and investment systems, establishing a macro-management system suited to the market economy. Remarkable achievements have been made in the deregulation of markets within the Chinese economy.

China actively discharges its obligations within the framework of the WTO, constantly improves its legal system regarding foreign trade, and has established a foreign trade system suited to the socialist market economy. It has clearly defined the rights and obligations of those engaged in foreign trade, and has improved the system of managing import and export of goods, technologies and the international service trade. It has established a foreign trade survey and promotion system with Chinese characteristics. In the light of WTO rules, China has improved its trade remedy system, customs supervision, and import and export commodity inspection and quarantine system, and established a unified and transparent foreign trade system. China's foreign trade has been expanding rapidly, and the ratio of its total export–import volume to the international trade volumes keeps rising. In 2010 the ratio of China's exports in the world's total was 10.4 %.

Social laws. China's social laws are the collection of laws and regulations with respect to the adjustment of labor relations, social security, social welfare, and protection of the rights and interests of special groups. It follows the principle of justice, harmony and appropriate state intervention. By performing their duties, the state and society provide necessary protection for the rights and interests of laborers, the unemployed, the incapacitated for work, as well as other special groups in need of help so as to safeguard social equity and promote social harmony. By the end of August 2011, China had enacted 18 laws in this particular field and a large number of administrative and local regulations to regulate labor relations and social security.

China's Labor Law deals with labor relations and other relationships closely related to them, such as labor protection, labor safety and hygiene, occupational training, labor disputes and labor supervision, thus establishing China's basic labor system. China has enacted the Law on Mine Safety, Law on Prevention and Control of Occupational Diseases, and Production Safety Law and some other laws, making provisions for safe production and prevention of occupational diseases, and strengthening the protection of the rights and interests of laborers. It has enacted the Labor Contract Law, Employment Promotion Law, and Law on Labor Dispute Mediation and Arbitration, thus establishing and improving the system, which is suited to the socialist market economy, of labor contract, employment promotion, and labor dispute settlement. It has enacted the Red Cross Society Law, Law on Donation for Public Welfare Undertakings and Regulations on Foundation Administration, thereby establishing and improving the system that promotes the development and administration of public welfare undertakings. It has formulated the Trade Union Law and revised it twice, defining the status of trade unions in the country's political, economic and social life, clarifying the rights and obligations of trade unions, and playing an active role in safeguarding laborers' legitimate rights and interests in accordance with the law.

China attaches importance to the building of its social security system. It has enacted the Social Insurance Law, established a social insurance system which covers both rural and urban residents, basic endowment insurance, basic health insurance, work-related injury insurance, unemployment insurance and maternity insurance, guaranteeing that all citizens can get necessary material aid and living allowances when they get old, sick, injured or unemployed, or give birth. It stipulates that the basic endowment funds should be managed at the national level, and other social insurance funds managed at the provincial level. It has set up a system for the inter-regional transfer of laborers' social security. The State Council has enacted the Regulations on Unemployment Insurance, Regulations on Work-related Injury Insurance, Provisional Regulations on Collection and Payment of Social Insurance Premiums, and Regulations on the Work Regarding the Rural Five Guarantees. It has decided to establish a new rural endowment insurance and new rural cooperative health care system. They all play an important role in promoting the building of a social security system. The gradual establishment of the social security system provides legal guarantee for the Chinese government to accelerate the building of the social security network in accordance with the law, safeguard social equality and build a harmonious society. At present, the coverage of China's social security is expanding from state-owned enterprises to various social and economic organizations, from workers and staff members of organizations to self-employed people and other residents, and from the urban areas to the rural areas. By the end of 2010 the endowment insurance system of urban workers covered 257 million people, an increase of 1.7 times compared with 2002, and the new rural endowment insurance system covered 103 million people. The basic health insurance for rural and urban residents covered 1.26 billion people, 13 times the number in 2002. Work-related injury insurance covered 161 million people. The coverage of unemployment insurance and maternity insurance is also expanding rapidly. The State Council has also formulated the Measures for Assisting Vagrants and Beggars with No Means of Support in Cities, Regulations on Legal Aid, Regulations on Natural Disaster Relief, and Regulations on Minimum Subsistence Allowance for Urban Residents, and has decided to set up a minimum subsistence allowance program for rural residents, thus basically establishing a social relief system covering both urban and rural areas. By the end of 2010 some 77 million residents with financial difficulties in China received minimum subsistence allowance. The level of China's social security is constantly improving, and people are sharing the fruits of development.

China pays great attention to the protection of the rights and interests of special groups. It has enacted the Law on the Protection of Disabled Persons, Law on the Protection of Minors, Law on the Protection of Rights and Interests of Women, Law on the Protection of the Rights and Interests of the Elderly, and Law on the Prevention of Juvenile Delinquency. It has developed a comparatively complete legal system to protect the rights and interests of special groups, which plays an important role in protecting the legitimate rights and interests of special groups, and in safeguarding social equity and justice.

Criminal Law. This is the law that defines crimes and penalties. It aims to punish crime and protect the people, maintain social order and public security, and safeguard national security through regulating the state's power of punishment. By the end of August 2011 China had enacted the Criminal Law and eight amendments to it, as well as decisions on punishing fraudulent purchase of foreign exchange, evading foreign exchange control, and illegal trade in foreign exchange, plus nine legal interpretations on the Criminal Law.

The Criminal Law defines clearly these basic principles: punishment of crimes is defined by law, everyone is equal before the law, and punishment should match the severity of the crime. It expressly stipulates that any act deemed by explicit stipulations of the law as a crime is to be convicted and given punishment by law, and that any act that is not deemed a crime by the explicit stipulations of the law is not to be convicted or given punishment. The law shall be equally applied to anyone who commits a crime. No one shall have the privilege of transcending the law. The degree of punishment shall be commensurate with the crime committed and the criminal responsibility to be borne by the offender. The Criminal Law of China defines various types of crime and types of punishment, including public surveillance, criminal detention, fixed-term imprisonment, life imprisonment and the death penalty. It also includes three accessory penalties—fine, deprivation of political rights and confiscation of property. In addition, it states the concrete application of punishments. It identifies ten criminal acts and corresponding criminal liability, namely the crimes of endangering national security, endangering public security, undermining the order of the socialist market economy, infringing upon the rights of the person and the democratic rights of citizens, encroaching on property, disrupting the order of social administration, endangering the interests of national defense, embezzlement and bribery, dereliction of duty, and servicemen's transgression of duties.

In the light of the actual situation brought about by economic and social development, China promptly revises and interprets its Criminal Law in an effort to improve the criminal legal system. Amendment VIII to the Criminal Law, passed in February 2011, made major revisions of the previous Criminal Law. It eliminates capital punishment for 13 non-violent economic-related offences, thus reducing the number of crimes subject to the death penalty by 19.1 %; it improves legal provisions that give more lenient punishment and non-custodial penalties to minors and elderly people who have reached the age of 75; it stipulates that refusing to pay wages, seriously infringing upon the legal rights and interests of laborers, and drunk driving are criminal offences; it gives harsher punishment for criminal offences in violation of citizens' personal freedom, life and health. All this has improved China's criminal justice system, strengthened the protection of human rights, reflecting the development of China's social civilization and progress in the spheres of democracy and rule of law.

Litigation and Non-litigation Procedure Laws. These are laws giving standard solutions to various litigation and non-litigation activities arising from social disputes. The litigation system aims to regulate the state's judicial activities in settling social disputes, and the non-litigation system aims to regulate arbitration agencies and people's mediation organizations in settling social disputes. By the end of August 2011 China had enacted ten laws in the fields of litigation and non-litigation procedure.

China's Criminal Procedure Law stipulates the basic system and principles of criminal procedures. For instance, the law applies equally to all citizens; the people's courts and people's procuratorates exercise judicial authority and procuratorial powers independently; the people's courts, people's procuratorates and public security organs divide their responsibilities, coordinate their efforts and check each other; ensure that criminal suspects and defendants obtain defense; and no one shall be convicted without a court decision. It also specifies the procedures such as jurisdiction, withdrawal, defense, evidence, enforcement measures, investigation, prosecution, trial and execution, which effectively guarantee the correct application of the Criminal Law, protect the personal, property, democratic and other rights of citizens so as to ensure the smooth progress of the cause of socialism.

China's Civil Procedure Law stipulates the following basic principles and system: the parties to civil litigation shall have equal litigation rights; mediation shall be conducted for the parties on a voluntary and lawful basis; the court shall follow the system of public trial and the court of second instance being that of last instance. It makes clear the litigation rights and obligations of the parties concerned, the use of evidence, the civil trial procedures such as ordinary procedure of first instance, procedure of second instance, summary procedure, special procedure, procedure for trial supervision, and procedure of execution and enforcement execution measures.

China's Administrative Procedure Law defines the legal remedy system in administrative lawsuits. It explicitly stipulates that a citizen, a legal person or other organization has the right to initiate an administrative lawsuit at a people's court in accordance with this law if they believe their lawful rights and interests are infringed upon by an administrative organ or staff working in it, and the people's court exercises judicial power independently with respect to administrative cases to protect the legal rights and interests of the citizens. Since the promulgation and implementation of the Administrative Procedure Law, the people's courts have accepted over 100,000 cases annually on average, protecting the lawful rights and interests of the citizens and making the administrative organs exercise their administrative powers according to law.

China's Arbitration Law has provisions for the establishment of domestic arbitration and foreign-related arbitration agencies, stipulates that an arbitration commission shall be independent of any administrative organ, which guarantees its independence. It also specifies that arbitration should be conducted upon a voluntary and independent basis, and that a system of a single and final award shall be practiced for arbitration. It also contains details about arbitration procedures. Since the promulgation of this law over 500,000 cases of economic disputes have been handled, involving a total sum of 700 billion yuan. It has played an important role in settling civil and economic disputes fairly, promptly and effectively, protecting the lawful rights and interests of the parties concerned, maintaining social and economic stability and promoting social harmony.

People's mediation is a Chinese way of resolving contradictions and settling disputes without resorting to legal proceedings. The Constitution and Civil Procedure Law specify the nature and fundamental principles of people's mediation, and the State Council has promulgated the Organic Regulations on the People's Mediation Commissions. In 2009 people's mediation organizations mediated over 7.67 million civil disputes, with a success rate of over 96 %. In order to further promote people's mediation work and improve the system, China has formulated the People's Mediation Law, making the good experience and practices accumulated in this field into law. At present, there are more than 820,000 people's mediation organizations in China, and 4.67 million people's mediators, forming a mediation network covering both rural and urban areas. They are playing an important role in preventing and reducing civil disputes, resolving social conflicts, and maintaining social harmony and stability.

In addition, China has formulated the Extradition Law, Special Maritime Procedure Law, Law on Labor Dispute Mediation and Arbitration, and Law on the Mediation and Arbitration of Rural Land Contracting Disputes, thereby establishing and improving the system of litigation and non-litigation procedure laws.

The above-mentioned laws and regulations made by legislative bodies cover all aspects of society, bring all the work of the state and all aspects of social life under the rule of law, laying a solid foundation for the rule of law and construction of a socialist country under the rule of law. Law has become an important means for Chinese citizens, legal persons and other organizations to resolve disputes and conflicts. It also provides an important basis for the people's courts at all levels to safeguard the lawful rights and interests of citizens, legal persons and other organizations.

Features of the Socialist System of Laws with Chinese Characteristics

The differences between countries in their historical and cultural traditions, actual situations and paths of development, their social, political and economic systems determine that their systems of laws have different features. The socialist system of laws with Chinese characteristics is the concentrated reflection of the institutionalization and codification of China's practice in its economic and social development since the founding of the People's Republic of China in 1949, and especially in the past 30-odd years since the adoption of the reform and opening up policy. As an important component of the socialist system with Chinese characteristics, it has distinct features.

1. *The socialist system of laws with Chinese characteristics embodies the essential requirements of socialism with Chinese characteristics*

The nature of a country's legal system depends on the nature of its social system established in law. China is a socialist country under the people's democratic dictatorship, led by the working class and based on the alliance of workers and peasants. In the primary stage of socialism, China practices a basic economic system with public ownership as the mainstay and the joint development of diverse forms of ownership, which determines that China's legal institutions are bound to be socialist ones and that China's legal system is bound to be a socialist one with Chinese characteristics. All legal norms covered in and all legal institutions established by the socialist legal system contribute to consolidating and developing socialism, reflect the people's common aspirations, safeguard their fundamental interests and make sure that the people are the masters of their own country. China proceeds from the essential requirement of socialism with Chinese characteristics and the will and long-term interests of the people in making its laws and determining the relevant provisions. The aim and outcome of all the work of the state are to realize, safeguard and expand the fundamental interests of the overwhelming majority of the people.

2. *Socialist system of laws with Chinese characteristics meets the demand of the reform, opening up and socialist modernization of the current times*

The most salient characteristic of this new period in China is reform and opening up. The socialist system of laws with Chinese characteristics comes into existence and develops along with reform and opening up, and they complement each other. The establishment of the socialist system of laws with Chinese characteristics is the inherent requirement for the progress of reform, opening up and socialist modernization. It is carried out on the basis of in-depth analysis of those practices. At the same time, the establishment of the socialist system of laws with Chinese characteristics provides a favorable legal environment for reform, opening up and socialist modernization, and serves as a good regulator, guide, guarantee and impetus for the latter. Meanwhile, by appropriately handling the relationship between the stability of law and the mobility of reform, the socialist system of laws with Chinese characteristics reflects the successful practice of reform, opening up and modernization, and leaves enough space for their future development.

3. *The socialist system of laws with Chinese characteristics reflects the requirements of an inherently unified and structurally multilevel legal system*

The constitution of a country's legal system is determined by its legal traditions, political and legislative systems, and other factors. China is a united multi-ethnic country as well as a state with a unified governmental system. Due to historical reasons, economic and social development is unbalanced among different regions. To accommodate the requirements of this national condition, the Constitution and laws define the unified and multilevel structure of China's legislative system with Chinese characteristics, which further determines the inherently unified and structurally multilevel feature of the socialist system of laws with Chinese characteristics. It reflects the inner logic of the legal system itself, and conforms to China's national conditions and practices. Therefore, the socialist system of laws with Chinese characteristics is headed by the Constitution, composed of multilevel legal norms, including laws, administrative and local regulations. The legal norms are laid down by various legislative bodies according to their respective legislative competence prescribed by the Constitution and laws. They have different legal effect, but together constitute the scientific, harmonious and unified whole of the socialist system of laws with Chinese characteristics as its organic parts.

4. *The socialist system of laws with Chinese characteristics meets the cultural demand of carrying forward the fine traditions of Chinese legal culture and drawing on the achievements of human legal civilizations*

All countries base and develop their legal systems on their historical and cultural traditions, and actual social conditions, and their legal systems' communication and exchange with and learning from each other as economic globalization deepens. The constitution of the socialist system of laws with Chinese characteristics is always based on China's national conditions, combining the inheritance of historical traditions, the introduction of the fruits of other civilizations with system innovations. It attaches great importance to the inheritance of fine traditional legal culture, carries out system innovations according to the requirements of reform, opening up and socialist modernization, thus realizing the integration of traditional culture and modern civilization; at the same time, it studies and draws on the good legislative experience of other countries and learns from their legislative achievements, but never slavishly imitates their models, which makes the current legal system conform to China's national conditions and practices as well as the trend of contemporary world legal civilization. China's legal system, featuring both inclusiveness and openness, has fully demonstrated its unique cultural characteristics.

5. *The socialist system of laws with Chinese characteristics reflects the development demand of being dynamic and open, and of advancing with the times*

A country's legal system is normally the reflection of its conditions at a specific historical stage. With the country's economic and social development, its legal system needs to be enriched and improved, and innovations introduced. Currently China is in the primary stage of socialism, and will remain so for a long time to come. The country is still in the stage of structural reforms and social transformation, and its socialist system calls for constant self-improvement and development, which determines that the socialist system of laws with Chinese characteristics is bound to have the features of both stability and mobility, both periodical variations and continuity, and both actuality and foresightedness. China's legal system is dynamic, open, developing, not static, closed or fixed; it will constantly improve with China's economic and social development and the practice of building a socialist country under the rule of law.

In the course of formulation of the socialist system of laws with Chinese characteristics, China's legislative bodies have integrated the leadership of the CPC, the people's status as masters of their country and the rule of law, actively exercised their legislative power, and carried out legislative work in a planned, focused and step-by-step manner, with attention always fixed on the priorities of the country. We have thereby accumulated some precious experience and successfully blazed a new path of legislation with Chinese characteristics.

Persisting in promoting legislation in a planned and phase-by-phase manner with clear objectives. In the practice of building socialism with Chinese characteristics under the leadership of the CPC over the past 30-odd years since the adoption of the reform and opening up policies, China's legislative bodies have, on the basis of their central tasks at different stages, proceeded from reality, focused on key issues, carried out careful organization work, established priorities, and formulated scientific, rational and practical 5-year legislation plans and annual legislation work plans. They have enacted laws and regulations urgently needed for economic and social development, promoted legislation actively and steadily, and gradually formulated methods of building a socialist legal system in a planned, focused and phase-by-phase manner with clear objectives. We should pool legislative resources, focus on key legislation work and promptly meet the requirements of the fast-developing reform and opening up, thereby providing an effective path for building a socialist system of laws with Chinese characteristics.

Persisting in promoting the side-by-side advancement of legislation at various levels. China is a united multi-ethnic country as well as a state with a unified government system, and economic and social development is unbalanced among different regions. In accordance with the national conditions, it is stipulated in the Constitution that under the guidance of the principle of giving full scope to the initiative and enthusiasm of the local authorities under the unified leadership of the central authorities, on the condition of maintenance of a unified legal system, the NPC and its Standing Committee exercise the legislative power of the state, the State Council formulates administrative regulations in accordance with the Constitution and the law, the people's congresses of provinces, autonomous regions, municipalities directly under the central government, comparatively larger cities and their standing committees may adopt local regulations, the people's congresses of ethnic autonomous areas have the power to enact regulations on the exercise of autonomy and other separate regulations, and the people's congresses or their standing committees of the provinces and cities where special economic zones are located may, upon authorization by the NPC, formulate regulations and enforce them within the limits of the special economic zones. A legislation work pattern of side-by-side advancement of legislation at various levels has gradually taken shape, which greatly accelerates the building of our legal system and at the same time takes into consideration the actual needs of economic and social development in various regions. This is a practical working model for the socialist system of laws with Chinese characteristics.

Persisting in the combination of various legislative forms. The building of the socialist system of laws with Chinese characteristics is a scientific and systematic project. Since the reform and opening up started, in accordance with the demands of economic and social development, China's legislative bodies have lost no time in enacting laws and regulations urgently needed for the development of all social undertakings, attached importance to their amendment or abolition, and explained and checked them in a timely manner. They have adopted various legislative forms, such as formulation, amendment, abolition and interpretation, and promoted legislation in an all-round way. In this way, we have improved the quality of legislation and guaranteed the scientific nature and harmony of the legal system while laying a solid foundation for the effective implementation of legal norms.

Improvement of the Socialist System of Laws with Chinese Characteristics

The task remains arduous to improve the socialist system of laws with Chinese characteristics which we have successfully built. To improve that system from a new starting point is an inherent requirement of promotion of the development and improvement of the socialist system with Chinese characteristics. This will also be the primary task for our legislation work in future.

China is now at a critical stage in deepening reform and opening up, and building a moderately prosperous society in an all-round way, as it has established the development goal for the first 20 years of the twenty-first century. The need for legal system improvement is urgent in order to meet the challenges of new domestic and international situations, and new demands and expectations of the people, as well as new issues and problems facing China's reform, development and stability. To realize scientific development, accelerate transformation of the economic development mode, and further guarantee and improve the people's livelihood, all need a legal system to promote and give guidance. There is a rising demand for more scientific and democratic legislation, as increasingly diversified stakeholders and complicated interest patterns make it harder to regulate social interests through legislation.

China will endeavor to meet the requirements of its basic strategies of promoting scientific development, improving social harmony and ruling the country by law. At present and for some time to come, and in accordance with the requirements of economic and social development, as well as scientific development, China will accelerate the transformation of the economic development mode, guarantee and improve the people's livelihood, improve social harmony, and continuously improve the laws and regulations, so as to build a better socialist system of laws with Chinese characteristics.

China will continuously improve legislation in the economic field. In order to meet the requirements of the development of socialist market economy, we will improve the legal institutions for civil and commercial affairs. To meet the requirements of deepening the reforms of the fiscal, taxation and financial systems, we will improve legal institutions concerned with budget management, fiscal transfer payment, financial risk control and taxation. We will, in particular, attach importance to taxation legislation, and turn taxation regulations made by the State Council on authorization into laws. We will also improve laws regarding the state's management and control of economic activities in order to safeguard the country's economic security, and promote the healthy development of the socialist market economy.

China will take active measures to strengthen legislation on socialist democracy. In order to meet the requirements of actively yet steadily advancing political reform, we will improve legal institutions concerning election, self-governance among people at the grassroots level and organization of state organs; we will improve legislation regarding administrative procedures to regulate administrative actions, and improve laws concerning audit supervision and administrative reconsideration. In order to meet the requirements of reforming the judicial system, we will revise the Criminal Procedure Law, the Civil Procedure Law and the Administrative Procedure Law, so as to improve the procedure law system. We will also improve the legal system concerning the exercise of power by state organs and the punishment and prevention of corruption, in order to expand socialist democracy, standardize and supervise the exercise of power, and continuously develop socialist democracy.

China will strengthen legislation in the social field. We will always put people first, guarantee and improve the people's livelihood, advance social undertakings, improve the social security system, encourage innovation in social management, gradually improve the legal institutions concerning employment, labor protection, social security, social assistance, social welfare, income distribution, education, medical care, housing and social organizations, constantly explore an innovative social management mechanism, and push forward the development of social undertakings.

China will attach more importance to legislation in the cultural, scientific and technological fields. In order to meet the requirements of promoting reform in the cultural system and advancing science and technology, we will improve the legal institutions which support public cultural undertakings, develop the culture industry, encourage cultural and scientific innovation, and protect intellectual property rights, so as to realize cultural prosperity and build an innovation-oriented country.

China will attach importance to legislation in the field of the environment. In order to meet the requirements of building an energy-saving and environmentally-friendly society, we will strengthen laws on energy saving and eco-environmental protection, and improve our institutions so as to accelerate the transformation of the economic development mode, solve the contradictions between socioeconomic development and environmental protection, and promote harmony between man and nature.

While improving various laws, we will attach importance to their implementation, working mechanism and supporting regulations. We will improve the channels and methods for the interpretation of laws, and make it our regular work. We will give timely legal interpretations when the specific meaning of certain provisions needs further clarification, or the application of laws in certain new circumstances needs further explanation. We need to improve the organization, mechanism and method for reviewing and filing regulations, rules, and legal interpretations. Meanwhile, we will improve the revision mechanism as applied to laws and regulations, and make it work on a regular basis in order to make our legal system more scientific and consistent.

We will work to promote scientific and democratic legislation, and improve legislation quality. We will improve the mechanism whereby NPC deputies are involved in legislation, and bring their role to the full. We will improve motion deliberation system and establish a scientific and democratic examination and voting mechanism. We will explore channels and forms for the public to participate in legislation activities in an orderly manner, improve panel discussions, feasibility study meetings, hearings on legislation and the gathering of public opinion through the publication of draft laws and regulations, and establish and improve the mechanism through which public opinion can be heard and feedback can be given, so as to let legislation reflect the will of the public. We will establish and improve a mechanism featuring feasibility studies before making legislation and evaluation after making legislation, constantly endeavor to make legislation more scientific and reasonable, and further improve the practicality of laws and regulations.

Concluding Remarks

Social practice is the foundation of laws, and laws encapsulate practical experience. Social practice is endless, and legislative work should also constantly move forward with the times. Building socialism with Chinese characteristics is a long-term historic task. Improving the socialist system of laws with Chinese characteristics is also a long-term and arduous historic task, and it must advance in tandem with the practice of socialism with Chinese characteristics.

The vitality of laws lies in their enforcement. The formation of the socialist system of laws with Chinese characteristics has generally solved the basic problem of having laws for people to follow. Now, the problem of ensuring that laws are observed and strictly enforced and that lawbreakers are prosecuted has become more pronounced and pressing. Therefore, China will take active and effective steps to guarantee the effective enforcement of the Constitution and laws, and accelerate the advance of the rule of law and the building of a socialist country under the rule of law.

Appendix IV
National Human Rights Action Plan of China (2012–2015)

Introduction

The formulation of the National Human Rights Action Plan is an important measure taken by the Chinese government to ensure the implementation of the constitutional principle of respecting and safeguarding human rights. It is of great significance to promoting scientific development and social harmony, and to achieving the great objective of building a moderately prosperous society in an all-round way.

Since the promulgation and enforcement of the National Human Rights Action Plan of China (2009–2010) in 2009, the Chinese citizens' awareness of human rights has been enhanced significantly; the protection of the citizen's economic, social and cultural rights and interests has been comprehensively strengthened; their civil and political rights have been more effectively safeguarded; the rights of ethnic minorities, women, children, senior citizens and the disabled have been further protected; international exchanges and cooperation in the field of human rights have been increasingly deepened; and human rights protection in all aspects has been constantly advanced along the orbit of institutionalization and rule by law. The cause of human rights in China has entered a new stage of development. In addition, the formulation, implementation and completion on schedule of the National Human Rights Action Plan of China (2009–2010) have been widely acclaimed by the Chinese public and highly regarded by the international community.

In recent years, the Chinese government has appropriately addressed the heavy toll brought about by the international financial crisis and the severe challenges posed by major natural disasters, vigorously solved the problems in development, perseveringly advanced the cause of human rights by putting people first, and had

---

Information Office of the State Council of the People's Republic of China
June 11, 2012

P. Sun, *Human Rights Protection System in China*,
DOI: 10.1007/978-3-642-39663-2, © Springer-Verlag Berlin Heidelberg 2014

its human rights conditions increasingly improved. The Chinese government has unswervingly combined safeguarding human rights with promoting scientific development and social harmony, kept improving its institutional arrangements for ensuring and improving its people's livelihood, vigorously boosted employment, speeded up the development of various social undertakings, promoted equal access to basic public services, gradually improved a social security system that covers both urban and rural areas, initially established a basic medical care and health service system benefiting both urban and rural residents, strived to develop cultural and educational undertakings, and effectively guaranteed the rights of all members of society to equal participation and development. The Chinese government has consistently combined protecting human rights with promoting democracy and the rule of law, actively and steadily pushed forward political reform, expanded citizens' orderly participation in political affairs, and carried out democratic election, decision-making, administration and supervision in accordance with the law to guarantee the people's rights to be informed, to participate, to be heard and to oversee. The Chinese government has integrated the principle of respecting and safeguarding human rights into its legislation, administration and law enforcement and strengthened supervision and restriction over the exercise of power. Consequently, a socialist legal system with Chinese characteristics has been established to provide legal support for all fields of social life and all aspects of human rights protection.

It should be remembered that China remains a developing country that is fraught with problems from unbalanced, uncoordinated and unsustainable development. Due to the influences and limitations of natural, historical and cultural factors, as well as the current level of economic and social development, China still confronts many challenges in the development of its human rights cause and it has a long way to go before it attains the lofty goal of full enjoyment of human rights.

The period 2012–2015 is a crucial period for implementing The Outline of the 12th Five-Year Plan for National Economic and Social Development of the People's Republic of China, deepening reform and opening-up and accelerating the transformation of the country's economic development pattern; it is also an important period for enhancing human rights and ensuring rapid development of the human rights cause. Therefore, on the basis of earnestly summing up past experience, the Chinese government has worked out this National Human Rights Action Plan of China (2012–2015) (hereinafter referred to as the Action Plan) to specify its aims and tasks in promoting and protecting human rights in the 2012–2015 period.

The Action Plan was formulated in accordance with the following guidelines: Holding high the flag of socialism with Chinese characteristics, taking Deng Xiaoping Theory and the important thought of "Three Represents" as guidance and thoroughly applying the Scientific Outlook on Development. In combination with the implementation of The Outline of the 12th Five-Year Plan for National Economic and Social Development of the People' s Republic of China, the Chinese government combines its human rights endeavors with economic, political, cultural, social and ecological construction. To satisfy the aspirations of its people of all ethnic groups for living a better life, it continuously prioritizes people's rights to subsistence and development, vigorously safeguards and improves people's livelihood, spares no efforts to solve the problems of the utmost and immediate concern to the people, practically safeguards the citizens' economic, political, social and cultural rights and promotes social equity and harmony, so as to ensure that every member of society live a happier and more dignified life.

The Action Plan was formulated in line with the following basic principles:

The principle of pushing forward the work according to law. In line with the constitutional principle that "the state respects and preserves human rights" and the spirit of the Universal Declaration of Human Rights and other relevant international conventions on human rights, the Action Plan sets out the goal of improving the laws and regulations and their implementation mechanisms for respecting and safeguarding human rights in legislation, administration and law enforcement, so as to promote the cause of human rights in China according to law.

The principle of comprehensive advances. Taking all types of human rights as interdependent and inseparable, the Chinese government determines to promote the coordinated development of economic, social and cultural rights as well as civil and political rights, and the balanced development of individual and collective human rights.

The principle of pursuing practicality. The Chinese government respects the principle of universality of human rights, but also upholds proceeding from China's national conditions and new realities to advance the development of its human rights cause on a practical basis.

The objectives in the implementation of the Action Plan are as follows:

Providing comprehensive protection to citizens' economic, social and cultural rights. The Chinese government will take proactive measures to protect more effectively the rights of all members of society to employment, basic living standard, social security, health care, education, culture and environment, striving to ensure that all the people enjoy their rights to education, employment, medical and old-age care, and housing, and ensuring that all people share the benefits of the nation's development.

Providing effective protection to the citizens' civil and political rights according to law. Efforts will be made to improve relevant laws and regulations to protect the citizens' basic rights; work will be done to strengthen judicial protection of human rights to promote judicial justice; and endeavors will be made to develop socialist democratic politics to expand citizens' orderly participation in political affairs, and to ensure people's rights to be informed, to participate, to be heard and to oversee.

Providing full protection to the lawful rights of ethnic minorities, women, children, senior citizens and the disabled. Further efforts will be made to ensure ethnic minorities enjoy equal economic, political, social and cultural rights; efforts will be made to promote gender equality and eliminate gender discrimination; practical work will be done to safeguard children's rights to subsistence and development, to be protected and to participate; the social security system for elderly people will be improved to speed up the building of an old-age service system; and efforts will be made to develop the cause of the disabled to promote their equal participation in social life.

Conducting extensive education in human rights. Education in human rights will be consistently carried out among civil servants; human rights education in various forms will be held in all types of schools and at all levels; and human rights knowledge will be publicized throughout the society to enhance the citizens' awareness in this respect.

Actively participating in international exchanges and cooperation on human rights. China will conscientiously fulfill its obligations to international human rights conventions, take an active part in the work of the United Nations human rights mechanisms, and continuously conduct human rights dialogue, cooperation and exchanges with other countries on the basis of equality and mutual respect.

Approved and authorized by the State Council, the National Human Rights Action Plan of China (2012–2015) is hereby promulgated.

Economic, Social, and Cultural Rights

The Chinese government will continue to give priority to the protection of the people's rights to subsistence and development. It will take proactive measures to ensure and improve the people's livelihood, spare no efforts to solve the problems of immediate concern to the people, and improve the level of protection of economic, social and cultural rights, so as to ensure that the benefits of development are shared by all members of society.

Right to Work

Efforts will be made to implement a more active employment policy, improve the wage system, fully carry out the labor contract system, improve working conditions, strengthen labor safety and protect the people's right to work.

- Implementing the "employment priority" strategy. From 2012 to 2015, the urban workforce will be increased by nine million on annual average, and the registered urban unemployment rate will be kept under 5 %. Efforts will be made to ensure equal employment opportunities for urban and rural residents, and promote the orderly outflow of rural labor force and local transfer and employment of rural labor force.
- Improving the wage system. A normal wage increase mechanism will be set up and the minimum wage level will be raised steadily. The minimum wage will increase by over 13 % annually, and the minimum wage level in most regions will reach over 40 % of the average wage of local urban employees. Efforts will be made to establish and improve the collective wage consultation mechanism

and wage payment security mechanism in enterprises, and to ensure that migrant workers and urban employees receive equal pay for equal work.

- Amending the Labor Contract Law and comprehensively introducing the labor contract system. By 2015, the labor contract signing rate of enterprises will reach 90 %.
- Improving working conditions. Efforts will be made to accelerate the construction of the system of labor standards, define management according to standard labor quotas and implement the paid vacation system.
- Implementing a safety production strategy, strengthening monitoring for workplace safety and preventing major accidents. By 2015, the completion rate of construction of enterprise emergency platforms at national, provincial (autonomous regions and municipalities directly under the central government) and city levels and for enterprises of high-risk industries will be 100 %; and that in the major counties, 80 %. By 2013, Grade III safety standards or above will be applied for non-coal mines and factories producing dangerous chemicals and fireworks as well as enterprises above a certain scale in the eight industrial and commercial trades of metallurgy, non-ferrous metals, building materials, machine-building, light industry, textiles, tobacco and commerce. By 2015, enterprises below a certain scale in the eight trades, including the metallurgical industry, as well as transportation and communications, construction and other industries, will reach the required safety standards. The death toll caused by various types of industrial accidents and the number of major accidents will fall markedly. Safety production information will be publicized, and complaints mailboxes and "12350" safe production report hotlines set up and standardized.
- Implementing the Law on the Prevention and Control of Occupational Diseases. The occupational health indicators prescribed in the National Occupational Disease Control Program (2009–2015) will be continuously implemented.
- Launching multiform vocational training to rural and urban workers. Efforts will be made to guarantee every new employee access to corresponding vocational training opportunities, ensuring that technical workers can take part in at least one skill-upgrading training program. The localities are encouraged to establish practical training bases. By 2015, the total number of skilled workers will reach 125 million, of which 34 million will be highly-skilled workers.
- Improving the labor security supervision and law-enforcing system and the labor dispute settlement mechanism. China will strengthen supervision over and law-enforcement for labor security. It will give full play to the role of labor dispute mediation and arbitration, and the closing rate of labor dispute arbitration will reach 90 %.

Right to Basic Living Standards

China will maintain steady and rapid economic development, adjust the income distribution pattern, implement poverty alleviation projects, improve the basic housing security system, protect farmers' rights and interests related to land according to law and improve the level of citizens' basic rights of life.

- The increase of rural and urban residents' income will keep pace with economic growth. From 2011 to 2015, the average annual growth rate of China's GDP is expected to be 7 %, and the annual growth rate of the per-capita disposal income of urban residents and per-capita net income of rural residents will be over 7 %. The income distribution pattern will be adjusted, the share of personal income in the distribution of national income will be increased, so will that of work remuneration in primary distribution; the proportion of middle-income earners will be expanded and the income of middle- and low-income earners will be increased.
- Implementing the Outline of Development-oriented Poverty Reduction for China' s Rural Areas (2011–2020). The state will gradually raise the standards for poverty alleviation. Key poverty reduction projects will be launched for 24,000 villages, where most of the villagers are hit hard by poverty. The government will also conduct training programs in practical skills for the impoverished laborers in rural areas. It will organize migration for people in areas with harsh living conditions on condition that they can do it out of their free will. It will continue to carry out poverty reduction pilot projects in border, endemic-disease-stricken and post-disaster reconstruction areas, and other poverty-stricken areas. It will continue to support such areas with science and technology, and send technicians there to help local people start businesses for the purpose of poverty reduction. Great efforts will be made to develop forestry in poor mountain areas, striving to increase the forest coverage by 1.5 % points over that at the end of 2010 and ensure that each impoverished household starts one income-generating project.
- Formulating basic housing security regulations, and improving the construction, distribution, management and exit system of indemnificatory housing. Efforts will be made to speed up the construction of low-rent housing, public rental housing, affordable housing and other types of indemnificatory house, and promote the rebuilding of shanty areas in cities. In so doing, China aims to basically solve the housing problem of low- and lower-middle-income urban families, lessen the housing difficulties of new employees and improve the living conditions of migrant workers. By 2015, the coverage of indemnificatory housing across the country will reach 20 %. China will speed up the transformation of shanty areas in forest, reclamation and coal-mining regions. It will renovate dilapidated housing for 815,300 families in forest areas during the 12th Five-Year Plan period.
- Helping impoverished farmer households solve housing safety problems. Efforts will be made to bring into play the guiding role of government financial subsidies in establishing a long-term mechanism for rural dilapidated house transformation. The government plans to help five million impoverished farmer households upgrade their dilapidated houses from 2012 to 2015.

- Implementing the Regulations on the Expropriation of and Compensation for Buildings on State-owned Land, enacting and improving policies and regulations related to housing expropriation to effectively protect the legitimate rights of the owners.
- Doing a good job in land right confirmation, registration and certification so as to effectively protect the farmers' rights to operate their contracted land, to use homesteads and to get income from distribution of collective gains. The state will formulate regulations concerning compensation from the expropriation of rural collective land.

Right to Social Security

China will improve the various forms of social insurance, and promote the equal coverage of the social relief system in both rural and urban areas to improve the social security level.

- Enacting and amending the supporting rules and regulations of the Social Insurance Law. The state will revise the Regulations on Unemployment Insurance, enact regulations on basic medical insurance and regulations on national security fund, and regulations on maternity insurance and rules regarding the registration, application and payment of social insurance, etc.
- Improving the pension system. By 2015, the number of urban workers and residents underwriting the basic old-age insurance policies will reach 357 million, and the eventual aim is to achieve full coverage of the new rural old-age insurance system and urban employees' pension insurance system. Migrant workers who have established stable labor relations with enterprises will be covered in the basic old-age and medical insurance schemes for urban employees. The state will guarantee the transfer of basic pension accounts for urban workers, and gradually promote the effectual bridging of the rural and urban old-age insurance systems. Efforts will be made to comprehensively implement unified planning in old-age insurance for urban employees and achieve national unified planning for basic old-age pensions. China will endeavor to improve the normal adjustment mechanism for basic pensions to steadily raise the basic pensions for enterprise retirees.
- Improving the basic medical insurance system to make medical insurance basically cover both rural and urban residents in 2015. The total number of people subscribing policies of medical insurance for urban employees, medical insurance for urban residents and new rural cooperative medical insurance will be increased by 60 million as compared with 2010, and the number of people subscribing urban and rural basic medical insurance policies will reach 1.32 billion. Financial grants to those taking policies of urban residents' basic medical insurance and new rural cooperative medical insurance will be raised. The medical treatment cost of inpatients covered by urban employees' medical insurance, urban residents' medical insurance and new rural cooperative

medical insurance will all be around 75 %. Urban residents' medical insurance and new rural cooperative medical insurance will cover all areas where unified planning in this regard is made, and their coverage of the outpatient expenses will be raised to over 50 %. By 2015, the government grant to each person subscribing urban residents' medical insurance and new rural cooperative medical insurance each year will be raised to over 360 yuan, while the coverage of the new rural cooperative medical insurance will be stabilized above 95 %.

- Amending regulations and supporting rules on unemployment insurance and further improving the unemployment insurance system. The level of unified planning for unemployment insurance funds will be elevated. By 2015, the number of subscribers to unemployment insurance will reach 160 million.
- Improving the work-related injury insurance system covering prevention, compensation and rehabilitation. Work-related injury insurance will be put first under unified planning at the municipal level, and gradually unified planning at the provincial level. Proactive and steady efforts will be made in the prevention and rehabilitation of work-related injuries. By 2015, the subscribers to work-related injury insurance will reach 210 million.
- Improving the maternity insurance system and by 2015 women subscribing maternity insurance will reach 150 million.
- Increasing subsistence allowances and level of social relief for rural and urban residents. Work will be done to improve the subsistence allowance determining mechanism and dynamic adjustment mechanism and ensure that the average annual growth rate of the subsistence allowances reach 10 %. And the subsistence allowances provided to rural residents enjoying the "Five Guarantees" (food, clothing, medical care, housing and burial expenses) will equal the average living standard of fellow villagers. Recipients of basic living allowances in both urban and rural areas will be classified, and more assistance will be granted to the aged, disabled, minors and seriously ill. By 2015, the urban and rural residents entitled to the subsistence allowances will make up around 6 % of the total population, covering everyone in need. Steps will be taken to gradually lower or cancel the minimum payment line for medical treatment, and popularize the one-stop settlement model. The Measures for Assisting and Managing Urban Vagrants and Beggars with No Means of Livelihood will be revised, and a temporary aid system will be established all over the country.

Right to Health

China will establish initially a basic medical and health system that covers the entire nation, and improve the medical insurance system, public health service system and medical care system to protect the citizens' right to health.

- Formulating a law on mental health, and making studies for the enactment of a law on basic medical and health care.

- Continuously increasing the average life expectancy so that it will reach 74.5 years by 2015.
- Strengthening the construction of primary-level medical and health care institutions and training bases for general practitioners. By 2015, China intends to train 150,000 general practitioners through job-transfer training, on-the-job training and standardized training.
- Promoting equality in the right to basic health services. Efforts will be made to ensure that the per-capita spending for public health services is no less than 25 yuan around the country, and see to it that it will be raised to over 40 yuan by 2015. The state will also provide such free services as establishing health records, and providing health education and vaccination. The state will encourage blood donation without compensation and secure blood safety, and make sure that emergency medical services are permanently available.
- Bringing infectious diseases under effective control. China will intensify efforts in prevention and control of major infectious diseases such as AIDS and cholera, and effectively control new infections and mortality caused by AIDS, viral hepatitis and tuberculosis. The rate of direct reporting on incidences of infectious diseases by medical and health institutions at/above the county level will be 100 %. Endeavors will also be made to strengthen the prevention and treatment of infectious diseases among passengers on public transportation vehicles such as trains. The mechanism of joint prevention and control of major epidemics at land and sea ports will be established and medical media monitoring and pathogen detection will be strengthened at the ports.
- Greater efforts will be made to prevent and treat chronic diseases. China will popularize knowledge in the prevention and treatment of chronic diseases, striving to achieve an awareness rate of 50 % among core members in this regard. China will improve early detection, intervention and management of major chronic diseases and high-risk people, making sure that the awareness rate of blood pressure and blood sugar level by people of 35 years old and above reach 75 and 50 %, respectively, and the management rate of hypertension and diabetes be no less than 40 %. China will institute early detection and treatment of major cancers in 30 % of areas with high incidences of cancer across the country.
- Ensuring the safety of drinking water. China will promote the construction of a monitoring network for the safety of drinking water, and make its coverage extend to all cities divided into districts and over 90 % of counties by 2015. The rural population with access to centralized water supply will be raised to 80 %. Efforts will be made to make safe drinking water accessible to an additional 60 million rural people every year.
- The Food Safety Law will be implemented, food safety monitoring system and food safety regulations and standards will be improved, and the responsibility will be determined for safe production of food. Stricter supervision will be enforced over all links of food processing and production, and the basic supervisory systems, such as the production licensing system, supervision and inspection system, recall system and label management system for food, food

additives and food-related production, will be improved, so will the emergency plan for food safety accidents, the accident investigation and handling system and rapid response and handling system. China will bridge mechanisms between administrative law enforcement and criminal justice to severely punish criminal acts harming food safety.

- Comprehensively implementing measures for prevention and control of endemic diseases, and basically eliminating such hazards. China will strive to eliminate iodine deficiency diseases in over 90 % of the counties (cities and districts) in Hainan, Tibet, Qinghai and Xinjiang, and make sure that iodine deficiency diseases are eliminated in 95 % of the counties (cities and districts) in other provinces (autonomous regions and municipalities directly under the central government). In areas with a high incidence of endemic fluorosis caused by coal burning, comprehensive preventive measures focusing on modifying and improving stoves will be adopted over 95 % of the households. China will basically complete projects to provide safe drinking water and improve water quality in areas afflicted by endemic fluorosis and arseniasis which have been proved to be caused mainly by unsafe drinking water. Efforts will be made to bring under effective control fluorosis caused by tea drinking. Over 90 % of the villages that are afflicted by Kaschin-Beck disease will have the disease eliminated, and over 90 % of the counties where Keshan disease remains an endemic will have it eliminated.
- Making studies for enactment of a law on traditional Chinese medicine and management methods of the standards of the medicinal materials. China will raise the national standards for drugs, improve the drug inspection and control system, strengthen drug safety monitoring and early warning, improve the drug safety emergency-response mechanism, fix in advance responsibility for the safe production and use of drugs, and ensure the quality and safety of basic drugs.
- Forming a national fitness public service network covering all urban and rural residents and carrying out the National Fitness Program (2011–2015). Sports venues of various kinds will add up to over 1.2 million, with per-capita sports area being above 1.5 m^2. To achieve this goal, venues with sports facilities will be built in all cities, counties (districts), neighborhoods (townships) and communities (administrative villages). National fitness centers will be built in over 50 % of the country's cities and counties (districts); convenient and practical fitness equipment will be installed in over 50 % of neighborhoods (townships) and communities (administrative villages). Fitness stations will be established in over 50 % of rural communities.

Right to Education

By implementing the Outline of the State Medium- and Long-term Program on Education Reform and Development (2010–2020), China will promote the balanced development of compulsory education throughout the country, develop pre-school education and vocational education, make senior high school education universal, improve the quality of higher education, achieve fairness in education, and raise the overall educational level of all Chinese citizens.

- Consolidating the achievements in 9-year compulsory education. The net enrollment rate in elementary schools will remain at above 99 %, gross enrollment rate in junior high schools will reach 99 %, and the number of students graduating from compulsory education will reach 93 % of the total enrollment. In addition, China will guarantee equal right to education for children of migrant workers, mainly relying on full-time public schools in cities they migrate to.
- Allocating educational resources in balanced manner. China will promote standardized construction of schools of 9-year compulsory education and step up efforts in the renovation of school buildings in poor conditions; encourage exchanges of teachers between different schools within an area to narrow the gap among schools; allocate more educational resources to central and western regions, rural areas, remote and border areas, ethnic-minority areas, as well as urban schools in poor conditions; and accelerate the construction of boarding schools in rural areas to meet the needs of rural children.
- Proactively developing pre-school education. The goal is to have 65 % of the children who will be starting school in 3 years enrolled in kindergartens, and 85 % of the children who will be starting school in one year enrolled in kindergartens. During the 12th Five-Year Plan period (2011–2015), the central government will appropriate 50 billion *yuan* for pre-school education development in rural areas of central and western China. Local governments at different levels will carry out the Pre-school Education Three-Year Action Plan and gradually build and improve pre-school education networks in urban and rural areas.
- Quickening steps in making senior high school education universal. China will improve the conditions of senior high schools, and enhance their teaching level and quality. By 2015, the gross enrollment rate of senior high schools will reach 87 %. Moreover, more support will be given to senior high schools in poor areas of central and western China.
- Making great efforts to develop vocational education. Secondary vocational education will have more or less the same enrollment as regular senior high schools. Support will be given to academic subjects that meet the needs of industry and enterprises. Teaching staff with theoretical knowledge, ability to teach, and practical experience and skills will be trained. The tuition fees for secondary vocational schooling will be gradually abolished.
- Boosting higher education. China will improve educational quality and innovation ability of institutions of higher learning in line with the requirements of its socio-economic development and national strategy. It will carry out a higher education rejuvenation program for central and western China. The areas of central and western China that are short of higher education resources will be given priority in the allocation of such resources. Institutions of higher learning in eastern China will enlarge their enrollments in central and

western China, and strengthen pair-up support by institutions of higher learning in eastern regions to those in western China.

- Further improving the policy system of assistance to poor students. China will improve the national allowance program for poor senior high school students and the dynamic adjustment mechanism of state scholarships to ensure that students do not drop out of school because of poverty.

Cultural Rights

The Outline of the National Plan for Cultural Reform and Development of the 12th Five-Year Plan Period will be implemented. Effective measures will be taken to accelerate the construction of public cultural facilities, promote the development of cultural undertakings, enrich the people's cultural life and guarantee the citizens' cultural rights.

- Strengthening legislation on culture and conducting research to formulate the Public Library Law, Museum Regulations, and other related laws and regulations, revising the Copyright Law, Law on the Protection of Cultural Relics and similar laws, and drawing up regulations and rules complementary to the Intangible Cultural Heritage Law.
- Improving public cultural facilities and cultural service networks. China will increase and improve public cultural facilities like culture centers, museums, libraries, art galleries, science and technology museums, memorial halls, workers' centers, and youth and children's palaces, and open them to the public free of charge. Radio and TV broadcasts will be available in all villages with no more than 20 households each and where electricity is available, covering 99 % of China's population. The cultural information resource sharing project will reach 530 TB in digital resources, shared by 50 % of all households. Mobile cinemas in rural areas will reach 50,000, showing one digital movie every month in every administrative village. Migrant workers will be brought into the urban public cultural service system; and enterprises and communities are guided to actively hold cultural activities geared towards migrant workers.
- Promoting culture coverage and popularization of science and technology. By 2015, each Chinese citizen will have, on average, 5.8 books and 3.1 periodicals every year; every 1,000 people will have 100 daily newspapers; every 10,000 people will share 1.3 publication outlets, and the number of people who read books or periodicals will reach 80 % of the total population. China will also accelerate the construction of farmers' libraries, and urban and rural newspaper reading boards. China will enact the Law on Science and Technology Progress and the Law on Popularization of Science and Technology, formulate standards on citizens' scientific knowledge, promote the building of venues for popularizing science knowledge and launch the construction of the National Demonstration Base for Science Popularization.

– Accelerating Internet construction. By 2015 over 45 % of China's population will have access to the Internet. The fixed broadband ports will exceed 370 million. The Internet connection speed for urban households will reach 20 Mb/s, and that for rural households, 4 Mb/s. Fiber optic Internet connection will cover 200 million households. In addition, China will build wireless broadband cities, and gradually spread Internet connections and usage throughout the rural areas.

Environmental Rights

China will strengthen its environmental protection work to guarantee the public's environmental rights, focusing on serious environmental pollution affecting the people's life, like heavy metal pollution, drinking water pollution, and air, soil and marine contamination.

– Amending the Law on Environmental Protection, preserving and improving the living environment and ecosystem, and preventing and controlling environmental pollution and other hazards.
– Effectively preventing and controlling heavy metal pollution by improving the prevention and control system, emergency response system, and environment and health risk assessment system as regards heavy metal pollution.
– Strengthening water pollution prevention and reversal efforts. China will improve the water quality and environment in trans-provincial areas, tackle seriously contaminated urban water systems and tributary rivers, slow the eutrophication of major lakes, further increase the rate of water functional zones that reach the required hygiene standards, and gradually restore the water ecosystem in certain water areas. China will also enhance protection of unpolluted lakes, and continuously reduce the total emission of major pollutants that contaminate the water. An underground water monitoring and control system will be established; the underground water pollution will be measured; underground water pollution sources will be initially controlled; and experiments to reverse underground water pollution will be launched.
– Improving air quality. By 2015, the country's chemical oxygen demand amount will be controlled at 23.476 million tons, and the total emissions of sulfur dioxide, ammonia nitrogen and nitric oxides will be controlled at 20.864 million tons, 2.38 million tons and 20.462 million tons, respectively. China will endeavor to reduce the concentration of inhalable particulate matter in the air in key regions year by year. By 2015, all cities at prefecture level and above will monitor particulate matter smaller than 2.5 μm.
– Pushing forward ecosystem construction. By 2015, China's land nature reserves will take up 15 % of its total land area so that 90 % of the key species under national protection and typical ecosystem types will be preserved. China's forest coverage will reach 21.66 %. Ten million ha of desertified land and 200,000 km^2 of land suffering from soil erosion will be treated. In urban and rural built-

up areas, the vegetation-coverage rates will reach 39 and 25 %, respectively.
- Strengthening marine ecosystem protection, pushing forward the construction of marine conservation areas, and tightening supervision for the environmental effects of marine projects and waste discharge into the sea.
- Intensifying prevention and control of radioactive waste pollution. China will push forward the decommissioning of obsolete nuclear facilities, and the prevention and treatment of radioactive waste. Civil radioactive-irradiation facilities will be decommissioned, and the waste will be reclaimed. The country will strengthen its ability to store, treat and dispose of radioactive waste, and basically eliminate the danger of contamination by low- and intermediate-level radioactive residue waste left over from history. The treatment of pollution by uranium mines and mines associated with radioactivity will be accelerated, and uranium mining and refining facilities that fall short of safety requirements will be shut down. At the same time, a long-term monitoring mechanism will be established for decommissioned uranium mining and refining facilities.
- Enforcing strict monitoring and control over dangerous chemicals. China will phase out chemicals that are highly poisonous, hard to degrade or highly hazardous to the environment, and strictly restrict the production and use of chemicals involving severe environmental risks.
- Improving environmental monitoring and supervision mechanisms, establishing a trans-regional and inter-departmental cooperative mechanism for the enforcement of environmental laws, and improving the accountability system for major environmental and pollution accidents.

Civil and Political Rights

China endeavors to develop socialist democracy, improve the socialist rule of law, expand the orderly political participation of citizens and guaranteeing people's civil and political rights in an all-round way.

Rights of the Person

All rights of the person are guaranteed by law in lawsuits and law enforcement.

- Criminal Procedure Law will be implemented. The applicable conditions and management stipulations for the adoption of such compulsory measures as arrest, release on bail pending trial and residential surveillance will be adjusted and specified in greater detail.
- All rights of the suspects in lawsuits will be guaranteed by law. The suspects will be informed of their rights and obligations in a timely fashion in accordance with the law, and conditions will be created actively for lawyers to get involved in a lawsuit from the stage of criminal investigation.

- Preventive and remedial measures against extortion of confession by torture and collecting evidence through other illegal methods will be enforced; and no one will be forced to prove himself or herself guilty.
- The people's procuratorates will pay greater heed to the self-defense of criminal suspects at the stage of approval for arrest. Procurators themselves should interrogate suspects when there are clues or evidences that prove the possibility of such serious violations of law as extortion of confession and collecting evidence through the use of force. If the criminal suspects request such an interrogation, the procurators should do so as required.
- Relevant mechanisms to facilitate the work of lawyers during criminal proceedings will be improved. When defense lawyers proffer written materials and evidence maintaining that no crime has been committed, an arrest is unnecessary, or the suspect should not be detained, or there have been violations of law in the investigation, the procurators must examine them seriously. When necessary, procurators may consult lawyers in person. The procurators should state clearly in the arrest warrant whether they are going to accept the lawyer's opinions and evidences and their reasons for doing so.
- The venues of law enforcement and case investigation by public security organs will be transformed according to defined standards step by step. The Standards for Venues of Law Enforcement and Case Investigation of Public Security Organs will be implemented strictly. Case investigation areas must be separated physically from other areas, and the function rooms of the case investigation areas will be established in line with the procedures of case investigation, where permanent sound and video recording as well as video surveillance systems will be installed for real-time monitoring and control over the whole course of law enforcement and investigation to prevent any violation of the legitimate rights and interests of citizens.
- The scope of application of the system of probationary suspension and community correction according to law will be expanded, appropriately reducing the application of imprisonment and clearly defining the scope of non-imprisonment punishment; improving the system of community-based correction, and enriching the contents of community-based correction, correction by education and measures to aid convicts in financial difficulties.
- Strengthening efforts in investigation and punishment of cases committed by state functionaries involving violations of a citizen's personal rights such as illegal detention by taking advantage of their functions and powers.

Rights of Detainees

China will further strengthen supervision over criminal proceedings, punishment execution and supervision, so as to guarantee the legal rights of detainees.

- Guaranteeing the rights and humane treatment of the inmates and improving legal stipulations concerning the management of prisons. The system of a bed for one inmate will be gradually adopted and medical care for prison inmates will be socialized so as to ensure an inmate to get timely treatment when ill.

- Preventing unnecessary detention. After a suspect or defendant is held in custody, the related people's procuratorate should review the necessity of the detention. Once it concludes the detention is not necessary, it should advise the organ that investigates the case to release the suspect or defendant, or change the compulsory measure adopted.
- Strengthening supervision over the time limit of criminal detention. The people's procuratorates should conduct supervision over the organs of criminal investigation to strictly implement the system of detention change, the warning and notifying system when the time limit of detention is going to expire and the accountability system for overdue imprisonment. Efforts will be made to prevent and settle cases involving prolonged detentions and urge the investigation organs to conclude cases that have long exceeded the time limit of detention.
- Improving mechanisms to guarantee the rights of detainees. The systems of physical examination for detainees when they are taken into custody, regular body surface examinations for detainees and notification of the rights and obligations of the detainees and emergency alarming will be strictly implemented, so will the system of interrogation and remand of criminal suspects. The systems of detainees' security risk assessment, psychological intervention and investigation and handling of their complaints will be improved. So will the system of inviting special supervisors to inspect the detention houses. Regulations regarding detainees' request to see the resident procurators, meetings between detainees and resident procurators and the establishment of procurator mailboxes will be improved to prevent and investigate violations of the rights of detainees, such as physical punishment, torture and insult by people working in the detention houses.
- Improving the system of examination and investigation in case of the death of a detainee in prisons and detention houses.

Right to Fair Trial

- China will improve the legal stipulations regarding judicial proceeding to guarantee litigants' right to fair trial.
- Guaranteeing criminal defendants the rights to plead, receive legal aid and request an avoidance (of a judge or witness).
- Guaranteeing the personal rights and right of defense of lawyers when they perform their duties.
- Further improving the system to have witnesses and expert witnesses appear in court and the system of protecting the witnesses.
- Improving the system of eliminating illegal evidence; all confessions by suspects and defendants extorted by torture or other illegal methods, as well as testimonies and statements of witnesses or victims collected by violence, threat or other illegal means will be eliminated and not used in working out the verdict. In addition, the stipulations on evidences used to examine and decide

cases of death penalty will be strictly observed, and more strict standards will be adopted in this regard.

- Implementing the Decisions of the Supreme People's Court on Audio-Visual Recordings of Court Trials. The system of producing audio-visual recordings of the whole process of suspect interrogating in major cases will be established.
- Continuing to push forward standardized measurement of penalty. The people's procuratorates will make suggestions on penalty measurement to the people's courts when handling criminal cases. The discretion in penalty measurement will be institutionalized. Guidelines on penalty measurement by the people's courts will be worked out, so will regulations of the Supreme People's Court, the Supreme People's Procuratorate and the Ministry of Public Security on standardizing procedures of penalty measurement to guarantee openness and fairness in penalty measurement.
- Observing more stringent judicial procedures for death penalty and review of death penalty. China will improve the trial procedures of death penalty cases. The trial of all death penalty cases of second instance will be open to the public. The review of death penalty should include the questioning of the defendant, and listening to the opinions of his/her attorney if the attorney so demands. Legal supervision by the Supreme People's Procuratorate over the review of death penalty will be strengthened. The Supreme People's Court will publicize typical cases to clarify the norms of application of death penalty.
- Amending the Law of Civil Procedure. China will further improve the procedures of bringing an action, case acceptance and pre-trial preparation, establish small-claim and public-interest litigation systems and improve the systems of preservation, evidence, service of litigation document, publicizing of court rulings and trial supervision to protect the litigants' litigation rights.
- Amending Administrative Procedure Law. China will further improve the rules regarding the acceptance of administrative cases, examination procedures and proofs to guarantee the right of individuals and organizations to legal aid in cases of administrative malfeasance.

Freedom of Religious Belief

China upholds the principle of freedom of religious belief stipulated in the Constitution and strictly implements the Regulations on Religious Affairs to guarantee citizens' freedom of religious belief.

- Protecting citizens from being forced to believe in or not to believe in any religion, and from discrimination due to religious belief.
- Protecting normal religious activities according to law.
- Improving the management measures of pilgrimage. China will improve the organization and management of, and service to pilgrimage to provide convenience and guarantee for Muslims to complete their pilgrimage smoothly.
- Encouraging religious believers to carry out charity activities.

- Helping the religious circles resolve difficulties encountered in the construction of some projects. The state will provide financial support to the construction of new school buildings in the Buddhist Academy of China and the improvement and expansion of the China Islamic Institute. The same support will be rendered to the rebuilding and expansion of venues for religious activities of the Tibetan-inhabited areas in Sichuan, Yunnan, Gansu and Qinghai provinces. Financial support will also be extended to the post-earthquake rebuilding of venues for religious activities in Yushu, Qinghai Province, and to mosques damaged during natural disasters.
- Working out methods for implementing the relevant regulations on social security for religious staff.
- Promoting cultural exchanges in religion. China will support friendly exchanges between Chinese religious circles and foreign religious organizations.

Right to Be Informed

The Chinese government will further efforts to make government affairs public, to expand the scope of right to be informed by proceeding from the angles of laws, regulations and policies, so as to enhance the level of guarantee to citizens' right to information.

- Pushing forward the disclosure of government information. China will implement the Provisions on the Disclosure of Government Information and the Opinions of the State Council on Strengthening Government Administration Based on the Rule of Law. The government will make public any government information that does not involve state or trade secrets, or individual privacy. Priority will be given to the disclosure of government information in the areas of financial budgeting, allocation of public resources, approval and implementation of major construction projects, and construction of social welfare undertakings.
- The state will make greater efforts in making public of administrative work. The system of making public of administrative work will be implemented in all government departments providing public services, and they will be asked to make public in accordance with the law the basis, prerequisites, requirements, progress and result of government administrative work, and provide adequate information.
- Proactive efforts will be made to steadily push forward the disclosure of auditing information. The state will uphold and improve the system of announcing auditing results, and standardize the form, content and procedure of such announcement; and uphold and improve the system of announcing the results of phased auditing of special-purpose auditing project and results of investigation of major cases.
- The government press conference system, spokesperson system and spokesperson system for Party committees will be improved continuously.
- The system of keeping the public informed of leading officials' appointment and dismissal will be established and improved. Vacant leadership positions and

related job responsibilities, as well as basic information of the candidates will be announced in due time to promote the institutionalization and standardization of appointment and dismissal of officials.

- The state will standardize and supervise the disclosure of work of enterprises and institutions that provide public services, including hospitals, schools, public transportation and public utilities. Priority will be given to the announcement of such contents as job responsibilities, service commitments, services for charges, job specifications, work discipline and channels of supervision.
- Effective measures will be taken to make enterprise affairs known to employees. By 2015, the system of disclosing enterprise affairs to their employees will be implemented in all state-owned and collective enterprises and state- and collective-controlled enterprises where trade union organizations are established, and in more than 80 % of non-public enterprises with trade union organizations, so as to ensure the employees' right to be informed.
- The state will make efforts to improve the transparency of village affairs. The emphasis will be placed on the disclosure of financial affairs, and a platform for open village affairs will be set up.

Right to Participate

Further efforts will be made to improve the systems, diversify the forms and open up the channels of democracy, to expand citizens' orderly participation in political affairs.

- Implementing the Electoral Law, and guarantee citizens' right to vote and to be elected.
- Ensuring and supporting the participation of non-Communist parties and figures without party affiliation in the exercise of state power, consultation on major state policies and choice of state leaders, administration of state affairs, and formulation and implementation of state policies, laws and regulations.
- Soliciting public opinion when formulating laws or regulations that concern major public interests and the vital interests of the people.
- Continuously supporting the trade unions, the Communist Youth League, the women's federations and other mass organizations in their participation in social management and provision of public services in accordance with the law. The government will wholeheartedly gather opinions from the mass organizations when formulating and amending relevant laws, regulations and public policies.
- Encouraging orderly participation by social organizations in social construction. The Law on Philanthropy will be formulated, and the Regulations on the Registration of Social Organizations, the Interim Regulations on the Registration of Private Non-enterprise Entities and the Regulations on the Management of Foundations will be amended. The government will standardize activities of voluntary services and expedite the development of voluntary services.

- Improving the system of workers' congress and the system of directors and supervisors from among workers, and giving support to trade unions in participating in the management of enterprises and public institutions on behalf of workers and staff. Efforts will be made to gradually realize the goal of full coverage of the system of workers' congress in state and collective enterprises and state- and collective-controlled enterprises where trade union organizations are established, and in more than 80 % of non-public enterprises with trade union organizations.
- Further developing and improving the system of self-governance at the primary level of society.

Right to Be Heard

The government will take effective measures to ensure that all channels of self-expression are unblocked, and citizens' freedom of speech and right to be heard are protected in accordance with the law.

- The state respects and guarantees the rights of all parties and groups and deputies from all ethic groups and all walks of life in the Chinese People's Political Consultative Conference (CPPCC) to voice their opinions, to go on inspection tours, to put forward motions, to reflect social conditions and public opinion, and to take part in investigation and inspection activities.
- Through communication with the public in various ways, state organs and their functionaries will earnestly learn what they want and solicit their opinions.
- The mechanism whereby the masses express their wishes will be improved, and the channels for people to make petitions in the form of letters and personal visits will remain unblocked and be broadened. Such practices as Green Post, online complaints, special telephone lines, video complaints and agencies which make complaints on behalf of others will be promoted and improved so as to ensure the implementation of the Regulations on Petitions in the Form of Letters and Visits. The state will persist in requiring leading cadres at all levels to read letters from the people and make comments or issue instructions concerning them, and improve the system in which leading cadres receive visitors who come to make complaints, and visit grassroots localities. Efforts will be made to enhance the construction, promotion and application of the complaint information system. We will further strengthen the building of a state-level complaint-handling center, and set up a comprehensive platform to deal with complaints quickly and efficiently.
- The state will guarantee employees' right to be heard. The making and revision of labor rules and regulations in enterprises will be discussed at workers' congress in advance, so as to ensure that channels are unblocked for employees to express appeals concerning their interests.
- The state will strengthen institutional guarantees for the legitimate rights and interests of news agencies and journalists, ensuring in accordance with the law

journalists' rights to be informed, to gather materials, to publish, to criticize, and to supervise, and safeguarding the legitimate rights and interests of news agencies, journalists, editors and other persons concerned.

Right to Oversee

The government will make unremitting efforts to improve the system of supervision, strengthen restraints on and supervision over the exercise of power, and earnestly guarantee citizens' right of democratic supervision.

- Strengthening the supervision over the people's governments, people's courts and people's procuratorates by people's congresses and their standing committees at all levels, and strengthening supervision over leading cadres, so as to ensure the correct exercise of power.
- Giving full play to the CPPCC's role in democratic supervision. Efforts will be intensified to strengthen supervision over the implementation of major policies and the performance of state organs and their functionaries by all participating parties and groups, and people from all ethnic groups and all walks of life in the CPPCC in the forms of making proposals and voicing criticisms.
- Improving the system of supervision over regulations and normative documents. Efforts will be made in seriously studying and handling suggestions by individuals and organizations for reviewing such regulations and documents in accordance with relevant rules. Work will be done to strengthen the filing and examination work regarding regulations and normative documents, so as to prevent illegitimate increase of the obligations of any individuals and organizations.
- Intensifying the supervision and restraint over the power of administrative examination and approval by pushing forward the publicizing of the process and results of such examination and approval, and strengthening monitoring throughout the whole process.
- Strictly implementing the administrative accountability system prescribed by the Civil Servant Law and the Law on Administrative Supervision, intensifying investigations regarding the accountability in accidents in production safety, food and drug quality, land requisition and environmental pollution, and punishing in accordance with the law those who infringe on the interests of the people because of dereliction of duty or malfeasance.
- Amending the Measures for Offence Reporting Work and Regulations on the Protection of Whistle-Blowers. The violations reported, the situation of the report and relevant information about informants will be kept confidential; acts obstructing, repressing and avenging the informants will be corrected timely so as to protect their legitimate rights and interests.
- Guaranteeing the right of citizens and social organizations in exercising supervision over administrative organs in accordance with the law by applying for administrative reconsideration or instituting administrative litigation.

- Expanding social supervision by enhancing the functions of special inspectors, supervisors and examiners, and strengthening the public's supervision over administrative, trial and procuratorial organs.
- Encouraging news media to play their unique role in supervision by public opinion, and opening up the channels for people to criticize, give advice to, complain of, accuse and impeach state organs and state functionaries.

Rights of Ethnic Minorities, Women, Children, the Elderly, and the Disabled

China will take further measures to protect the legitimate rights and interests of ethnic minorities, women, children, elderly people and the disabled.

Rights of Ethnic Minorities

China is a unified multi-ethnic country, where all ethnic groups are equal, and the state protects the lawful rights and interests of ethnic minorities.

- The right of ethnic minorities to participate in the management of state and social affairs on an equal footing is guaranteed by the state according to law. The state will make sure that minority groups have a proportionate number of representatives in organs of state power and administrative, judicial and procuratorate organs at both the central and local levels. Ethnic-minority citizens will enjoy favorable treatment when they apply to take the national civil service examinations.
- The state attaches importance to the training and utilization of talented people from ethnic minorities. Greater efforts are made to cultivate and select ethnic-minority personnel for Party and administrative work. The state supports areas inhabited by ethnic minorities in compact communities in their implementation of the national revitalization program for highly-skilled personnel and the support program for talented people in rural areas. The state will continue to train general medical practitioners and employ professional medical practitioners for rural areas in places where ethnic minorities live in compact communities on the state budget, and cultivate professionals of ethnic-minority medicine.
- The state guarantees that ethnic minorities enjoy equal right to public services. The state constantly strengthens the capacity of public services in ethnic autonomous areas. The gaps in the incomes of urban and rural residents, compulsory education, medical care, social security between ethnic-minority areas and the national average level will be significantly narrowed; existing problems in education, medical care, drinking water, communication, employment and other areas will be significantly alleviated; the production and living conditions of the farmers and herdsmen in pasturing areas, border

areas, areas inhabited by ethnic minorities with small populations, and impoverished ethnic-minority areas will be improved significantly.

- The right of ethnic minorities to economic development is guaranteed. The state will implement policies and special programs for promoting the socio-economic development of the five autonomous regions, i.e. Inner Mongolia, Xinjiang, Guangxi, Ningxia and Tibet, and for supporting the development of other ethnic-minority regions, and work to make sure that the main indices of economic development for ethnic-minority regions are higher than those of the national average. The state will continue to formulate and implement special programs to support the development of minority ethnic groups with small populations, vitalize border areas and bring prosperity to their residents, and develop special undertakings of ethnic minorities and other programs. In major pastoral areas, the state will establish a subsidy and bonus mechanism for the protection of steppe ecosystem, guaranteeing that the income growth of herdsmen is not lower than that of the farmers in the same province (autonomous region). Vigorous efforts will be made to promote ethnic-minority trade and the production of ethnic consumer products, implement relevant preferential policies, and satisfy the special production and life needs of ethnic minorities. Emphasis will be put on the protection of the ecological environment in ethnic-minority regions.
- Education for ethnic minorities is to be promoted. The state will transfer more public education resources to ethnic-minority regions, quicken the development of preschool education, support the standardized construction of compulsory-education schools in border counties and poverty-stricken counties of ethnic autonomous areas, strengthen the construction of boarding schools in ethnic-minority regions, actively and steadily promote bilingual education, vigorously promote the development of vocational education, make greater efforts in the training and cultivation of teachers, and strengthen pair-up assistance in education.
- Cultural rights of ethnic minorities are guaranteed. The state will make greater efforts to protect the special cultures of ethnic-minority groups, strengthen the protection of their cultural relics, carry out emergency protection of endangered projects and representative inheritors who are aged or otherwise feeble, and implement overall protection for areas where intangible cultural heritage of ethnic minorities is concentrated. Traditional sports of ethnic minorities will also be given state support.
- Ethnic minorities' right to learn, use and develop their own spoken and written languages is guaranteed in accordance with the law. The state will promote the standardization and information processing of the spoken and written languages of ethnic minorities, and build databases of China's endangered ethnic-minority languages.

Women's Rights

China implements the Law on the Protection of Women's Rights and Interests, promotes gender equality, and guarantees the lawful rights and interests of women.

- The state will continue its efforts to promote women's equal participation in the management of state and social affairs. The state will gradually increase the proportion of women representatives in the national and local people's congresses and political consultative conferences, and make sure that the people's congresses, governments, and political consultative conferences at the provincial and municipal levels as well as county-level governments include at least one female member in the leadership. The state will gradually increase the proportion of women holding principal positions in the leadership of local governments and departments at/above the county level, the proportion of women on boards of directors and boards of supervisors as well as the leadership of enterprises, and the proportion of women representatives at workers' conferences and faculty congresses. There should also be a certain proportion of women members in village committees and community committees.
- The state makes efforts to eliminate gender discrimination in employment and realize equal payment for men and women doing the same work. The state will strengthen special labor protection for female workers, timely revise the standards of special labor protection for women workers, and encourage the signing and implementation of special collective contracts for the protection of female workers' rights and interests in enterprises that have established labor unions.
- Women's right to having equal access to economic resources and to participating in economic development is guaranteed. The state will make sure that women in rural areas enjoy equal rights with men in the contracting and management of land, use of rural homesteads and distribution of collective income.
- The level of reproductive health services for women will be raised. The state will improve the maternity service system in urban and rural areas, and make sure that maternity insurance covers all employing units. The state will increase the proportion of women giving birth in hospitals, lower mortality rate during delivery, increase the screening rate of common gynecological diseases, and increase the rate of early diagnosis and treatment of cervical cancer and breast cancer to lower the mortality rate in this regard. The state will gradually provide free folic acid and other nutrients to women of childbearing age in rural areas as a pre-gestational and early-pregnancy supplement, promote trial programs of free pre-gestational checkups, and provide free technical service to women who plan for pregnancy in rural areas, including relevant health care education.
- The state will prevent and prohibit domestic violence against women. The state will formulate a law on domestic violence, and improve the inter-departmental cooperative mechanism for the prevention and prohibition of domestic violence, and the integrative work mechanism of prevention, prohibition and assistance.

- The state will crack down on the crimes of abducting and trafficking in women. The state will stick to the principles which stress prevention as the major measure, integrate crackdown with prevention, put people first and exert comprehensive control, improve the vigilance of the whole society against abduction and women's precautionary awareness, provide physical and mental rehabilitation services to rescued women, and help them return to society.
- The state will strengthen the statistical work on gender data, and improve the collecting and publishing of gender-specific data in the fields of economic and social development.

Children's Rights

China implements the Law on the Protection of Minors, promotes the legislation process regarding children's welfare, preschool education, family education and other issues, and effectively guarantees children's rights to life, development, protection and participation for their best interests.

- Children's right to health is guaranteed. The state will constantly lower the mortality rates of infants and children under the age of five, and make sure to lower the rate of severe and frequently-occurring birth defects that lead to disabilities, and lower the disability rate due to birth defects. It will control the rate of low birth weight at under 5 %. Ninety-five percent of the children in the country's central and western cities, and the entire eastern part will be vaccinated in the national immunization program, and the figure for rural areas in the central and western regions will reach 90 %. The state will implement a nutrition enhancement program for students receiving compulsory education in rural areas, and make sure that students in primary and secondary schools generally reach the basic requirements of the National Standard of Students' Physical Health, and that students' endurance, strength, speed and other physical qualities realize significant improvement. During school time, students will be given at least 1 h of sports and exercise every day, and the rates of nearsightedness, dental caries, obesity and malnutrition will be put under control.
- Administration of school buses and campus safety will be strengthened.
- Children's right to leisure and entertainment will be guaranteed. Children's services will be established in urban and rural areas to provide venues and facilities for games, recreation, education, health care, social and psychological support for children and their families. The state will make sure that at least one professional or part-time children's social worker is employed in a local community, village or town.
- Children's right to participate will be protected. The state encourages and supports children's participation in family and social life according to the degree of their physical and psychological development, and works to create a favorable social environment for children's participation.

- Discrimination against girls will be eliminated. The state will implement the reward-and-support policy for families with girls only, and try out support schemes for such families in impoverished areas. It bans identification of the sex of a fetus for other than medical purposes and termination of pregnancy in the case of a female fetus.
- The state will gradually expand the coverage of children's welfare. The state will improve the security system for orphans, increase the proportions of fostered and adopted orphans, and gradually bring unsupported children, children with severe or rare diseases and severely disabled children into the security system. The state will increase the emergency rehabilitation rate of disabled children under 6 years old, and guarantee the rights to life, education, health care and other rights of AIDS-affected children and convicts' children under 18 years old. The state will increase the number of institutions providing professional services for the upbringing and protection of orphans, protection of homeless children and rehabilitation of disabled children.
- Children's personal rights will be protected. The state will crack down on the abduction, maltreatment and abandonment of children, and the forcing of children into begging and other illegal activities and crimes that infringe upon the personal rights of children. The state will protect children from all forms of sexual abuse, and provide physical and psychological services to rescued children before properly resettling them.
- The state will prohibit the employment of child labor and exploitation of children, and will severely punish such illegal activities according to law.
- The legal proceedings in criminal cases involving juveniles will be improved. A conditional non-prosecution mechanism and criminal record sealing mechanism will be established. A good job will be done in community-based corrections of juvenile delinquents, and juveniles will be guaranteed legal service and assistance in accordance with the law.

Senior Citizens' Rights

China implements the Law on the Protection of the Rights and Interests of the Elderly, gradually improves the old-age security system, pushes forward the construction of old-age service system, and guarantees the legitimate rights and interests of the elderly.

- The state will improve the old-age social security system that covers both urban and rural residents. The government will provide basic pensions for rural residents and unemployed urban residents above 60 years old, and issue reward and support subsidies to parents in rural areas who are both above 60 and who have only one child or two daughters, preliminarily realizing universal coverage for all senior citizens.
- The state will improve preferential treatment measures for the elderly, actively providing various forms of preferential treatment and prioritized and

preferential services to the elderly, and gradually increasing the level of social welfare for senior citizens.

- The state will improve the support policy for home-based old-age care. The state will improve the administrative policy of household registration transfer for elderly people, thus creating conditions for the transfer of senior citizens along with their providers. It will also improve policies that support and encourage home-based care and security services for elderly people.
- The state implements the Program for the Construction of Old-age Social Service System (2011–2015). By 2015, the state will increase the number of beds in day-care facilities and nursing homes by 3,420,000, and extend support to the establishment of not-for-profit nursing homes by private businesses.
- The state will improve the basic medical insurance for the elderly. Grassroots-level medical care services will provide health management services to local residents above 65 years old, and establish and keep health profiles for them.
- The state will enrich senior citizens' cultural lives. The state will increase financial investment into the construction of colleges for senior citizens, enlarge the scale of such schools, increase the supply of public cultural products for the elderly, organize public fitness activities for them and provide convenience for their participation in voluntary programs. In order to promote senior citizens' participation in social life, the state will make sure that at least 95 % of urban communities and 80 % of rural communities have their own senior citizens' associations by 2015.
- The state will promote the construction of elderly-friendly cities and livable communities for senior citizens. The state will comprehensively implement the technological standards of urban and rural construction projects related to senior citizens, as well as the standards of renovation of barrier-free facilities and the construction of facilities for the elderly in newly-built communities.
- The state will expand channels of legal assistance for the elderly and the emphasis is to provide legal services to citizens of advanced age, and senior citizens who live alone, are disabled or have any other physical difficulty.

Rights and Interests of the Disabled

China develops undertakings relating to the disabled, improves social security and services for them, and protects their lawful rights and interests.

- The state will implement the Law on the Protection of the Rights and Interests of the Disabled and improve relevant supporting laws and regulations. The state will formulate regulations on the construction of barrier-free environments, research and formulate regulations on the rehabilitation of the disabled, and research and revise the regulations on education for the disabled.
- The state will include the disabled people in both urban and rural areas in the basic endowment insurance and basic medical insurance according to relevant regulations. The state will establish a life subsidy system for the financially-challenged disabled population and nursing care allowances for the severely

disabled, in an effort to supply a steady institutional guarantee for the basic life of the disabled.

- The state will comprehensively carry out community-based rehabilitation services. The state will help 13 million disabled people obtain rehabilitation to various degrees through the implementation of key rehabilitation programs, organize the supply of five million pieces of supporting devices of various types and provide basic supporting devices for those in need. It will also provide subsidies on 1.6 million occasions for community or household services for people suffering from mental disabilities and diseases, as well as for seriously disabled people.
- The state will raise the education level of the disabled. The state will make sure that school-age disabled children generally receive compulsory education. It will promote compulsory education for disabled children in such a way that they attend the same classes as other healthy children where convenient, providing education for disabled people that suits their needs and capacities. The state will develop pre-school rehabilitation education for disabled children and vocational education for the disabled, promoting senior high-school education and higher education for the disabled, and reducing illiteracy among the young and middle-aged disabled population.
- The state will stabilize and expand employment for the disabled. The state will provide employment services and vocational training for disabled people who seek employment, and make sure that an additional 800,000 disabled people will be employed by 2015.
- The state will strengthen development-oriented poverty reduction programs for the disabled population in rural areas. The state will help eight million needy disabled people in rural areas to improve their living conditions, increase their incomes and enhance their abilities for development. The state will provide skills training for 800,000 disabled people in rural areas, and continue to implement the "sunshine housing project" to improve the housing conditions of impoverished disabled people in rural areas.
- The state will require public cultural facilities to give access to the disabled free of charge or at preferential rates. The state encourages the construction of digital reading rooms for the blind in public libraries in areas that are capable of doing so, opens public sports facilities to the disabled gratis or at preferential rates, and carries out mass cultural and sports activities that conform to the physical and psychological characteristics of the disabled.
- The state will quicken the construction and renovation of barrier-free facilities. It will create barrier-free cities, counties and districts nationwide, strengthen the construction of barrier-free facilities of public transport including the railway, as well as the construction of information accessibility. The state will carry out renovation of barrier-free facilities for families of the disabled and subsidize those who have financial difficulties in the renovation.
- The state will expand the scale of publications in braille. It will strengthen the construction of publishing bases of braille books, and realize the annual production goal of 700,000 copies of such books and periodicals in 1,600 titles.

It will also develop music scores for the blind, as well as reference books, periodicals, digital audio books and encyclopedias for them.
- The state will improve a coordinating work mechanism of legal assistance to the disabled. It will improve legal assistance to the disabled to protect their rights and interests by law.

Human Rights Education

China will carry out extensive human rights education and training in various forms, and promote human rights awareness and publicize human rights knowledge throughout the Chinese society.

- China will include human rights education in the training programs of civil servants to strengthen human rights education and training for civil servants. The state supports human rights research institutes in their efforts to develop teaching materials for training in human rights and participate in the training work.
- China will strengthen human rights education in primary and middle schools. The state will make sure that human rights knowledge is integrated into relevant courses and included in the legal education curriculum. It will also carry out human rights promotional activities that suit juveniles, promote school management by law and democratic administration, and create an education environment that honors human rights.
- China will encourage institutions of higher learning to offer public courses and specialized courses on human rights, support the development of related disciplines and majors, and encourage studies on human rights theories.
- China will encourage and promote the publicity of human rights knowledge in enterprises and public institutions, and develop corporate cultures that honor and protect human rights.
- China will encourage the dissemination of human rights knowledge via the media. It will enhance human rights awareness among the whole populace to create an atmosphere of public opinion that human rights is emphasized by all.
- China will give full play to the role of national human rights education and training bases. By 2015, at least five new such bases will be opened.

Fulfillment of Obligations to International Human Rights Conventions, and Exchanges and Cooperation in the Field of International Human Rights

China continues to earnestly fulfill its obligations to the international human rights conventions to which it has acceded, and actively conducts exchanges and cooperation in the field of international human rights.

Fulfillment of Obligations to International Human Rights Conventions

China cherishes the important role played by international instruments on human rights in promoting and protecting human rights. It submits timely reports on implementing the conventions to the treaty bodies concerned, holds constructive dialogues with these treaty bodies, takes into full consideration the proposals raised by them, and adopts rational and feasible ones in the light of China's actual conditions.

- China completed the sixth report on implementing the "Convention against Torture and Other Cruel, Inhuman or Degrading Treatment or Punishment," and submitted it to the United Nations Committee against Torture for consideration.
- China completed the 14th report on implementing the "International Convention on the Elimination of All Forms of Racial Discrimination," and submitted it to the United Nations Committee on the Elimination of Racial Discrimination for consideration.
- China renewed the second report on implementing the "International Covenant on Economic, Social and Cultural Rights," and participated in the deliberation meeting held by the UN Committee on Economic, Social and Cultural Rights.
- China attended the deliberation meeting held by the Committee on the Rights of the Child concerning China's third and fourth combined report on implementing the "Convention on the Rights of the Child."
- China attended the deliberation meeting held by the Committee on the Rights of the Child on China's first report on implementing the "Optional Protocol to the Convention on the Rights of the Child on the Involvement of Children in Armed Conflict."
- China attended the deliberation meeting held by the Committee on the Elimination of Discrimination Against Women on China's seventh and eighth combined report on implementing the "Convention on the Elimination of All Forms of Discrimination Against Women."
- China attended the deliberation meeting held by the Committee on the Rights of Persons with Disabilities on China's first report on implementing the "Convention on the Rights of Persons with Disabilities."
- China has continued to carry out administrative and judicial reforms and prepare the ground for approval of the "International Covenant on Civil and Political Rights."

Exchanges and Cooperation in the Field of International Human Rights

China is committed to holding exchanges and cooperation in the field of international human rights and promoting the healthy development of international human rights on the basis of equality and mutual respect.

- China implements the related suggestions of United Nations Human Rights Council's (HRC) first Universal Periodic Review for China, prepares for and actively participates in the second Universal Periodic Review.

- China takes an active part in the work of the HRC, and helps that body to solve human rights problems in a fair, objective and non-alternative way.
- China continues its cooperation with the Special Procedures of the United Nations Human Rights Council, answers letters from it, and considers inviting special reporters to visit China while taking into account the principle of balancing various human rights and China's reception abilities.
- China continues its good cooperation with the Office of the United Nations High Commissioner for Human Rights.
- China continues to hold dialogues and exchanges on human rights with various countries on the basis of equality and mutual respect. China also increases consultation and cooperation on human rights with developing countries.
- China continues to participate in human rights activities in the framework of the Asian-Pacific Region and Sub-region, including the Informal ASEM Seminar on Human Rights.

Implementation and Supervision

The joint meeting mechanism for the National Human Rights Action Plan, headed by the Information Office of the State Council and Ministry of Foreign Affairs, is responsible for the implementation, supervision and evaluation of the Action Plan.

- Related departments of the CPC Central Committee and Central Government, and local governments at all levels will attach the utmost importance to the Action Plan, and while taking into consideration the specific responsibilities of each department and regional characteristics, will take effective measures to achieve the aims and complete the tasks of the Action Plan.
- The joint meeting mechanism for the National Human Rights Action Plan will conduct research and examination, and have a final evaluation and publicize the evaluation report.
- In the process of implementing the Action Plan, China will respect and give full play to the public's initiative and creativity. It will innovate the social management mechanism and promote the constructive role of NGOs in human rights protection.
- China will make the Action Plan an important part of human rights education and training, and effectively raise people's consciousness in implementing the Action Plan.
- China will encourage the mass media to play a positive role in the publicizing, implementation and supervision of the Action Plan.

Appendix V
Judicial Reform in China

Preface

The judicial system is a major component of the political system, while judicial impartiality is a significant guarantee of social justice.

Since the founding of New China in 1949, and especially since the reform and opening-up policies were introduced some three decades ago, China, proceeding from its national conditions, carrying on the achievements of Chinese traditional legal culture and learning from other civilizations regarding their rule of law, has been building and improving its socialist judicial system with Chinese characteristics, safeguarding social justice and making significant contributions to the rule of law of the mankind.

China's judicial system is generally consistent with its basic national conditions at the primary stage of socialism, its state system of people's democratic dictatorship, and its government system of the National People's Congress. With the further development of China's reform and opening up, particularly due to the development of the socialist market economy, the comprehensive implementation of the fundamental principle of rule of law, and the increasing demands of the public for justice, China's judicial system urgently needs to be reformed, improved and developed.

In recent years, China has been promoting the reform of the judicial system and its work mechanism vigorously, steadily and pragmatically. Aiming to safeguard judicial justice and focusing on optimizing the allocation of judicial functions and power, enhancing protection of human rights, improving judicial capacity, and practicing the principle of "judicature for the people," China has been striving to improve its judicial system with Chinese characteristics, expand judicial

---

Information Office of the State Council, the People's Republic of China
October 2012, Beijing

P. Sun, *Human Rights Protection System in China*,
DOI: 10.1007/978-3-642-39663-2, © Springer-Verlag Berlin Heidelberg 2014

democracy, promote judicial openness and ensure judicial impartiality. This provides a solid judicial guarantee for China's economic development, social harmony and national stability.

Judicial System and Reform Process

The founding of the People's Republic of China in 1949 ushered in a new era for the building of China's judicial system. The Common Program of the Chinese People's Political Consultative Conference, which functioned as a provisional Constitution, and the Organic Law of the Central People's Government of the People's Republic of China, both promulgated in September 1949, laid the cornerstone for legal construction in New China. The Constitution of the People's Republic of China promulgated in 1954, the Organic Law of the People's Courts of the People's Republic of China, the Organic Law of the People's Procuratorates of the People's Republic of China among other laws and regulations, defined the organic system and basic functions of the people's courts and procuratorates, established the systems of collegiate panels, defense, public trial, people's jurors, legal supervision, civil mediation, putting into place the basic framework of China's judicial system.

Toward the end of 1950s, especially during the 10-year tumultuous "cultural revolution" (1966–1976), China's judicial system suffered severe damage. Since the reform and opening-up policies were introduced in 1978, China, after summing up its historical experience, established the fundamental policy of promoting socialist democracy and improving socialist legal construction, restored and rebuilt the judicial system, and formulated and amended a range of fundamental laws. In the 1990s, China established the fundamental principle of governing the country in accordance with the law, and quickened the step to build China into a socialist country under the rule of law. During the process of promoting social progress, democracy and the rule of law, China's judicial system is continuously improving and developing.

Basic Characteristics of China's Judicial System

China is a socialist country with a people's democratic dictatorship led by the working class and based on the alliance of workers and peasants. The people's congress system is the organic form of its state power. China's state system and system of government decide that its judicial power comes from the people, belongs to the people and serves the people. The people's courts and the people's procuratorates are created by the people's congresses at various levels, to which they are responsible and by which they are supervised.

The people's court is the basic judicial organ in China. The state has set up the Supreme People's Court, local people's courts at different levels and special people's courts such as military courts. They adjudicate civil, criminal and administrative cases in accordance with the law, and carry out law enforcement activities including the execution of civil and administrative cases and state compensation. The Supreme People's Court supervises the judicial work of all local people's courts and special people's courts. The people's court at a higher level supervises the judicial work of the people's court at the next lower level. In litigious activities, China adopts the systems of public trial, collegiate panels, challenge, people's jurors, defense, and judgment of the second instance as final, among others.

The people's procuratorate is the procuratorial organ in China. The state has set up the Supreme People's Procuratorate, local people's procuratorates at different levels and special people's procuratorates such as military procuratorates. The Supreme People's Procuratorate directs the work of local people's procuratorates at different levels and special people's procuratorates. A people's procuratorate at a higher level directs the work of a people's procuratorate at the next level below it. The people's procuratorate exercises legal supervision over criminal, civil and administrative litigations in accordance with the law.

The people's court and the people's procuratorate exercise their adjudicative power and procuratorial power independently and impartially in accordance with the law. Their exercise of power is subject to the supervision of the National People's Congress, the Chinese People's Political Consultative Conference and the general public.

The people's courts, the people's procuratorates and the organs of public security handle criminal cases according to their respective functions, and collaborate with and check each other, so as to ensure the accurate and efficient implementation of law. The organs of public security take charge of the investigation, detention, arrest and pretrial in criminal cases; the people's procuratorates conduct procuratorial work, approve proposals for arrest, investigate cases directly accepted by them, and initiate public prosecution; and the people's courts are responsible for conducting trials.

Objectives, Principles, and Process of China's Judicial Reform

Since the introduction of the reform and opening-up policies, China has witnessed rapid economic and social development, and the public's awareness of the importance of the rule of law has been remarkably enhanced. Due to the profound changes in the judicial environment, judicial work in China is facing new situations and problems. The defects and rigidity in China's current judicial system and its work mechanism are becoming increasingly prominent, and they need to be improved gradually through reform.

The fundamental objectives of China's judicial reform are to ensure that the people's courts and people's procuratorates exercise adjudicative power and procuratorial power fairly and independently; to establish an impartial, efficient and authoritative socialist judicial system; and to provide solid and reliable judicial guarantee for safeguarding the legitimate rights and interests of the people, social equity and justice, and lasting national stability.

China carries out judicial reform based on its national conditions. It draws on the sound practices of other countries but does not blindly copy them; it keeps pace with the times but does not advance rashly and blindly. It sticks to the line of relying on the people, strives to meet their expectations, tackles problems of particular concern to the people, and subjects itself to their supervision and examination, so as to ensure the reform is for the people, relies on the people and benefits the people. It pushes forward the reform in accordance with the law, abiding by the Constitution and other laws and regulations, while those measures that contravene the laws in force should only be implemented after the laws are revised. It adheres to the principle of overall planning and coordination, comprehensive designing, and proceeding in an orderly and gradual way.

As early as in the 1980s, China started reforms in court trials and ensuring professionalism in judicature, focusing on enhancing the function of court trials, expanding the openness of trials, improving attorney defense functions, and training professional judges and procurators.

In 2004, China launched large-scale judicial reforms based on overall planning, deployment and implementation. Starting with issues that caused complaints from the public and the key links that hamper judicial justice, according to the demands of promoting judicial impartiality and strict enforcement of the law, and proceeding from the regular pattern and characteristics of judicial practice, China improved the structure of its judicial organs, division of judicial functions and system of judicial management, to establish a judicial system featuring clearly defined power and responsibilities, mutual collaboration and restraint, and highly efficient operation. Thereby, China's judicial reform entered a phase of overall planning and advancing in an orderly way.

Since 2008, China has initiated a new round of judicial reform, and entered a stage of deepening in key areas and overall advancement. The reform proceeds from the demands of the public for justice, with safeguarding the people's common interests as its fundamental task, promoting social harmony as the main principle and strengthening supervision and restraint of power as priority. China aims to tackle problems in the key links that hamper judicial justice and restrain judicial capability, remove existing barriers in the institutional setup and operational mechanism as well as provision of legal guarantee, and put forward the specific tasks for judicial reform in four aspects—optimizing the allocation of judicial functions and power, implementing the policy of balancing leniency and severity, building up the ranks of judicial workers, and ensuring judicial funding. Currently, the tasks of this round of judicial reform have been basically completed, as relevant laws have been amended and improved. As China is making continuous progress in economic and social development, its judicial reform is bound to advance further.

Maintaining Social Fairness and Justice

Maintaining social fairness and justice is the value to be enforced in China's judicial reform. China aims its judicial reform at strengthening its judicial organs' capability in maintaining social justice by optimizing the structure of the judicial organs and allocation of their functions and power, standardizing judicial acts, improving judicial proceedings, and enhancing judicial democracy and legal supervision.

Optimizing the Allocation of Judicial Functions and Power

The rationalization and optimization of judicial functions and power has a direct bearing on the materialization of justice. China, starting from removing the institutional barriers that affect judicial impartiality, has enhanced internal checks in judicial organs, clarified the work relationship between the people's courts and the people's procuratorates at different levels, standardized and improved retrial procedures, and established consistent law-enforcement system and judicial authentication management system. These reforms have improved judicial organs' capacity for maintaining fairness, helped to safeguard social equity and justice, and fulfilled the public's new expectations and demands for the judicial system in maintaining justice.

Separation of filing, trial and execution of cases. The people's courts at all levels have established case-filing tribunals, execution bureaus and other departments in addition to the original criminal, civil and administrative adjudication tribunals. Case-filing, trial and execution are handled separately by different offices, which act independently and exercise a mutual-check function to ensure the fair exercise of adjudicative and execution power.

Standardizing the retrial of remanded cases and designated cases. To correct the irregular practices in the procedures regarding retrial of remanded cases and designated cases, the Civil Procedure Law amended in 2012 revised and improved the procedure for the retrial of remanded cases. The new provisions clearly state that after the original people's court makes its ruling in the retrial of a remanded case, if the litigant makes an appeal, the people's court of second instance shall not send the case back for a retrial. The Criminal Procedure Law, amended in 2012, articulates that a criminal case designated for retrial by a lower-level people's court shall be tried by one other than the original court in principle.

Regularizing and improving a unified execution mechanism for civil and administrative cases. Full and effective execution of a judgment or verdict given by the court bears on effective protection of the lawful rights of all parties involved and the expression of judicial authority. In recent years, local people's courts have established a mechanism of execution that works closely with departments in charge of public security, procuratorial work, finance, land resources, construction, business and commerce, as well as exit-entry administration. The people's courts exercise separation of jurisdiction from execution. The higher and intermediate people's courts have established execution command centers for unified management and coordination of execution, and, when necessary, can have their power elevated or allow them to carry out the execution beyond the prescribed region. The reform of the execution system has further strengthened the internal checks on the exercise of execution power, promoted impartial and standardized execution, and effectively protected the legitimate rights of the parties concerned.

Reforming the procedures for examining and approving arrests in power-abuse cases. To prevent arrests by mistake, China has reformed the procedure for examining and approving arrests in power-abuse cases. For power-abuse cases filed with and investigated by a people's procuratorate below the provincial level, the approval for an arrest shall be examined and determined by the people's procuratorate at the next higher level. This reform has strengthened the supervision of a people's procuratorate at a higher level over one at a lower level on law enforcement.

Improving the system of judicial authentication management. Judicial authentication refers to the activity of an authenticator applying scientific technology or specialized knowledge to identify and determine the specialized issues involved in a lawsuit and giving authentication opinions. Before the judicial reform, the judicial authentication system in China had problems as legislation was incomplete, management was not standardized and standards were not consistent. To solve these problems, China's legislative organ promulgated the Decision on the Management of Judicial Authentication in 2005, thereby establishing a uniform management and registration system for judicial authentication. The judicial administrative departments of the State Council take charge of the registration and management of judicial authenticators and judicial authentication institutions in China, while the judicial administrative departments of the people's governments at the provincial level are responsible for the registration upon examination, roster formulation and roster announcement of judicial authenticators and judicial authentication institutions. The people's courts and judicial administrative departments do not have judicial authentication institutions any longer; judicial authentication institutions already set up by investigation organs to meet the needs of their work will not provide judicial authentication services to the public. The state promotes a mechanism that combines administrative management with trade associations' self-disciplinary management, and adopts the system of judicial authenticators' independent practice in accordance with the law, which ensures that judicial authentication is standardized and neutral. By the end of 2011, there were 5,014 judicial authentication institutions and 52,812 judicial authenticators approved and registered in China.

Standardizing Judicial Acts

Social fairness and justice shall be ensured in the trial of every case and in each judicial act. Due to the country's unbalanced economic and social development, different law-enforcement capabilities of judicial personnel and remnants of local protectionism, there are still problems like non-transparent exercise of judicial discretion and non-standardized judicial acts. In recent years, China's judicial organs have vigorously pushed forward the standardization of penalties, established the case guidance system, and enhanced case management, all of which have promoted standardization of judicial acts.

Standardizing penalties. To regulate acts in giving out a sentence, the Supreme People's Court, by summarizing pilot experiences, has formulated the Guiding Opinions on Sentencing by the People's Courts (Trial Implementation) and Opinions on Several Issues Concerning the Regulation of Sentencing Procedures (Trial Implementation). Both documents clarify the sentencing processes, subdivide the range of statutory sentencing and clarify the quantification standards for different circumstances when giving out a sentence. For cases of public prosecution, the people's procuratorate provides suggestions on sentencing in accordance with the law, while the litigant, the defender and the procurator may give opinions on the penalty. Comparatively independent sentencing procedures have been established for court trials, so as to facilitate investigations and debates over the facts and evidence concerning conviction and sentencing in a case. The people's courts should explain the reasons for sentencing in their documents of criminal judgment. These reforms have further standardized sentencing jurisdiction, and maintained transparency and impartiality of sentencing.

Establishing the case guidance system. In 2010, China's judicial organs issued regulations on building a case guidance system, marking the establishment of a case guidance system with Chinese characteristics. Different from the system of case judgment in the common law, China's case guidance system—under the statutory law—uses cases to give directions for the accurate understanding and appropriate application of the provisions of laws. In recent years, judicial organs have made public cases that are typical in the application of laws as guiding cases and references for judicial personnel at all levels to settle similar cases. The case guidance system has improved the standardized exercise of judicial discretion, and enhanced uniformity in the application of the law.

Enhancing case management. The people's courts and people's procuratorates have set up special case management institutions to improve the management of case-handling procedures and quality. By the end of May, 2012, nearly 1,400 people's courts had set up special trial management institutions, and nearly 1,600 people's procuratorates had set up special case management institutions. Public security organs have arranged for full-time/part-time legal personnel at the basic-level law enforcement organs to supervise and examine the process of case handling. Judicial organs have widely established information platforms for case management, which have realized online case handling, supervision and appraisal, and improved the level of standardized case handling.

Expanding Judicial Openness

In view of multiple social conflicts, large numbers of cases, and newly emerging problems and situations, China's judicial organs, while building up their judicial capacity, are comprehensively promoting judicial openness, so as to ensure that judicial power is exercised openly, fairly and impartially under the supervision of all the people.

Expanding the items and content of judicial openness. People's courts extend judicial openness in court trial to all other processes such as case-filing, execution, hearing, issue of documents, and jurisdiction affairs. The people's procuratorates make fully public case-handling procedures, case review procedures, litigation participators' rights, interests and obligations, and results of legal supervision in accordance with the law. Public security and judicial administration organs make known to the public their main functions and responsibilities, the basis, procedures and results of law enforcement, and discipline in the case of police affairs.

Diversifying the forms and carriers of judicial information disclosure. The form of judicial openness has been changed from separate information release by each judicial department to unified information disclosure through a designated information service platform. The carriers of judicial information disclosure have been extended from the traditional public notice boards, newspapers, periodicals and pamphlets, to websites, blogs, microblogs, instant communication tools, and other newly emerging online media. A press spokesman news briefing mechanism has been established and improved for timely judicial information release.

Enhancing the effectiveness of and guarantee for judicial openness. The reasoning and argumentation of all documents in relation to judgments, procuratorial work and public security affairs will be strengthened. Ordinary people and experts are invited to attend hearings and arguments. Email boxes are opened as a means of communication with the people and hotlines of the same number across the country are created for people to report offences. There are designated days when heads of judicial departments meet with visitors. The state has strengthened the manpower and material guarantees for judicial openness. All these measures have ensured that judicial openness advances in an orderly way and achieves positive results.

Enhancing Judicial Democracy

The people's courts as the judicial organs and the people's procuratorates as the legal supervisory organs also need to promote democracy to ensure judicial impartiality. China is striving to establish and improve the systems of people's jurors and people's supervisors. This provides a significant guarantee for developing socialist democratic politics, and realizing the people's participation in the administration of state affairs in accordance with the law.

Improving the system of people's jurors. The system of people's jurors is a major way for the public to directly participate in and supervise judicial work. In

2004, China's legislative organ promulgated the Decision on Improving the System of People's Jurors. The state has expanded the sources of people's jurors to all walks of life, and determine the people's jurors for cases by random selection from the rosters. In a collegiate panel, people's jurors have the same power as the judges, except that they cannot serve as chief judges, and exercise the right to vote independently for the findings of fact and the application of law. The people's courts at all levels have held training sessions for people's jurors, mainly focusing on judicial procedure, professional skills and awareness of the rule of law, so as to improve their capability to perform their duties.

The graphics shows cases with the Participation of People's Jurors from 2006 to 2011, according to China's white paper on judicial reform published by the Information Office of the State Council on October 9, 2012. (Xinhua) (Table E.1)

Attempt to establish the system of people's supervisors. In 2003, the Supreme People's Procuratorate launched a pilot program to establish the system of people's supervisors. In October 2010, this system is comprehensively implemented in procuratorial organs throughout the country. People's supervisors are selected from all walks of life who supervise and assess, according to supervisory procedures, the following situations in power-abuse cases handled by the people's procuratorates: failure in putting a case on file for investigation, wrongfully putting a case on file for investigation, and withdrawing a case or stopping prosecution. From October 2003 to the end of 2011, people's supervisors in China supervised 35,514 cases, and gave opinions different from the original ones of the people's procuratorates in 1,653 cases. People's supervisors' votes in 908 cases were adopted by the people's procuratorates, accounting for 54.93 % of the total.

Strengthening Legal Supervision by Procuratorial Organs

The people's procuratorates exercise legal supervision over judicial activities, such as investigation, trial and execution. China sets enhancing supervision over judicial power as the focus of its judicial reform, and has taken a range of measures to strengthen legal supervision.

Table E.1 Cases with the participation of people's jurors (2006–2011)

Years	Number of cases with participation of people's jurors	Proportion of cases with participation of people's jurors in regular cases of first instance (%)
2006	339,965	19.73
2007	377,040	19.31
2008	505,412	22.48
2009	632,006	26.51
2010	912,177	38.42
2011	1,116,428	46.50

Strengthening legal supervision over case-filing and activities of the investigation organs. The people's procuratorates and organs of public security have established a briefing system and information-sharing platform for criminal cases. By means of examining and approving for arrest, handling people's petitions and visits, complaints of litigants, public opinion and media reports, the people's procuratorates and organs of public security can promptly find clues to failures in putting a case on file for investigation, or wrongfully putting a case on file for investigation, so that they can review and deal with such situations in accordance with the law. When accepting a case, a charge or a reported offence, or discovering that investigation personnel have collected evidence illegally, the people's procuratorates give suggestions for correction based on investigation and affirmation, and in the meantime, enhance supervision over the examination and approval of an arrest, the extension or recalculation of an investigation or detention. In 2011, the procuratorial organs in China supervised the filing of 19,786 cases. They urged the correction of unlawful procedures during the investigation of 39,432 cases.

Strengthening legal supervision over the judicial activities of the people's courts. For criminal, civil and administrative judgments, rulings and mediation decisions that have come into effect, if mistakes are found in them or which might damage the national or public interest, or contravene legal procedures and affect judicial justice, the procuratorial organs are entitled to lodge a protest or give procuratorial suggestions and take other supervisory measures. The people's courts shall deal with the matter and give a written reply within a month after receiving the procuratorial suggestion.

Strengthening legal supervision over penalty execution and surveillance and control process. In view of the exposure of some pernicious incidents in detention houses and prisons in recent years, the procuratorial organs, along with related departments, have launched a campaign to review law-enforcement work in detention houses and to "remove hidden dangers of accidents and promote safe custody" in prisons, in order to ensure the implementation of surveillance and control according to law. The procuratorial organs have intensified supervision over prison and other places of surveillance by regulating and strengthening the work on resident procurator's offices established at these places, building up a network to share information on law enforcement and monitoring in these places, and improving and implementing mechanisms for supervision over detention procedures and for on-site inspections. In addition, the procuratorial organs have intensified supervision over commutation of punishment, parole and temporary execution of sentences outside prison, worked to establish a supervision mechanism for the punctual implementation of penalty changes, and conducted special checks on the implementation of medical parole and the use of enforcement tools and punishing confinement at detention houses. The newly amended Criminal Procedure Law promulgated in 2012 stipulates that prisons, detention houses and other surveillance agencies, when giving suggestions or written proposals to the people's courts for commutation of punishment, release on parole or execution of sentence outside prison, should send the written proposals or copies of them to the people's procuratorates, which can submit their opinions to the people's courts in writing.

Strengthening supervision over judicial functionaries' acts of dereliction of duty. The Supreme People's Procuratorate, together with the Supreme People's Court and other relevant organs, have formulated Some Regulations on Intensifying Legal Supervision over Judicial Functionaries' Dereliction of Duty in Litigation Activities. It makes clear that procuratorial organs can exercise their supervision over 12 acts of dereliction of duty (including bending the law for personal gains) on the part of judicial functionaries by investigating and confirming the alleged violations, giving rectification opinions, and suggesting that the judicial functionaries in question be replaced, in order to punish dereliction of duty, to curb judicial corruption and safeguard justice.

Strengthening Human Rights Protection

To strengthen the protection of human rights is an important goal of China's judicial reform. China's legislative body promulgated its 2004 amendments to the Constitution, adding "the state respects and protects human rights" to it. The Criminal Procedure Law amended in 2012 included "respecting and protecting human rights" in the general provisions. China's judicial organs are taking effective measures in accordance with the law to deter and prohibit extorting confessions by torture, protect the rights to defense of criminal suspects and defendants, protect attorneys' rights to exercising their duties, limit the applicable measures of detention to protect the lawful rights of detainees, strengthen the protection of the legal rights and interests of detainees, strengthen the protection of juvenile suspects and defendants, strictly control and prudently apply the death penalty, improve the systems of community rehabilitation for inmates and assistance for persons released after serving their terms, and improve the state compensation system and establish systems including the criminal victim relief system, in an attempt to materialize efforts in human rights protection in the sphere of criminal justice.

Prohibiting and Deterring Extortion of Confessions by Torture

To improve the investigation and questioning system is a prerequisite for building the rule of law, and it is also an important method for strengthening judicial supervision and protecting the legal rights and interests of criminal suspects in accordance with the law. China is constantly improving its laws to prohibit the exacting of evidence through torture or other illegal means by judicial officials.

Banning self-incrimination. The Criminal Procedure Law amended in 2012 clearly stipulates that no person may be forced to prove his or her own guilt, and no criminal suspects or defendants may be forced to confess.

Excluding illegally obtained evidence. The Criminal Procedure Law amended in 2012 makes it clear that confessions by a suspect or a defendant obtained through extortion or other illegal means and witness's testimony and victim's statements obtained through the use of violence, threats or other illegal means should be excluded from evidence. If physical or documentary evidence is collected in ways violating legal procedures and severely affecting judicial justice, such evidence should be excluded if no correction or justification is provided. It also stipulates the specific procedure for exclusion of such evidence. Once evidence that should be excluded is found by public security organs, people's procuratorates or people's courts during the course of investigation, prosecution review or trial, such evidence should be excluded in accordance with the law.

Improving the system of detention, taking a person into custody after arrest, and interrogation. A person who has been detained must be sent to a house of detention within 24 h. When a person is arrested, he/she must be taken into custody immediately in a house of detention, where the interrogation shall be conducted. With advances in the IT-based law enforcement by judicial organs, interrogation, detention, court trials and activities happening in places of custody are recorded and video taped. The practice of recording and videotaping investigation and questioning processes is widely adopted. The law explicitly states that for crimes punishable by life imprisonment or death and other serious crimes, audio or video recording of the interrogation process is mandatory. The audio or video recording should cover the entire process of the questioning and should be complete.

Protecting the Right to Defense of Suspects and Defendants

The system of advocacy set up for implementing the right to defense as stipulated in China's Constitution is a basic system in China's criminal litigation. It demonstrates the respect of the state for human rights such as those to life and freedom. In recent years, China has been reforming and improving its system of advocacy, aiming to change the old conception of "stressing fighting crimes, but ignoring human rights protection" in judicial practice, and make the system of advocacy play its due role in human rights protection.

Ensuring timely defense. The Criminal Procedure Law of 1979 stated that a defendant is not entitled to appoint a defender until he/she is undergoing court trial. The amended version in 1996 stipulated that a criminal suspect is entitled to hire an attorney for legal assistance during the investigation period, and appoint a defender when the case is handed over to a prosecution organ when the investigation is concluded. And the newly amended Criminal Procedure Law of 2012 went further to specify that a criminal suspect has the right to appoint a defender at any time as of the date when he/she is interrogated for the first time or from the day on which compulsory measures are adopted against him/her. A defendant is entitled to hire a defender any time he/she wants. If a criminal suspect or defendant in custody requests the appointment of a defender, the people's court, the people's procuratorate or the public security organ should convey the message promptly, and a defender may also be appointed by his/her guardian or a close relative on his/her behalf.

Expanding the scope of legal assistance. In order to further protect the rights to defense and other relevant rights of criminal suspects and defendants, the Criminal Procedure Law amended in 2012 expanded the scope of legal assistance in criminal litigation, to make it cover the investigation and prosecution review processes as well as trials, and expanded the scope of people entitled to receive such assistance. If the criminal suspect is blind, deaf or mute, or is a minor or is a mentally ill person who has not completely lost his/her capacity to comprehend or to control his/her behavior, or if a criminal suspect may be sentenced to life imprisonment or death, but he/she has not appointed a defender, the relevant people's court, people's procuratorate or public security organ should inform the legal assistance agency to assign a defense attorney.

Stressing witness's duty to testify in court. Witness testimony in court is crucial to improving the quality of a court trial. In order to have more witnesses testify in court, the Criminal Procedure Law amended in 2012 defines the scope of witness appearance at a court and sets up an assistance mechanism for their appearance at court. It stipulates that if the prosecutor and the defender disagree upon the testimony of a witness that bear significantly on sentencing, the witness should attend the court. A witness should be compensated for transportation, accommodation and meal expenses related to his/her court duties by the government. The employer of the witness may not reduce or reduce in disguise the witness's remuneration, bonuses or other social benefits in the period he/she is absent from work providing testimony.

Improving protection for witnesses. In cases involving serious crimes, if the personal safety of a witness, expert witness, or victim or a close relative of the same is at risk because of court testimony, the relevant people's court, people's procuratorate and public security organ should withhold the personal information, and disguise the appearance and voice of such persons during testimony, prohibit certain persons to be in contact with the witnesses, or their close relatives, and take special measures for personal and residential protection.

Protecting Lawyers' Rights to Practice

The protection of lawyers' rights to practice in the course of criminal litigation is essential to protecting the lawful rights and interests of the criminal suspect or defendant and ensuring that such cases are dealt with impartially. China is revising related laws to provide a legal guarantee for lawyers to overcome difficulties in meeting with the suspect or defendant, accessing to materials concerning the case and obtaining evidence through investigation.

The Law of the People's Republic of China on Lawyers, amended in 2007, supplemented and stressed lawyers' rights in the course of litigation, particularly criminal litigation. It stipulates that the representation or defense opinions presented in court by a lawyer shall not be subject to legal prosecution so long as they do not compromise national security, maliciously defame others or seriously disrupt court order. These measures have effectively promoted the exercise of the defense function of lawyers. From 2006 to 2011, lawyers throughout the country provided defense for a total of 2,454,222 cases, an increase of 54.16 % over the period 2001–2005.

A timely meeting with a client in custody, access to case materials and obtaining evidence through investigation bear directly on the practice of the defense attorney in criminal litigation. The Criminal Procedure Law amended in 2012 specifies that, except for few cases, a defense attorney who holds a license for practicing law, a certificate of his law firm and a letter of attorney or an official legal assistance letter may meet a detained suspect or defendant. Such a meeting is not to be monitored. Starting from the date of the review by the people's procuratorate, a defense attorney may have access to, extract and copy filed materials concerning the case. A defender may apply to the relevant people's procuratorate or people's court for evidence of the innocence of the defendant or the insignificance of the alleged crime collected by the public security organ or the people's procuratorate. It also specifies that if a defender thinks the public security organ, the people's procuratorate, the people's court or their staff hinders him/her from exercising his/her litigation right, he/she has the right to make a petition/accusation to a people's procuratorate at the same level or at the next higher level. The people's procuratorate must review the petition/accusation in a timely fashion. If the petition/accusation is true, the people's procuratorate will notify the relevant department to make corrections to its acts.

Restrictions on Application of Custody

In order to safeguard public safety and guarantee the smooth conduct of criminal case investigation, Chinese law specifies both custodial and non-custodial measures to be imposed on a criminal suspect or defendant as well as the strict conditions of their application. To further regulate the application of these compulsory measures and strengthen the protection of civil rights, the Criminal Procedure Law amended in 2012 further improves the compulsory custodial measures.

Refining conditions and approval procedures for arrest. The newly revised Criminal Procedure Law clearly defines social risk criteria of offences, stipulating that when a people's procuratorate reviews and approves an arrest application it may question the suspect. It must question the suspect when it doubts whether the conditions for arrest are met, or the suspect requests to give a statement to the prosecutor face to face, or the investigation may have been in serious violation of the law. If the defense attorney asks to express his opinion, this request should be granted. These provisions help investigators and the investigating authorities get a thorough understanding of the case, and an accurate grasp of the conditions for arrest, thus avoid putting someone in custody by mistake.

Establishing a system of review over the necessity of detention. After a criminal suspect or defendant is arrested, the people's procuratorate should still check the necessity for detention. If the detention is found to be not necessary, the judicial authorities concerned should be advised to release the detainee or alter the compulsory measures.

Improving the procedures for terminating and altering compulsory measures imposed on detained suspects or defendants. The people's court, people's procuratorate or public security organ shall cancel or alter the compulsory measures promptly or release the detained person upon expiration of the statutory period for custody or as soon as they find that the custody measures imposed on a suspect or a defendant are not appropriate. The criminal suspect, defendant, his statutory representative, close relative or defender are entitled to request an alteration of the compulsory measures imposed, and the relevant authority shall respond within 3 days.

Expanding application of residential surveillance and reducing application of detention. The Criminal Procedure Law revised in 2012 defined residential surveillance as an alternative to detention. It puts under residential surveillance those who meet the conditions for arrest but are seriously ill and unable to take care of themselves, or pregnant women or women currently breastfeeding their own babies, or someone who is the only caregiver of a person who cannot take care of himself/herself.

Protecting the Legal Rights and Interests of Detainees

A house of detention is a criminal custody institution for detaining persons who have been arrested and taken into custody in accordance with the law. Protecting detainees' legal rights and interests not only demonstrates the level of civilized and standardized legal enforcement of the house of detention but is also the need for human rights protection.

China attaches great importance to improving the surveillance level of houses of detention, prohibits extorting confessions by torture and overdue custody, improves the conditions for detention and surveillance, improves the living conditions of detainees and protects their lawful rights and interests. A body surface examination will be conducted on a detainee daily within 7 days after he/she is sent to a house of detention, and this examination system is also strictly implemented before and after a round of interrogation, as well as before and after a detainee is sent away from or back to a house of detention. The system of one bed for each inmate will be gradually adopted, and medical care for prison inmates will be socialized, so as to ensure that an inmate gets timely treatment in case of illness. The system of investigation and handling of complaints by detainees will be improved, so will the system of detainees' meeting with the police, officials of detention houses or resident procurators upon their requests, so as to receive and investigate complaints and accusations by detainees on time. When the term of detention for a detainee is to expire, the house of detention should submit a written report to the resident procurator's office, which in turn will supervise whether the release of the detainee or alteration of the compulsory measures by the investigation authorities are carried out promptly. From 2008 to 2011, procuratorial organs conducted supervision and examination of houses of detention throughout the country, and corrected 5,473 cases of illegal detention. Efforts are being made to crack down on bullying rogues in prisons, and alarm devices are installed in each cell so that the detainees can call the police on time in case of abuse. The practice is adopted whereby officials talk to detainees upon their release from the house of detention, with follow-up observations and meetings with them for better monitoring over bullying rogues in houses of detention. A responsible system is implemented for chief and assistant policemen in management of prison cells, and those concerned shall be held accountable if there are serious injuries or deaths of detainees inflicted by bullies because of lax management. The system of inviting special supervisors to inspect detention facilities will be established whereby invited special supervisors may come and inspect the performance of duties and law enforcement by the police in the houses of detention during working hours without notification in advance. In 2010, the number of accidents in houses of detention fell by 31.6 % compared with 2009. Video meetings with detainees is being introduced in houses of detention across the country to facilitate family visits. The systems of security risk assessment and separate management of detainees have been established, and psychological intervention has been strengthened for detainees. The working principle of "education, persuasion and rehabilitation," which integrates educational measures with management and care for detainees, is upheld in order to help them foster again a positive attitude towards life and healthy lifestyle.

Protecting the Legal Rights and Interests of Juvenile Suspects and Offenders

China adopts the measure of combined punishment and protection to help juvenile offenders and does the utmost to rehabilitate them and get them reintegrated into society. China specifies the principle of "education, persuasion and rehabilitation" for juvenile offenders, sticking to the principle of applying primarily educational measures, and taking punitive sanctions as ancillary means. The judicial organs assign officials who have a good knowledge of the physical and psychological characteristics of minors to handle juvenile cases. If a minor defendant has not appointed a defender, the judicial organs should notify a legal assistance agency to assign an attorney to defend him/her. There are strict rules regarding the arrest of a juvenile suspect or defendant. When a people's prosecutor's office reviews and approves an arrest and a people's court decides on the arrest of a minor, the minor shall be questioned and the defense attorney's opinion shall be heeded. Minors held in custody, arrested or are under criminal punishment shall be detained, administered and educated separately from adults. During the interrogation and trial of juvenile criminal cases, the legal representative of the minor should be present. The court may also inform the minor's other adult relatives or

Table E.2 Punishments meted out by people's courts on Juvenile criminals, 2009–2011

Years	Number of Juvenile criminals	Decline from previous year (%)	Proportion of Juvenile criminals in all criminals (%)
2009	77,604	12.69	7.78
2010	68,193	12.13	6.77
2011	67,280	1.33	6.40

representatives of his/her school, work unit, place of residence or juvenile protection organizations of the trial so that they shall be present. If the legal representative or any other relevant person present believes that the legitimate rights and interests of the minor have been infringed upon during the interrogation or trial, he/she may express his/her opinion thereon. The interrogation or court records shall be made available on the spot to the legal representative or other relevant person present to read or be read out to them. When female juvenile suspects are interrogated, a female officer shall be present. For a minor whose offence is not serious, therefore may be sentenced to less than one year in prison but who has shown remorse, the people's procuratorate may decide not to proceed with prosecution, with conditions attached. The judicial organs may take into consideration the family and school background, cause of crime, guardianship and education of a juvenile offender and use them as reference when handling the case. Trial of cases in which the offenders are under the age of 18 shall not be open to the public. If the offender is under 18 at the time of the crime and sentenced to less than 5 years of imprisonment, the records of the crime shall be sealed. These records shall not be disclosed to any institution or individual unless they are required by judicial authorities for handling cases or by relevant institutions for inquiry in accordance with state regulations. Amendment Eight to the Criminal Law promulgated in 2011 makes clear the conditions under which probation is applicable to a minor. It also stipulates that juvenile offenders do not constitute recidivists. By July 2011, a total of 2,331 juvenile courts had been set up across the country. From 2002 to 2011, thanks to efforts from all sectors of society, the rate of recidivism of China's juveniles remained at 1 to 2 %. In recent years, cases of juvenile delinquency have been falling, and the proportion of juvenile offenders among the criminal population is gradually decreasing.

The graphics shows punishments meted out by people's courts on juvenile criminals from 2009 to 2011, according to China's white paper on judicial reform published by the Information Office of the State Council on October 9, 2012. (Xinhua) (Table E.2)

Strict Control Over and Prudent Application of the Death Penalty

China retains the death penalty, but strictly controls and prudently applies it. China's Criminal Law stipulates that the death penalty shall only be applied to criminals who have committed extremely serious crimes, and has very strict stipulations on its application. Amendment Eight to the Criminal Law promulgated in 2011 eliminated the death penalty for 13 economy-related non-violent offences, accounting for 19.1 % of the total death penalty charges. It stipulates that death penalty shall generally not be used for people who are already 75 years old at the time of trial. It also established the system of death penalty with a suspension of execution and put restrictions on reduction of sentences. These are attempts to create conditions in legislation and system to gradually reduce the use of the death penalty.

The death penalty bears directly on the citizen's right to life, so it must be applied in a very prudent manner. Starting in 2007, only the Supreme People's Court has the right to approve death penalty. In China, court trials of all death penalty cases of the second instance are open to the public. The state has improved the death penalty review procedure and strengthened supervision over the death penalty review. When the Supreme People's Court reviews a death sentence, it shall question the defendant, and hear the opinion of the defense attorney if the attorney makes the request. During the review of a death sentence, the Supreme People's Procuratorate may advise the Supreme People's Court of its opinions. The reform of the death penalty review procedure guarantees fairness in handling death penalty cases. Since 2007, when the Supreme People's Court began to exercise the right to review death sentences, the standard for the application of the death penalty has been more uniform and the number of death sentences in China has dropped gradually.

Improving Community Correction System for Persons Serving Sentences and Assistance System for Persons Released from Prison

Improving law-enforcement conditions of prisons and results of education and reform. China is striving to build a just, clean, civilized and efficient prison system, realizing its reform objective of "full-sum guarantee, separation of administrative and business functions, separation of revenues and expenditures, and standardized operation" of prisons. The expenses for jail administration, criminal reformation, prisoners' cost of living, and jail facilities are all guaranteed by the government budget. Inmates are required to work in prison and get paid. Every week, they work for 5 days, receive classroom education for one day and rest for one day. Attempts are made to strengthen moral, cultural, and technical education to inmates and give them vocational training so as to enhance their ability to make a living after being released. Since 2008, a total of 1.26 million inmates have completed literacy and other compulsory education courses while serving their sentences, and over 5,800 people have acquired college diplomas recognized by the state. Over 30,000 skill-training courses of various kinds have so far been conducted by prisons across the country, and over 75 % of inmate trainees have received related certificates, made about 14,000 technological innovations and obtained over 500 invention patents.

Carrying out community correction. In recent years, China has committed itself to reforming and improving the punishment system. It launched this effort in 2003 to introduce community correction experiments first, and then spread it across the country in 2009, putting criminals who have been under surveillance, received a suspended sentence, been released on parole or temporarily served a sentence outside prison into community correction organizations. The aim of this is to correct their crime-prone mentality and harmful behavior with the assistance of social forces and help them reintegrate into society. Community correction has been established as a legal system by China's Criminal Law and Criminal Procedure Law. By June 2012, a total of 1.054 million people had received community correction, and 587,000 people had been released from such correction. The recidivism rate of those undergoing community correction is around 0.2 %.

Improving the system of assistance to people released from prison. The Chinese government pays great attention to helping solve difficulties encountered by people released from prison in life and employment. Those who are eligible for the minimum subsistence allowance are covered by this system. Others who face economic difficulties but ineligible for the minimum subsistence allowance are given temporary assistance. People released from prison who are starting their own businesses and enterprises providing jobs for them can enjoy tax breaks and reduction of administrative fees. According to available statistics, people who are released from prison and receive social assistance across the country increased 2.7-fold from 2008 to 2011. The recidivism rate of such people remains low.

Improving the State Compensation System

China has established a state compensation system to compensate citizens, legal persons or other organizations if their lawful rights and interests are damaged by state organs or their functionaries in the course of enforcing their power in accordance with the law. The State Compensation Law of the People's Republic of China amended in 2010 sets up necessary offices responsible for state compensation, opens up the channels for claiming compensation, expands the compensation scope, specifies the burden of proof, adds compensation for psychological injury, increases the compensation standards, and guarantees the timely payment of compensation. This has further improved the system of administrative compensation, criminal compensation, and non-criminal judicial compensation. In recent years, the standard of state criminal compensation has been rising along with social and economic development. The daily payment for infringement upon a citizen's right to freedom was increased from 17.16 *yuan* in 1995 to 162.65 *yuan* in 2012. In 2011, a total of 6,786 cases concerning administrative compensation (first instance), criminal compensation and non-criminal judicial compensation were concluded by people's courts at all levels. Among them, 868 were criminal compensation cases, with the aggregate amount of compensation standing at 30.67 million *yuan*, representing increases of 16.04 and 42.9 % respectively as compared with 2009.

Establishment of Assistance System for Crime Victims

In recent years, China has been actively exploring ways to establish an assistance system for crime victims. The government will provide appropriate financial support to crime victims who are not able to get effective and timely compensation, live in poverty and particularly to those violent crime victims who are severely injured, disabled or dead or to their immediate family members. The assistance standard and scope for crime victims shall be set in the light of the local economic and social conditions. The crime victim assistance work should be done in combination with related measures, such as legal assistance, judicial assistance and social security, improving the guarantee system for the rights and interests of crime victims. From 2009 to 2011, the judicial authorities issued assistance funds worth a total of 350 million *yuan* to 25,996 crime victims, and provided legal assistance in 11,593 cases.

Enhancing Judicial Capabilities

Improving judicial capabilities is an important goal of China's judicial reform. In recent years, China has continuously improved its qualification system for the legal profession, strengthened occupational and ethical training, and improved its funding guarantee, thus effectively improving judicial capabilities and laying a solid foundation for enhancing the public credibility of the judiciary.

Implementing a unified national judicial examination system. China has established and constantly improved its national judicial examination system by incorporating qualification examinations for junior judges, junior prosecutors, lawyers and notaries. The national judicial examination system for access to the legal profession plays an important role in regulating qualifications for legal personnel, improving the overall quality of judicial staff and promoting the professionalism of legal personnel. Since 2002, the national judicial examination has been held annually. Organized and implemented nationwide, it has evolved into a unified system for access to the legal profession. By the end of 2011, nearly 500,000 people had passed the national judicial examination and were qualified to work in the field of law.

Establishing a tiered law-enforcement qualification examination system for the police. To enhance the capabilities of its police officers, China requires all on-the-roster police officers in public security organs to take a qualification examination on law enforcement. Those who fail shall not be entitled to enforce the law. In 2011, the examination was taken by a total of 1.73 million police officers, of whom over 1.69 million passed.

Strengthening occupational training for judicial staff. To keep up with the times and meet the public's increasing demands on the judiciary, China pays increasing attention to improving the occupational training system for judicial staff and elevating their capabilities. The central and provincial-level judicial organs have now established training agencies, formulated training plans, and extended training for all judicial staff, while setting up various specific training systems, including required training for junior officials and officials prior to promotion. The training programs have changed the traditional mode that focused on higher academic degrees and theoretical knowledge, but selected judges, prosecutors and police officers who have rich practical experience and a relatively high level of theoretical knowledge to serve as teachers. This educational training is designed to tackle the key, difficult points and newly emerging conditions and problems, and constantly improve practicability. Over the past 5 years, China has trained some 1.5 million judges, 750,000 prosecutors and 6 million police officers.

Intensifying professional ethical training for judicial staff. In light of different features of their work, judicial organs have formulated basic work ethics, setting forth specific requirements for judicial staff in such aspects as moral values, conduct in performing duties, discipline, style and etiquette in work, and conduct off duty. In 2011, a campaign for spreading core values was launched among China's judicial staff, taking "loyalty, for the people, justice and incorruptibility" as the common values to be held by them.

Strengthening professional ethics training for lawyers. This training, which highlights "always following the law, observing good faith, working diligently, and ensuring justice," is being carried out to build up the professional ethics of lawyers. Attempts are made to consolidate the self-discipline of the lawyers association, to establish a credibility system for practicing lawyers, and to improve the mechanism for evaluating and supervising the credibility of practicing lawyers and for punishing dishonest practicing lawyers so as to spur lawyers to increase their sense of responsibility in safeguarding the lawful rights and interests of the recipients of their services, to guarantee proper enforcement of the law, and to uphold equity and justice and ultimately to improve the moral standards and credibility of lawyers (Chart E.1).

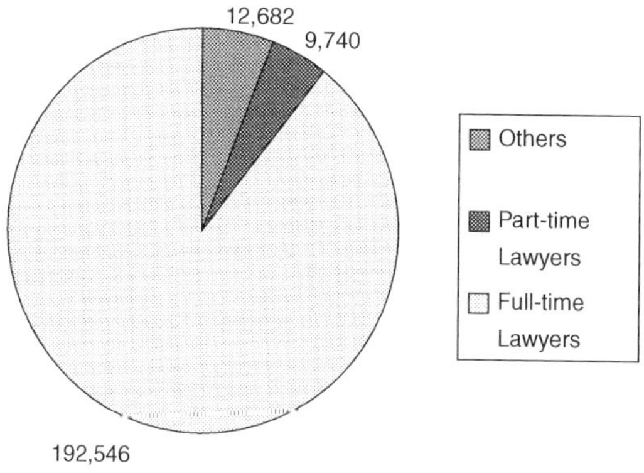

Chart E.1 Composition of lawyers in China, 2011

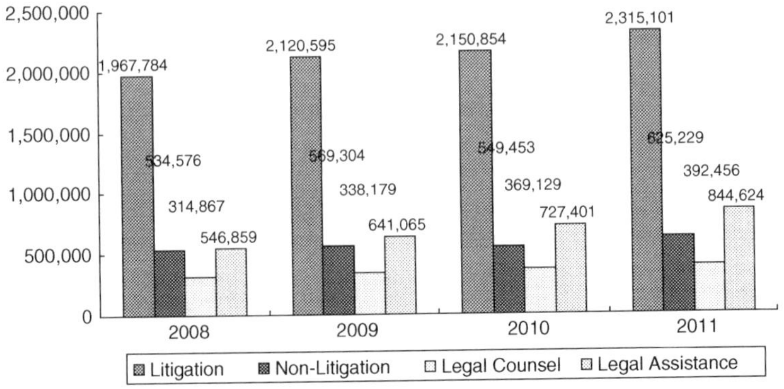

Chart E.2 Cases undertaken by lawyers from 2008 to 2011

The graphics shows composition of lawyers in China in 2011, according to China's white paper on judicial reform published by the Information Office of the State Council on October 9, 2012.

Expanding space in which lawyers play their role. China has borrowed international experience in establishing the systems of public defenders and corporate lawyers. Since 2002, the country has trial-established the systems to provide legal counsel for government decision-making and major corporate operations, thus improving the structure of the law business that is composed of public defenders, corporate lawyers as well as lawyers in the common sense (including full-time and part-time ones). The Lawyers Law, revised in 2007, improves the organizational form of law firms, allowing individuals to open law firms. Thus, a setup of state-funded, partnership and individually owned law firms has been established. By the end of 2011, China had had 18,200 law firms, an increase of 31.6 % compared with 2008. Among them, 13,500 were partnerships, 1,325 state-funded ones and 3,369 individually owned ones. There had been more than 210,000 lawyers, of whom full-time lawyers accounted for 89.6 %, part-time ones made up 4.5 %, while the rest were corporate lawyers, public defenders, legal-assistance lawyers and military lawyers. In 2011, China's lawyers acted as legal counselors for 392,000 clients, an increase of 24.6 % compared with 2008; they handled 2.315 million litigation cases, 625,000 non-litigation cases and 845,000 legal-assistance cases, up by 17.7, 17 and 54.5 % respectively as compared with 2008 (Chart E.2).

The graphics shows cases undertaken by lawyers from 2008 to 2011, according to China's white paper on judicial reform published by the Information Office of the State Council on October 9, 2012.

Reforming the funding guarantee system for judicial organs. China initiated a new round of judicial reform in 2008, clearly proposing that a funding guarantee system for judicial organs will be established, featuring "funding by category, separate management of income and expenditure, and full-sum coverage." The central and provincial governments have increased their funding for judicial organs, ensuring full-sum coverage for the expenses of judicial organs at all levels, resulting in great improvement in the performance capacity of grassroots judicial organs. Litigation fees collected by judicial organs in accordance with the law and revenues from fines and confiscations are all turned over to the national treasury to ensure the separation between income and expenditure as well as between penalty decisions and penalty payments, so as to halt wanton collection of fees and fines that are driven by the hunger for economic gains. The state has also formulated standards for the construction of basic facilities and equipment for judicial organs to improve their working conditions and information and technological levels, providing concrete guarantees for enhancing judicial capabilities.

Judicial Power Serving the People

Putting the people first and exercising judicial power for the people are the fundamental starting point and ultimate objective of judicial work in China. In recent years, in light of new situations and requirements coming along with the rapid socioeconomic development, China has made continuous efforts in promoting the development of the grassroots judicial organs by intensifying service consciousness in judicial work, extending work platforms and improving work procedures, so as to provide more convenience for people to exercise their rights.

Strengthening the Development of Grassroots Judicial Organs

Most of the cases handled by the judicial bodies take place at grassroots level, and grassroots judicial institutions are the frontline platforms providing judicial services to the public. The local grassroots courts, procuratorates, public security organs and judicial administrative bodies are strengthening such agencies as people's tribunals, procuratorial offices, police stations and judicial offices to make judicial services close to the people and provide better service to them.

Strengthening the construction of grassroots people's courts. Every year grassroots people's tribunals try an average of 2.4 million cases, accounting for one-third of all cases tried by the people's courts of first instance across the country. In recent years, to facilitate litigation, local grassroots people's courts have resumed, built or improved the people's tribunals, and promoted a mechanism for people's tribunals to directly place cases on file for investigation by simplifying this procedure. Currently, China has nearly 10,000 people's tribunals, covering almost all towns or townships and urban neighborhoods. Convenient litigation offices and liaison points have been set up in remote villages and litigation liaisons are appointed. Circuit tribunals have been set up in places where there is relative concentration of population, and they are encouraged to receive and hear cases as they go the rounds so as to serve the people as best they can.

Strengthening the construction of grassroots procuratorial offices. Local grassroots people's procuratorates have established sub-offices in some major townships or towns to receive reports from the masses about offences, their complaints and petitions, to find clues to crimes involving government functionaries, to exercise legal supervision over illegal practices in litigation, to do publicity work on crime prevention and the rule of law, to participate in social security comprehensive management and safety building, and to supervise and coordinate with community correction work. So far, China's procuratorates have set up 2,758 such offices, and 9,622 other procuratorial agencies like liaison stations and work stations.

Strengthening the construction of grassroots police stations. Public security organs are promoting a community policing strategy in urban and rural areas. Now China has more than 50,000 police stations and over 170,000 sub-stations, covering all the townships, towns and neighborhoods, making police services and distribution of police forces closer to the grassroots and the public. Public security organs have remarkably improved their capabilities to prevent and crack down on crimes, control security situation and serve the people. Since 2006, cases of serious violent crimes in eight categories handled by public security organs nationwide, including murder, robbery, rape, kidnapping and personal injury, have kept going down, by 9 % in 2010 from 2009, and by 10 % in 2011 from 2010.

Strengthening the construction of grassroots judicial offices. In recent years, in addition to the functions of legal publicity, legal assistance, mediation guidance and grassroots legal services, the grassroots judicial offices have taken upon themselves such new functions as community correction, and settling down and rehabilitating those committing minor offences. Currently, China has more than 40,000 such offices, covering most of the country's townships or towns and urban districts. In the 2004–2011 period, the judicial offices solved 2.84 million disputes, assisted in the mediation and settlement of 46.77 million difficult and complex disputes, participated in resettlement of 2.69 million ex-convicts, and guided the handling of 1.12 million legal-assistance cases.

Simplifying Case-Handling Procedures

Recent years have seen a sharp rise in litigation cases. On the basis of giving comprehensive consideration to the nature and complexity of the cases, the people's courts classified the cases into complex ones and simple ones and adopted different hearing procedures for different cases, thus applying different hearing procedures to cases of different natures to optimize judicial resources and enhance litigation efficiency.

Extending the scope of application of the summary procedures for criminal cases. The Criminal Procedure Law amended in 2012 extends the scope of application of the summary procedures from cases punishable by no more than 3 years in jail to all criminal cases under the jurisdiction of grassroots people's courts.

Promoting the reform of small-claim litigation. To safeguard the legitimate rights and interests of the parties concerned promptly and fairly, small-claim litigations are heard using simple procedures on a trial basis in some grassroots people's courts. If both parties involved agree to use simple procedures, when the people's court hears a civil case in which the facts, rights and obligations are clear, and involves a small sum of money, the trial of first instance will be final. Based on the previous experiences, the Civil Procedure Law amended in 2012 stipulates that among the simple civil cases heard by the grassroots people's courts, if the sum of money involved is less than 30 % of the annual average wage of employees in the previous year in the province (autonomous region or municipality directly under the central government) in question, then the trial of first instance will be final. This legislation affirms the reform of small-claim litigation.

Summary procedure for administrative cases. For an administrative case of first instance in which the basic facts are evident and the dispute is trivial in character, involving a small amount of property, the people's court may, on the premise of mutual agreement between the parties concerned, have a single judge try the case, simplify the litigation procedures, and conclude the case within 45 days after it is placed on the docket.

Establishing Multiple Dispute Resolution Mechanisms

In response to the frequently occurring conflicts and disputes in a period of rapid social development, in 2010 the legislative organ of China promulgated the Law of the People's Republic of China on Mediation, and relevant department issued Several Opinions on Establishing and Improving Conflict and Dispute Resolution Mechanisms by Linking Litigation and Non-litigation Cases and Guidelines on Encouraging the Use of Mediation to Solve Conflicts and Disputes. They encourage the development and improvement of non-litigation dispute resolution mechanisms, thus establishing multiple dispute resolution mechanisms suited to the national conditions. Provisions such as mediation should be used first and mediation agreements shall be accepted by judicial organs are added to the Civil Procedure Law amended in 2012, reaffirming the achievements in judicial reforms.

Giving play to people's mediation. People's mediation is a Chinese way for resolving non-litigation disputes. China has established people's mediation committees in village (neighborhood) committees, townships or towns (urban districts), enterprises and public institutions, as well as industries and sectors with a high frequency of occurrence of disputes. By the end of 2011, China had 811,000 people's mediation organizations and 4.336 million mediators. In 2011, a total of 8.935 million conflicts were resolved through mediation, with a 96.9 % resolution rate.

Giving play to administrative mediation. Out of the volition of the parties involved, an administrative organ may mediate administrative disputes under its jurisdiction and civil disputes relating to its functions and powers, enabling the parties concerned to reach agreement through consultation on an equal footing. Such mediation is conducive to the timely and reasonable settlement of disputes.

Giving play to judicial mediation. A people's court shall, according to its functions and powers or at the request of the involved parties, mediate civil cases lodged to it and resolve disputes under the presiding of a judge. In 2011, the people's courts in China mediated 2.665 million civil cases and had 1.746 million cases withdrawn by the parties after mediation. The people's procuratorates have established and improved a mechanism to link prosecution with mediation. With respect to a minor criminal case or a civil appeal that meets certain requirements, a people's procuratorate will ask a people's mediation organization to mediate first before it makes a decision in accordance with the law on the basis of the mediation result to jointly resolve the conflict or dispute.

Strengthening conflict or dispute resolution mechanisms by linking litigation and non-litigation cases. Highlighting the role of people's mediation organizations, social groups, lawyers, experts and arbitration agencies, China endeavors to establish a "large mediation" work system that integrates people's, administrative and judicial mediation, and improves coordination among the three in terms of procedure linkage, validity confirmation and legal guidance. As for non-litigation dispute resolution mechanisms like arbitration, the people's courts respect their own rules and provide support in such aspects as evidence and property preservation, and compulsory execution.

Improving litigation procedures for cases of public prosecution involving conciliation between the parties. For some minor crimes arising from civil disputes and for negligent crimes (excluding dereliction of duty) that may be given sentences of less than 7 years, when criminal suspects or defendants repent of their crimes and obtain the forgiveness of the victims through such means as compensation for losses or apologies, and the victims wish to be reconciled with the perpetrators on a voluntary basis, both parties may be reconciled. For cases in which the parties concerned reach conciliation agreements, the people's procuratorate may recommend lenient penalties to the people's courts; and for minor crimes that do not entail criminal punishment, the people's procuratorate may issue non-litigation decisions. The people's courts may give a lenient penalty to defendants in accordance with the law.

Reducing Litigation Costs for Parties Concerned

China has expedited the reform and improvement of its litigation fee collection system. In 2006, China promulgated the Rules on Litigation Fee Payment, and the Methods for Management of Collection of Lawyer Service Fees. These measures markedly lowered the cost of litigants, thus mitigating the difficulty of lodging a lawsuit and hiring a lawyer, while guaranteeing normal judicial work and preventing abuse of litigation rights.

Lowering litigation charges. China has clarified the payment scope concerning litigation fees, with people's courts collecting only fees for case registration and application. China has sharply adjusted the threshold, percentage and standard of fees for cases involving property, divorce and labor disputes whose occurrence is fairly frequent, resulting in a great reduction in actual charges. Case registration fees are exempted for such cases as administrative compensation. For administrative cases, whether involving property or not, a fixed fee is collected.

Reducing and exempting litigation fees. When a party has difficulty paying a litigation fee it may apply to a people's court for judicial assistance. The state makes clear the circumstances, procedures and percentages for exemption, reduction and deferment of litigation fees, ensuring that parties with economic difficulties are able to fully exercise their litigation rights in accordance with the law.

Regulating lawyers' charges. While expanding the scope of lawyers' charges to market-adjusted prices, China continues to implement government-guided prices for service fees collected by lawyers when they act as representatives in state compensation cases and other law-suits, and rigorously standardizes the links and procedures for lawyers' charges. This effectively guarantees litigants' lawful rights and interests, as well as the state's interests while promoting the healthy development of the law profession.

Facilitating litigation. Judicial organs have generally established litigation service centers, and case registration and reception centers, and initiated and improved such systems as first inquiry responsibility, service commitment, open work and polite reception. They have improved such services as litigation guidance, search and inquiry, mediation prior to litigation, and meeting with people who report offences. They provide a suitable litigation environment for the public by opening hotlines and making use of information technology to provide online services such as case registration, serving a document, court sessions and inquiries.

Providing Legal Assistance

China attaches great importance to legal assistance. Since the implementation of the Regulations on Legal Assistance promulgated in 2003, China has gradually extended its coverage of legal assistance, and established and improved its funding guarantee system, providing free legal services for citizens with economic difficulties and parties to special cases of lawsuits, making it possible for more and more impoverished people to protect their legitimate rights and interests through legal assistance. In recent years, legal assistance has extended from criminal defence to areas involving people's livelihood, such as seeing a doctor, seeking employment and obtaining education; the standards of economic difficulty have been established in reference to local subsistence allowance standards; the subsidies for handling cases have been improved; and specific funding guarantee systems have been established for five special groups: migrant workers, the

Table E.3 Number of legal assistance cases, consultation, and total funding in recent years

Years	Number of cases	Amount (cases) of consultation	Total funding (thousand yuan)
2004	190,187	1,919,448	245,774.4
2005	253,665	2,663,458	280,523.0
2006	318,514	3,193,801	370,297.8
2007	420,104	4,069,972	532,317.9
2008	546,859	4,322,329	682,498.6
2009	641,065	4,849,849	757,603.7
2010	727,401	4,874,083	1,022,897.0
2011	844,624	5,036,814	1,277,280.3

disabled, the elderly, minors and women. By the end of 2011, China had more than 3,600 legal-assistance agencies, 14,000 full-time legal-assistance personnel, 215,000 lawyers and 73,000 grassroots legal service personnel. A total of 28 provinces (autonomous regions and municipalities directly under the central government) have formulated local statutory regulations on legal assistance. Since 2009, funding for legal assistance has increased at an annual rate of 26.8 %, reaching 1.28 billion *yuan* in 2011. The work of legal assistance has constantly improved along with socioeconomic advances.

The graphics shows the number of legal assistance cases, consultation and total funding in recent years, according to China's white paper on judicial reform published by the Information Office of the State Council on October 9, 2012 (Table E.3).

Facilitating Channels of Communication between Judicial Organs and the Public

Judicial organs in China attach great importance to listening to the public's opinions, and make proactive efforts to guarantee the people's rights to know, participate in, be heard and supervise in terms of judicial affairs. They have established special departments to strengthen communication with members of the people's congresses and members of the Chinese People's Political Consultative Conference, and handle proposals and recommendations related to judicial work. They invite members of the democratic parties, personages without party affiliation and representatives from among the general public to act as special supervisors and procurators, people's supervisors, and specially-invited consultants to oversee their work and provide comments and advice. They have built websites and microblogs to establish mechanisms for the online expression of public opinion and opinion polls, so as to facilitate communication with the general public. They also approach the public through such activities as receiving visitors, handling petitions and hosting open days.

Conclusion

Through judicial reform, China has constantly improved the socialist judicial system with Chinese characteristics, enhancing rigorous, just, polite and incorruptible law enforcement by the country's judicial organs, promoting the country's scientific development of judicial work and personnel, and winning the public's approval and support.

As circumstances keep changing, there is no end to innovation. Judicial reform is regarded as an important part of China's political system reform; it is the self-improvement and development of a socialist judicial system with Chinese characteristics. It remains a long and arduous task, and we will deepen the reform along with economic and social development. Establishing a just, effective and authoritative socialist judicial system with Chinese characteristics is the goal of our reform, and China will make continuous efforts to achieve this goal.

Appendix VI
Major Articles and Works of the Author in the Past 10 Years

- 2002 年发表的论文 (Articles published in 2002)

1. 孙平华, 2002a, 国外英语教材评价标准综述, 《中小学英语活页文选》(15) 第5–9页。 (Sun, Pinghua. 2002a. 'Review of criteria for evaluating English textbooks abroad'. *English for Primary and Middle Schools* 15: 5–9.) (注:本文被中国人民大学书报资料中心全文收入《中学外语教与学》2003年第3期, 第9–13页。—This article was included in *Foreign Language Teaching and Learning in Middle Schools* 2003/3: 9–13, by Information Center for Social Sciences, RUC.)
2. Sun, Pinghua. 2002b. 'Middle school English teachers' self-development in China'. *Teaching English in China* 25/3: 21–23.

- 2003 年发表的论文 (Articles published in 2003)

3. Sun, Pinghua. 2003a. 'Communicative competence and its dilemma in the Chinese context'.《基础英语教育研究》第2期, 第1–5页。 (Sun, Pinghua. 2003a. 'Communicative competence and its dilemma in the Chinese context'. *Journal of Basic English Education* 2: 1–5.)
4. 孙平华, 2003b, 国外英语教材评价标准综述, 全文被中国人民大学书报资料中心收入《中学外语教与学》第3期, 第9–13页。 (Sun, Pinghua. 2003b. 'Review of criteria for evaluating English textbooks abroad'. Included in *Foreign Language Teaching and Learning in Middle Schools* 3: 9–13, by Information Center for Social Sciences, RUC.)

- 2004 年发表的论文 (Articles published in 2004)

5. 孙平华, 2004a, 怎样成为更加成功的语言学习者导读, In J. Rubin and I. Thompson, *How to Be a More Successful Language Learner*, 北京:外语教学与研究出版社。 (Sun, Pinghua. 2004a. 'Introductions to How to Be a More Successful Language Learner'. In J. Rubin and I. Thompson, *How to Be a More Successful Language Learner*. Beijing: Foreign Language Teaching and Research Press.) (http://www.fli.com.cn/expertdialogue.htm)

P. Sun, *Human Rights Protection System in China*,
DOI: 10.1007/978-3-642-39663-2, © Springer-Verlag Berlin Heidelberg 2014

6. Sun, Pinghua. 2004b. 'Principles for evaluating English textbooks in the Chinese context'. Presented at the Fourth International Conference on ELT in China. Beijing: May 21–25, 2004.
7. Sun, Pinghua. 2004c, 'The influence of new ELT materials on teacher development', 《山东师范大学外国语学院学报——基础英语教育》第6卷第2期, 第80–87页。 (Sun, Pinghua. 2004c. 'The Influence of New ELT Materials on Teacher Development'. *Elementary English Teaching Journal* 6/2: 80–87.)
8. 孙平华, 2004d, 英语教师在职培训的原则、问题和策略, 《中小学外语教学》第27卷第8期, 第21–24页。 (Sun, Pinghua. 2004d. 'Principles, problems and strategies associated with INSET'. *Foreign Language Teaching in Schools* 27/8: 21–24.)
9. 孙平华, 2004e, 英语新教材对教师发展的影响, 《中小学英语活页文选》(28) 第1–10页。 (Sun, Pinghua. 2004e. 'The influence of new ELT materials on teacher development'. *English for Primary and Middle Schools* 28: 1–10.) (注:本文被中国人民大学书报资料中心全文收入《中学外语教与学》2005年第2期, 第49–53页。—This article was included in *Foreign Language Teaching and Learning in Middle Schools* 2005/2: 49–53, by Information Center for Social Sciences, RUC.)
10. 孙平华, 2004f, 英语教师在职教育和培训的原则、问题和策略, 《基础教育外语教学研究》第8期, 第43–48页。 (Sun, Pinghua. 2004f. 'Principles, problems and strategies associated with INSET'. *Foreign Language Teaching & Research in Basic Education* 8: 43–48.) (注:论文全文见北京外国语大学主办的中国高校人文社会科学信息网基地期刊《中国英语教育》2004年第5期 (http://www.sinoss.net/qikan/2010/1115/7542.html)。
11. 孙平华, 2004 g, 制定英语语言教育政策的影响因素和基本原则, 《中小学英语教学与研究》第12期, 第1–5页, (Sun, Pinghua. 2004g. 'Influential factors and basic principles in developing policy for ELE'. *English Language Teaching & Research Notes* 12: 1–5.)

- 2005 年发表的论文 (Articles published in 2005)

12. 孙平华, 2005a, 教师就学生语言错误应持的对策, 《广东外语外贸大学学报》第16卷第1期, 第85–92页。 (Sun, Pinghua. 2005a. 'Strategies for teachers towards learners' errors'. *Journal of Guangzhou University of Foreign Studies* 16/1: 85–92.)
13. 孙平华, 2005b, 英语新教材对教师发展的影响, 全文被中国人民大学书报资料中心收入《中学外语教与学》第2期, 第49–53页。 (Sun, Pinghua. 2005b. 'The influence of new ELT materials on teacher development'. Included in *Foreign Language Teaching and Learning in Middle Schools* 2: 49–53, by Information Center for Social Sciences, RUC.)
14. 孙平华, 2005c, 我国高考英语测试的理论基础和实际面临的主要问题, 《基础教育外语教学研究》第5期, 第27–40页。 (Sun, Pinghua. 2005c. 'Theoretical foundation of NMET and major problems encountered'. *Foreign Language Teaching & Research in Basic Education* 5: 27–40.)

- 2006 年发表的论文 (Articles published in 2006)

15. 孙平华, 2006a, 开展教师行动研究, 实现持续性专业发展,《高师英语教学与研究》第1期, 第13–19页。 (Sun, Pinghua. 2006a. 'Action research for teachers' continuous professional development'. *English Teaching and Research for University and College* 1: 13–19.)
16. 孙平华, 2006b, 雅思考试对英语教师的几点启示,《英语考试研究》第1卷第1期, 第29–33页。 (Sun, Pinghua. 2006b. 'Several revelations for teachers of English from IELTS'. *English Language Testing Research* 1/1: 29–33.)
17. 孙平华, 2006c, 英语语言教学相关因素分析,《法大教育教学研究》第1–2期, 第38–45页。 (Sun, Pinghua. 2006c. 'Analysis of relevant factors in English language teaching'. *Education and Teaching Research of CUPL*: 1–2: 38–45.)
18. 孙平华, 2006d, 论我国中小学英语教材的评价标准,《课程·教材·教法》第26卷第4期, 第49–55页。 (Sun, Pinghua. 2006d. 'On the criteria for evaluating primary and secondary English textbooks in China'. *Curriculum, Teaching Material and Method* 26/4: 49–55. (http://www.pep.com.cn/200503/ca707347.htm)
19. Sun, Pinghua. 2006e. 'Influential factors and fundamental principles in developing policy for ELE'. *Teaching English in China* 29/5: 89–95.
20. 孙平华, 蒋晓萍, 2006, 教学实习——走向课堂教学的第一步,《基础教育外语教学研究》第8期, 第28–34页。 (Sun, Pinghua and Jiang Xiaoping. 2006. 'Teaching practicum—The first step towards classroom teaching'. *Foreign Language Teaching & Research in Basic Education* 8: 28–34.)
21. 孙平华, 2006f, 论英语语言教学艺术 (上),《中小学英语教学与研究》第9期, 第1–4页。 (Sun, Pinghua. 2006f. 'Arts in English language teaching (I)'. *English Language Teaching & Research Notes* 9: 1–4.)
22. 孙平华, 2006g, 论英语语言教学艺术 (下),《中小学英语教学与研究》第10期, 第1–4页。 (Sun, Pinghua. 2006g. 'Arts in English language teaching (II)'. *English Language Teaching & Research Notes* 10: 1–4.)
23. Sun, Pinghua. 2006h. 'Principles, problems and strategies associated with INSET'. In T. Bao (ed.), *IATEFL China 2005 Conference Paper Selections (II)*, International Association of Teachers of English as a Foreign Language, China Branch: 234–345. (Note: This article won the First Prize at the conference.)
24. 孙平华, 2006i, 开展教师行动研究, 实现持续性专业发展, 载于北京市昌平区前锋学校主编的《科研引领特色之路——英语课堂教学模式初探》, 中国戏剧出版社2006年版, 第49–69页。 (Sun, Pinghua. 2006i. 'Action research for teachers' continuous professional development'. Included in Qianfeng Middle School of Changping District, Beijing (Ed.), *Special Approach Led by Scientific Research—Exploring the Modes of English Classroom Teaching*. Beijing. Chinese Drama Press. pp. 49–69.)

25. 孙平华, 2006j, 英语新教材对教师发展的影响, 载于北京市昌平区前锋学校主编的《科研引领特色之路——英语课堂教学模式初探》, 中国戏剧出版社2006年版, 第70–82页。 (Sun, Pinghua. 2006j. 'The influence of new ELT materials on teacher development'. Included in Qianfeng Middle School of Changping District, Beijing (Ed.), *Special Approach Led by Scientific Research—Exploring the Modes of English Classroom Teaching*. Beijing: Chinese Drama Press. pp. 70–82.)

- 2007 年发表的论著 (Articles and the monograph published in 2007)

26. 孙平华, 2007a, 培养英语教师写作能力, 突破英语教学科研瓶颈, 《基础教育外语教学研究》第3期, 第53–58页。 (Sun, Pinghua. 2007a. 'Developing English teacher's writing ability and breaking through the bottleneck of English teaching and research'. *Foreign Language Teaching & Research in Basic Education* 3: 53–58.)
27. 孙平华, 2007b, 英语学习过程中的合作学习, 《中小学英语教学与研究》第5期, 第7–10页。 (Sun, Pinghua. 2007b. 'Cooperative learning in English learning process'. *English Language Teaching & Research Notes* 5: 7–10.) (注:本文被中国人民大学书报资料中心全文收入《中学外语教与学》2007年第9期, 第4–7页。—This article was included in *Foreign Language Teaching and Learning in Middle Schools* 2007/9: 4–7, by Information Center for Social Sciences, RUC.)
28. 孙平华, 蔡清月, 2007, 英语自主学习、合作学习和研究性学习模式, 《基础教育外语教学研究》第6期, 第29–35页。 (Sun, Pinghua & Cai, Qingyue. 2007. 'The modes of English autonomous learning, cooperating learning and research-based learning'. *Foreign Language Teaching & Research in Basic Education* 6: 29–35.)
29. 孙平华, 2007c, 英语学习过程中的研究性学习, 《高师英语教学与研究》第4期, 第13–17页。 (Sun, Pinghua. 2007d. 'Research-oriented learning in English learning process'. *English Teaching & Research in Normal Colleges and Universities* 4: 13–17.)
30. 孙平华, 2007d, 英语学习过程中的自主学习, 《中小学英语教育》第2卷第11期, 第16–19页。 (Sun, Pinghua. 2007d. 'Autonomous learning in English learning process'. *English Education for Schools* 2/11: 16–19.)
31. 林生香, 孙平华, 2007a, 论新形势下中学英语教师的素质 (上), 《基础教育外语教学研究》第9期, 第17–21页。 (Lin, Shengxiang & Sun, Pinghua. 2007a. 'On English teachers' quality of middle schools in the new situations (I)'. *Foreign Language Teaching & Research in Basic Education* 9: 17–21.)
32. 林生香, 孙平华, 2007b, 论新形势下中学英语教师的素质 (下), 《基础教育外语教学研究》第10期, 第20–28页。 (Lin, Shengxiang & Sun, Pinghua. 2007b. 'On English teachers' quality of middle schools in the new situations (II)'. *Foreign Language Teaching & Research in Basic Education* 10: 20–28.)
33. 孙平华, 2007e, 英语教师职业发展的制约因素与对策, 《中小学外语教学》第12期, 第16–19页。 (Sun, Pinghua. 2007e. 'Influential factors and strategies adopted in English teachers' professional development'. Language

Teaching in Schools 12: 16–19.) (注:全文被中国人民大学书报资料中心复印报刊资料全文收入《中学外语教与学》2008年第5期, 第14–16页。 (—This article was included in *Foreign Language Teaching and Learning in Middle Schools* 2008/5: 14–16, by Information Center for Social Sciences, RUC.)

34. Sun Pinghua (Trans.). 2007f. 'Bases of human rights guarantee in contemporary China'. *China Legal Science*. Pp. 11–15. (原文作者:陈佑武, 论当代中国人权保障的基础, 《中国法学》2007年卷, 第11–15页。)
35. Sun Pinghua (Trans). 2007g. 'On environmental rights in ICESCR'. *China Legal Science*. P16–21. (原文作者:杨松才, 论经社文权利公约中的环境权, 《中国法学》2007年卷, 第16–21页。)
36. Sun, Pinghua. 2007h. Criteria for evaluating English textbooks abroad. In Sun, Pinghua, *Focusing on Teaching and Research in English Education*. "New Coursebook of Basic Education for Teacher Education". Beijing: Higher Education Press. pp. 202–219.
37. Sun, Pinghua. 2007i. Principles, problems and strategies associated with INSET. In Sun, Pinghua, *Focusing on Teaching and Research in English Education*. "New Coursebook of Basic Education for Teacher Education". Beijing: Higher Education Press. pp. 220–233.

——被转载的论文 (Articles included):

38. 孙平华, 2007j, 英语学习过程中的合作学习, 全文被中国人民大学书报资料中心全文收入《中学外语教与学》2007年第9期, 第4–7页。 (Sun, Pinghua. 2007j. 'Cooperative learning in English learning process'. Included in *Foreign Language Teaching and Learning in Middle Schools* 9: 4–7, by Information Center for Social Sciences, RUC.)

——出版的专著 (Monograph published):

39. 孙平华著, 2007 k, 《聚焦英语教育中的教学与科研》, 北京:高等教育出版社。 (Sun, Pinghua. 2007k. *Focusing on Teaching and Research in English Education*. Beijing: Higher Education Press.)

• 2008 年发表的论文 (Articles published in 2008)

40. 孙平华, 2008a, 论生命权的国际人权法保护, 《人权》第3期, 第24–28页。(Sun, Pinghua. 2008a. 'International protection of the right to life'. *Human Rights* 3: 24–28.) (注:本文被中国人民大学书报资料中心复印报刊资料全文收入《国际法学》2008年第9期, 第19–23页。本文篇目被收入《新华文摘》2008年第19期第169页法学"篇目辑览"。 (—This article was included in *International Law* 2008/9: 19–23, by Information Center for Social Sciences, RUC; This tile of this article was reprinted in *Xinhua Digest* 2008/19:169. http://www.xinhuawz.com/zw.asp?title_id=54952)
41. 李立, 孙平华, 2008, 大学生公共英语语言学习模式的研究报告, 《外语界》第5期, 第78–84页。(Li Li and Sun Pinghua. 2008. 'Research on the learning modes of college English'. *Foreign Language World* 5: 78–84.)

42. Sun Pinghua. 2008b. 'International protection of the right to life'. *Human Rights* 5: 23–27.
43. 孙平华, 2008c, 《世界人权宣言》诞生的背景和过程, 《人权》第5期, 第20–25页。 (Sun, Pinghua. 2008c. 'Background and process of the birth of UDHR'. *Human Rights* 5: 20–25.)
44. 孙平华, 2008d, 论《世界人权宣言》的思想基础和权利体系, 《法学家》第6期, 第76–81页。 (Sun, Pinghua. 2008d. 'Ideological foundation and rights system of UDHR'. *Jurists Review* 6: 76–81.)
45. 孙平华, 2008e, 论英语课堂教学的基本特征, 《课程·教材·教法》第28卷第7期, 第53–57页。 (Sun, Pinghua. 2008e. 'On fundamental features of English classroom teaching'. *Curriculum, Teaching Material and Method* 28/7: 53–57.) (注:本文被中国人民大学书报资料中心全文收入《中学外语教与学》2008年第11期, 第24–27页。—This article was included in *Foreign Language Teaching and Learning in Middle Schools* 2008/11: 24–27, by Information Center for Social Sciences, RUC.)
46. 包天仁, 2008, 孙平华教授访谈录, 《基础教育外语教学研究》第7期, 第5–14页。 (Bao, Tianren. 2008. 'Interview with Professor Pinghua Sun'. *Foreign Language Teaching & Research in Basic Education* 7: 4–24.)
47. 孙平华, 2008f, 论英语教材及其分析和评价, 《英语教师》第10期, 第9–13页。 (Sun, Pinghua. 2008f. 'Analysis and evaluation of English textbooks'. *English Teachers* 10: 9–13.)

——出版的译著 (Works translated):

48. Sun, Pinghua & Wang, Xiangfeng (Trans.). 2008. 'Human rights, culture and their reconstruction in the Chinese context'. *China Legal Science*. Vol. 1. Pp. 51–57. (原文作者:肖君勇, 唐健飞, 中国语境下的人权、文化及其重构, 《中国法学》2008年卷1, 第51–57页。)
49. Sun, Pinghua & Zhao, Haixiu (Trans.). 2008. 'On the implication of the right of claim in the civil right system'. *China Legal Science*. Vol. 2. Pp. 191–197. (原文作者:辜明安, 试论民事权利体系中请求权的含义, 《中国法学》2008年卷2, 第191–197页。)
50. 孙平华译, 《中学英语文化背景知识手册》, 北京: 人民教育出版社2008年版。 (Sun, Pinghua (Trans.). 2008. *Background Knowledge for Secondary English Coursebooks*. Beijing: People's Education Press.)

——被转载的论文 (Articles included):

51. 孙平华, 2008g, 英语教师职业发展的制约因素与对策, 被中国人民大学书报资料中心复印报刊资料全文收入《中学外语教与学》2008年第5期, 第14–16页。 (Sun, Pinghua. 2008g. 'Influential factors and strategies adopted in English teachers' professional development'. Included in *Foreign Language Teaching and Learning in Middle Schools* 2008/5: 14–16, by Information Center for Social Sciences, RUC.)

52. 孙平华, 2008i, 论生命权的国际人权法保护, 被中国人民大学书报资料中心复印报刊资料全文收入《国际法学》2008年第9期, 第19–23页。本文篇目被收入《新华文摘》2008年第19期第169页法学"篇目辑览"。 (Sun, Pinghua. 2008i. 'International protection of the right to life'. Included in *International Law* 2008/9: 19–23, by Information Center for Social Sciences, RUC; The tile of this article was reprinted in *Xinhua Digest* 2008/19:169. (http://www.xinhuawz.com/zw.asp?title_id=54952)
53. 孙平华, 2008j, 论英语课堂教学的基本特征, 被中国人民大学书报资料中心全文收入《中学外语教与学》2008年第11期, 第24–27页。 (Sun, Pinghua. 2008j. 'On fundamental features of English classroom teaching'. Included in *Foreign Language Teaching and Learning in Middle Schools* 2008/11: 24–27, by Information Center for Social Sciences, RUC.)

- 2009 年发表的论文 (Articles published in 2009)

54. 孙平华, 2009a, 《世界人权宣言》两个中文本语言差异研究, 载于徐显明主编, 《人权研究》第八卷 (2008年卷), 第348–390页。 (Sun, Pinghua. 2009a. 'Research on main language differences of two Chinese versions of UDHR'. In Xu, Xianming (Ed.), *Human Rights Research*. Volume VIII (Volume 2008): 348–390.)
55. 孙平华, 马丽娟译, 2009, 论教师的信念, 《英语教师》第2期, 第3–6页。 (Sun, Pinghua. and Ma, Lijuan. (trans.). 2009. 'On teachers' beliefs'. *English Teachers* 2: 3–6.)
56. 孙平华, 2009b, 论具有人权史里程碑意义的英国《自由大宪章》, 《菏泽学院学报》 (社会科学版) 第31卷第3期, 15–22页。 (Sun, Pinghua. 2009b. 'On the significant milestone in human rights history: British Magna Carta'. *Journal of Heze University* 31/3: 15–22.) (本文被中国人民大学书报资料中心复印报刊资料全文收入《宪法学、行政法学》2009年第8期, 第82–86页。—This article was included in *Constitutional and Administrative Law* 2009/8: 82–86, by Information Center for Social Sciences, RUC.)
57. Sun, Pinghua. 2009c. 'The significance of the birth of the Universal Declaration of Human Rights'. *Human Rights* 4: 19–24.
58. 孙平华, 王春, 2009, 《世界人权宣言》中文本翻译的主要问题研究, 《外语与外语教学》第6期, 第58–61页。 (Sun, Pinghua and Wang, Chun. 2009. 'Central issues of the UDHR in the Chinese versions'. *Foreign Language and Foreign Language Teaching* 6: 58–61.)

——被转载的论文 (Articles included):

59. 孙平华, 2009d, 论具有人权史里程碑意义的英国《自由大宪章》, 被中国人民大学书报资料中心复印报刊资料全文收入《宪法学、行政法学》2009年第8期, 第82–86页。 (Sun, Pinghua. 2009d. 'On the significant milestone in human rights history: British Magna Carta'. Included in *Constitutional and Administrative Law* 2009/8: 82–86, by Information Center for Social Sciences, RUC.)

- 2010 年发表的论文 (Articles published in 2010)

60. 孙平华, 2010a, 论《世界人权宣言》的实体内容及历史局限性, 《人权研究》（第9卷）, 第228–260页。 (Sun, Pinghua. 2010a. 'The substantive content and historical limitations of UDHR'. In Xu, Xianming (Ed.), *Human Rights Research*. Volume IX (Volume 2010) : 228–260.)
61. 孙平华, 2010b, 论美洲人权保护和实施机制, 《菏泽学院学报》第32卷第3期, 第79–83页。 (Sun, Pinghua. 2010b. 'American regional human rights protection and implementation mechanism'. *Journal of Heze University* 32/3: 49–54.)
62. 孙平华译, 2010c, 论外语教师的职业发展策略——团队教学, 《基础教育外语教学研究》第11期, 第67–71页。 (Sun, Pinghua (Trans.). 2010c. 'On strategies of foreign language teachers' professional development—Team teaching'. *Foreign Language Teaching & Research in Basic Education* 11: 67–71.)

• 2011 年发表的论著 (Articles published in 2011)

63. 孙平华, 2011a, 张彭春——享誉全世界的人权活动家, 《人权》第6期, 第40–45页。 (Sun, Pinghua. 2011a. 'P. C. Chang—The world-known human rights activist'. *Human Rights* 6: 40–45.)
64. Sun, Pinghua. 2011b. 'Zhang Pengchun, a globally famed Chinese human rights activist'. *Human Rights* 10/6: 29–30.
65. 孙平华, 2011c, 第二讲, 论英语课堂教学的基本特征 (第一编), 载于王松美、李宝荣主编:《英语新课程教学与教师成长》, 北京: 中国人民大学出版社2011年版, 第12–19页。 (Sun, Pinghua. 2011c. 'Lecture II—On fundamental features of English classroom teaching'. In Wang, Songmei & Li, Baorong (eds.), *English Teaching of New Curriculum and Teacher's Development*. Beijing: Press of Renmin University of China. pp. 12–19.)
66. 孙平华, 2011d, 第一讲, 英语教师职业发展的制约因素与对策 (第四编), 载于王松美、李宝荣主编: 《英语新课程教学与教师成长》, 中国人民大学出版社2011年版, 第241–246页。 (Sun, Pinghua. 2011c. 'Lecture I—Influential factors and strategies adopted in English teachers' professional development'. In Wang, Songmei & Li, Baorong (Eds.), *English Teaching of New Curriculum and Teacher's Development*. Beijing: Press of Renmin University of China. pp. 241–246.)

——出版的专著 (Monograph published):

67. 孙平华著, 2011e, 《中国人权保障制度研究》, 北京: 中国对外翻译出版有限公司。 (Sun, Pinghua. 2011e. *The Study of Human Rights Protection System in China*. Beijing: China Translation & Publishing Corporation.) (英文专著/English Monograph) (本书系中国政法大学"211三期工程"子项目"从司法语言看中国司法实践的公平正义、效率与人权保护", 的标志性成果之一。项目码:10108329。—This book is an indicative achievement of a subprogram of the third stage of "211 Program" of China University of Political Science and Law. The subprogram is: *Equity and Justice, Efficiency*

and Human Rights Protection of Chinese Judicial Practice Viewed from the Perspective of Judicial Language. The Subprogram No.: 10108329.)

- 2012 年发表的论著 (Articles and the monograph published in 2012)

——出版的专著 (Monograph published):

68. 孙平华著, 2012a, 《世界人权宣言研究》, 北京:北京大学出版社。 (Sun, Pinghua. 2012a. *The Study of the Universal Declaration of Human Rights*. Beijing: Peking University Press.) (该书为"国家社科基金后期资助项目"的最终成果, 项目编号: 10FFX010。—This book is the ultimate achievement of "National Social Science Foundation Post-funded Projects", the number of approval: 10FFX010).

——发表的论文 (Articles published):

69. SUN, Pinghua. 2012b. 'Specific measures to improve human rights protection standards in China'. *Proceedings of the First International Conference on Law, Translation and Culture: Advances in Law and Languages*. USA and China: The American Scholars Press. (Indexed by ISSHP) .
70. SUN, Pinghua. 2012c. 'Fundamental principles to achieve international human rights standards in China'. Paper Presented at International Academic Conference Entitled *Fundamental Rights in Europe and China* on 28 and 29 May 2012 in the University of Bologna, Italy.
71. 孙平华, 2012d, 论具有里程碑意义的《国家人权行动计划》, 《人权》第3期, 第29–35页。 (SUN Pinghua. 2012d. 'On the *National Human Rights Action Plan* which represents a landmark'. *Human Rights* 3: 29–35.) (注: 本文被中国人民大学书报资料中心复印报刊资料全文收入《中国政治》2012年第9期, 第3–9页。—This article was included in *Politics of China* 2012/9: 3–9, by Information Center for Social Sciences, RUC.)
72. Sun, Pinghua. (Trans.). 2012e. To be adept at rule-by-law thinking and legal means to manage state affairs. *Chinese Law* 4: 60–63. (原文作者: 姜明安, 要善于运用法治思维和法律手段治国理政, 《中国法律》第4期, 第2–5页。) (Original author: Jiang, Ming'an from Peking University)
73. 孙平华, 2012f, 论我国提高人权保障水平应采取的具体措施, 《人权》第5期, 第35–42页。 (Sun, Pinghua. 2012f. 'Concrete measures to take for the improvement of human rights protection standards in China'. *Human Rights* 5: 35–42.)
74. Sun, Pinghua. 2012g. National Human Rights Action Plan as a milestone. *Human Rights* 5: 15–24.
75. Sun, Pinghua and Gong, Mingyu (Trans.). 2012. An epic work filling blanks in human rights research in China's academia: review of *The Study of the Universal Declaration of Human Rights* by associate professor Sun, Pinghua. *Chinese Law* 5: 97–99. (原文作者: 黄进, 2012, 一部填补我国学术界研究空白的扛鼎之作——评孙平华老师所著的《〈世界人权宣言〉研究》, 《中国法律》第5期, 第38–40页。) (Original author: Huang Jin, President of

China University of Political Science and Law; Professor; Doctoral tutor; and Director of National Human Rights Education and Training Base)
76. 孙平华, 2012h, 论我国实现国际人权标准的基本原则, 《安徽大学学报》第6期第117–125页。 (Sun, Pinghua. 2012h. 'Fundamental principles to achieve international human rights standards in China'. *Journal of Anhui University* 6: 117–125.)
77. 孙平华, 2012i, 论"国家尊重和保障人权"载入宪法, 《人权》第6期, 第34–39页。 (Sun, Pinghua. 2012i. '"The state respects and guarantees human rights" Included in the Constitution'. *Human Rights* 6: 34–39.)
78. Sun, Pinghua. 2012j. Measures to improve China's human rights protection. *Human Rights* 6:15–22.
79. Sun, Pinghua. (Trans.). 2012k. Foreign-related jurisdiction by agreement and the principle of genuine link. *Chinese Law* 6: 100–108. (原文作者: 程冰, 2012, 涉外协议管辖与实际联系原则, 《中国法律》第6期, 第40–43页。) (Original author: Cheng Bing from China University of Political Science and Law)
80. 孙平华, 2012l, 大学英语"四位一体"能力培养模式研究, 载入李立主编、孙平华副主编的《高等教育外语能力培养模式研究》, 北京: 光明日报出版社, 第133–143页。 (Sun, Pinghua. 2012l. 'Research into the developing mode of college English "four in one" ability'. In Li, Li and Sun, Pinghua. (Eds.). 2012. *The Modes of Tertiary Education on Foreign Language Competence*. Beijing: *Guangming Daily* Press. pp. 133–143.)

——被转载的论文 (Articles included);

81. 孙平华, 2012m, 论具有里程碑意义的《国家人权行动计划》, 被中国人民大学书报资料中心复印报刊资料全文收入《中国政治》2012年第9期, 第3–9页。(Sun, Pinghua. 2012m. 'On the *National Human Rights Action Plan* which represents a landmark'. Included in *Politics of China* 2012/9: 3–9, by Information Center for Social Sciences, RUC.)

——其他学者的书评 (Reviews by other scholars):

82. 黄进, 2012, 一部填补我国学术界研究空白的扛鼎之作——评孙平华老师所著的《〈世界人权宣言〉研究》, 《中国法律》第5期, 第38–40页。 (Huang, Jin. 2012. 'An epic work filling blanks in human rights research in China's academia: Review of *The Study of the Universal Declaration of Human Rights* by associate professor Sun Pinghua'. *Chinese Law* 5: 97–99. (Original author: Huang Jin, President of China University of Political Science and Law; Professor; Doctoral tutor; and Director of National Human Rights Education and Training Base.)

——参与编辑图书 (Books edited):

83. 孙平华 (副主编), 2012, 《高等教育外语能力培养模式研究》 (李立主编), 北京: 光明日报出版社。 (Li, Li and Sun, Pinghua. (Eds.). 2012. *The Modes of Tertiary Education on Foreign Language Competence*. Beijing: Guangming Daily Press.)

- 2013 年出版的论著 (Articles and the monograph published in 2013)

——发表的论文 (Articles published)

84. Sun, Pinghua. 2013a. On the Constitutional Prescription to "Respect and Ensure Human Rights". *Human Rights* 1: 23–28.
85. Sun, Pinghua. 2013b. 'Fundamental principles for achieving international human-rights standards in China'. Rossi, L. S. and Federico, G. D. (Eds.), *Fundamental Rights in Europe and China: Regional identities and universalism*. Italy: Editoriale Scientifica.
86. Sun, Pinghua and Xie, Yan. 2013. Human trafficking and sex slavery in the modern world. *Albany Government Law Review* 1: 18–26. (Attend the Spring Symposium: Human Trafficking and Sex Slavery in the Modern Era, New York, February 2013, as a Panelist of both International Perspectives on Human Trafficking and Issues in Domestic Law Enforcement of Human Trafficking.)
87. Sun, Pinghua. 2013c. The development of human rights in China. A speech delivered to the Professors and students in Albany Law School of Union University, the United States. (27 January 2013.).

——发表的译文 (Translated-articles published)

88. Sun, Pinghua. (Trans.). 2013. Budget supervision system reform of the people's congresses at the new stage. *Chinese Law* 1: 77–80. (原文作者: 刘剑文, 论新阶段人大预算监督制度改革, 《中国法律》2013年第1期, 第17–19页。) (Original author: Liu, Jianwen from Peking University)
89. Sun Pinghua. (Trans.). 2013. Where Does the 2013 Government Reform Show a Sword? *Chinese Law* 2: 54–59. (原文作者:石亚军, 2013政府改革亮剑何处, 《中国法律》第2期, 第2–5页。) (Original author: Shi, Yajun from China University of Political Science and Law, Secretary of CPC Committee of China University of Political Science and Law, Chairman of the School Board, Professor, Doctoral Tutor, Head Expert of National Social Science Fund Project—Investigation of current situations and reform of the Chinese administrative system.)
90. Sun, Pinghua (Trans.) 2013. Improvement of legal system as a permanent strategy against corruption. *Chinese Law* 2: 66–69. (原文作者:姜明安, 2013, 完善法制是反腐的治本之策, 《中国法律》第2期, 第11–13页。) (Original author: Jiang, Ming'an from Peking University)
91. Sun, Pinghua and Gong, Mingyu (Trans.). 2013. A Comparative Analysis of Property Preservation System in Mainland China and Hong Kong. *Chinese Law* 3: 65–69. (原文作者：温嘉明，梁凯恩，蔡佩瑶，2013，中港财产保全制度比较，《中国法律》第3期，第26–34页。)

——其他学者的书评 (Reviews by other scholars):

92. 肖宝兴, 2013, 世界人权宣言研究的崭新成果, 《人权》第1期, 第52–53页。 (Xiao Baoxing. 2013. Span-New Fruit in the study of the Universal Declaration of Human Rights. Human Rights 1: 52–53.)
93. Xiao, Baoxing. 2013. Latest results on studying the Universal Declaration of Human Rights. Human Rights 2: 31–32.

——出版的译著 (Translated-works published)

94. 孙平华, 曲欣汉译, 2013, 《论内心生活》, (英) 托马斯·厄·肯培著, 北京:中国对外翻译出版有限公司。 (Sun, Pinghua and Qu, Xin (Trans.). 2013. *The Inner Life*. (Written by) Thomas a Kempis. Beijing: China Translation & Publishing Corporation.)
95. 孙平华, 何珊汉译, 2013, 《乌托邦》, (英) 托马斯·莫尔著, 北京:中国对外翻译出版有限公司。 (Sun, Pinghua and He, Shan (Trans.). 2013. *Utopia*. (Written by) Thomas More. Beijing: China Translation & Publishing Corporation.)
96. 孙平华, 韩宁汉译, 2013, 《语言的滥用》, (英) 约翰·洛克著, 北京:中国对外翻译出版有限公司。 (Sun, Pinghua and Han, Ning. (Trans.). 2013. *On the Abuse of Words*. (Written by) John Locke. Beijing: China Translation & Publishing Corporation.)
97. 孙平华, 宫明玉汉译, 2013, 《沉思录》, (法) 笛卡尔著, 北京:中国对外翻译出版有限公司。 (Sun, Pinghua and Gong, Mingyu. (Trans.). 2013. *Meditations*. (Written by) René Descartes. Beijing: China Translation & Publishing Corporation.)
98. 孙平华, 钱金美汉译, 2013, 《驳自由之敌》, (意) 西塞罗著, 北京:中国对外翻译出版有限公司。 (Sun, Pinghua and Qian, Jinmei. (Trans.). 2013. *An Attack on an Enemy of Freedom*. (Written by) Cicero. Beijing: China Translation & Publishing Corporation.)
99. 孙平华, 曾娟汉译, 2013, 《奇迹与偶像崇拜》, (法) 伏尔泰著, 北京: 中国对外翻译出版有限公司。 (Sun, Pinghua and Zeng, Juan. (Trans.). 2013. *Miracles and Idolatry*. (Written by) François Voltaire. Beijing: China Translation & Publishing Corporation.)
100. 孙平华, 方丹丹汉译, 2013, 《阴谋论》, (意) 马基雅维利著, 北京: 中国对外翻译出版有限公司。 (Sun, Pinghua and Fang, Dandan. (Trans.). 2013. *On Conspiracies*. (Written by) Machiavelli. Beijing: China Translation & Publishing Corporation.)
101. 孙平华, 储春艳汉译, 2013, 《会饮篇》, (希腊) 柏拉图著, 北京: 中国对外翻译出版有限公司。 (Sun, Pinghua and Chu, Chunyan. (Trans.). 2013. *Symposium*. (Written by) Plato. Beijing: China Translation & Publishing Corporation.)
102. 孙平华, 于艳芳汉译, 2013, 《作为一种艺术工作的国家》, (瑞士) 雅各布·布克哈特著, 北京: 中国对外翻译出版有限公司。 (Sun, Pinghua and Yu, Yanfang. (Trans.). 2013. *The State as a Work of Art*. (Written by) Jacob Burckhardt. Beijing: China Translation & Publishing Corporation.)

103. 孙平华、石伟东汉译, 2013, 《女作家写的蠢故事》, (英) 乔治·埃略特著, 北京: 中国对外翻译出版有限公司。 (Sun, Pinghua and Shi, Weidong (Trans.). 2013. *Silly Novels by Lady Novelists*. (Written by) George Elliot. Beijing: China Translation & Publishing Corporation.)

——出版的论著 (Monograph published)

104. Sun, Pinghua. 2013. *Human Rights Protection System in China*. Heidelberg/New York/Dordrecht/London: Springer. (Sponsored by Chinese Fund for the Humanities and Social Sciences——本书获中华社会科学基金资助). (It is a final achievement for China Academic Translation Project of the National Social Science Fund—*Socialist Protection System of Human Rights with Chinese Characteristics*, its number of approval: 12WFX001. 本书为2012年"国家社会科学基金中华学术外译项目"——"中国特色社会主义人权保障制度研究"的最终成果, 项目编号: 12WFX001。)

Further Reading

Chapter I

Chang, Y. (1995). Thoughts on my beloved father. In H. C. Ruth & S.-C. Cheng (Eds.), *Peng Chun Chang 1892–1957: Biography & collected works*. Privately Printed.

Dante. (1999). *Monarchy* (Translated and edited by Prue Shaw). Cambridge: Cambridge University Press.

Donnelly, J. (1985). *The concept of human rights*. London/New York: Croom Helm Ltd.

Donnelly, J. (1998). *International human rights* (2nd ed.). Westview Press.

Glendon, M. A. (1998). Knowing the Universal Declaration of Human Rights. *Notre Dame Law Review, 73*(5), 1153–1190.

Glendon, M. A. (2001). *A world made new: Eleanor Roosevelt and the Universal Declaration of Human Rights*. New York: Random House.

Han, Y. (1996). Legal protection of human rights in China. In P. R. Baehr et al. (Eds.), *Human rights: Chinese and Dutch perspectives* (pp. 91–101). The Hague/London/Boston: Martinus Nijhoff Publishers.

Hobbins, A. J. (Ed.) (1994). *On the edge of greatness: The diaries of John Humphrey, first Director of the United Nations Division of Human Rights, Volume 1. 1948–1949*. Montreal: McGill University Libraries.

Humphrey, J. P. (1983). The memoirs of John P. Humphrey, the first Director of the United Nations Division of Human Rights. *Human Rights Quarterly, 5*(4), 387–439.

Humphrey, J. P. (1984). *Human rights and the United Nations: A great adventure*. New York: Transnational Publishers.

Li, B. (2005). *Human rights law*. Beijing: Higher Education Press.

Li, T. (Trans.) (1991). *The analects of confucius*. Jinan: Shandong University Press.

Malik, H. C. (Ed.). (2000). *The challenge of human rights: Charles Malik and the Universal Declaration*. Oxford: Centre for Lebanese Studies.

Morsink, J. (1999). *The Universal Declaration of Human Rights: Origins, drafting, and intent*. Philadelphia: University of Pennsylvania Press.

Nickel, J. W. (2007). *Making sense of human rights* (2nd ed.). Oxford: Blackwell Publishing.

Ruth, H. C., & Cheng, S.-C. (Eds.) (1995). *Peng Chun Chang 1892–1957: Biography & collected works*. Privately Printed.

Sun, P. (2011). Zhang Pengchun, a globally famed Chinese human rights activist. *Human Rights, 6*, 29–30.

Sun, P. (2012). *The study of the Universal Declaration of Human Rights*. Beijing: Peking University Press.

P. Sun, *Human Rights Protection System in China*,
DOI: 10.1007/978-3-642-39663-2,

Twiss, S. B. (2007). Confucian ethics, concept-clusters, and human rights. In M. Chandler & R. Littlejohn (Eds.), *Polishing the Chinese mirror: Essays in honor of Henry Rosemont, Jr* (pp. 50–67). New York: Global Scholarly Publications.
Twiss, S. B. (2009). Confucian contributions to the Universal Declaration of Human Rights: A historical and philosophical perspective. In A. Sharma (Ed.), *The World's Religions after September 11*. Volume 2: Religion and human rights (Chapter 14, pp. 153–173). Westport, CT and London: Praeger.
Vincent, R. J. (1986). *Human rights and international relations*. Cambridge: Cambridge University Press.
Waltz, S. (2002). Reclaiming and rebuilding the history of the Universal Declaration of Human Rights. *Third World Quarterly, 23*(3), 437–448.
Wang, Z. (2010). Several issues on the formation of a socialist legal system with Chinese characteristics. *People's Daily*, November 15th, p. 6.
Xia, Y. (1992). *The origin of the concept of human rights—A historical philosophy of rights*. Beijing: China University of Political Science and Law Press.
Xia, Y. (1996). Human rights and Chinese tradition. In P. R. Baehr et al. (Eds.), *Human rights: Chinese and Dutch perspectives* (pp. 89–90). The Hague/London/Boston: Martinus Nijhoff Publishers.
Xu, X. (2004). An endless study of human rights—Speech at the closure of seminar between Chinese and American academics. *Tribune of Political Science and Law, 2*, 36–38.
Xu, X. (2006). The right to harmony: The fourth generation human rights. *Human Rights, 2*, 30–32.
Yang, Y. (2008). *Influence on Chinese criminal and judicial reform by international human rights law*. Beijing: China Legal Press.
Zhuo, Z. (2003). *Rule of law and the state*. Beijing: Law Press.

Chapter II

Angle, S. C. (2008). Human rights and harmony. *Human Rights Quarterly, 30*(1), 76–94.
Guo, D. (2009). The original intention of Mao for launching the movement of rectifying the incorrect style of work. *Yanhuang Chunqiu, 2*, 10–16.
Han, Y. (1996). Legal protection of human rights in China. In P. R. Bachr et al. (Eds.), *Human rights: Chinese and Dutch perspective* (pp. 91–101). The Hague/London/Boston: Martinus Nijhoff Publisher.
Hu, J., & Han, D. (1993). *Contemporary human rights protection system*. Beijing: China University of Political Science and Law Press.
Ouyang, Z. (Ed.). (1998). *Collected works of Hushi 5*. Beijing: Peking University Press.
Qi, Y., & Zang, Z. (2008). Progress and reflection: China's human rights in the past 30 years. *Human Rights, 3*, 19–26.
Qu, X. (2009). Main doctrines for human rights over the past three decades after the opening up and reforming. In X. Xu (Ed.), *Human Rights Research* (Vol. 8, pp. 1–66). Jinan: Shandong People's Press.
Wang, C. (2008). China's human rights have made a historic progress. *Human Rights, 6*, 2–7.
Wang, C. (2009). Major measures to advance the all-round development of human rights in China. *China Daily*, April 15th, p. 8.
Wang, Z. (2010). Several issues on the formation of a socialist legal system with Chinese characteristics. *People's Daily*, November 15th, p. 6.
Xu, X. (Ed.). (2008). *Human rights principles*. Beijing: China University of Political Science and Law Press.
Yu, Z. (Ed.). (2004). *Constitutional jurisprudence*. Beijing: China University of Political Science and Law Press.

Chapter III

Beitz, C. (2003). What human rights mean. *On International Justice, 132*(1), 36–46.

Dong, Y. (2002). Major landmark in the history of China's human rights. *Human Rights, 1*, 24–29.

Donnelly, J. (2002). *Universal human rights in theory and practice* (2nd ed.). Ithaca, NY: Cornell University Press.

Glendon, M. A. (1992). Law, communities, and the religious freedom language of the constitution. *The George Washington Law Review, 60*, 672–684.

Glendon, M. A. (1998). Knowing the Universal Declaration of Human Rights. *Notre Dame Law Review, 73*(5), 1153–1190.

Glendon, M. A. (2000). John P. Humphrey and the drafting of the Universal Declaration of Human Rights. *Journal of the History of International Law, 2*, 250–260.

Glendon, M. A. (2003). The forgotten crucible: The Latin American influence on the universal human rights idea. *Harvard Human Rights Journal, 16*, 28–39.

Glendon, M. A. (2004). The rule of law in the Universal Declaration of Human Rights. *Northwestern Journal of International Human Rights, 2*, 2–19.

Humphrey, J. P. (1945). On the foundations of international law. *The American Journal of International Law, 39*, 231–243.

Humphrey, J. P. (1958). Human rights: New directions in the U.N. program. *New York Law Forum, 4*, 391–397.

Humphrey, J. P. (1965). The United Nations and human rights. *Howard Law Journal, 11*, 373–378.

Humphrey, J. P. (1968). The United Nations sub-commission on the prevention of discrimination and the protection of minorities. *The American Journal of international Law, 62*, 869–888.

Humphrey, J. P. (1974–1975). The revolution in the international law of human rights. *Human Rights, 4*, 205–216.

Humphrey, J. P. (1975–1976). The International Bill of Rights: Scope and implementation. *William and Mary Law Review, 17*, 527–541.

Humphrey, J. P. (1978–1979). The implementation of international human rights law. *New York Law School Law Review, 24*, 31–61.

Humphrey, J. P. (1981). La nature juridique de la Déclaration Universelle des Droits de l'homme. *Revue Générale de Droit, 12*, 397–400.

Humphrey, J. P. (1986). Preventing discrimination and positive protection for Minorities: Aspects of international law. *Les Cahiers de Droit, 27*, 23–29.

Humphrey, J. P. (1989). Revue de droit de McGill. *McGill Law Journal, 34*(2), 191–202.

Humphrey, J. P. (1992). Peace on earth and goodwill to men. *Human Rights Quarterly, 14*(3), 429–444.

Hunt, L. (2007). *Inventing Human Rights: A history*. New York: W. W. Norton and Company.

James, S. A. (2007). *Universal human rights: Origins and development*. New York: LFB Scholarly Publishing.

Lauren, P. G. (2003). *The evolution of international human rights: Visions seen*. Philadelphia: University of Pennsylvania Press.

Liu, H. (2009). Establishment and development of rule of law of human rights in China. *Nandu Journal* (College Social-science Journal), *1*, 75–90.

Moravcsik, A. (2000). The origins of human rights regimes: Democratic delegation in postwar Europe. *International Organization, 54*(2), 217–252.

Normand, R. (2008). *Human rights at the U.N.: The political history of universal justice*. Bloomington: Indiana University Press.

Power, S., & Allison, G. (Eds.) (2001). *Realizing human rights: Moving from inspiration to impact*. New York: St. Martin's Press.

Sen, A. (2004). Elements of a theory of human rights. *Philosophy & Public Affairs, 32*(4), 315–356.
Waltz, S. (2002). Reclaiming and rebuilding the history of the Universal Declaration of Human Rights. *Third World Quarterly, 23*(3), 437–448.
Welch, C. E, Jr (Ed.). (2000). *NGOs and human rights: Promise and performance*. Philadelphia: University of Pennsylvania Press.

Chapter IV

China Society of Human Rights Studies. (2005). The significance of "the state respects and guarantees human rights" being written into the Constitution. *China Daily*, August 3, p. 9.
Dong, Y. (2004). Human rights into the Constitution: An important milestone in China's human rights development. *Human Rights, 2*, 31–35.
Dong, Y. (2006). Respecting and protecting human rights is the foundation for the construction of a harmonious socialist society. *The Forum of Party and Administrative Cadres, 9*, 53–54.
Freeman, M. (2002). *Human rights: An interdisciplinary approach*. Cambridge: Polity Press.
Jiao, H. (2004). Constitutional analysis on "the state respects and guarantees human rights". *China Legal Science, 3*, 42–49.
Liu, Y. (2004). On the significance of human rights becoming constitutional. *Journal of the Party School of Wulumuqi, 4*, 61–63.
Xin, C. (2004). The state respects and guarantees human rights: The significance of human rights becoming constitutional. *Seeking the Truth, 9*, 36–38.
Xu, X. (2005). Human rights concepts in China in the past hundred years. *Social Sciences Forum, 3*, 26–32.
Xu, X. (2000). The system and categories of human rights. *China Social Sciences, 6*, 95–104.
Yan, H. (2006). The normative connotations of "the state respects and guarantees human rights". *Legal Studies, 4*, 141–143.
Yang, Y. (2008). *The effects of international human rights law on the reform of China's criminal judicature*. Beijing: China Legal Press.
Yu, P. (2007). An interpretation of the legal relations "the state respects and guarantees human rights". *Legal Studies, 6*, 28–31.
Zhong, R. (2005). From white paper to being constitutional: The development and choices of China's cause of human rights. *Henan Social Sciences, 1*, 10–15.

Chapter V

Hu, J. (2007). *Hold high the great banner of socialism with Chinese characteristics and strive for new victories in building a moderately prosperous society in all respects*—Report to the Seventeenth National Congress of the Communist Party of China, Part VIII, October 15.
Hu, Jintao's congratulation letter to China Society for Human Rights Studies. *People's Daily* (Oversea Version). December 12, 2008. p. 1.
The Information Office of the State Council. (2008). *China's efforts and achievements in promoting the rule of law*. Released on February 28.
The Information Office of the State Council. (2009). *National Human Rights Action Plan of China (2009–2010)*. Released on April 13.
Wan, M. (2007). Human rights lawmaking in China: Domestic politics, international law, and international politics. *Human Rights Quarterly, 29*(3), 727–753.
Wang, C. (2009). Important measures to facilitate the development of Chinese human rights career in all aspects—Wang Chen's answering the journalists' questions regarding *National Human Rights Action Plan of China*. *People's Daily*, April 15, p. 8.

Chapter VI

Alston, P. (1994). The UN's human rights record: From San Francisco to Vienna and beyond. *Human Rights Quarterly,16*(2), 375–390.

Alston, P., & Quinn, G. (1987). The nature and scope of states parties' obligations under the International Covenant on Economic, Social and Cultural Rights. *Human Rights Quarterly, 9* (2), 156–229.

Barsh, R. L. (1993). Measuring human rights: Problems of methodology and purpose. *Human Rights Quarterly,15*(1), 87–121.

Burgers, J. H. (1992). The road to San Francisco: The revival of the human rights idea in the twentieth century. *Human Rights Quarterly,14*(4), 447–477.

Carozza, P. G. (2003). From conquest to constitutions: Retrieving a Latin American tradition of the ideal of human rights. *Human Rights Quarterly,25*(2), 281–313.

Central Compilation & Translation Bureau for Works of Marx, Engels, Lenin and Stalin. (Ed.) (1972). *Selected works of Marx and Engels* (Vol. 2). Beijing: People's Publishing House.

Central Compilation & Translation Bureau for Works of Marx, Engels, Lenin and Stalin. (Ed.) (1972). *Selected works of Marx and Engels* (Vol. 3). Beijing: People's Publishing House.

Chan, S. (2002). Human rights in China and the United States: Competing visions and discrepant performances. *Human Rights Quarterly,24*(4), 1035–1053.

Cohen, R. (1987). People's Republic of China: The human rights exception. *Human Rights Quarterly,9*(4), 447–549.

Chen, L. (2007). "Reform of UN Human Rights Institutions—On UN Human Rights Commission". *Commentary on Human Rights Law* (Vol. 2). Beijing: Peking University Press.

China Foundation for Human Rights Development. (Ed.). *China's basic position and point on human rights*. Beijing: New World Press.

Deng, X. (1993). *Deng Xiaoping anthology* (Vol. 3). Beijing: People's Publishing House.

Dong, Y. (1998). Universal Declaration of Human Rights—The important milepost in the world history of human rights". *People's Daily*, December 10th.

Donnelly, J., & Howard, R. E. (1988). Assessing national human rights performance: A theoretical framework. *Human Rights Quarterly,10*(2), 214–248.

Forsythe, D. P. (2006). *Human rights in international relations* (2nd ed.). Cambridge: Cambridge University Press.

Gu, C., & Zheng, H. (Eds.). (1999). *Human rights: From the world to China—Theory and practice of human rights in contemporary China*. Beijing: Party Building Books Publishing House.

Gu, C. (2004). *The cluster of democracy, human rights and rule of law*. Beijing: China Procuratorial Press.

Han, D., & Li, L. (Eds.). (1995). *On theory and practice of human rights*. Wuhan: Wuhan University Press.

Lawson, E. (1996). *Encyclopedia of human rights* (2nd ed.). Washington/London: Taylor & Francis.

Lawson, E. (1997). *Encyclopedia of human rights*. Chengdu: Sichuan People's Publishing House.

Li, B. (2000). *Jurisprudence*. Beijing: Economic Science Press.

Li, B. (2003). *Jurisprudential exploration*. Changsha: Hunan People's Publishing House.

Li, Y. (2005). "China human rights development path and the basic experience". In China Society of Human Rights Studies. (Ed.), *Human rights in China in the new century*. Beijing: Unity Press.

Milne, A. J. M. (1986). *Human rights and human diversity: An essay in the philosophy of human rights*. New York: State University of New York Press.
The national cadre training materials editing steering committee. (Ed.) (2006). *Cadre Chrestomathy on human rights knowledge*. Beijing: People's Publishing House/Party Building Books Publishing House.
Zheng, H. (1993). *New theory of human rights*. Beijing: China Youth Press.

Chapter VII

Angle, S. C. (2008). Human rights and harmony. *Human Rights Quarterly, 30*(1), 76–94.
Gao, L. (2008). Do Chinese farmers own their properties—Concurrently discussing the problem of compensation for the contracted land of farmers. *Yanhuang Chunqiu, 9*, 4–12.
Liu, H. (2005). Construction and development of the rule of law of China's human rights. *Academic Forum of Nandu* (Journal of Humanities and Social Sciences), *1*, 75–90.
Liu, J. (2004). Legal value of human rights into the Constitution. *Law Science Magazine, 2*, 6–8.
Qi, Y. (2005). The national responsibility for protection of human rights and establishment of National Human Rights Institutions. *Legal System and Social Development, 3*, 3–9.
Wang, Z. (2010). Several issues on the formation of a socialist legal system with Chinese characteristics. *People's Daily*, November 15th. p. 6.
Xu, X. (2006). The five "obstacles" to a harmonious society. *People's Daily*, August 9th.
Yun, X. (2005). Discussions by the NPC representative Xu Xianming on the five major changes of the development of human rights in China. *Human Rights, 2*, 20–21.
Zhong, R. (2005). From white paper to human right into the Constitution: Unfolding and choice of China's human rights undertaking. *Henan Social Sciences, 1*, 10–15.

Chapter VIII

Englehart, N. A. (2000). Rights and culture in the Asian value argument: The rise and fall of Confucian ethics in Singapore. *Human Rights Quarterly, 22*(2), 548–568.
Hu, S. (1998). "Human rights and conventions". In W. Zhu (Ed.), *Self-reflection and Trial*. Shanghai Literary and Art Press.
Hu, S. (1998). "What way do we take?" In W. Zhu (Ed.), *Self-reflection and Trial*. Shanghai: Shanghai Literary and Art Press.
Liu, H. (2005). Construction and development of the rule of law of China's human rights. *Academic Forum of Nandu (Journal of Humanities and Social Sciences), 1*, 75–90.
Liu, J. (2004). Legal value of human rights into the Constitution. *Law Science Magazine, 2*, 6–8.
Qi, Y. (2005). The national responsibility for protection of human rights and establishment of National Human Rights Institutions. *Legal System and Social Development,3*, 3–9.
Wang, Z. (2010). Several issues on the formation of a socialist legal system with Chinese characteristics. *People's Daily*, November 15th, p. 6.
Xu, X. (2002). Culture and subjects of human rights. In J. Wang (Ed.), *Human rights and 21st century*. Beijing: China Legal Publishing House.
Xu, X. (2006). The five "obstacles" to a harmonious society. *People's Daily*, August 9th.
Yun, X. (2005). Discussions by the NPC representative Xu Xianming on the five major changes of the development of human rights in China. *Human Rights,2*, 20–21.
Zhong, R. (2005). From white paper to human right into the Constitution: Unfolding and choice of China's human rights undertaking. *Henan Social Sciences,1*, 10–15.

Chapter IX

Arat, Z. F. K. (2006). Forging a global culture of human rights: Origins and prospects of the International Bill of Rights. *Human Rights Quarterly,28*(2), 416–437.
Bell, D. A. (1996). The East Asian challenge to human rights: Reflections on an East West dialogue. *Human Rights Quarterly,18*(3), 641–667.
Brems, E. (2001). *Human rights: University and diversity*. The Netherlands: Kluwer Law International.
Cowan, J. K., Dembour, M.-B., & Wilson, R. A. (2001). *Culture and rights: Anthropological perspectives*. Cambridge: Cambridge University Press.
Donnelly, J. (1998). *Universal human rights in theory and practice*. Ithaca: Cornell University Press.
Fields, A. B., & Narr, W.-D. (1992). Human rights as a holistic concept. *Human Rights Quarterly,14*(1), 1–20.
Jin, Y. (2002). On China's "modernization" and "modernity". In Y. Jin (Ed.), *Self-selections of Jin Yaoji*. Shanghai: Shanghai Education Press.
Monshipouri, M. (2002). Islam and human rights in the age of globalization. In A. Mohammadi (Ed.), *Islamic encountering globalization*. London: Routledge Curzon.

Chapter X

Drinan, R. F. S. J., & Kuo, T. T. (1992). The 1991 battle for human rights in China. *Human Rights Quarterly,14*(1), 21–42.
Falk, R. (1979). Comparative protection of human rights in capitalist and socialist third world countries. *Universal Human Rights,1*(2), 3–39.
Forsythe, D. P. (1980). American foreign policy and human rights: Rhetoric and reality. *Universal Human Rights,2*(3), 35–53.
Fraser, A. S. (1999). Becoming human: The origins and development of women's human rights. *Human Rights Quarterly,21*(4), 853–906.
Fraser, D. M., & Salzberg, J. P. (1979). Foreign policy and effective strategies for human rights. *Universal Human Rights,1*(1), 11–18.
Freeman, M. (1994). The philosophical foundations of human rights. *Human Rights Quarterly,16*(3), 491–514.
Gallagher, A. (2001). Human rights and the new UN Protocols on Trafficking and Migrant Smuggling: a preliminary analysis. *Human Rights Quarterly,23*(4), 975–1004.
Goldstein, R. J. (1986). The limitations of using quantitative data in studying human rights abuses. *Human Rights Quarterly,8*(4), 607–627.
Han, Y. (1996). Legal protection of human rights in China. In P. R. Bachr et al. (Eds.), *Human rights: Chinese and Dutch Perspective* (pp. 91–101). The Hague/London/Boston: Martinus Nijhoff Publisher.
Henderson, C. W. (1988). Human rights and regimes: A bibliographical essay. *Human Rights Quarterly,10*(4), 525–543.
Johnson, M. G. (1980). Historical perspectives on human rights and U.S. foreign policy. *Human Rights Quarterly,2*(3), 1–18.
Kent, A. (1991). Waiting for rights: China's human rights and China's Constitutions 1949–1989. *Human Rights Quarterly,13*(2), 170–201.
Kent, A. (1995). China and the international human rights regime: A case study of multilateral monitoring, 1989–1994. *Human Rights Quarterly,17*(1), 1–47.
Kent, A. (2001). States monitoring states: The United States, Australia, and China's human rights, 1990–2001. *Human Rights Quarterly, 23*(3), 583–624.

Kolodner, E. (1994). Religious rights in China: A comparison of international human rights law and Chinese domestic legislation. *Human Rights Quarterly,16*(3), 455–490.
Marks, S. P. (1998). From the "single confused page" to the "Decalogue for six billion persons": The roots of the Universal Declaration of Human rights in the French Revolutions. *Human Rights Quarterly,20*(3), 459–514.
Mitoma, G. (2008). Civil society and human rights: The commission to study the Organization of Peace and the origins of the UN human rights regime. *Human Rights Quarterly,30*(3), 607–630.
Morsink, J. (1991). Women's rights in the Universal Declaration. *Human Rights Quarterly,13* (2), 229–256.
Morsink, J. (2003). World War Two and the Universal Declaration. *Human Rights Quarterly,15* (2), 357–405.
Robinson, M. (1993). Human rights at the dawn of the twenty-first century. *Human Rights Quarterly,15*(4), 629–639.
Rybak, B. (1982). La formalization du droit avec application aux droit de l'humme. *Human Rights Quarterly,4*(2), 261–274.
Zhou, Q. (2005). Human rights conflicts: China and the United States. *Human Rights Quarterly,27*(1), 105–124.

Chapter XI

Chen, D. (2002). Administration of justice and democracy: A critique of the democratization of the Chinese judiciary. *Social Sciences in China (Special Issue: Judicial Reform in China), 2*, 89–95.
Chen, R. (2002). Major issues concerning the reform of criminal judicature in China. *Social Sciences in China (Special Issue: Judicial Reform in China), 2*, 131–139.
He, W. (2002). Three key issues in the reform of the judicial system in China. *Social Sciences in China (Special Issue: Judicial Reform in China), 2*, 116–122.
Ji, W. (2002). Judicial independence and the value of procedure. *Social Sciences in China (Special Issue: Judicial Reform in China), 2*, 96–106.
Xin, C. (2002). Judicial reform in China: A mission that could not be avoidable. *Social Sciences in China (Special Issue: Judicial Reform in China), 2*, 84–88.
Xu, X., & Qi, Y. (2002). The ethics of and oversight over the judiciary. *Social Sciences in China (Special Issue: Judicial Reform in China), 2*, 107–115.
Zhang, W. (2002). Basic ideas for the reform of the civil justice system in China. *Social Sciences in China (Special Issue: Judicial Reform in China), 2*, 123–130.

Book Summary and Scholars' Comments

Human Rights Protection System in China (Pinghua Sun 2013)

I. Book Summary

This book discusses China's human rights protection system systematically, starting with the concept of human rights, discussing the role of human rights in China's traditional culture and the concept of human rights as understood in Confucian philosophy. It briefly introduces China's main human rights movements in modern history, having a systematic analysis of the first white paper on *Human Rights in China*, "the state respects and guarantees human rights" into the Constitution, and the National Human Rights Action Plan as a milestone. It puts forward ten fundamental principles for achieving international human rights standards in China and suggests how these principles might form the basis of systematic theory for human rights protection. Important measures are suggested to improve human rights protection in China. After analyzing four aspects of human rights protection in contemporary China, it discusses human rights, culture and its reconstruction in the Chinese context. It studies not only the issues on the formation of a socialist legal system with Chinese characteristics, but also the judicial protection of human rights in China, showing the dynamic development of human rights protection system in China.

This is the first book on human rights protection system in China published in English sponsored by Chinese Fund for the Humanities and Social Science, which opens a window for the world to have a better understanding of the development of human rights protection system in China, and will promote the mutual communication and exchanges between China and the rest of the world.

——Pinghua Sun
BA, MAs (BNU; Warwick),
PhD (CUPL, First PhD in human rights law in China);
Associate Professor at China University of Political Science and Law;
Visiting scholar to the School of Law, the University of Exeter, UK;

P. Sun, *Human Rights Protection System in China*,
DOI: 10.1007/978-3-642-39663-2, © Springer-Verlag Berlin Heidelberg 2014

II. Scholars' Comments

Based on the teaching module of LAWM706 run by Professor Sun at the Law School of the University of Exeter (2011–2012), the book systematically introduces human rights protection system in China to the world, opening a window for the Western scholars to have a better understanding of the system and achievements made by China in human rights.

——Michael K. Addo
School of Law, University of Exeter
Member, United Nations Working Group on the Issue of Human Rights and Transnational Corporations and Other Business Enterprises

This is the first book systematically discussing human rights protection system in China. This book is great significant for the understanding the achievements and progress made by the Chinese government, opening a window for the Western scholars in human rights research world.

——XU Xianming
Professor of Law and President at Shandong University

This book objectively and systematically introduces the socialist legal system with Chinese characteristics and judicial protection in China to the world, which is a significant contribution both to the research of human rights protection system in China and to the research of international human rights regime.

——HUANG Jin
Professor of Law and
President at China University of Political Science and Law

This book not only explores the historical development of human rights in China, but also puts forth ten principles for achieving the international human rights standards. Specific measures suggested in it will play a significant role in promoting the realization of human rights in China.

——Benjamin Liebman
Professor of Law and
Director of the Center for Chinese Legal Studies at Columbia Law School

About the Author

Pinghua Sun, male, born in 1964, Shandong, MA in English Language and Literature (Beijing Normal University), MA in Arts of English Language Teaching (the University of Warwick), PhD in Human Rights Law (China University of Political Science and Law), a visiting scholar to School of Law, the University of Exeter, UK. He is an Associate Professor (China University of Political Science and Law) and MA Supervisor. His research interests include: human rights law, applied linguistics, teacher's professional development, curriculum and pedagogy.

He has presided over and completed one of the "National Social Science Foundation Post-funded Project", presided over one of the "National Social Science Fund, China Academic Translation Project", and presided over or participated in more than ten research projects at the provincial and ministerial level. More than 80 journal articles in either Chinese or English have been published in various types of core journals (such as "*Curriculum, Teaching Material and Method*", "*Foreign Language World*", "*Foreign Language and Foreign Language Teaching*", "*Jurist*", "*China Legal Science*", "*Human Rights Research*", "*Journal of Anhui University*", and "*China Law*", *etc.*), 8 of which are included in "*Politics of China*", "*International Law*", "*Constitutional Law, Administrative Law*" and "*Foreign Language Teaching and Learning in High School*" by the Information Center for Social Sciences, Renmin University of China (RUC).

In 2006, he served as an editorial director of *Foreign Language Education in Schools*, the journal of the National Foreign Language Teaching Professional Association. In 2007, his monograph—*Focusing on Teaching and Research in English Education* was published by Higher Education Press. In 2008, his teaching achievements—"College English 'Four-in-One' Teaching Mode, Innovation and Practice" won the second prize of the fruits of education and teaching in Beijing (awarded by Beijing Municipal People's Government). His doctoral thesis (Sun, 2009)—*The Study of the Universal Declaration of Human Rights* applied for the inclusion of the first "National Philosophy and Social Science Research Excellence Library" in 2010 and was successfully incorporated into the "National Social Science Foundation Post-funded Projects" (its number of approval: 10FFX010).

P. Sun, *Human Rights Protection System in China*,
DOI: 10.1007/978-3-642-39663-2, © Springer-Verlag Berlin Heidelberg 2014

In 2011 he was a visiting scholar in the United Kingdom and ran a postgraduate course "Human Rights in China" (LAWM706) for the Law School, the University of Exeter. In the same year, he was invited to participate in the 47th Session of the United Nations Committee on Economic, Social and Cultural Rights in Geneva.

In May 2012, he was invited to attend the International Conference of the China-EU Fundamental Rights at the University of Bologna, Italy, and delivered a speech entitled "*Fundamental Principles for Achieving International Human Rights Standards in China*", which is included in Rossi, L. S. and Federico, G. D. (Eds.). *Fundamental Rights in Europe and China: Regional identities and universalism* published by Editoriale Scientifica in Italy (2013).

As the final fruit of the National Social Science Foundation Post-funded Projects, his academic monograph: *The Study of the Universal Declaration of Human Rights* (474 thousand characters) published by Peking University Press in August 2012, has filled a gap of academic research in China. Meanwhile, he succeeded in applying for China Academic Translation Project of the National Social Science Fund—*Socialist Protection System of Human Rights with Chinese Characteristics*, its number of approval: 12WFX001. This is his second important national research project sponsored by Chinese Fund for the Humanities and Social Sciences. The present book entitled *Human Rights Protection System in China* (Sun, 2013) published by Springer is the final achievement of the above-mentioned project.

In February 2013, he accepted the invitation to be a panelist of the International Human Rights Symposium—"Human Trafficking and Sex Slavery in the Modern World" held in Albany, New York, the United States, attending two panels including both "International perspectives on human trafficking" and "Issues in domestic law enforcement of human trafficking" as a panelist, and making two speeches. Based on the panel speeches, he wrote an article entitled "Human Trafficking and Sex Slavery in the Modern World", which will be published in the journal *Albany Government Law Review* in 2013. During his stay in New York, he was invited to pay a visit to both the Columbia Law School and Albany Law School of the Union University, meeting with Professors and students there for further communication. At Albany Law School, he was invited to give a speech entitled "The development of human rights in China" to the law students.

He is now committed to "Chinese Wisdom in Establishing International Human Rights System—Viewed from the perspective of P. C. Chang's contributions to the drafting of the UDHR", which was appraised by Michael K. Addo, the global leading human rights expert: "This is an original research to fill the gaps in the academic research field of international human rights". The draft based on the present research has been included in the publishing agenda of Springer.

Index

P. Sun, *Human Rights Protection System in China*,
DOI: 10.1007/978-3-642-39663-2, © Springer-Verlag Berlin Heidelberg 2014